The Civil War in Arizona

The Civil War
in Arizona

THE STORY OF THE CALIFORNIA
VOLUNTEERS, 1861–1865

Andrew E. Masich

UNIVERSITY OF OKLAHOMA PRESS : NORMAN

Also by Andrew E. Masich

(with Jean Afton, et al.) *Cheyenne Dog Soldiers: A Ledgerbook History of Coups and Combat* (Niwot, Colo., 2000)

(with David Fridtjof Halaas) *Halfbreed: The Remarkable True Story of George Bent: Caught between the Worlds of the Indian and the White Man* (Cambridge, Mass., 2004)

Library of Congress Cataloging-in-Publication Data
Masich, Andrew Edward.
    The Civil War in Arizona : the story of the California Volunteers, 1861–1865 / Andrew E. Masich.
        p. cm.
    Includes bibliographical references and index.
    ISBN 978-0-8061-3747-6 (cloth)
    ISBN 978-0-8061-3900-5 (paper)
    1. United States. Army. California Column. 2. California—History—Civil War, 1861–1865—Regimental histories. 3. United States—History—Civil War, 1861–1865—Regimental histories. 4. Arizona—History—Civil War, 1861–1865—Campaigns. 5. United States—History—Civil War, 1861–1865—Campaigns. 6. Soldiers—California—Correspondence. I. Title.
E497.4.C35M37 2006
973.7'494—dc22

                                                                    2005054914

The paper in this book meets the guidelines for permanence and durability of the committee on Production Guidelines for Book Longevity of the Council on Library Resources. ⊗

2 3 4 5 6 7 8 9 10

For Deb, Matt, Molly, and Max

Contents

Illustrations

FIGURES

MAPS

Acknowledgments

The genesis of this book came more than twenty-five years ago while I was a student at the University of Arizona in Tucson. Professor Harwood P. Hinton nurtured my budding interest in Arizona's Civil War and patiently tolerated my fascination with museum objects and archaeological specimens—the stuff of history—that lured me from academe into a museum career. Still, he never gave up hope that this book would someday be written.

Research at repositories in California, Arizona, and at the National Archives in Washington, D.C., yielded a wealth of primary-source material relating to the service of the California Volunteers in Arizona. In California the staff of the Bancroft Library, University of California, Berkeley; the Huntington Library; the California Historical Society; the California State Library; the California State Archives; and the Los Angeles City Library were all most helpful in ferreting out information pertinent to this study. The staff of the Arizona Historical Society in Tucson and Yuma; the University of Arizona Library and its Special Collections Department; the Arizona Historical Foundation at Arizona State University; the Sharlot Hall Museum; the recorder's offices of Mohave, Yavapai, and Yuma counties; and the staff of the San Augustin Cathedral in Tucson also provided valuable assistance.

Many individuals, including Sidney Brinckerhoff, Jim Hutchins, Cameron Laughlin, Boyd Finch, Bruce Dinges, Lori Davisson, Carol Brooks, Jay Van Orden, Arnie Franks, Rick Collins, Tom Peterson, Roman Mallach, and Pat Callahan, provided information, tips on sources, clues to interpretation, and thoughtful comments. The late Don Bufkin always offered keen observations and encouragement. Henry P. Walker, Art Woodward, Constance Wynn Altshuler, and the irascible Yuma historian Harvey Johnson are also gone now, though not forgotten. Amanda Dunyak Gillen read the manuscript with a sharp and unbiased eye; she deserves much credit for transforming rough drafts into readable chapters. David Fridtjof Halaas, a friend and a scholar, provided expert reading and wise counsel. Copyeditor Kevin Brock and the entire team at the University of Oklahoma Press all deserve my heartfelt thanks. My wife, Deborah, assisted in more ways than I can count—from research to moral support—and my children, Matthew, Molly, and Max, all helped in their own ways.

Abbreviations

AAG	assistant adjutant general
Alta	*San Francisco Daily Alta California*
CAH	Center for American History, University of Texas at Austin
CV	California Volunteers
GO	General Orders
NARA	National Archives and Records Administration, Washington, D.C.
OR	*War of the Rebellion: The Official Records of the Union and Confederate Armies,* 139 vols. (Washington, D.C.: Government Printing Office, 1880–1901). All references are to series 1 unless otherwise stated.
SO	Special Orders

The Civil War in Arizona

Prologue

Lieutenant James Barrett sat his horse easily, as one accustomed to the saddle. His black army hat shaded his pale gray eyes as he scanned the northern horizon, hoping to catch sight of the California infantry column on the old stage road snaking through the wide valley of the Santa Cruz River. The dry, clean Arizona air allowed a man to see fifty, even one hundred, miles across the desert. But Barrett saw no sign of the column as he and his men hid low in the chaparral. Scrubby mesquite, grease-wood, and an astonishing variety of cacti—barrels, chollas, prickly pears, and saguaros—grew miraculously from the rocky soil. The saguaros, in particular, cap-tured the imagination of the soldiers from California. The men admired these green giants rising more than fifty feet, their ponderous arms lifted toward the sun, sentinels of the desert.

Sentinels. Barrett turned his gaze toward the jagged red mountain that dominated the landscape. He knew the Rebels guarded the pass. They would be watching from El Picacho (Spanish for "peak"), if they knew their business.

These Arizona Rangers did know their business. Just weeks earlier, on March 6, 1862, they had captured Captain William McCleave and nine picked men. Barrett still could not believe it. How could McCleave have been taken? They had served together for more than five years—U.S. dragoons they were, and proud. Yes, these Rebels knew their business, and he was sure they were watching from Picacho.

Old Powell Weaver, a mountain man and denizen of the desert, had scouted ahead. The Rebels were there all right, not far from the abandoned Butterfield stage station, an adobe shack with a ramshackle corral nestled in the dense chaparral at the base of the mountain. Weaver had stayed behind with the main column, but an express rider from Yuma, John W. Jones, had replaced him as scout—Barrett did not trust this man, who seemed reluctant to press on. But perhaps the party had eluded the searching eyes of the Rebel picket.

Barrett looked to his thirteen men—dismounted, quiet, disciplined—their blue uniforms covered in the fine dust that inevitably coated travelers in this country. These California Volunteers were good men. Most were in their twenties, tall and strong, and tough beyond their years. Hard labor in the California gold fields did that to a man.

Compared to his men, Barrett felt like an old hand. Although only twenty-eight, he had served as an enlisted man in the First Dragoons ever since his ship arrived at New York City from County Mayo, Ireland. It seemed almost a dream that he was now an officer leading men—this command was his alone. As a dragoon he had taken orders from the likes of McCleave, a first sergeant (hard as they come) and then captain of Company A, First California Cavalry. But now the Rebels had McCleave, and it was Barrett's job to get him back.

According to the plan drawn up the night before, Captain William Calloway would strip the white canvas covers from his wagons to make the column less visible. He would then march down the road to Tucson with the infantry and a mountain howitzer battery packed on mules while Lieutenant Ephraim Baldwin's cavalry circled Picacho from the west. Barrett's platoon would ride wide to the east. By reining in their horses to keep the dust down and walking as much as possible, Barrett hoped the Rebels would not observe his approach. Calloway had ordered the mounted flankers to coordinate their attack, then dash in and cut off the retreat to Tucson— and hopefully grab McCleave, if he was there. The plan was simple, but timing was everything.

It was past noon now. Even in April the Arizona sun burned with intensity. The tangled mesquites offered little shade, and the waiting was hard. The Rebels must be aware of them by now—if the pickets escaped, the Confederate garrison in Tucson would be warned and McCleave lost. Jones urged caution, but Barrett could wait no longer for Baldwin and Calloway.

Through parched lips he ordered the men to mount and move toward Picacho station. Then he saw them: Rebel rangers, no uniforms—just broad-brimmed hats and the practical garb of the frontier—but armed to the teeth with revolvers, rifles or shotguns, and Bowie knives. Without warning, Barrett drew his revolver and fired a shot in the air while demanding that the Rebels throw down their arms and surrender.

Those caught out in the open obeyed immediately, but as Barrett and his men rushed into the clearing, shots boomed from the surrounding thicket, dropping four of the Californians. Barrett's troopers wasted no time returning fire with their carbines and revolvers, shooting wildly at phantom puffs of white gun smoke.

His heart pounding, the lieutenant dismounted to help tie one of three captured Rebels. Intent on flushing the remaining rangers, he quickly remounted and shouted *an order, cut short by a rifle blast. A ball smashed through the back of Barrett's neck—he was dead before his body hit the ground.*[1]

Thus began the skirmish at Picacho Pass on April 15, 1862. Today Picacho is a stopping place on I-10, the U.S. highway between Phoenix and Tucson. The rugged volcanic outcropping still marks the site of the best-remembered Civil War action to take place on Arizona soil. In fact, for most people residing in the state, the "Battle of Picacho Pass" is all they know of the Civil War in the Far West. Few today realize how the Civil War influenced the early development of Arizona.

The years 1861–65 saw the creation of the Arizona Territory and the beginnings of its progress on a path toward economic independence, social change, and eventually statehood. During these years California played a critical role in the process. The legacy of this influence can be clearly seen in the nature of Arizona's growth, its laws and institutions, and the character of its people.

The California Volunteers who served in Arizona during the war years became agents of change. They not only facilitated Arizona's development as a distinct geopolitical unit but also explored, prospected, fought Confederates, established mail and other essential services, made maps, and promoted the territory. These men provided political leadership, invested in Arizona businesses, and established laws and institutions based on California models. At the same time they guarded the border with Mexico from encroachment by Louis Napoleon's French forces and, tragically, decimated native tribes through relentless campaigning.

The troops from California were a unique body of men. A majority emigrated west during the 1849 gold rush and exhibited traits seen in many

1. When James Barrett enlisted in 1854, he was five feet, nine inches tall, with brown hair and gray eyes. Altshuler, *Cavalry Yellow and Infantry Blue*, 21; Clothing Account Books of CV Regiments, 1861–66, California State Library, Sacramento; J. H. Carleton, GO 3, Hdqrs. Dist. of Southern Calif., Feb. 11, 1862, *OR*, 50(1):858–59; N. J. Pishon and B. F. Harvey to J. R. West, Pimos Villages, May 11, 1862; William P. Calloway to J. R. West, Pimos Villages, May 9, 1862; and J. R. West to Ben C. Cutler, Hdqrs. Advance Guard, CV, Pimos Villages, May 11, 1862, William P. Calloway Consolidated Service Record, RG 94, NARA; E. A. Rigg to J. H. Carleton, Mar. 25, 30, 1862, *OR*, 50(1):950–52, 965–66; Julius Hall, "Wild West"; Sherod Hunter Jacket, Compiled Service Records of Confederate Soldiers, Microcopy 323, Roll 182, NARA, cited in Finch, "Sherod Hunter," 203; *Sacramento Union*, May 23, 1862; J. H. Carleton, SO 15, June 15, 1862, Hdqrs. Column from Calif., *OR*, 50(1):142; *Alta*, May 14, 1862; E. E. Eyre to R. C. Drum, May 14, 1862, *OR*, 50(1):120; "Knapsack" [James P. Newcomb], untitled clipping, *San Francisco Herald and Mirror*, May 9, 1862, in James P. Newcomb Papers, CAH; Finch, *Confederate Pathway*, 141–44; J. H. Carleton to J. R. West, May 3, 1862, *OR*, 50(1):1048–49.

peoples undertaking voluntary migrations. Big and strong, hardy and hale, adaptable and intelligent, these men provided the foundation upon which the new territory was built.

There are no book-length treatments of the Civil War in Arizona. Historians who have dealt with the subject have concentrated primarily on the Confederate invasion of the territory or the ousting of the Rebels by the California Column in 1862. Others have focused entirely on the New Mexico phase of the struggle for the Southwest. There are books that detail the Navajo war of 1863 and the army's campaigns against other Arizona tribes. Broad-brush treatments of the Army of the Pacific and the Civil War in the Far West have touched upon Arizona, but none has dealt exclusively with the war from the perspective of the soldiers from California.

The story of the California Volunteers is more important and more interesting than the historical record leads one to believe. For this reason I have endeavored to set down an account of their formation, organization, and equipping; the invasion of Arizona and clash with Confederates; campaigning against tribes deemed hostile to the United States; occupation of the fledgling Arizona Territory and contributions to settlement and economic development; service along the border with Mexico during a time of international tension; and, finally, mustering out at the end of the Civil War. I have avoided duplicating information available to researchers in the *Official Records of the War of the Rebellion* and other published sources. The reader will find in this volume more detail on logistics and equipage—a subject critical to understanding the Civil War in the Southwest. I have also compiled and annotated letters written by California Volunteer correspondents that tell the soldiers' story of the Civil War in Arizona in their own words. These remarkable eyewitness accounts have been gleaned from the pages of the *San Francisco Daily Alta California,* the most influential newspaper in the Far West. The *Alta* provided the most consistent reporting from the territory, and these letters from the field are presented just as eager readers on the home front found them. The letters complement the narrative history found in the first part of this book and give voice once again to the all-but-forgotten men of the California Column.

ONE

The California Volunteers in Arizona, 1861–65

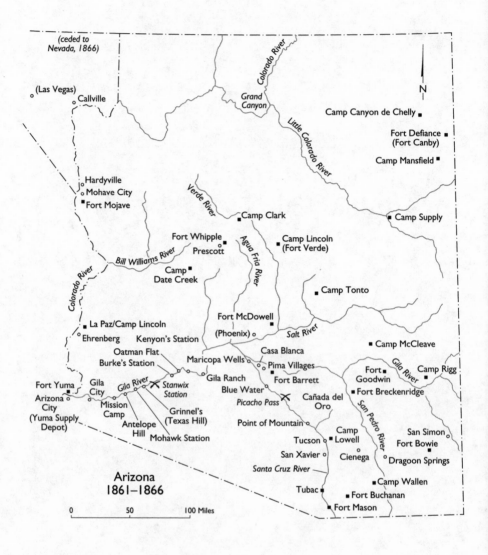

(ceded to
Nevada, 1866)

(Las Vegas) ○
○ Callville

Colorado River

*Grand
Canyon*

Little Colorado River

■ Camp Canyon de Chelly

■ Fort Defiance
(Fort Canby)

■ Camp Mansfield

○ Hardyville
○ Mohave City
■ Fort Mojave

Verde River

● Camp Clark

■ Camp Supply

Fort Whipple ●
Prescott ○

Agua Fria River

■ Camp Lincoln
(Fort Verde)

■ Camp
Date Creek

■ Camp Tonto

Bill Williams River

La Paz/Camp Lincoln ■
○ Ehrenberg

Colorado River

Kenyon's Station ●

Fort McDowell ■

(Phoenix) ○

Salt River

■ Camp McCleave

Gila River

Casa Blanca
● ○ Pima Villages

Maricopa Wells ●

Oatman Flat ○
Burke's Station ●

Gila Ranch ○

Fort ●
Goodwin

● Fort Breckenridge

Camp Rigg ■

Fort Yuma ■
Gila
City ○

Gila River

✕ Stanwix
Station

Fort Barrett ●

San Pedro River

Arizona
City
(Yuma Supply
Depot)

Mission
Camp

Grinnel's
(Texas Hill)

Blue Water ○

Cañada del
Oro

San Simon ○

Antelope
Hill

Picacho Pass ✕

Fort Bowie ■

Mohawk Station

Point of Mountain ○

Camp
Lowell ■

Dragoon Springs ○

Tucson ○

San Xavier ○

Cienega ○

Santa Cruz River

■ Camp Wallen

Tubac ■

● Fort Buchanan

Fort Mason ■

Arizona
1861–1866

0   50   100 Miles

N

CHAPTER 1

Column from California

In the spring of 1862, a large contingent of U.S. Volunteers from California crossed the Colorado River and entered that portion of New Mexico Territory popularly known as Arizona. During the next four years, the men composing the "Column from California," and other California regiments that followed, endured exhausting marches, brushed aside minor resistance from Confederate troops, restored mail service, built military posts, subdued warring Indian tribes, guarded against foreign invasion, and enabled the establishment and growth of the Arizona Territory. The war in the East largely overshadowed these efforts in the Far West, and the California soldiers never got the chance to test themselves against Rebel armies. Nonetheless, the efficiency, energy, and military successes of the California Volunteers helped secure the Southwest for the Union and profoundly influenced Arizona's early social, economic, and political development.

In July 1861, after the fall of Fort Sumter and the secession of eleven Southern states, the U.S. government called on California for volunteer troops. The army needed soldiers to suppress the rebellion that seemed to be brewing in southern California and protect the transcontinental mail routes from secessionists and Indian raiders. President Abraham Lincoln endorsed the Volunteer Employment Act the day after the Bull Run disaster of July 21. This emergency legislation specified that volunteers would be enlisted for terms of not less than six months and no longer than three years. Later that month Congress amended the law to allow soldiers to enlist for the duration of the war. Following calls in July and August, California enrolled and mustered two regiments of cavalry and five regiments of infantry for Federal service. Two mountain-howitzer batteries, trained in Arizona, composed the California artillery complement.[1] By the end of the war, the state had raised three additional regiments of infantry, a battalion of "Native California Cavalry," and a battalion of mountaineers. When enlistment terms began to expire in 1864, state authorities organized a battalion of "Veteran Volunteers" for continued service in New Mexico and Arizona.

The 15,725 volunteers raised by the state of California from 1861 to 1865 represented a military force as large as the entire U.S. Army at the time the Civil War began. These soldiers replaced the regular troops sent east to the "seat of the rebellion," provided a bulwark against Confederates in the West, and patrolled the territories to ensure the safety of U.S. citizens and overland mail routes. California Volunteer regiments served as far north as Fort Colville, Washington Territory, and as far east as Fort Leavenworth, Kansas. They also garrisoned New Mexico, pursued Rebels in Texas, and made forays from Arizona deep into French-occupied Sonora and Chihuahua, Mexico.[2]

While the first regiments of California infantry and cavalry mobilized under the direction of Brigadier General George Wright, news of a Confederate invasion of New Mexico and Arizona reached the San Francisco headquarters of the U.S. Army's Department of the Pacific. Confederate lieutenant colonel John R. Baylor's companies of mounted riflemen, recruited in Texas and the territories, captured Major Isaac Lynde's entire command of regulars as they fled from Fort Fillmore, New Mexico, in July 1861. Even before this humiliating defeat, the Lincoln administration had ordered the abandonment of most of the military posts in the Southwest and the consolidation of forces in New Mexico under Colonel Edward R. S. Canby, an experienced and capable officer.[3]

Unwilling to let supplies and munitions fall into enemy hands, Federal troops in Arizona destroyed all the government property they could not haul away and then marched for New Mexico. On August 1, 1861, Lieutenant Colonel Baylor proclaimed a "Territory of Arizona" for the Confederacy, marking the first time any government recognized the area (then considered western New Mexico Territory) as a separate political unit. In Richmond, Confederate president Jefferson Davis confirmed Baylor's self-appointed gover-

1. Orton, *California Men*, 12; Wright, *Civil War in the Southwest*, 10.
2. The Third and Sixth California Infantry and the unusual Battalion of Mountaineers were the only California Volunteer units that did not serve in Arizona. Orton, *California Men*, 5.
3. I. Lynde to AAG, Hdqrs. Dept. of New Mexico, Aug. 7, 1861, *OR*, 4:5–6.

Confederate Col. John R. Baylor was responsible for early Rebel victories along the Rio Grande, and he assigned Capt. Sherod Hunter to capture Tucson. Baylor proclaimed himself governor of Arizona, but Jefferson Davis did not approve of his Apache extermination program, which included poisoning the tribesmen and selling captive women and children into slavery. Courtesy of the Arizona Historical Society, Tucson, AHS 28440.

norship. On February 28, 1862, Captain Sherod Hunter arrived in Tucson with about one hundred men of Company A, Second Texas Mounted Volunteers and elements of other Confederate territorial ranger companies. Colonel James Reily, the special envoy of Confederate general Henry Hopkins Sibley, now commanding in New Mexico, accompanied Hunter to Arizona. On March 3, 1862, Reily left Tucson with twenty of Hunter's men under Lieutenant James Tevis for Ures, Sonora, to contact Governor Ignacio Pesqueira and seek Mexican recognition of and supplies for the Confederate government.[4]

4. The portion of the Gadsden Purchase south of the Gila River had been known since the Spanish entrada as "Arizonae," probably a Basque word meaning "the good oak tree." Garate, *Juan Bautista de Anza,* 164. For other theories on the origin of Arizona, see Will C. Barnes, *Arizona Place Names,* rev. and ed. Byrd H. Granger (Tucson: University of Arizona Press, 1985), xv. See also Finch, "William Claude Jones," 410–11. From 1854, when the Senate ratified the Gadsden Purchase, to 1860, no fewer than ten bills were introduced in Congress calling for the creation of an Arizona separate from New Mexico Territory. The proponents of these bills all imagined an east-west division of New Mexico from the Colorado River to the Rio Grande. In 1863 Abraham Lincoln finally signed into law the bill that created Arizona Territory divided on a north-south line in order to separate what was thought to be a voting block sympathetic to the Confederacy. Walker and Bufkin, *Historical Atlas of Arizona,* 25; J. R. Baylor, "Proclamation to the People of the Territory of Arizona," Aug. 1, 1861, *OR,* 4:20–21; Sherod Hunter to Col. J. R. Baylor, Apr. 5, 1862, ibid., 9:707–8.

Hunter's small but independent command promptly seized the initiative in Arizona. No Union forces opposed the arrival of the Rebel horse soldiers. The settlers, it seemed, even welcomed them as a means of protection from the increasingly aggresive Apaches. Attacks by Chiricahua and other western Apaches, as well as eastern Mimbreño and Mescalero bands, took their toll on civilian miners between Tucson and the Rio Grande. Emboldened by the earlier withdrawal of U.S. troops, Apache war leaders raided with impunity. They even attacked the heavily armed rangers under Hunter's command, making no distinction between Union and Confederate whites. While Baylor and Hunter began the tasks of occupation and control of the natives, the movement of California Volunteer units to Fort Yuma along the Colorado River was already underway.[5]

In August 1861 President Lincoln and senior officers at the War Department debated the practicability of a column from California striking Texas by way of Mexico. Brigadier General Edwin V. Sumner, then commanding the Department of the Pacific, began planning such an operation. Civil unrest in southern California, however, diverted the California regiments. December brought news of Confederate victories in New Mexico and a Rebel invasion of Arizona. General Wright, who by then had succeeded Sumner, proposed to invade the territories with a force of California troops that would cross the Colorado River at Yuma and proceed to New Mexico along the Gila River on the old Butterfield Overland Mail route. General in Chief George B. McClellan, in a rare moment of decisiveness, approved the operation.[6]

General Wright selected forty-seven-year-old James Henry Carleton, colonel of the First California Infantry and formerly major of the First U.S. Dragoons, to lead the column into Arizona. Wright wanted an aggressive field commander to find and strike the Confederates as quickly as possible. He knew Carleton to be a tough and efficient officer with many years of

5. Edwin A. Rigg to James H. Carleton, Mar. 25, 1862, *OR*, 50(1):950–52. The term "Apache" is frustratingly inadequate for the historian, but it is used here because this is how the Californians referred to the nomadic bands of Apachean (Southern Athabaskan) speakers they encountered in Arizona and New Mexico. The soldiers applied "Apache" to Chiricahuas, Mescaleros, Mimbrenos, Jicarillas, Western Apaches, and even Yavapais. If their identities were known, it would be more appropriate to refer to specific bands. The Chiricahuas, for example, comprised the Bidanku, Chihene, Chukanen, and Ndendai bands. Yet it is nearly impossible to identify Apache bands with any sort of precision based on contemporary accounts, so period terminology has been retained in most cases to avoid confusing the issue with speculative identifications.

6. George Wright to Lorenzo Thomas, Dec. 9, 1861, *OR*, 50(1):752–53.

frontier experience. After more than twenty years in the saddle, Carleton had earned a reputation as an uncompromising disciplinarian. Lean, sharp-featured, and ramrod straight, he could command obedience with a flash of his steel gray eyes. He was also energetic, articulate, and always demonstrated foresight in both the logistic and strategic aspects of organizing, equipping, and deploying troops. Wright developed the plan for the Arizona expedition only after the War Department rejected as politically inexpedient the idea of attacking the Confederates in Texas by way of the Mexican states of Sonora and Chihuahua. The leadership in Washington had originally intended that Carleton command the soldiers assigned to guard the overland mail on the central route through Nevada, Utah, and Wyoming territories—he had led his dragoons over this country following the Mormon War of 1857—but rescinded these orders when the Confederate threat in the Southwest became apparent.[7]

A thrust from southern California across Arizona and New Mexico to the Rio Grande would serve several purposes. It would block a junction of Texas Rebels and California secessionists, reopen the southern overland mail route, provide garrisons for abandoned posts, and furnish protection to the citizens of the territories. Many of these citizens were miners taking advantage of the tremendous mineral wealth—gold and silver—already evident in Colorado, New Mexico, and most recently Arizona. The Californians would also be in a position to fall upon the flank and rear of Sibley's Texans, who seemed invincible as they pushed up the Rio Grande toward Santa Fe and the Colorado goldfields. Wright advised McClellan that, "under the command of Colonel Carleton, an officer of great experience, indefatigable and active, the expedition must be successful."[8]

Carleton's force included ten companies of his own regiment, the First California Infantry; five companies of the First California Cavalry under Lieutenant Colonel Edward E. Eyre; and Light Battery A, Third U.S. Artillery. First Lieutenant John B. Shinn commanded the battery, which mounted four bronze field pieces (six-pounder guns and twelve-pounder howitzers) manned by regulars. Wright assigned Captain John C. Cremony's Company B, Second California Cavalry to Carleton's contingent before the column set out across the desert. Later Colonel George W. Bowie's ten companies of the Fifth California Infantry and two improvised mountain-howitzer batteries,

7. Hunt, *James Henry Carleton.*
8. Report of James M. McNulty, Oct. 1863, *OR,* 50(1):137; Wright to Thomas, ibid., 752–53.

Obsessed with the minutiae of arming and equipping his "Column from California," Brig. Gen. James H. Carleton secured Arizona for the Union. Aloof and imperious— he could stop a man dead in his tracks with his steel gray eyes—he ruled the southwestern territories with an iron hand. Courtesy of the Arizona Historical Society, Tucson, AHS 41550.

commanded by Lieutenants Jeremiah Phelan and William A. Thompson, joined Carleton's command, bringing the total force to 2,350 men. Before the war's end some 6,000 additional California soldiers would follow this advance column.[9]

Experienced regular-army officers raised and trained the regiments destined for Arizona. Lieutenant Colonel Benjamin F. Davis, formerly captain of Company K, First U.S. Dragoons, drilled the First California Cavalry into a sharp outfit. But by the time the Californians marched for the territory in late 1861, Davis and many of the other regular officers had gone east to fight, and civilian appointees led the volunteers. The men benefited greatly from the training provided by their original cadre of officers, and these professionals agreed that no finer material for soldiers could be found anywhere. Recruits from every part of California flocked to enlistment centers at forts and camps. Nearly half of the state's population comprised men of military age. They were a hardy lot, used to working outdoors in the harshest conditions imaginable. Most of them were laboring in the mines and goldfields of the mother-lode country of northern California when the war

9. Richard C. Drum, AAG, to Carleton, Dec. 19, 1861, *OR*, 50(1):772; Pettis, *California Column*, 11, 8.

Capt. Benjamin F. Davis of Company K, First Dragoons, fought Apaches in Arizona before the Civil War. As lieutenant colonel of the First California Cavalry, he whipped raw recruits into first-class horse soldiers. Fearful that he would miss out on the action, Davis transferred to the eastern theater, where he was killed in 1863. From the Collection of Photographs of Civil War Officers compiled by Bvt. Lt. Col. George Meade. Courtesy of the J. David Petruzzi Collection.

broke out. In the 1850s they had rushed to California from every state in the Union and many European countries. They were risk-takers and tended to be bigger and stronger than their stay-at-home eastern counterparts. Intelligent and self-reliant, most had undertaken the difficult journey to California—by land or sea—and then survived the rough-and-ready life of a miner; other occupations appearing on the regimental descriptive lists include laborer, farmer, mechanic, printer, and seaman. The men ranged in age from eighteen to forty-five, and most had some formal education. These volunteer soldiers represented a true cross section of California's male population.[10]

The men enlisted for a variety of reasons, from a patriotic desire to preserve the Union to the lure of three regular meals a day. Others found the pay, eleven dollars a month, an inducement. In the ranks there was little

10. Hunt, *Army of the Pacific*, 24; Altshuler, *Cavalry Yellow and Infantry Blue*, 94; Orton, *California Men*, 68, 87; Hulse, "Migration and Cultural Selection," 1–21; Lord, *They Fought for the Union*, 227. A survey of "Descriptive Lists" for California regiments shows that the height of the average western soldier was more than an inch taller than his eastern counterpart. Quartermaster records indicate that the hat, coat, and shoe sizes were also larger. Lieutenant Colonel Crosman, commanding the Philadelphia Depot, noted: "The tariff for boots and bootees has been in operation for twenty years, with slight variations, but I have discovered that it does not suit the men of the West and those of the East equally well. In the western departments larger sizes are needed than in the East. The men are generally larger and have larger feet in the West." *OR*, 19(2):505. See CV Descriptive Lists and CV Clothing Accounts, RG 95, NARA.

talk of the slavery issue, but occasionally tempers flared between proslavery and antislavery men. Californians generally agreed that whether or not Americans tolerated slavery, the Union must be preserved. Native Californians—"Californios" descended from Spanish and Mexican pioneers—adopted a wait-and-see attitude as the sectional strife escalated. Most felt that this was not their war yet.

In many ways the California Volunteers proved to be superior to the soldiers of the regular army. Although well officered, illiterate immigrants and Americans from the lowest rung of the socioeconomic ladder filled the regular ranks. Alcoholism, a 33 percent desertion rate, malingering, and a host of social diseases crippled the strength and effectiveness of the standing army. The regulars lacked the diverse talents of the volunteers, who viewed military service as a temporary break from their civilian occupations. The volunteers quickly adapted to new people, environments, and challenges, while the regulars looked to their officers and the security of military routine. All things considered, the Californians seemed ideally suited for the arduous service they would face in Arizona.[11]

Although the California regiments lost most of their regular officers before departing for Arizona, able and experienced volunteer officers quickly took their places. Virtually all of the men awarded a major's commission or higher, including Joseph R. West, Edwin A. Rigg, Clarence E. Bennett, and Edward Eyre, had served in California's large and active militia during the 1850s. Others had seen service in volunteer regiments during the Mexican-American War (1847–48). Oscar M. Brown, William P. Calloway, Charles W. Lewis, John Martin, and Edmond D. Shirland could all claim war experience.[12]

California governor John Downey confirmed commissions for a number of outstanding officer candidates who had served as enlisted men in the regular army before the war. William McCleave served as Carleton's first sergeant in Company K, First U.S. Dragoons, during the decade preceding the Civil War, and Carleton pushed for his old friend's appointment to command Company A, First California Cavalry. McCleave had left the service in 1860 to oversee the army's experimental camel herd at Fort Tejon, California. Now he jumped at the chance to serve as an officer under Carleton. Similarly, Emil Fritz received a commission to lead Company B, First California Cavalry. Fritz had previous military training in Germany before arriv-

11. Orton, *California Men;* Utley, *Frontiersmen in Blue,* 12–18; Utley, *Frontier Regulars,* 23–24.
12. Dayton, "California Militia," 398; Altshuler, *Chains of Command,* 24.

ing in California in 1849; he succeeded McCleave as first sergeant of Company K, First Dragoons in October 1860. Second Lieutenant James Barrett of Company A, First California Cavalry, served beside McCleave and Fritz as a corporal in the First Dragoons before the war. Chauncey Wellman, a first sergeant in the First U.S. Cavalry before the war, also won a California Volunteer commission. Cavalry commands were the most sought after in the patriotic rush that followed the opening of hostilities. Carleton made certain that these plum commissions went to men of proven ability.[13]

But even the rigid Carleton could be swayed by political favoritism and friendship. Nathaniel J. Pishon, Carleton's brother-in-law and a former sergeant in the First Dragoons, landed the captaincy of Company D, First California Cavalry after the Pacific Department ordered that unit to accompany the Arizona expedition. Carleton kept his relationship quiet but later confided to McCleave that he had secured Pishon's appointment. Although the governor approved all commissions, a military board, established early in the war, reviewed all officer candidates as a safeguard against unqualified appointments. Later in the war many veteran volunteers with demonstrated aptitude were promoted from the ranks. A soldier in the First California Infantry lamented, "there has [*sic*] been about 15 or 16 sergeants in our column promoted to Second Lieut. Our sergeant went among the rest." The volunteer army, more so than the regular army, recognized and rewarded ability.[14]

U.S. Army regulations made no special provisions for the California Volunteers destined for service in Arizona. The army expected these troops to be organized, uniformed, armed, and equipped the same as the regular regiments they replaced. In practice, however, the availability of matériel, the personal preferences of officers and men, the anticipated enemy, and

---

13. Hunt, *Army of the Pacific*, 94; Altshuler, *Cavalry Yellow and Infantry Blue*, 209. Gulton, *Lincoln County War*, 46.

14. Wallace, "Fort Whipple," 114; Carleton to William McCleave, Mar. 15, 1862, *OR*, 50(1):931–32; Dayton, "California Militia," 400–401; Altshuler, *Chains of Command*, 24. Late in the war enlisted men competed fiercely for commissions. Cpl. Aaron Cory Hitchcock, First California Cavalry, wrote home asking "if you can fit in a word for me with the Governor in any shape I shall be much obliged. The Lieutenant Governor has promised me his influence for a position when ever an opportunity offers. . . . I would rather not let any person know that I have any promise or that I want anything for the reason that there are a great many old volunteers that think they are first on the list and if they know of any one attempting to get promoted they will throw everything in the way that they can." C. A. Hitchcock to W. M. Smyth [brother-in-law], Oct. 7, 1863, Aaron Cory Hitchcock Letters, Joanne Grace Private Collection (copies in author's possession).

Comrades in arms and close friends, these men of the First Dragoons had their photograph made just before the war. Sgts. Emil Fritz and William McCleave (*standing, left to right*) commanded California cavalry companies, while Lts. Leroy Napier and Henry B. Davidson (*seated, left to right*) went east and joined the Confederate army. Courtesy of the Arizona Historical Society, Tucson.

the desert environment influenced the formation and outfitting of the California regiments. Most of the regular troops returning to the East in 1861 deposited their arms and equipage at government arsenals and forts in California. Ordnance officers inspected and quickly reissued serviceable equipment to the newly formed California regiments. Armorers and artificers at Benicia Arsenal near San Francisco repaired unserviceable equipment as fast as possible, and stocks of unused weapons and accoutrements, some obsolete, were issued in the rush to arm the new soldiers.[15]

Carleton realized that the expedition across miles of uncharted Arizona desert, populated with Rebel and Indian enemies, would only be successful if he could properly equip his men. He understood that the campaign was as much about logistics as fighting. Fortunately his organizational skills and penchant for military minutiae were equal to the task.

The first cavalry volunteers to answer the call received the arms turned over by the regulars. These weapons included .54-caliber Model 1853 and 1859 Sharps breechloading carbines, the heavy 1840 pattern saber, and the cumbersome Model 1847 .44-caliber Colt "Dragoon" revolver. When the supply of carbines ran out, ordnance officers issued "3rd class" common rifles of the 1817 pattern, recently altered from flintlock to the new percussion system. Only the most expert horsemen and noncommissioned officers received sabers when the supply ran low.[16] Anxious about the arms issued to his mounted troops, Carleton knew from experience that uniformity of armament would be critical when it came to supplying ammunition in the field. His ordnance officers would have a hard time keeping track of and supplying ammunition for two different models of Sharps carbines as well as muzzleloading rifle cartridges. After more regulars left for the East and the workers at Benicia repaired unserviceable weapons, all of the horsemen with Carleton's column, and most of the subsequent California cavalry companies serving in Arizona, received the Sharps New Model 1859 carbine.[17]

This short-barreled carbine shot true at ranges up to one hundred yards. A trained trooper could load a combustible linen cartridge into the open breech, aim, and fire every ten seconds. By comparison, an infantryman with a muzzleloading rifle musket could fire only three rounds per minute. The carbine, designed for use on horseback, attached to a snap hook on a broad leather strap slung across the trooper's chest. Cavalry officers generally preferred the carbines and considered long rifles or muskets too unwieldy for mounted service.[18]

Carleton understood the need to balance firepower with the capacity of horses and men to carry the weapons. Accordingly he requested that the

15. George Wright to Thomas, Dec. 9, 1861, *OR*, 50(1):752–53.

16. J. McAllister to Drum, Nov. 20, 1861, Benicia Arsenal Letters Sent, 1861–63, p. 65, RG 156, NARA; Carleton to Drum, Dec. 21, 1861, *OR*, 50(1):775. Even after Carleton took up his duties as department commander in New Mexico, subsequent commanders of the California Volunteers in Arizona followed his carefully crafted guidelines.

17. Ordnance Return, California Cavalry, Office of the Chief of Ordnance, 1861–65, RG 156.

18. Carleton to Drum, Dec. 21, 1861, *OR*, 50(1):775.

commander of Benicia Arsenal provide his cavalry with the lightweight Colt Navy revolver instead of the heavy, four-and-a-half-pound .44-caliber Dragoon pistol. Although the Navy was .36 caliber and its small powder charge rendered it effective only at close range, Carleton preferred it because of the weight savings in the weapon itself and the ammunition. His soldiers would wear the gun in a holster on the saber belt rather than strapped to the saddle in pommel holsters as regulations prescribed for the heavier pistol. The Navy revolver also had the reputation of being accurate and a natural pointer, a decided advantage, considering that most of the volunteers were not accomplished pistol shots and little ammunition could be spared for practice. Despite Carleton's insistence, some of the Second California Cavalry companies had to carry the heavy Dragoon pistol when supplies of the Navy revolver ran out.[19]

Carleton preferred the heavy 1840 cavalry saber to the newer, lighter 1860 pattern for the mounted troops. All of his experience had been with the old pattern, and he felt that if the soldiers kept their sabers razor sharp, they could cut through the clothing of enemy cavalrymen and inflict serious casualties in close-quarter fighting. Cold steel, he contended, would win out against the pistol in a melee.[20]

Infantry regiments destined for Arizona carried .58-caliber rifle muskets of the 1855 pattern. These single-shot muzzleloaders fired expanding lead bullets, a deadly innovation recently developed by Captain Claude Minié of the French army. A paper cylinder contained the bullet and powder until the soldier tore open the tail of the cartridge with his teeth and rammed the contents down the gun barrel in a nine-step process that took twenty to thirty seconds to complete. Hoping to shave a few seconds off the loading time, the army adopted the Maynard patent tape-priming system, but experience had taught Carleton that the exploding paper caps misfired when wet. He ordered his troops to use the tried-and-true brass percussion caps in place of the newfangled Maynard primers.[21]

Each infantryman carried an eighteen-inch triangular socket bayonet for his rifle musket, but as the first volunteers were being equipped, a shortage of the proper leather scabbard for this weapon caused supply officers to issue the shorter and wider 1842 pattern scabbards. The loose fit resulted in

19. Ibid.
20. Carleton to West, May 2, 1862, *OR*, 50(1):1045.
21. Carleton to R. W. Kirkham, Apr. 11, 1862, *OR*, 50(1):1000. Later regiments received Model 1861 or 1863 rifle muskets, which no longer employed the unreliable Maynard system.

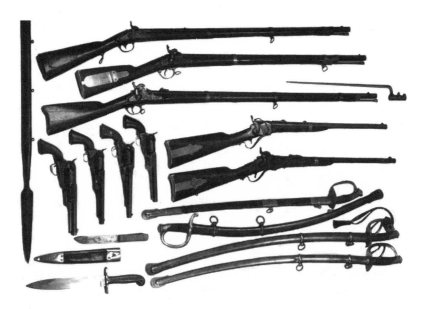

Weapons of the California Volunteers in Arizona (*top to bottom, left to right*): Benicia Arsenal lance; .54-caliber 1817 "Common Rifle" (marked "Native" on patchbox); .54-caliber 1841 Mississippi Rifle; .58-caliber 1855 Springfield Rifle Musket with bayonet; .44-caliber 1847 Colt Army "Dragoon" Revolver (ser. no. 13858, George W. Oaks, Co. I, First California Infantry); .44-caliber 1860 Colt New Model Army Revolver (ser. no. 32281, George Hand, Co. G, First California Infantry); .44-caliber 1858 Remington New Model Army Revolver (ser. no. 79296, Fritz Martin, Co. G, First California Infantry); .36-caliber 1851 Colt Navy Revolver; .52-caliber 1853 Sharps "Slanting Breech" Carbine (ser. no. 12817, "G 10 CV" on barrel); .52-caliber 1859 Sharps "New Model" Carbine; "Green River" knife; 1849 Rifleman's Knife and scabbard; 1850 Foot Officer's Sword ("Presented to Lieut. C. S. Whitney" Co. F, Fifth California Infantry); 1840 Light Artillery Saber; 1840 Heavy Cavalry Saber; 1860 Light Cavalry Saber. Photo by Angela Bayardo; Arizona Historical Society.

bayonets being dropped and lost on the march. Increased production of scabbards at Benicia Arsenal corrected the shortage, but only following heated exchanges between the Ordnance Department and frustrated volunteer officers.[22]

Selected infantrymen and unassigned recruits received training in the use of the four brass twelve-pounder mountain howitzers, which constituted the volunteer portion of the California artillery complement. Adopted by the

22. McAllister to Carleton, Sept. 10, 1861, *OR*, 50(1):616.

army in 1841, these lightweight howitzers could be packed on mules or mounted on "prairie carriages," wide-axled wheeled carriages that could be pulled by mules and were better suited for Arizona's vast and rugged deserts. Some of the infantrymen-turned-cannoneers retained their rifle muskets, unwilling to enter hostile country without some means of self-defense. These motley volunteer crews contrasted sharply with Captain Shinn's polished regulars of Battery A, Third U.S. Artillery, with their two full-sized twelve-pounder howitzers and two six-pounder guns.[23]

Newly commissioned California infantry officers eagerly sought to complete their personal equipage, only to discover that arsenal officers could not supply sufficient quantities of the standard 1850 pattern sword prescribed by army regulations. These men needed something as a symbol of rank and command, so the officer in charge at Benicia granted them permission to purchase the model 1840 light artillery saber and saber belts normally issued to enlisted men. This saber, with its dangerous-looking curved blade, came complete with a polished steel scabbard and only cost $5.50, which could be deducted from the purchaser's uniform allowance. Many officers who could not afford to buy swords from private dealers or were not presented swords by friends or civic organizations also took advantage of this bargain.[24]

Carleton wanted to ensure that civilian teamsters could defend themselves in case of attack by Confederates or Apaches. They received the heavy Model 1847 Dragoon revolver, deemed unsuitable for cavalry, and the 1849 pattern riflemen's sheath knives that had been stored for years at Benicia. The teamsters also brought along obsolescent Mississippi Rifles for use in an emergency. This muzzleloading weapon, adopted in 1841 and made famous by Jefferson Davis's Mississippi troops during the war with Mexico, was not as long as the infantry rifle musket. It fired a .54-caliber ball, though government arsenals had reamed and re-rifled many of these older weapons in order to use the standard .58-caliber Minié cartridge.[25]

The troops would be required to carry much of the ammunition needed for their weapons. For this purpose the depots in California issued two types

23. Carleton to Canby, May 3, 1862, *OR,* 50(1):95; Carleton to Rigg, Mar. 25, 1862, ibid., 950–51; *Ordnance Manual,* 20, 74.

24. McAllister to H. M. Judah, Oct. 3, 1861, Benicia Arsenal Letters Sent, 41, RG 156.

25. Carleton to Drum, Dec. 21, 1861, *OR,* 50(1):777; Ordnance Returns, California Cavalry, Office of the Chief of Ordnance, RG 156. In 1865, when many Sharps carbines became unserviceable through hard use, ordnance officers issued Mississippi Rifles to cavalry companies in Arizona. Single-shot Maynard carbines, designed to use brass cartridges, replaced these obsolete rifles in 1866.

of leather cartridge boxes. The foot soldiers received large boxes with removable tin compartments holding forty paper cartridges. The men wore these boxes suspended from broad leather shoulder belts. Each cavalryman had a shorter box, worn on the saber belt, containing a wooden block bored through with twenty holes that held the paper or linen cartridges used in the carbines. Both foot and horse soldiers received small leather pouches, which held the percussion caps needed to fire the carbines, pistols, and muskets they carried.[26]

To load their pistols, the men inserted powder and ball into the front of each of the revolving cylinder's six chambers and compressed the charge by cranking a loading lever. Then six thimble-shaped copper percussion caps had to be pinched onto the nipples, which automatically aligned under the hammer when the pistol was cocked. The whole operation took about five minutes—too time consuming to be done in combat—so most soldiers packed pistol cartridges in their pockets or saddlebags.[27]

Although the Californians received both dress and fatigue uniforms while on the West Coast, Carleton ordered them to bring only their fatigue uniforms to Arizona. Utility won out over looks, and unnecessary items were left behind or packed into escort wagons, two of which followed each company. The obsessive Carleton itemized every article his soldiers would wear or carry:

  I. Each soldier will carry one greatcoat, one blanket, one forage cap, one woolen shirt, one pair of drawers, one pair of stockings, one towel, two handkerchiefs, one fine [louse comb] and one coarse comb, one sewing kit, one piece of soap, one toothbrush.

  II. Each soldier will wear his uniform hat without trimmings, one blouse, one pair trousers, one pair stockings, one woolen shirt, one pair drawers, and may wear a cravat in lieu of the leather [neck] stock.

  III. Each soldier, whether of cavalry or infantry, will have one canteen, one haversack, and one tin cup. In his haversack he will carry one fork, spoon, and plate. He will wear a good sheath knife.

  IV. Each company, whether of cavalry or infantry, will have only enough mess pans and camp kettles (in nests) for absolute requirements; also a few short-handed frying pans, some large tin pans in which to

26. Ordnance Returns, California Cavalry, Office of the Chief of Ordnance, RG 156.

27. Ibid. Late in the war some of the horse soldiers would receive cartridge boxes for their pistol ammunition, but when Carleton's Arizona expedition set out, he did not deem this item essential.

mix bread, one or two strong coffee-mills, a 6-gallon keg for vinegar [to prevent scurvy], a few pounds of black-grained pepper, four axes, four camp hatchets, six spades, six shovels.

V. Officers will not take mess-chests, or trunks, or mattresses on the march. It is suggested that each mess of officers of not less than three be provided with two champagne baskets covered with painted canvas for their mess furniture. These can be packed upon a mule. Their necessary clothing can be carried in a small hand-valise, or pair of saddlebags.[28]

Carleton had no use for ornamentation and instructed the men to wear the regulation 1858 pattern black felt uniform hat—a flat-crowned, broad-brimmed affair—devoid of the brass trimmings that designated branch of service, regiment, and company. Carleton also deleted the prescribed black ostrich plume (one for enlisted men, two for officers) and directed that soldiers wear the hat brim folded down rather than looped up on the side according to regulation. The old dragoon knew that his men would need their hats for protection from the burning desert sun.[29]

The wool fatigue uniform consisted of a loose-fitting sack coat of dark blue wool, sky blue kersey trousers, and a forage cap. Undergarments were also woolen, though occasionally the men drew cotton drawers. The burgeoning California wool industry provided much of the raw material for the army clothing produced by contractors, who augmented their work force with inmates from the military prison on Alcatraz Island. Shipments from eastern manufacturers filled shortages, but especially in the later years of the war, overworked or corrupt government inspectors approved much shoddy clothing produced in New York sweatshops.[30]

Carleton paid particular attention to the men's shoes. He ordered that ankle-high "bootees" be made with sewn rather than pegged soles. The wooden pegs, he knew, had a tendency to shrink in the hot desert sands. When the pegs fell out, the sole detached and the soldier went barefoot. Mounted men had the option of drawing calf-high boots instead of the bootee. In practice, however, most soldiers accepted whatever the quartermaster had available, pegged or sewn, boots or bootees.[31]

28. GO 3, Hdqrs. Dist. of Southern Calif., Feb. 11, 1862, *OR*, 50(2):858–59.
29. Ibid.
30. Wright to Thomas, Oct. 21, 1861, *OR*, 50(1):668; Clothing Account Books of CV Regiments, 1861–66, California State Library, Sacramento; *Alta*, 1863.
31. Carleton to Drum, May 10, 1862, *OR*, 50(1):1060.

Carleton required cavalrymen and infantrymen to carry "Green River" sheath knives. Experience had taught him that this versatile tool would be indispensable in the field. Before leaving California, church and temperance organizations provided some volunteer regiments with "butcher knives" and other necessities such as sewing kits, toothbrushes, and shoe blacking.[32]

Horses and horse equipment would prove vital to successful operations in Arizona. Although the army tried to procure fifteen-and-one-half-hand "American" or Morgan horses, most volunteers found themselves astride smaller "California" horses of Spanish stock. The California mounts were famed for their endurance but could not carry the weight larger horses bore. Several companies of the First California Cavalry reluctantly relinquished their American horses, turned in by the regulars, for use with the artillery batteries and the freight wagons.[33]

Cavalry regiments received three types of saddles. The "Grimsley" dragoon saddle, adopted in 1847, was too wide and flat in design to fit the small California horses; these saddles went back to the arsenal for reissue to the artillery. The volunteers soon learned an ill-fitting saddle would gall and ruin a good horse, so a new pattern, inspired by a popular Mexican style, went into production. The San Francisco firm of Main and Winchester, as well as some smaller contractors, manufactured these "California," or "Ranger," saddles in large numbers. This distinctive western saddle had a horn, like a stock saddle; Mexican hooded stirrups; and a leather cover, called a *mochila*. The Californians also used the relatively new 1859 McClellan saddle. With its spare, rawhided wooden seat, the McClellan proved to be an acceptable alternative for use with the California horses.[34]

Mounted soldiers received wool saddle blankets and bridles, either the old dragoon style or the new 1859 pattern. Picket pins and lariats, hobbles, or side lines—all designed to secure horses while camped—completed the trooper's horse equipment. The horsemen carried leather-reinforced canvas nosebags for feeding their mounts measured rations of grain. Carleton ordered seamless burlap gunny bags, capable of holding one hundred pounds of barley, manufactured for the march to Fort Yuma. He directed

32. *Downieville (Calif.) Sierra Democrat*, Nov. 30, 1861; GO 3, Hdqrs. Dist. of Southern Calif., Feb. 11, 1862, *OR*, 50(2):858. For riflemen's knives issued to teamsters, see Hutchins, "Mounted Rifleman's Knife," 20–21.

33. Carleton to Thomas, Dec. 19, 1861, *OR*, 50(1):777.

34. McAllister to Carleton, Sept. 10, 1861, *OR*, 50(1):616; Drum to McAllister, Sept. 9, 1861, Dept. of the Pacific Letters Sent, 381, RG 393, NARA; Carleton to H. K. Craig, Oct. 18, 1861, First California Infantry Letter Book, RG 94, NARA.

officers to make certain the men soaked the grain in water before feeding in order to maintain the animals' strength during the difficult desert march.[35]

Most of the Californians would have been familiar with the doggerel verse popularized by Benjamin Franklin in *Poor Richard's Almanack:*

For the want of a nail the shoe was lost
For the want of a shoe the horse was lost
For the want of a horse the rider was lost
For the want of a rider the battle was lost
For the want of a battle the kingdom was lost—
And all for the want of a horse-shoe nail.

But for Carleton, this might have been his mantra. In fact the colonel seemed obsessed with horseshoe nails. He required that only hand-forged iron horseshoes be taken on the expedition. Machine-made steel shoes, he believed, would require too much hand fitting on his "quick thrust" into Arizona. Each soldier carried in his saddlebags two spare shoes, with nails, ready to set, and farriers prepared special steel-toed mule shoes in anticipation of Arizona's rocky terrain.[36]

Every man carried nearly sixty pounds of clothing, arms, supplies, and equipage. Little space could be spared in the company wagons for creature comforts for the California soldiers. Each hundred-man company had only two teepee-shaped Sibley tents. But the most important cargo was water. The company wagons each packed two six-gallon water kegs from which the men would fill their three-pint tin canteens. "Have the men drink heartily before setting out on a march," Carleton ordered, "and husband their canteens of water." Theoretically the company wagon carried enough water to enable one hundred men to travel eighty miles—a real possibility if a well were found poisoned or dry. Before leaving Fort Yuma, coopers fashioned huge six-hundred-gallon rolling water tanks to supply Carleton's column. The expedition could not wait for zinc lining material from San Francisco, so the enterprising soldiers stripped the tin linings from arms and ammunition boxes and soldered them together to make the tanks watertight.[37]

35. Carleton, "Memorandum B," *OR,* 50(1):780.

36. Benjamin Franklin, *Poor Richard's Almanack* (Philadelphia, 1758); Carleton to Drum, Dec. 17, 1861, *OR,* 50(1):769.

37. Carleton to George Bowie, Apr. 28, 1862, *OR,* 50(1):1036–37; Benjamin C. Cutler to Rigg, Mar. 15, 1862, ibid., 930; Rigg to Carleton, Feb. 14, 1862, ibid., 866; Carleton to West, Oct. 22, 1861, ibid., 672. Weight (in pounds) of equipment carried by a California infantry

California Volunteer cavalryman (*left*) and infantryman wearing wool fatigue uniforms, fully equipped for service in Arizona. This reconstruction depicts the soldiers of Col. James Carleton's Column from California as they might have appeared in 1862. The clothing, arms, and equipage of a fully outfitted California foot soldier totaled fifty-eight pounds. Photo by Michael Sahaida Photography; items from the author's collection.

---

man, under arms, in heavy marching order: CLOTHING: 0.25 hat (without trimmings other than worsted cord), 2.50 blouse (lined), 2.50 trousers, 4.00 bootees, 1.00 drawers (2), 1.00 shirts (2 woolen), 0.50 stockings (2 pairs), 0.05 cravat, 5.25 greatcoat, 0.25 forage cap; ARMS AND ACCOU-TREMENTS: 9.25 1855 rifle musket, 0.50 musket sling, 0.75 bayonet, 0.75 bayonet scabbard, 1.74 waist belt and plate, 4.00 cartridge box with shoulder belt and plates, 3.20 forty cartridges (.58-caliber elongated ball), 0.50 percussion cap box (with caps); OTHER EQUIPMENT: 2.00 knapsack, 5.25 blanket, 0.50 haversack, 5.25 ten days' rations, 4.00 canteen (w/3 pints water), 0.25 plate, 0.50 cup, 0.20 fork and spoon, 0.25 towel, 0.05 handkerchiefs (2), 0.05 combs (2, fine and coarse), 0.20 sewing kit, 0.20 soap, 0.05 toothbrush, 1.00 sheath knife. TOTAL: 57.75 pounds. Only items specifically mentioned in orders or known to have been carried by California Column companies are included.

Advance units of the expedition began the difficult march from Camp Wright, at Oak Grove, and Camp Latham, at Wilmington, to Fort Yuma on the California side of the Colorado River in late October 1861. One of Carleton's able subordinates, Lieutenant Colonel Joseph West, commanded the 180-mile tramp across the desolate basin and sandy dunes of the Colorado Desert. West carefully planned the movement, requisitioning supplies for men and animals and deploying advanced guards to clean out wells and collect the precious water. He staggered the departure of his command—no more than one hundred men moved at a time—to avoid overtaxing the capacities of the wells. The dry desert, however, was not the only obstacle in the path of the Californians.[38]

There seemed to be no happy medium when it came to water during the winter of 1861. Rains drenched southern California and the lower Colorado River region. Roads became mud bogs, making the movement of men and supplies virtually impossible. Soon after West's command reached the Colorado, the river overflowed its banks. Torrents of muddy water carved a channel around Fort Yuma, making it an island, and swept away tons of stockpiled supplies. Despite these conditions, by February 1862, ocean-going vessels and river steamers had delivered all of the expedition's supplies, now safely stored on high ground at Fort Yuma.[39]

Situated on a bluff overlooking the confluence of the Gila and Colorado rivers, Fort Yuma guarded that strategic crossing on the southern overland route. Carleton remained in southern California to expedite the movement of troops and supplies. Expresses left his headquarters nearly every day carried by cameleers Hi Jolly (Hadji Ali) or Greek George, both of whom had come to America with the camels imported by Secretary of War Jefferson Davis in 1857. Although the War Department had discontinued the camel experiment, Carleton relied on the animals and their able handlers for the frequent desert crossings. The colonel sent detailed instructions for the proper placement of field and siege artillery to command all river and land approaches to Fort Yuma. His men sank, or brought within range of the guns, the ferries at the crossings above and below the fort. Carleton ordered his officers to watch the steamboat men for signs of treachery. No

38. McNulty's Report, OR, 50(1):138.

39. Ibid.; Rigg to Carleton, Jan. 23, 1862, ibid., 815–18. Rigg wrote in exasperation, "I have the honor to report to you that Fort Yuma is now an island." For flood details, see Alta, Feb. 17, Mar. 5, 1862.

A camel stands beside a horse at the U.S. government depot in Los Angeles. After Chief Camel Herder William McCleave joined James Carleton's command, other California officers took charge of the herd. Camels were occasionally used to carry dispatches across the desert to Forts Yuma and Mojave until the army auctioned off the animals in 1864. Courtesy of the Bancroft Library, University of California, Berkeley.

one was to cross the river in either direction without the knowledge and approval of the army.[40]

Carleton insisted that the officers "Drill, drill, drill, until your men become perfect as soldiers, as skirmishers, as marksmen." When the first California infantry companies arrived at Fort Yuma, Major Edwin Rigg began drilling the men in earnest. They loaded their muskets with blanks and practiced firing by company and battalion—by rank, by file, and all at once in crashing volleys. Late into the night the officers memorized the pages of William Hardee's and Philip St. George Cooke's tactics manuals. Carleton forwarded additional instructions to Rigg. Each night, after taps, the officers were to recite passages by rote. Every morning they would drill their companies in compact linear formations, then in the afternoon, dispersed as skirmishers.[41]

40. Carleton to Joseph R. West, Oct. 22, Nov. 5, 1861, *OR*, 50(1):672, 704–5.
41. Carleton to Rigg, Nov. 4, 1861, *OR*, 50(1):700; Rigg to Carleton, Feb. 15, 1862, ibid., 870.

A flat-bottomed ferry at Yuma Crossing yawed across the Colorado River between two tall masts (*center*) arranged so the guide rope could be drawn up to allow river steamers such as the *Mohave* (*right*) to pass. California Volunteers established a quartermaster depot (*left*) and graded the landing (*foreground*) on the Arizona side of the river while manning the guns of Fort Yuma on the California side. Courtesy of the Arizona Historical Society, Yuma.

In March 1862, as Carleton consolidated his forces at Fort Yuma, scouts rode toward Tucson to learn the strength of the enemy there. Rumors filtered back that Confederate cavalry would soon be riding down the Gila in force. Both Carleton and Rigg had spies in Tucson. These men traveled via Sonora to avoid suspicion and carried a secret code, the key to which Rigg kept safely locked at Fort Yuma. Writing under the pseudonym of George Peters, Peter Brady, the former post interpreter at Fort Mojave, sent Rigg information concerning the Rebels. One of Carleton's agents, Frederick C. Buckner, made the five-hundred-mile round trip from Yuma to Tucson in twenty-two days. He returned with a letter from merchant Solomon Warner reporting that attacks by Apache bands around Tucson grew bolder and

During the Civil War, Arizona City was the largest town in the territory and served as the jumping-off point for the California Volunteers. This view looks north toward the ferry crossing and Fort Yuma's fortified bluffs on the other side of the Colorado River. Courtesy of the Arizona Historical Society, Yuma.

more frequent with each passing day and that "protection . . . would be favourably received here from any quarter."

Rigg worried even more about the rumors of Rebel raiders. He particularly feared for the safety of Ammi White, a loyal Union man who operated a flour mill at the Pima Villages along the Gila River, about ninety miles northwest of Tucson. White had stockpiled fifteen hundred sacks of wheat at his mill for the subsistence of the California troops. The major also fretted about the piles of hay that volunteer parties from Fort Yuma had cut and stacked along the Gila River, knowing full well that lack of forage for horses and mules would stall Carleton's supply trains and doom the expedition from the start.[42]

Captain McCleave took action to deal with these concerns. His dragoon service with Carleton before the war had earned him the commander's fullest

42. Carleton to Rigg, Feb. 9, 1862, *OR*, 50(1):854; Rigg to Carleton, Mar. 27, 1862, ibid., 958; Rigg to Carleton, Feb. 14, 1862, ibid., 865; P. R. Brady to Rigg, Mar. 4, 1862, ibid., 911–12; Brady, "Portrait of a Pioneer," 171–94; S. Warner to F. Hinton, Jan. 31, 1862, *OR*, 50(1):867.

confidence; in fact the two men had become close personal friends. Late in February McCleave's Company A, First California Cavalry rode for Fort Yuma in two sections. The captain must have breathed a sigh of relief upon seeing the adobe fort perched on the Colorado River bluffs, realizing that his men had made the first leg of the desert crossing without incident. But Fort Yuma also brought back painful memories: Elizabeth, his bride of only a year, had died there three years earlier as the dragoons rode from Fort Buchanan, Arizona, to California. Eager to leave Yuma behind, McCleave did not wait for the second detachment of his California Cavalry company to catch up. He crossed the river and started up the north bank of the Gila with an escort of only nine men, heading for the Pima Villages and White's Mill. Perhaps the captain was too eager and not nearly cautious enough. On March 9 he left six of his men at the Tanks, the last stage station before reaching the mill, and arrived late that night at White's with just three troopers.[43]

McCleave—Carleton's most trusted officer—had unwittingly ridden into a trap. The resourceful Confederate captain Sherod Hunter had scouts of his own, and they learned that the California troops were crossing the Colorado and marching up the Gila. Soon after Colonel Reily left on his mission to Sonora, Hunter rode to the Pima Villages, took White prisoner, and disabled the mill. Hunter did not have enough wagons to haul off all of the captured wheat, so he distributed it to the Pimas, from whom it originally came, figuring he would need all the friends he could get as the Californians approached. When McCleave brazenly rode up to White's house and pounded on the door, one of Hunter's men greeted him. None of the Confederates lounging about the house wore recognizable uniforms. After his hosts put him at ease, McCleave introduced himself to Hunter, who represented himself as White. After gleaning what intelligence he could from the unwary officer, Hunter suddenly revealed his true identity as his men leveled cocked revolvers on the astonished captain. At first McCleave refused to surrender, but Hunter pressed the matter by threatening, "If you make a single motion I'll blow your brains out." The Californian gave up without a fight, and within a matter of hours, the Confederates surprised his six men

43. Carleton to Henry W. Halleck, Nov. 14, 1862, OR, 50(2): 222–23; Carleton to Eyre, Feb. 8, 1862, OR, 50(1): 851; Carleton to McCleave, Mar. 15, 1862, OR, 50(1): 931; Carleton to R. C. Drum, Mar. 30, 1862, OR, 50(1): 962; McCleave to Eyre, Feb. 17, 1862, OR, 50(1): 871; Rigg to Carleton, Feb. 20, Mar. 20, Mar. 30, 1862, OR, 50(1): 884, 939–40, 965–66; Altshuler, Cavalry Yellow and Infantry Blue, 209.

Capt. William McCleave (pictured here as a major in 1865) was James H. Carleton's favorite—the two men had served together as U.S. dragoons before the war. McCleave's zeal, however, proved to be his downfall as Confederates captured him at White's Mill along the Gila River in March 1862. Carleton exclaimed, "a whole staff could not compensate for the loss of McCleave." When later exchanged, the humiliated captain refused to accept his army pay for the period he had been a prisoner. Courtesy of the Arizona Historical Society, Tucson, AHS 50110.

waiting at the Tanks. The Rebels had won the first encounter in Arizona, much to Carleton's disbelief and McCleave's humiliation.[44]

Hunter followed up this initial success by sending a platoon of his mounted rangers down the Gila to burn the haystacks along the route. Meeting no opposition, they successfully fired the hay at six stations. On March 29 at Stanwix Station, some eighty miles east of Fort Yuma, the Confederates encountered two California vedettes. The Rebel riders shot first, hitting Private William Semmilrogge of Company A, First California Cavalry in the shoulder. The wounded man and his comrade rode for help without returning fire, and Hunter's men wheeled and rode for Tucson after realizing that they had encountered the advance guard of Carleton's column.[45]

44. Hunter to Baylor, Apr. 5, 1862, *OR,* 9:708; Rigg to Carleton, Mar. 30, 1862, *OR,* 50(1):965–66; Hunter reported that nine California cavalrymen were taken with McCleave, while Union records report only eight. See Finch, *Confederate Pathway,* 129. For variations on the composition of the nine-man squad, see *Alta,* June 8, 23, 29, 1862.

45. Hunter to Baylor, Apr. 5, 1862, *OR,* 9:708; Rigg to Carleton, Apr. 12, 1862, *OR,* 50(1):978–79.

Although the forward units suffered at the hands of the Arizona Confederates, the Californians at Fort Yuma eagerly awaited an opportunity to prove themselves in battle. While the soldiers anxiously anticipated skirmishes with Rebels and possibly Indians, their company commanders worried about logistics and the difficulties of getting their men across the Arizona desert. The march would tax them all to the limits of endurance.

CHAPTER 2

Arizona

The impossibly blue desert sky showed clear against the distant mountain peaks as the men of the First California Infantry marched in column, four abreast, down the winding road from the Fort Yuma bluffs to the ferry crossing at the narrows below. Regimental musicians shrilled and beat their fife-and-drum version of "The Girl I Left Behind Me," a lilting Irish tune popular with the men. The formidable Colorado rushed a muddy torrent as officers herded their men onto the ferry, taking care to balance the load to prevent capsizing. Equipped in heavy marching order, with full pack and weapons, a tumble into the water would mean certain death. The flatboat yawed across the river as the ferrymen hauled on the stout hemp rope lowered from the high masts planted at the landings. Everyone involved in the expedition—soldiers, surgeons, teamsters, contractors—thrilled at the day's activity, understanding that the crossing into Arizona meant their war was about to begin in earnest.[1]

When he learned that Hunter's Confederates had captured Captain McCleave, Carleton appointed Captain William P. Calloway of Company I, First California Infantry, to command the advance into Arizona. Calloway's force totaled 272 men and included his own company of foot soldiers and Captains McCleave and Pishon's companies, A and D respectively, of the First Cavalry. Young Lieutenant James Barrett commanded McCleave's men now, and Second Lieutenant Jeremiah Phelan drilled a detachment of

---

1. James P. Newcomb Diary, May 15, 1862, CAH. "The Girl I Left Behind Me" was traditionally played when a command left a military station for the field.

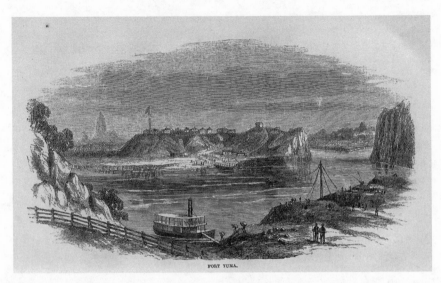

Fort Yuma, 1864. By J. Ross Browne, from *Adventures in the Apache Country*.

unattached recruits until they could service the two mule-packed mountain howitzers the Californians dubbed the "Jackass Battery."

Hoping to throw off Confederate spies, Carleton announced that his Arizona invasion aimed to chastise the Tonto Apaches. He instructed the advance guard, "When you leave Fort Yuma, you are to say you go and campaign against the Tontos." It was true that Western Apache bands had stepped up their attacks on overland travelers and the farms of the Pimas and Maricopas along the Gila River, but Carleton had no intention of allowing the Tontos to distract him from his real mission—the destruction of Rebel forces in the territories. In fact Calloway and all company commanders received specific instructions *not* to engage any Indians encountered on the road to Tucson. Confused soldiers held their fire when they stumbled upon war-painted warriors. Fearing Carleton's wrath more than the Indians, the troops gave the tribesmen an opportunity to fire first. A solider correspondent wrote of one such encounter between an Apache and Private David Carver, a member of Carleton's escort, near Grinnell's Ranch along the Gila River:

> Just as he reached the river, an Apache sprang from the bushes, gun in hand, and the muzzle directed full upon Carver, who, fortunately, saw him at the same moment, and brought his Colt to bear upon the savage. The latter stood ready for a few seconds, Carver likewise, both with weapons leveled and both, doubtless, anxious to fire; but the

Indian seemed to think the odds too great, at the short distance between them, some twelve feet, and Carver had positive orders not to fire first. The savage, who was in his full panoply of war paint, then dropped his muzzle and said, "How de do?" "How do you do?" replied Carver. "You Captain?" asked the Indian. "No," answered Carver, "Are you a Chief?" "No," growled the ring-streaked and spotted Apache, and without further parley he plunged into the river and swam across, bearing his gun up out of the water as he went. The temptation to shoot was a sore one for Carver, but he would not disobey his orders.[2]

Sam Hughes, a Tucson citizen traveling with the column, thought Carleton's policy absurd. Hughes refused to respect the ceasefire with regard to Apaches and bet the colonel a new pair of boots that the natives would run off at least one-third of the command's horses before they reached Tucson. But Carleton was nobody's fool. His "Tonto campaign" was only intended to confuse the Confederates in Arizona and New Mexico as his column marched toward the Rio Grande.[3]

The colonel kept his own counsel and demanded the same of others. From the time he accepted command of the Arizona expedition, he attempted to mask the movements and intentions of his troops. He strictly forbade soldiers to correspond with newspapers. Obsessed with secrecy, he wrote messages to Fort Yuma in code or occasionally in Greek. He sent some dispatches on tissue paper for easy concealment and, if necessary, destruction. Trusted couriers, including the camel rider Greek George and expressman John W. Jones, often carried fake correspondence in addition to genuine dispatches. If captured, the messenger could eat the real thing and turn the phony papers over to the enemy. Carleton intended to deceive the Confederates for as long as possible about his expedition's true purpose, hoping to surprise them in Tucson or pitch into Sibley's rear somewhere along the Rio Grande.

Calloway's advance troops prepared well for the long desert trek to Tucson. The march to Fort Yuma, where some soldiers had been waiting as long as five months, had been good practice. Both officers and enlisted men benefited from the journey and the experience of desert living at Fort Yuma while the column slowly grew, one company at a time. Carleton's command began the march across Arizona using the same survival skills learned while

2. *Alta,* June 11, 1862.
3. Lockwood, *Life in Old Tucson.*

crossing the Colorado Desert. Small parties went out to fill water tanks and cut hay at the abandoned stage stations in advance of the column. It made sense to follow the old Butterfield Overland Mail route so that soldiers and draft animals could take advantage of the wells at the way stations. The rough wagon road followed the Gila trail across the Sonoran desert of southern Arizona. Annual rainfall averaged only five or ten inches in this region, yet the soldiers discovered an amazing variety of life. Scorpions and rattlesnakes taught them to watch their steps and shake out their bedrolls; coyotes dogged their trail in search of scraps; and antelope fell prey to their rifle muskets. The Californians began to appreciate the desert flora too— barrel cacti with fishhook thorns, prickly pears topped with colorful flow-ers, and the occasional giant saguaros. The men marched with knapsacks and carried ten days' rations in their haversacks. Company commanders made certain their wagons had full water kegs and sufficient forage to travel without having to resupply at one of the stations.

Carleton hoped that Calloway's command would move rapidly up the Gila, surprise Hunter's company at Tucson, and recapture McCleave and his party. The advance companies moved along cautiously with civilian scouts, including mountain man Powell Weaver and expressman Jones in the lead. When the two vedettes from McCleave's Company A ran into Hunter's rangers at Stanwix Station, Captain Pishon gave chase with his cav-alry, but the well-mounted Rebels made good their escape.[4]

On April 12, 1862, Calloway's command reached the Pima Villages, where the stage road left the Gila to follow the broad valley of the Santa Cruz River into Tucson. The Pimas gladly resold the wheat given back to them by Hunter. The Indians traded for "manta," a cotton cloth that had become their principal medium of exchange, and handkerchiefs that Car-leton had wisely ordered taken along. Here Calloway learned of a Confed-erate outpost in Picacho Pass, about forty-five miles northwest of Tucson. Picacho, a volcanic plug of red rock rising nearly a thousand feet from the flat Santa Cruz valley, stood alone at the end of a range of rugged moun-tains. Just west of the peak, the river sank beneath its sandy bed, leaving only a dry wash to mark its path to the Gila. A ten-man Rebel picket post guarded the pass, while Hunter sent Lieutenant Jack Swilling, with another

4. West to Carleton, Nov. 4, 1861, *OR*, 50(1):698–99; Rigg to Carleton, Mar. 25, 1862, ibid., 950–52. Powell Weaver was known to Spanish-speaking Arizonans as Paulino and others called him Pauline (apparently he answered to all of these variants with good humor).

On March 19, 1862, the first shots of the Civil War in Arizona were fired at Stanwix Station, a stop on the old Butterfield Mail route along the Gila River eighty miles east of Fort Yuma. Courtesy of the Arizona Historical Society, Tucson, AHS 6624.

detachment, east to Mesilla to escort Ammi White and Captain McCleave to Confederate authorities at the Rio Grande.[5]

Although ordered to push on to Tucson by way of abandoned Fort Breckenridge, Calloway diverted his whole command to Picacho instead. If he could capture the Rebel outpost there, the shorter stage road to Tucson would give him a better chance of rescuing the hapless McCleave. On April 15 he instructed Lieutenants Barrett and Baldwin each to take twelve mounted men around the Rebel position in an attempt to cut off the escape to Tucson. But the two units failed to link up, and Barrett's unsupported detachment engaged Captain Hunter's picket, a sergeant and nine privates, in the chaparral near the base of "Picacho Mountain."[6]

Barrett's men, taking the shorter route, got into position long before Baldwin's platoon arrived at the rendezvous point south of the peak. Calloway had assigned John Jones to accompany young Barrett. Jones knew the country and possessed survival skills honed by numerous close calls in Apache territory. He sensed danger and urged caution. But Lieutenant Barrett pressed on, without dismounting his men, until he discovered the

5. Hunter to Baylor, Apr. 5, 1862, *OR*, 9:707–8.
6. Report of the Battle of Picacho Pass, Sherod Hunter Jacket, Compiled Service Records of Confederate Soldiers, Microcopy 323, Roll 182, NARA, cited in Finch, "Sherod Hunter," 203.

El Pecacho, 1864. By J. Ross Browne, from *Adventures in the Apache Country.*

Rebel pickets playing cards and resting in a small clearing not far from the old Butterfield stage station. Before Jones could prevent it, the excited lieutenant fired his pistol into the air and called upon the Confederates to surrender. A volley from the chaparral knocked four of the Californians from their saddles. The Union men then charged into the thicket, capturing three of the Rebels, who had thrown down their arms. Barrett had just finished tying one of the prisoners when a bullet struck him in the neck, breaking it and killing him instantly. The fighting continued for more than an hour, but when the smoke cleared, two of Barrett's men lay dead or dying and three others wounded. The Confederates suffered no losses other than the three prisoners taken early in the fight.[7]

By late afternoon Calloway's entire command reached the scene of the skirmish, too late to overtake Hunter's well-mounted rangers, who were now well on their way to Tucson. Lieutenant Phelan selected some high ground

7. *Sacramento Union,* May 23, 1862. The Rebel rangers fired at close range and with deadly accuracy. Barrett and his men were all shot in the head or upper body. Two men, Cpl. James Botsford and Pvt. Peter Glann, suffered gunshot wounds to their left shoulders. Botsford soon returned to duty and earned his sergeant stripes, while Glann never fully recovered; he was discharged at Camp Drum for disability on January 6, 1863. Pvt. William C. Tobin was a lucky man. A bullet had smashed into the brass crossed sabers pinned to the front of his uniform hat, then raked across the top of his head, resulting in an ugly wound. Tobin convalesced at Forts Barrett and Yuma before being discharged for disability on January 6, 1863. George H. Pettis to Annie [wife], Apr. 30, 1862, George H. Pettis Papers, Western Americana Collection, Beinecke Library, Yale, New Haven, Conn.; Orton, *California Men,* 69, 90, 98, 107, 109, 120.

and unpacked his howitzers to protect the column against a counterattack, but the Rebel prisoners confirmed that the pickets were unsupported and that McCleave was no longer in Tucson. This news added to the despondency of the Californians, who had been bested once again by the Confederates. Dark and early the following morning, Private William S. Leonard succumbed to an agonizing neck wound that had left him moaning throughout the night. Now the only sounds were the howling coyotes and the metallic clank and scrape of picks and shovels on the rocky earth. Calloway's men rolled their dead comrades in their blankets and buried them alongside the stage road where they had fallen. In the moonlight the burial detail used crackerbox boards to mark the cactus-covered mounds of earth and stone:

> Lieut. Jas Barrett
> 1st Cav. Cal. Vols
> Killed in action
> April 15th 1862
> aged 28 years
>
> Geo. Johnson, Co. A
> 1st Cav. Cal. Vols
> Killed April 15th 1862
> aged 25 years
>
> W. S. Leonard, Co. D
> 1st Cav. Cal. Vols
> died of wounds April 16, 1862[8]

Unnerved by the ordeal and worried his supplies would not be sufficient if the Rebels in Tucson held their ground, Calloway ordered his men to retreat to the Pima villages, more than forty miles distant, against the wishes of his subordinates and much to the consternation of the men.[9]

8. Newcomb Diary, Oct. 19, 1862; Julius Hall, "Wild West"; "William S. Leonard," Hayden Arizona Pioneer Biography Files, Arizona State University Library, Tempe.

9. "William S. Leonard," Hayden Arizona Pioneer Biography Files, Arizona State University Library; Orton, *California Men*, 47; Col. J. H. Carleton to Col. J. R. West, May 3, 1862, *OR*, 50(1):1048–49. The best account of the skirmish at Picacho may be found in Finch, *Confederate Pathway*, 139–48. All who passed the graves of the fallen California cavalrymen paid homage. See "Mr. Greeley's letters from Arizona," *Alta*, Mar. 15, 1864; and *Calaveras (Calif.) Chronicle*, July 1, 1865. In June 1862 Carleton and Captain Shinn noted that the graves were on the left of the road to Tucson near a mesquite thicket and dry *chalcos* (water holes) on the right of the road. He recorded the distance as 13.9 miles from Blue Water Station, south of the Pima Villages, and

Old Powell Weaver, disgusted by the inept handling of the affair, took leave of the outfit at White's Mill, remarking as he rode west to prospect on the Colorado, "If you fellers can't find the road from here to Tucson, you can go to hell!"[10] Two weeks later, when Colonel West arrived at the Pima villages with the second contingent of the expedition, he found that Calloway's men had already dug in. West ordered the construction of a more substantial earthen fortification and named it in honor of Lieutenant Barrett. From Fort Yuma, Carleton attempted to boost morale by remembering those who had fallen "in defense of the colors." He ordered that "until the end of the war [the names Johnson and Leonard] be called at every stated roll-call of their respective companies, and a comrade shall always respond, 'He died for his country!'" Carleton later designated Camp Barrett a subdepot, the only source of supply between Yuma and Tucson. On the march the men ate jerked beef, pemmican, and hardtack while the horses and draft animals fed on barley soaked in water and the gramma and galleta grass that grew wild along the Gila. With the exception of their encounters with Rebels, both men and animals had come through the first leg of the journey in good shape.[11]

Surgeon James McNulty, the acting medical director of the column, attributed the excellent condition of the troops to good planning and the fact that the men composing the column were "inured to mountain life in California, pioneers and miners; self-reliant and enduring; men equal to any emergency, if guided by a firm hand and a clear head." Carleton marched his men at night, starting at four or five in the afternoon and end-

1 mile from Picacho Station. J. H. Carleton, SO 15, June 15, 1862, Hdqrs. Column from California, *OR*, 50(1):142; *Alta*, Mar. 15, 1864. Privates Johnson and Leonard were reinterred at the post cemetery in Tucson but were moved again when Fort Lowell was relocated northeast of the growing town in 1884. When the post was deactivated in 1892, the remains were dug up yet again and moved to the national cemetery in San Francisco. Barrett's remains were never reinterred. The army tried to locate next of kin, but his only known relative, Ellen Brady of Albany, New York, never claimed the body, and it remained in the mesquite thicket near Picacho until all traces of the grave were lost. In 1928 the Arizona Historical Society and the Southern Pacific Railroad erected a fifteen-foot stone obelisk in the railroad right of way between the tracks and the peak on a spot a railroad signal superintendent believed to be Barrett's burial site. The original bronze plaque on the monument was stolen, prompting the Arizona State Parks Department to move the marker nearer to the entrance of Picacho Peak State Park in 1975. E. E. Eyre to R. C. Drum, May 14, 1862, *OR*, 50(1):120; *Arizona Daily Star*, Apr. 27, 1959; Edith C. Tomkins Manuscript, Small Collection, John Spring Papers, Arizona Historical Society, Tucson; Hunt, *James Henry Carleton*, 214; *Oakland Tribune*, Apr. 16, 1961.

10. George Oakes Reminiscence, Arizona Historical Society.

11. GO 8, Hdqrs. Dist. of Southern Calif., May 10, 1862, *OR*, 50(1):1061.

ing before dawn the next day. The sandy roads and choking alkali dust made the march almost unbearable at times, but the men did endure and pressed on.[12] In fact they were in good spirits, despite McCleave's capture and the dismal Picacho affair. Most of the soldiers believed that the expedition had been handled well, and they were proud of their remarkable record of marches from Los Angeles toward Tucson—nearly six hundred miles—averaging about twenty miles a day.

Camp or Resting Place	Miles
Camp Latham (Los Angeles)	18
Reed's Ranch	15
Chino	18
Temescal	17
Laguna Grande	13
Temecula	21
Giftaler's	13.5
Camp Wright (Warner's Ranch, San Diego)	25
San Felipe	13
Vallecito	17
Carrizo Creek	16.5
Sackett's Well	17.5
Indian Wells	15
New River Station	15
Alamo Station	14
Salt or Seven Wells	18
Pilot Knob	25
Fort Yuma, Colorado River	10
Gila City	17.5
Mission Camp	11.5
Filibuster Camp	6
Antelope Peak	9.25
Mohawk Station	13
Texas Hill	11
Lagoon Camp	5

12. McNulty's Report, *OR*, 50(1):136; Cremony, *Life among the Apaches*, 181. One soldier wrote from Tucson on July 7, 1862, that every man lost from eight to ten pounds on the march, but aside from some fevers, the California Volunteers enjoyed remarkably good health. See *San Francisco Evening Bulletin*, July 30, 1862.

Camp or Resting Place	Miles
Grinnell's Ranch	11.25
Grassy Camp	3
Burkes Station	6.5
Oatman Flat	11.25
Kenyon Station	13.5
Shady Camp	10
Gila Bend	4
Desert Station	22
The Tanks	7.5
Maricopa Wells	11.25
Pima Villages	11.25
Sacaton Station	12
Oneida Station	11
Blue Water Station	10
Barrett's Grave	13.9
Picacho Station	1
Point of Mountain	25
Tucson	15[13]

Carleton made certain that the officers made meticulous notes of all they observed, paying special attention to water (alkalinity, depth of wells, time to replenish wells), grass, shade, game, and the condition of the road. He also required them to carefully record distances. Shinn's artillery battery had an odometer attached to one of the caissons that measured distances to the nearest hundredth of a mile. Infantry officers relied on the tried-and-true method of pace counting. A reliable soldier in each company was assigned the unenviable task of counting each step and reporting to the first sergeant at every halt. Of course the man had to have a regular stride and measured pace of twenty-eight inches from heel to heel. A knotted string helped him keep track of his count, but he had to forgo socializing on the march or doing anything that might break his concentration.[14]

13. SO 15, Hdqrs. Column from California, June 16, 1862, *OR*, 50(1):138–42; GO 6, Hdqrs. Dist. of Southern Calif., May 7, 1862, ibid., 1056; J. R. West to B. C. Cutler, Fort Yuma, Nov. 7, 1861, ibid., 709–14.

14. Scott, *Military Dictionary*, 451; Bowman, "Diary of Corporal A. Bowman, Pace-counter, Co. B., 5th Infantry, California Volunteers," University of Arizona Library Special Collections, Tucson.

The marching men seemed unaware that their route through the low desert country along the Gila to Tucson's Santa Catalina Mountains rose nearly a mile in elevation. The climb was gradual, nearly imperceptible, but the teamsters needed to urge their tired draft animals on and occasionally double-teamed overloaded wagons over steeper grades. Some observant soldiers noted the altitude change and its effect on the native flora—from creosote, sage, and prickly pear cactus in the Colorado lowlands to the mesquite, palo verde, and saguaros of the high desert.

By the time the Californians regrouped and began the final push from the Pima Villages to Tucson on May 14, there was little chance they might overtake Hunter's men. From the Rebel prisoners taken at Picacho Carleton had learned that McCleave and Ammi White had been sent to the Rio Grande escorted by Lieutenant Jack Swilling. McCleave had given up an opportunity to be paroled because he refused to swear that he would not take up arms against the Confederacy. Knowing that it would now be impossible to rescue his friend, Carleton resumed his methodical preparations for subsisting his troops. Before leaving Fort Yuma he ordered Colonel West to secure Tucson and establish a supply line to Sonora, Mexico, as soon as possible. Carleton impressed upon his subordinates that on this campaign logistics mattered more than fighting. He wrote to Sonora governor Ignacio Pesqueira urging him to make supplies available to the California troops. As a gesture of goodwill, Carleton removed his earlier immigration ban on Mexicans who desired to cross the border to work in the rich new mines on the lower Colorado River. In accordance with orders West did not take the Picacho route to Tucson but instead traveled the longer Fort Breckenridge trail by way of the Gila and San Pedro rivers.[15]

Carleton saw Tucson as the key to Arizona, and his plan for its capture left nothing to chance. He would not be embarrassed again and cautioned West not to make any move against the town unless the chances for success were nearly all in his favor. Carleton counseled him to keep his sabers very sharp and not to underrate the Confederates. The commander drew on his Mexican War experiences and offered advice on how to take the town if Hunter's men decided to fight it out from entrenchments or forted up in loopholed adobes. As the Californians got closer to Tucson, Carleton's old

15. Yuma is just above sea level, and the road from Fort Breckenridge to Tucson passes along the base of the Santa Catalina Mountains, nearly a mile high; McNulty's Report, *OR*, 50(1):140; S. Hunter to J. R. Baylor, Apr. 5, 1862, *OR*, 9:707–8; E. A. Rigg to J. H. Carleton, Mar. 30, 1862, *OR*, 50(1):965–66.

confidence returned, and he warned West that Colonel Bowie's Fifth California Infantry, following close behind but not considered part of the original column, "must have equal chances" for glory with the First Infantry.[16]

On May 20, 1862, Captain Emil Fritz's Company B, First California Cavalry dashed into sleepy Tucson with drawn pistols at the ready. One platoon entered from the east and another from the north, meeting in the town's plaza without incident. Actually there was one embarrassing incident. As Fritz's men galloped through the dusty streets, they saw what appeared to be gun barrels projecting from the rooftops. According to Lieutenant George H. Pettis, Company K, First California Infantry, "Captain Fritz and his gallant troops, as they rode through the vacant streets of Tucson, threw themselves over on the sides of their horses when they saw the long water spouts [canales] protruding from the casas . . . pointing in their direction." The California cavalrymen quickly regained their composure and secured the town. The following day the infantry marched down the narrow streets with flags snapping and fifes and drums echoing "Yankee Doodle" off the adobe buildings that crowded the pueblo. The Californians stacked arms in the plaza and slapped the dust from their blue uniforms. From sympathetic locals they learned that all but a handful of Hunter's men had evacuated a week earlier. Only five hundred people remained in town, a third of the former population, along with a surprisingly large number of cats and dogs.[17]

By the end of May, Colonel West had regarrisoned Fort Breckenridge, which he renamed Fort Stanford in honor of Leland Stanford, the new governor of California, and Fort Buchanan, forty-five miles southeast of Tucson. But West soon abandoned these posts—the regulars had destroyed the buildings when they withdrew in 1861—for occupying forts had no place in Carleton's strategy to reach the Rio Grande and the real war in New Mexico.[18]

On June 6 Carleton himself arrived in Tucson. Lieutenant Shinn's four-gun battery boomed an impressive salute as the commander's entourage rode into the dusty adobe pueblo. Apparently Carleton arranged for Shinn to arrive early in order to perform such a ceremony, ordering his own

16. Carleton to West, May 2, 1862, OR, 50(1):1047.

17. Pettis, California Column, 11; Tucson Arizona Citizen, May 19, 1883, Sept. 27, 1884. Lieutenant Pettis contends that the canales that frightened Fritz's men became a standing joke with the California Column. Bowman, "Diary," May 21, 1862, University of Arizona Library. The Californians surprised Lt. James Tevis and a few Confederate sentinels who rode out from the opposite end of town. Finch, Confederate Pathway, 153; Lt. George H. Pettis to Annie (wife), May 26, 1862, Pettis Papers.

18. Carleton to Drum, June 10, 1862, OR, 50(1):1128–29.

On May 20, 1862, Capt. Emil Fritz's California cavalrymen, with pistols at the ready, dashed through Tucson's deserted streets. Expecting to find Sherod Hunter's Confederates waiting for them, the Californians ducked and dodged the *canales* (rainspouts) projecting from the adobe walls, mistaking them for Rebel rifles. Soon the wagons of the California Column clogged the streets of the "Old Pueblo." Courtesy of the Arizona Historical Society, Tucson, BD 68.

escort to make a fatiguing detour that enabled the artillery contingent to travel straight through. Undeniably the normally straight-laced Carleton had a flair for the dramatic. Just before leaving Fort Yuma on May 15, he issued General Orders No. 1, which declared that his expedition would hereafter be known officially as the "Column from California." Although unorthodox, the name caught on immediately with the men, and soon all official correspondence reflected the change or clipped it to the more manageable "California Column."[19]

After Arizona City, on the banks of the Colorado River across from Fort Yuma, Tucson was the largest permanent settlement in the territory. The

19. *Alta,* June 10, 1862; GO 1, Hdqrs. Column from California, May 15, 1862, *OR,* 50(1):1075.

people remaining in the town were a resilient lot—undeterred by Apache raids or the Rebel occupation. Most had been born Mexican citizens, but the Gadsden Purchase (1854) had made Americans of them—no matter, as long as the new government allowed them to practice their religion, tend their flocks, and till their fields. Some of the Mexican American population profited as merchants and freighters. Others offered important services such as blacksmithing—essential for the maintenance of army rolling stock. Captive Apaches toiled alongside the Tucsonans, just as many Mexican American captives had been adopted into Apache families. Pima, Maricopa, and Papago Indians could be found in the town as well. Some worked as farmers, teamsters, scouts, or domestic servants.

Tucson's white inhabitants, though a minority, dominated the political and economic life of the community. They were mostly young and middle-aged men—outnumbering the women five to one—who had emigrated from the "States" to seek fortunes as miners, tradesmen, and entrepreneurs. Some subsisted by gambling or some other illicit trade, and more than a few were fugitives from justice.[20]

Carleton had been feeling sorry for himself as he became aware that officers junior to himself had received promotions. But shortly before reaching Tucson, the news arrived that President Lincoln had confirmed Carleton's appointment as brigadier general. Now the new general provisionally proclaimed Arizona a U.S. territory and just as quickly imposed martial law in Tucson on June 8, 1862. He immediately established a supply depot that could support the other posts in the territory as well as the column that would continue to New Mexico. While the rear guard filed into town, Carleton, now also military governor, set about rectifying matters in Arizona. "A number of notorious characters were arrested . . . and sent to Fort Yuma. Order sprang from disorder, and in a short time a den of thieves was converted into a peaceful village." Such was the glowing account of Carleton's reign as related by Surgeon McNulty. Not everyone, however, was as well pleased with the new military government.[21]

20. Senate, *Federal Census—Territory of New Mexico and Territory of Arizona*, Tucson, 1864. Carleton's proclamation may be found in *OR*, 50(1):96–97. The United States acquired present Arizona north of the Gila River with the Mexican Cession of 1848. Gadsden's treaty, which included Tucson and the land south of the Gila, was amended and ratified by the Senate in June 1854—though this new territory was not occupied by U.S. troops until November 1856. See Sonnichsen, *Tucson*, 40.

21. Carleton to E. R. S. Canby, June 15, 1862, *OR*, 50(1):96–97; McNulty's Report, ibid., 142.

Ramrod straight and tough as nails, James H. Carleton served in the U.S. Dragoons before accepting a commission as colonel of the First California Infantry and commander of the Arizona expedition he dubbed the "Column from California." He plagued subordinates with his obsessive attention to detail, relentlessly pursued Indian adversaries, and established a military government in Arizona. Courtesy of the Bancroft Library, University of California, Berkeley.

Carleton sent a detachment under Colonel Eyre to arrest Sylvester Mowry, an ex–army officer, mining entrepreneur, and avowed Confederate sympathizer, at his Patagonia Mine south of Tucson near the Mexican border. Eyre brought Mowry and the occupants of the mine back to Tucson. A military commission tried the men and sent them in shackles to Fort Yuma for incarceration. Carleton extended his heavy-handed style of government to Tucson's gambling-hall and saloon owners by imposing a monthly one-hundred-dollar tax on all tables used for monte or games of chance. He ordered that the tax revenue raised be used to benefit the sick and injured members of the California Column. He also instituted a military pass system that monitored all citizens entering or leaving town. Although many Southern sympathizers had decamped with Sherod Hunter, Carleton would not tolerate any saboteurs or Rebel spies.[22]

He directed that until the territorial government could organize civil courts, martial law would prevail. Regulations for army courts-martial pertained to all

22. Orton, *California Men*, 44–45; SO 142, Sept. 10, 1863, Tucson, Commands of J. R. West, Special, General and Post Orders, 1861–66, Records of the U.S. Army Continental Commands, RG 393, NARA; E. E. Eyre to Benjamin C. Cutler, acting AAG, Column from California, June 16, 1862, *OR*, 50(1):1142–43; Proclamation, Executive Dept., Ariz. Terr., by Order of General Carleton, June 17, 1862, *OR*, 9:693.

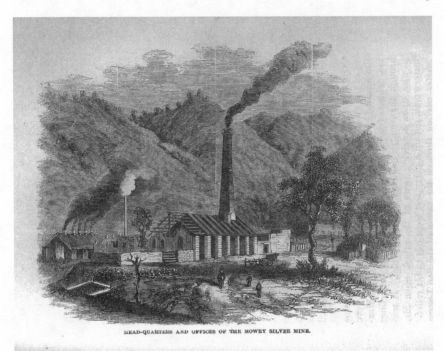

HEAD-QUARTERS AND OFFICES OF THE MOWRY SILVER MINE.

Headquarters and offices of the Mowry Silver Mine, 1864. By J. Ross Browne, from Adventures in the Apache Country.

public trials. A commission of not more than five and no fewer than three officers presided over the court. Only when the territorial government could establish civil courts would appeals be granted. A number of Tucson desperados, no doubt, breathed a sigh of relief when Carleton added, "no execution shall follow conviction" without orders from the president.[23]

While the California Column regrouped in Tucson, General E. R. S. Canby's Union forces in New Mexico, recently augmented by volunteer troops from Colorado, were pursuing General Sibley's Texans southward. On March 26, 1862, the Confederates met with a serious reverse at Glorieta Pass, just east of Santa Fe in northern New Mexico. After three days of fierce fighting, the Texans discovered that Coloradans under the command of Major John M. Chivington had destroyed their entire supply train and with it all hope of reaching Fort Union and the Colorado gold fields. While the

23. Carleton to Canby, June 15, 1862, *OR*, 50(1):97.

struggle for New Mexico raged, Carleton tried repeatedly to communicate with Canby.[24]

Finally on June 15, Carleton dispatched three expressmen in an attempt to reach Canby's command on the Rio Grande. John W. Jones; Sergeant William Wheeling of Company F, First Infantry; and a Mexican guide named Chavez left Tucson and rode hard for three days until a large party of Chiricahuas attacked them near Apache Pass in southeastern Arizona. Jones alone escaped with his life, but Confederate troops at another El Picacho, about six miles from Mesilla, captured him before he reached Canby. Incredibly, although imprisoned, Jones somehow managed to get word to Canby that the California Column was on its way. Carleton's passion for secrecy paid off. The expressman surrendered his false dispatch—intended for Confederate consumption in case of capture—and smuggled the tissue paper version to Canby.[25]

By June 21 the Californians began to move forward to the Rio Grande. Colonel Eyre pressed on with two companies of the First Cavalry on a "forced reconnaissance." This command met with no Confederate resistance, but it did encounter Cochise's Chiricahua Apaches, with whom Eyre had been admonished to "avoid collision." The advance companies encamped in Apache Pass, a narrow defile through the Chiricahua Mountains midway between Tucson and Mesilla. The Californians had ridden into the heart of Cochise's domain, hoping to treat with the chief while showing good faith by offering to share food and tobacco. Eyre little understood the enmity forged just the year before when an inexperienced regular-army lieutenant named George Bascom had hanged Chiricahua prisoners thought to be responsible for crimes actually committed by Coyotero Apaches from the White Mountains to the north. Some of Cochise's own family members had been among those executed in the Bascom affair, and the Chiricahua leader now reversed his peace policy toward Americans, intent on exacting a measure of revenge.[26]

So it was that while Eyre offered a gift of pemmican and attempted to parley, Chiricahua warriors killed, stripped, and mutilated three troopers from Fritz's Company B. Fritz was furious that Eyre would not allow him to avenge the slaughter of his men, throwing down his saber and carbine and

24. Orton, *California Men*, 44–45.
25. Jones's Statement, July 22, 1862, *OR*, 50(1):119–20.
26. Mulligan, "Apache Pass and Old Fort Bowie," 5–10; Sweeney, *Mangas Coloradas*, 391–412; and *Cochise*, 142–60.

arguing openly with his superior. The offending Apaches could still be seen on the adjoining hills just out of range. But Eyre was determined that the incident would not delay him. He tightened camp security and allowed the enraged Fritz to calm down. The Apaches fired a volley into the soldiers' camp that night, but the advance continued without further trouble. The pass had proven itself the bane of more than one expedition. At Dragoon Springs, just west of the pass, Sherod Hunter had lost four of his rangers and fifty-five animals as they fled eastward from the California Column weeks earlier. The graves of the Union and Confederate dead ominously marked the trail near the abandoned stage station.[27]

Just a month after Eyre's skirmish, the Apaches ambushed Captain Thomas L. Roberts's command in the pass. This fight resulted in the largest armed conflict ever to take place between U.S. troops and the Apaches in Arizona. On July 16, 1862, Roberts's command, which included a company of infantry, a detachment of cavalry, and Lieutenant Thompson's two mountain howitzers manned by infantrymen, met several hundred Chiricahua and Mimbreño Apaches under the joint leadership of Cochise and Mangas Coloradas. The volunteers suffered two men killed and two seriously wounded after a four-hour fight for the spring in the pass. Only the effective deployment of the artillery saved the command. With but brief respite beside the cool water of the spring, the men of the strung-out California Column continued on toward the Rio Grande.[28]

The danger of Apache attack in the pass decreased after Major Theodore A. Coult and a company of the Fifth California Infantry established a post there on Carleton's orders. Coult named this strategic post Fort Bowie in honor of the regiment's colonel, George W. Bowie. Carleton also created the District of Western Arizona, with headquarters at Tucson. He entrusted Major David Fergusson, chief commissary of the California Column, with the command of the district, which encompassed the region between Fort Yuma and Fort Bowie and provided for the protection of travelers, settlers, and miners. A detachment of Californians was already on the way to relieve the civilians at the Pinos Altos mines in southwestern New Mexico, where Apaches had killed so many of the miners that their families and others faced death by starvation.[29]

27. Carleton to Eyre, June 17, 1862, OR, 50(1):98; McChristian and Ludwig, "Eyewitness to the Bascom Affair," 277–300.

28. Report of Thomas L. Roberts, July 19, 1862, OR, 50(1):128–29.

29. Carleton to West, Aug. 6, 1862, OR, 50(1):105.

Carleton authorized a military mail, or "vedette service," to run from Tucson to Los Angeles. Modified in March 1861, the Butterfield Overland Mail contract permitted stage coaches and Pony Express riders to carry the mail on the safer central route along the Platte River and across the high plains, after which the San Antonio–San Diego Mail Line secured the contract for the southern route. The "Jackass Mail," as it was known, did not last long, for the sectional hostilities and the threat posed by Apache raiders forced it to cease operations by May. Carleton's elite corps of vedettes, using the best riders in the California Column, reestablished deliveries on the southern route. The general recruited small men, to lessen the fatigue of the horses, with a lot of grit. These mail carriers often rode without an escort, relying on their instincts and their animals to carry them safely through Apache ambushes and an unforgiving desert. Although Carleton appealed to Postmaster General Montgomery Blair to restore regular mail service along the route, the U.S. government did not resume operations until after the war. In 1864 Arizona territorial governor John N. Goodwin expressed his appreciation to the Californians in his report to the first legislature, stating, "We have been indebted to the courtesy of the military authorities for the means of communication between the principal points in the territory and the mail routes in New Mexico and California."[30]

By August 1862 the California Column had reached the Rio Grande, and Carleton succeeded Canby as commander of the Department of New Mexico. At the same time, Carleton received permission from Washington to retain command of the California Column, which had previously reported to General Wright's Department of the Pacific. Although supplies continued to pour into the depot at Tucson along the Yuma route, Carleton now commanded the whole operation from his headquarters at Santa Fe.[31]

In September Carleton defined the District of Arizona as stretching from the Colorado River to the Rio Grande. The District of Western Arizona, now commanded by Major Coult, became a subdistrict, supporting the frontline troops closing in on Sibley's retreating Texans. Carleton's change in command and the redefinition of the existing districts resulted in considerable confusion over departmental jurisdiction and the District of Western Arizona. Coult found himself in a decidedly difficult position, receiving

30. Wright, *Civil War in the Southwest*, 8; GO 11, Order of Brigadier General Carleton, July 21, 1862, *OR*, 50(1):92.

31. John N. Goodwin, Report to the First Arizona Territorial Legislature, Prescott, Sept. 1864, cited in Hunt, *Army of the Pacific*, 133–34.

conflicting orders from the Department of the Pacific and the Department
of New Mexico. Washington finally resolved the problem by officially at-
taching the District of Western Arizona to Carleton's department in January
1863.[32]

Although the California Column had skirmished with Rebel pickets and
fought Apaches in Arizona, Carleton's men encountered no serious opposition from the Confederates in New Mexico. Sibley had been defeated by
his inability to resupply his troops in the southwestern desert and the
relentless pressure from Canby's troops from the north and Carleton's command from the west. With the Rebels on the run, General in Chief Henry
W. Halleck wrote from Washington on October 13, 1862, that the desert
trek of the California Column was "one of the most creditable marches on
record. I only wish our Army here had the mobility and endurance of the
California troops." But the volunteers remaining in Arizona had only
begun the arduous task of securing and occupying the territory.[33]

32. Pettis, *California Column*, 18–19; Orton, *California Men*, 669–70.
33. Henry W. Halleck, Oct. 13, 1862, quoted in Hunt, *James Henry Carleton*, 236.

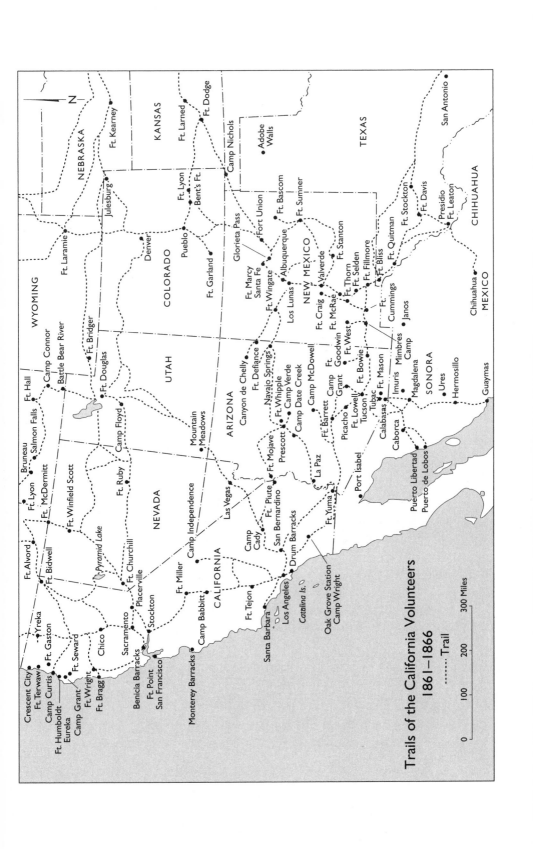

Trails of the California Volunteers
1861–1866

.... Trail

0   100   200   300 Miles

N

NEBRASKA

KANSAS

WYOMING

COLORADO

UTAH

NEVADA

CALIFORNIA

ARIZONA

NEW MEXICO

TEXAS

CHIHUAHUA

MEXICO

SONORA

Ft. Kearney

Ft. Larned

Ft. Dodge

Camp Nichols

Adobe Walls

San Antonio

Julesburg

Ft. Lyon

Bent's Ft.

Ft. Laramie

Denver

Pueblo

Ft. Garland

Glorieta Pass

Fort Union

Ft. Bascom

Ft. Sumner

Ft. Stockton

Ft. Davis

Presidio
Ft. Leaton

Camp Connor

Battle Bear River

Ft. Bridger

Ft. Marcy
Santa Fe

Ft. Wingate

Albuquerque

Los Lunas

Valverde

Ft. Stanton

Ft. Thorn
Ft. Selden

Ft. Fillmore

Ft. Bliss

Ft. Quitman

Chihuahua

Ft. Hall

Ft. Douglas

Camp Floyd

Mountain Meadows

Canyon de Chelly

Ft. Defiance

Navajo Springs

Ft. Whipple

Camp Verde

Camp Date Creek

Camp McDowell

Ft. Craig
Ft. McRae

Ft. West

Camp Goodwin

Ft. Bowie

Cummings

Janos

Bruneau

Salmon Falls

Ft. Ruby

Camp Independence

Las Vegas

Ft. Mojave

Prescott

Ft. Piute

La Paz

Ft. Barrett

Picacho

Ft. Grant

Tubac

Ft. Lowell
Tucson

Ft. Mason

Calabasas

Camp Mimbres

Imuris

Magdalena

Caborca

Ures

Hermosillo

Fort Alvord

Ft. Lyon

Ft. McDermitt

Ft. Winfield Scott

Pyramid Lake

Ft. Churchill

Placerville

Ft. Miller

Camp Babbitt

Yreka

Ft. Gaston

Ft. Seward

Chico

Sacramento

Stockton

Ft. Tejon

Camp Cady

San Bernardino

Drum Barracks

Ft. Yuma

Port Isabel

Catalina Is.

Oak Grove Station
Camp Wright

Los Angeles

Santa Barbara

Crescent City

Ft. Terwaw

Camp Curtis

Eureka

Ft. Humboldt

Camp Grant

Ft. Wright

Ft. Bragg

Benicia Barracks

Ft. Point
San Francisco

Monterey Barracks

Ft. Bidwell

Puerto Libertad
Puerto de Lobos

Guaymas

CHAPTER 3

Campaigning

During 1863 General Carleton devoted his attention to establishing the newly appointed civil government of Arizona Territory, consolidating his command and supply lines, and subduing the Indians considered guilty of depredations. The question of jurisdiction over the forts in the territory continued to cause problems, however, and logistics remained an administrative nightmare.

On February 24, 1863, Arizona became an official U.S. territory, no longer a provisional territory ruled by a military governor. Its boundaries included all of the present state of Arizona and part of southern Nevada, but the new political map did not correspond with nor alter the military boundaries of the District of Arizona within the Department of New Mexico. Nevertheless, in the spring of 1863, General Wright ordered the reactivation of Fort Mojave along the upper Colorado River in Arizona Territory and directed Companies B and I, Fourth California Infantry to garrison the post. Carleton at that time had his hands full overseeing the subjugation of the Navajos, who desperately defended their homes in the canyon lands of northern Arizona and New Mexico. He did not dispute Wright's reestablishment of Fort Mojave as an encroachment on his district and made no formal objection. The fort, he reasoned, could be more easily supplied through the District of Southern California. A short time later, though, Wright again stretched the bounds of his authority across the Colorado River to establish Camp Lincoln near the Arizona mining town of La Paz, with none but tacit approval from Carleton's New Mexico headquarters.[1]

1. For details on the evolution of the military districts and departments of Arizona, see Altshuler, *Chains of Command*.

In central Arizona Carleton ordered the establishment of Fort Whipple near the new gold fields discovered by Joseph R. Walker's prospecting party in 1863. The increased civilian and military activity in this area prompted him to create the District of Northern Arizona as well. This subcommand included all land north of the Gila within Arizona Territory except for Fort Mojave and La Paz, which continued operating under the Department of the Pacific. Carleton built Fort Whipple in northern Arizona to protect the miners and preserve order there until the newly appointed territorial officials arrived. Fort Whipple remained subordinate to the Department of New Mexico and received its supplies by way of a tortuous wagon road from Albuquerque.

The Yuma-Tucson route continued to supply most of the District of Arizona, though this arrangement proved less than satisfactory. Seagoing vessels carried supplies from San Francisco or Los Angeles to the mouth of the Colorado River. On the tidal mudflats at Port Isabel, hardworking stevedores lightered the cargo to shallow-draft steamers capable of navigating the unpredictable river. Only experienced pilots could navigate the muddy Colorado, especially when seasonal floods or drought affected the river's flow. Once the goods arrived at the Yuma depot, they had to be freighted east across the desert to Tucson.

From the very beginning, supplying the California troops in Arizona proved difficult under the best of circumstances and nearly impossible when things went awry. Generals Wright and Carleton planned at first to support the California Volunteers, even those in New Mexico, from the Pacific coast. They believed that purchases in Sonora would supplement the San Francisco-Yuma-Tucson supply line, but the Mexican connection never materialized, and the complicated system soon broke down. To make matters worse, the freight wagons deteriorated in the hot, dry desert almost as quickly as the horses and mules.

Deficiencies in supplies also heightened petty jealousies over jurisdiction. When the advance units of the California Column arrived on the Rio Grande in 1862, Canby complained that the new arrivals would eat up his already meager subsistence stores. Carleton, seething, responded that it was not his intention to "embarrass you to keep it [the California Column] supplied" and that he and his command did not come all this way "to split hairs" over how the several departments ought to be supplied. When the wagon train from Tucson could catch up with the advance guard of the column that had rushed to New Mexico to help drive out the Texans,

Carleton promised to replace the stores that the Californians had already consumed.[2]

Even though he planned the Arizona campaign carefully, Carleton had not given much thought to supplying his troops for an extended period once the Rebels had been whipped. Evidently he believed that Arizona and New Mexico could be supplied from the east when lines of communication were reestablished. Until then, experienced wagon masters commanded each of the California Column's forty-wagon trains. The most experienced teamsters were appointed as assistant wagon masters. Carleton named Captain Nicholas S. Davis "chief of transportation" to oversee the efficient operation of the trains. The California Column left Yuma with two hundred wagons and nearly twelve hundred mules, but the rough terrain, scarce water, and lack of forage resulted in unexpected problems, breakdowns, and delays.[3]

The question of jurisdiction plagued all of the post commanders serving in Arizona. Major Fergusson, commanding the Tucson garrison in 1863, was forced to purchase food from Sonora because the officer commanding Fort Yuma would not supply a post that, technically, was no longer part of the Department of the Pacific. The situation only got worse as the war dragged on.

General Carleton accused one-time friend and subordinate General Joseph West of dereliction of duty, believing that he did not adequately supply the District of Arizona. The seriousness of the situation forced fresh companies of the First California Cavalry, destined for New Mexico, to return to Fort Yuma or face starvation on the desert. Fergusson dispersed the Tucson garrison to feed off of far-flung posts throughout the district when his food stores ran out. Carleton considered this state of affairs the result of a "flagrant and criminal neglect of duty" on West's part and so reported to General in Chief Halleck. West, a capable and well-liked officer, thankfully received his transfer orders east before the bickering and legal posturing could get any worse. Colonel Bowie of the Fifth California Infantry succeeded West to command of the District of Arizona.[4]

2. Carleton to Canby, Aug. 2, 1862, Hdqrs. Column from California, *OR*, 50(1):92–95.

3. GO 20, Sept. 5, 1862, Hdqrs. Column from California, Las Cruces, Commands of J. R. West, Special, General, and Post Orders, 1861–66, Records of the U.S. Army Continental Commands, RG 393, NARA.

4. Carleton to West, Dec. 2, 1863, *OR*, 34(2):673; Carleton to Halleck, Mar. 20, 1864, ibid., 671–72; Nelson H. Davis to Carleton, Mar. 1, 1864, Tucson, *OR*, 34(1):674, 677.

Inspector General Nelson H. Davis reported a host of other reasons for the supply problems. Want of coin, he said, was a critical factor—contractors simply would not accept government scrip. Drought in Sonora resulted in a poor crop yield and starving cattle, while Arizona farmers, mostly Indians and Mexican Americans, would not tend their fields for fear of attack by Apaches. At the same time, the territory's population boomed as miners headed for the new gold fields. Major Davis cited poor roads, long distances, and the lack of reliable contractors as the main reasons for the failure of the district's supply system.[5]

Occupation duties soon centered on Indian fighting, or "hunting," as the volunteers disdainfully termed it. Carleton launched expeditions against the Navajos and the Mescalero Apaches in northeastern Arizona and New Mexico. From Fort Defiance, Arizona, and Fort Wingate, in northwestern New Mexico, California and New Mexico troops marched to strike the Indians. Under Carleton's direction, Colonel Christopher "Kit" Carson, the famed mountain man turned soldier, waged a relentless campaign. By the end of 1863 the Mescaleros of New Mexico and most of the Navajos of northeastern Arizona had been defeated and moved to the Bosque Redondo Reservation on the Pecos River. Although Carleton's reservation experiment ultimately proved to be a failure, these tribes never again posed a threat to settlements, Indian or white, in Arizona and New Mexico.[6]

Carleton's campaign against the Navajos destroyed their ability to wage war and their fighting spirit. Fort Defiance, supplied only with difficulty, provided a base of operations in Arizona, but most of the expeditions originated at Fort Wingate. The general had found in Carson a man who not only could expertly coordinate the efforts of the California and New Mexico volunteers but who also understood the ruthless brand of warfare required. Carson waged a war of attrition against the Navajos, who had successfully defended their strongholds for two hundred years against attacks by Spanish, Mexican, and U.S. soldiers. Tactics such as burning crops and orchards, capturing livestock, and destroying stockpiles of food forced the majority of the beleaguered Navajos to surrender.[7]

5. Davis to Carleton, Mar. 1, 1864, *OR*, 34(2):675; Davis to Carleton, Apr. 4, 1864, *OR*, 34(3):208.

6. Carleton to Drum, May 24, 1864, *OR*, 50(1):1094–95; Pettis, *California Column*, 18; Orton, *California Men*, 669–70.

7. For details on the Navajo war and the Bosque Redondo experiment, see McNitt, *Navajo Wars;* Gerald Thompson, *Army and the Navajo;* and Dunlay, *Kit Carson and the Indians,* 228–342.

In 1864 the adjutant general reported that "the Navajos soon found that they had no place of security from such determined adversaries, and being pressed on every hand by unexampled rigor, the spirit of the tribe was soon broken." As the Navajo campaign came to a close, other tribes began to feel the pressure of the increasingly aggressive military policy. Chief Iretaba of the Mojaves kept his Colorado River warriors in check by recounting stories of the white man's might; the chief had traveled to San Francisco and then to Washington, at government expense, accompanied by Pima chief Antonio Azul and Indian agent John Moss. The trip, intended to awe the chiefs and inspire loyalty, was deemed a success by soldiers and Arizona civilians. The Paiutes and Chemehuevis to the north, however, defiantly resisted incursions by white miners, freighters, and travelers on the Mojave–Fort Whipple road across central Arizona. Troops retaliated, though with limited success. Unprepared for the hit-and-run style of warfare, one soldier commented that the Indians "were too fleet of foot for infantrymen and gave us wide berth when we got after them."[8]

An increase in Arizona's population and a corresponding increase in Apache raids in central Arizona during 1864 prompted Carleton to establish Fort Goodwin in May. This post on the Gila River in the eastern part of the territory became the base of operations for an all-out campaign against the Western Apaches. Volunteer units stationed near the Mexican border at Tubac cooperated in this effort, and from April to July the number of soldiers in Arizona increased from 233 to 1,076. Carleton planned to launch a coordinated campaign against the hostile Chiricahua, Gila, Mogollon, and Mimbres Apaches. Troops would attack simultaneously from Fort Goodwin, Fort Whipple, Fort Bowie, Tubac, and Tucson. In an unprecedented move to crush the Arizona tribes once and for all, the general even requested the assistance of the Mexican governors of Sonora and Chihuahua in an effort to cut off the Apaches' escape routes, authorizing Mexican militia to "come over the line into our territory in pursuit of Apaches when, where, and as far as they please."[9]

8. GO 4, Feb. 18, 1865, Hdqrs. Dept. of New Mexico, *OR*, 48(1):909; Tuttle, "River Colorado," 60–61; Davis, "Pioneer Days in Arizona," Arizona State University Library, 52.

9. GO 12, May 1, 1864, Hdqrs. Dept. of New Mexico, *OR*, 34(1):387; abstract of troop returns, *OR*, 34(3):372; *OR*, 41(2):495. U.S. officers dealt only with the Republican governors of Mexico, even though the French-backed Conservatives were waging their own civil war against Pres. Benito Juárez. In July 1864 Napoleon III installed Austrian archduke Maximilian as the puppet emperor of Mexico.

In the spring of 1864, Carleton hounded his field commanders to make certain everything was in readiness for an all-out offensive against the Western Apaches. He eased up on his standing orders to husband ammunition and ordered "systematic target practice to the extent of twenty rounds per man with musket and carbine and eighteen rounds with revolver" each day. The soldiers would be trained to fight as individuals, taking advantage of Arizona's broken terrain, instead of drilling in compact formations and volley firing. The general was convinced that "the Apaches in Arizona are very hostile, and unless vigorous measures are pursued against them right away the miners will become panic-stricken and leave the country."[10]

The Apache bands of central and northern Arizona and the Yavapais continued to attack the settlers and miners flocking to the gold fields near Lynx Creek and the Walker diggings. The Indians found it increasingly difficult to hunt and forage as the encroaching whites not only frightened away game but also attacked rancherias without discriminating between warring and peaceful bands. Newly elected territorial legislators, as well as most of the citizens, were admitted exterminationists. They clamored for protection from the "savages." Yet as the three-year enlistments of many California soldiers began to expire, the District of Arizona faced a critical manpower shortage. A company of New Mexico Volunteer Cavalry helped fill the vacant ranks of the Fort Whipple garrison until California Veteran Volunteers and some Arizona volunteers arrived.

The Chiricahua and Mimbreño Apaches of southeastern Arizona and western New Mexico continued their attacks along the road between Tucson and Mesilla. Although Carleton had strategically located Fort Bowie in Apache Pass, the heart of Cochise's Chiricahua country, the garrison could rarely muster enough strength to take the offensive. Protecting their livestock as well as overland travelers fully occupied the volunteers stationed there. In April 1863 a war party of nearly two hundred Apaches attacked the Fifth California Infantry company assigned to guard the pass. The soldiers beat off the determined warriors after a two-hour fight. The activity of the Mimbreños abated somewhat in Arizona after the capture of their war leader Mangas Coloradas. California Volunteers deceived and captured the charismatic Apache under a flag of truce near Fort West, New Mexico. The soldiers assigned to guard the chief taunted and tortured him until he ran

10. Carleton to George W. Bowie, Apr. 15, 1864, *OR*, 50(2):820.

for his life. His bullet-riddled body became a thing of curiosity for the Californians, who expressed little remorse for their role in the affair.[11]

The California soldiers who had so confidently marched into Arizona ready to do battle soon came to despise their Apache adversaries. "I abhor the idea of fighting Indians," wrote one volunteer, "let me fight an enemy that is worthy of my steel." Fantastic rumors of terrible tortures, perpetrated by a "cowardly and inhuman" foe, circulated in the ranks. Captive children, it was said, had been found nailed to spiny cacti, and Apache warriors ornamented their bridles not only with the scalps of slain soldiers but with their severed mustachioed lips as well. Sympathy for "Lo, the poor Indian" evaporated, and the Californians set to the task of extermination with hard hearts and grim determination.[12]

Officers reported killing hundreds of "hostile" Indians, including men, women, and children, in Arizona between 1862 and 1866, far more than at any other period in history. The Californians lost forty officers and men in battles, skirmishes, or ambushes while traveling singly or in small parties. Carleton believed his men better armed than the natives, and he placed his trust in "the gallantry of small parties against any number [of Indians]. Large parties move snail-like, are seen at once, and are avoided; generally are laughed at by these Apaches. Small parties move secretly, cover more ground, move with celerity, emulate to do better than all others, and in the end either destroy or worry the Indians into submission."[13]

In March 1864, Chiricahua raiders ran off with a herd of government mules corralled at Cow Springs, near the Arizona–New Mexico border. Captain James H. Whitlock, Company F, Fifth California Infantry, with a mixed command of cavalry and foot soldiers, set out in pursuit but deliberately held his men back, allowing the raiders to get a good lead. When the Chiricahuas thought they had eluded the Californians, they no longer attempted to mask their trail, which headed straight to a large village in the Sierra Bonita Mountains thirty-five miles northwest of Fort Bowie. Splitting his command and striking out with a fast-moving force, Whitlock tracked the Chiricahuas by moonlight and attacked at daybreak on April 7. Although outnumbered, the Californians killed twenty-one warriors, recaptured the stolen stock, and completely destroyed the Apaches' food supplies and

11. Colton, *Civil War in the Western Territories,* 133.

12. *San Francisco Evening Bulletin,* Mar. 11, 1863. The author of this letter is most likely Manson A. Mesenheimer, a saddler in Company B, Second California Cavalry.

13. Carleton to Lorenzo Thomas, AG, USA, Washington, Apr. 17, 1864, *OR,* 34(3):200.

camp equipage—all without loss to Whitlock's command. Carleton congratulated Colonel Bowie and Whitlock while bragging about the rare victory to the high command in Washington.[14]

The California soldiers believed themselves, man for man, to far surpass their Indian adversaries. One volunteer wrote: "The superiority of the Californians over the Apaches at their own style of fighting, was shown in the case of Corporal [Charles] Ellis of Company A [First Cavalry], who crawled to a rock behind which was an Indian, and, giving a short cough, the Indian raised his head to discover his course, when a bullet from Ellis's rifle dashed through his brain."[15]

Captain T. T. Tidball's expedition against the Arivaipa Apaches epitomizes the type of warfare waged against the warring bands within the territory. Tidball's command consisted of twenty-five picked men of Companies I and K, Fifth California Infantry; ten "American citizens"; thirty-two "Mexicans"; twenty Papagos from San Xavier; and about nine "tame Apaches." They left Tucson for the "Cajon de Arivaypa" in May 1864 to "chastise" the Apaches. The troops marched only at night, in silence, and did not light a fire for five days. Tidball's caution enabled his command to completely surprise an Apache village of men, women, and children. The savage attack killed at least fifty Apaches and wounded as many more. The soldiers escorted ten women and children back to Tucson as prisoners of war. Thomas C. McClelland, a Tucsonan, was the only one of Tidball's men killed in the raid. Colonel Fergusson, commanding at Tucson, praised the "brilliant little affair," regarding it as "something for emulation to others in future campaigns against Apaches."[16]

Colonel Oscar M. Brown wrote a poem that the men of his First California Cavalry soon adopted as their marching song:

We'll whip the Apache
We'll exterminate the race
Of thieves and assassins

14. Carleton to Lorenzo Thomas, Apr. 24, 1864, *OR*, 50(2):826; Bowie to Carleton, Apr. 15, 1864, ibid., 826–27; James H. Whitlock to Capt. C. A. Smith, Apr. 13, 1864, ibid., 827–29.

15. Orton, *California Men*, 72.

16. GO 8, May 12, 1863, Tucson, *OR*, 50(2):432–33; Fergusson to T. T. Tidball, May 2, 1863, ibid., 422–23; Orton, *California Men*, 671; *Los Angeles Star*, Aug. 30, 1864. Others followed Tidball's example during the war years. As late as 1871, men who had accompanied Tidball instigated the infamous Camp Grant Massacre. Their route, method of attack, and results were almost identical; the main difference was that, in 1871, Chief Eskiminzin's Arivaipa Apaches had surrendered to the officer commanding Camp Grant and supposedly enjoyed his protection.

A California forty-niner and newspaper editor, Thomas T. Tidball commanded Company K, Fifth California
Infantry. From his base at Fort Bowie,
Tidball led a number of deadly raids
against Apache bands and won the
gratitude of Arizona's white settlers.
Courtesy of the Arizona Historical
Society, Tucson, AHS 11255.

Who the human form disgrace
We'll travel over mountain
And through the valley deep,
We'll travel without eating,
We'll travel without sleep.[17]

The Apache war had devolved into something more akin to a blood
feud. Noncombatants suffered the most. Both whites and Indians perpetrated atrocities without regard for sex, age, or guilt. In June 1865 Captain
Martin H. Calderwood had been in Arizona for only a month when his company of the Seventh California Infantry responded to a call for help from
Pedro Saavedra's "Spanish Ranch" near Tubac. Calderwood remembered
the grisly aftermath of the Chiricahua attack:

17. *Santa Fe Gazette*, Dec. 17, 1864.

Here I beheld one of the most sickening and cruel sights I ever witnessed during the whole of my campaign against the Apaches. The Indians had stripped naked the four women they had captured and after disembowelling them while still alive, had on the first sight of our approach lanced them through the heart. One of the lance heads had been pulled from its shaft and still remained in the woman's body. I pulled the lance from the woman and the still warm blood flowed from it.

The two small children were lying dead near a mesquite log. The savages had taken them by the feet and smashed their heads to a pulpy mass on the log which was besmeared with their blood and brains. Sevadra, who was as brave a man as ever lived and who was esteemed by all who knew him, had purportedly been shot through his kidneys with an arrow; We found him alive but in awful agony. He lived for two days and then died.[18]

Carleton's far-reaching Apache campaign of 1864 did not live up to expectations. Some citizens claimed that repeated military forays only agitated the Indians, prompting bloody revenge raids. In fact only one of four expeditions or scouts resulted in any significant damage to the warring tribesmen. The Californians measured success in pounds of mescal, the dietary staple of the Western Apaches, destroyed; the number of weapons and animals captured; and of course, body counts.[19]

Some Arizona tribes chose to ally themselves with the army rather than fight. Longstanding enemies of the Apaches, the Pimas and the Maricopas not only supplied the Californians with food and fodder but also performed valuable service as guides and auxiliaries in campaigns against the common enemy. In May 1862 Carleton requested that General Wright send to the Pimas and Maricopas "100 stand of the old muskets (percussion), with 10,000 rounds of buck and ball cartridges." He added that "this would be a great favor to this worthy people, who have always been our fast

18. *Arizona Enterprise,* June 13, 1891; Capt. M. H. Calderwood to J. F. Calderwood, June 27, 1865, in *Dutch Flat Enquirer,* Aug. 12, 1865. The killings at Saavedra's ranch outraged both soldiers and civilians in Arizona. See Farish, *History of Arizona,* 6:130–31. After Mangas Coloradas's death in 1863 at the hands of the California Volunteers, Cochise became the most aggressive and pursued Apache leader. See Report of Lt. Col. C. E. Bennett, July 6, 1865, *OR,* 50(1):415–19.

19. Utley, *Frontiersmen in Blue,* 259.

Pima chief Antonio Azul provided assistance to the California Volunteers in Arizona. Pima wheat fed the California troops, and later in the war Pima warriors joined with the soldiers to combat Apache raiders. Courtesy of the Arizona Historical Society, Tucson, AHS 49894.

friends." Carleton trusted these peaceful native farmers but had little confidence in their marksmanship. He ordered the buck and ball cartridges in the belief that these multi-projectile loads would increase the effectiveness of his warrior allies.[20]

Almost everybody connected with the army in Arizona saw the wisdom of arming native auxiliaries. The friendly tribes repeatedly requested arms and ammunition. Citizens and legislators agreed that the Pimas, Maricopas, and Papagos would perform well if given the opportunity. Every commander of the District of Arizona advocated it, as did a majority of rank-and-file California Volunteers. Army red tape, however, bogged down the implementation of the concept for nearly four years. Between September and November 1865, the territorial legislature recruited four companies of Arizona Volunteers. This battalion comprised two companies of "Mexicans," one of Pimas, and one of Maricopas, some 350 men all told. White officers commanded, some of whom had until recently served as enlisted men in the ranks of the California Volunteers.

With only one-year terms of enlistment, the Arizona Volunteers had orders to scout central Arizona and kill Apaches. On several occasions they cooperated successfully with the few California companies still in the field. The native troops exceeded all expectations, and when their enlistments expired, the territorial legislature and the California Volunteer district commander, Colonel Clarence E. Bennett, extolled their value and requested an extension of their service. Bennett even suggested that they be allowed to keep their weapons if orders came to disband. These native Arizonans were highly motivated to carry on the war for their homes, even without government assistance. But by late 1865, Federal authorities had focused their energies on demobilizing the tremendous war machine created during the rebellion. Thus the War Department ignored pleas from Arizona for new regiments and extensions.[21]

The California Volunteers campaigned against Arizona's Indians on a scale and with a ferocity unequalled before or after the Civil War. Just like the Pimas, Maricopas, and Mexican American Arizonans, many of the volunteers became exterminationists after experiencing warfare with Apache raiders on the unsettled frontier. The Californians reasoned that before they could develop the territory, they would have to eliminate any Indians considered hostile. Previous waves of European and American soldiers and settlers had the same idea, but the Californians had not only the willingness to execute such a plan but also the mental, physical, and technological wherewithal. John C. Cremony wrote soon after the war:

> It is my conviction that the many signal triumphs obtained over the Apaches and Navajoes could only have been achieved by Californian soldiers, who seem gifted in a special manner with the address and ability to contend advantageously against them. This assertion has been so frequently admitted by the resident populations that it is not deemed necessary to dilate further than mention the names of such men as Roberts, McCleave, Fritz, Shirland, the two Greens, Tidball, Whitlock, Thayer, Pettis, and many others, who rendered good service and compassed the security and peace of the two Territories during their term of service. With the retirement of the Californian troops another series of robberies and massacres was instituted by the Indians, and maintained until the present time [1865] without apparent hindrance.[22]

In truth the California Volunteers performed remarkably well during their service in Arizona, against both Confederate and Indian opponents. As Carleton understood from the outset, the territory would be won with good planning and proper equipment. Arms and equipage played an important

21. For a complete history of the Arizona volunteers, see Underhill, "Arizona Volunteers."
22. Cremony, *Life among the Apaches*, 198.

May. John C. Cremony

1st Nat. Cal. Cavalry.

San Francisco newspaperman John C. Cremony accompanied the California Column to Arizona as captain of Company B, Second California Cavalry. Promoted to major in 1864, Cremony commanded the California Native Cavalry Battalion, which saw service patrolling the Mexican border in 1865. Courtesy of the Maine State Archives, CW Photo #1150.

role in the success of the Californians, influencing both operations and tactics, while Arizona's desert environment forced the soldiers to adapt to service under harsh and (for the Civil War) unusual conditions.[23]

As Carleton had predicted when outfitting the California Column, the Sharps carbines issued to the cavalry performed well in Arizona. These reliable breechloading arms made the difference in more than one encounter with Apaches. When Private John Teal's horse was killed near Apache Pass in 1862, the lone trooper held a large party of Apaches at bay with his carbine. The warriors would not risk a rush when they saw that he had a revolver and a saber as well as his rapid-fire Sharps. The fight ended abruptly when a shot from Teal's carbine seriously wounded Mangas Coloradas himself.[24]

23. Orton, *California Men*, 5–12.

24. J. C. Cremony to Roberts, July 16, 1862, *OR*, 50(1):133. In 1864 Cpl. Aaron Cory Hitchcock, First California Cavalry, encountered Confederate cavalry in Las Cruces, New Mexico, and wrote home that "at the best their arms were not much of a force in comparison to ours. While theirs were common rifles loading at the muzzle ours was Sharps rifles loading at the breech, and we have splendid Colts Revolvers while many of their pistols was the old fashioned

But by 1864 attrition through hard service had reduced the number of serviceable carbines to the point that newly organized companies, such as the California Native Battalion, received the muzzleloading "Common Rifles," labeled by Carleton as "worthless as weapons for mounted men." The demand for carbines was so great in the East, however, that in 1864 even veteran California troopers had to make do with Mississippi Rifles when they could not replace their broken-down Sharps carbines. Colonel Edwin Rigg, commanding the First Cavalry, pleaded for his men to be reissued carbines to replace the cumbersome muzzleloading rifles. "If well armed," he wrote, "the Men go with confidence and will do effective service, with [their] present arms they have not the confidence to make them when in small parties effective." The California cavalrymen finally received breechloading Maynard carbines in 1865, but shortages of the unique brass cartridges required by these weapons delayed issue to troops on duty in Arizona.[25]

Carleton believed the heavy .44-caliber Dragoon revolver unfit for cavalry, but when supplies of the lighter .36-caliber Navy revolver gave out, some California troops wound up carrying them. Horse soldiers armed with the heavier pistol complained of the additional weight on their already overburdened belts. In reality the soldiers rarely got close enough to Apache warriors to use handguns, and as the war wore on, ammunition resupply in Arizona proved not to be as critical as Carleton had feared. With rare exceptions, there always seemed to be plenty of ammunition for the various weapons issued to the Californians.[26]

In 1862 Carleton had fantasized that his men would dash into Tucson, sabers at the ready, and clash with the Confederates. Their razor-sharp blades would slash enemy bridles, unhorsing the Texans, and slice through clothing to inflict terrible wounds. In fact the only saber-inflicted wounds suffered in Arizona were on the volunteers themselves. Occasional duels and accidents among the men drew blood, and the cavalry mounts, no doubt, suffered at the hands of inexperienced saber-wielding soldiers. Some veterans said that one might identify a new recruit's horse by its bobbed ears—the result of sloppy saber work. By 1863, cavalry companies

flint locks. Besides these advantages we have a sabre to their nothing." A. C. Hitchcock to Thomas and Naomi Hitchcock, July 20, 1864, Aaron Cory Hitchcock Letters, Joanne Grace Private Collection (copies in author's possession).

25. Wright to Drum, Mar. 23, 1865, *OR*, 50(2):1169; Rigg to W. R. Shoemaker, July 15, 1865, Regimental Letter Book, First California Cavalry, Co. L, RG 94, NARA.

26. Carleton to Drum, Dec. 21, 1861, *OR*, 50(1):775.

received issues of the lighter 1860 pattern saber, which, though easier to handle than the old 1840 pattern "wrist breaker," was rarely drawn in combat.[27]

Several of the Native California Cavalry companies recruited in 1864 and 1865 were armed with lances in addition to sabers and firearms. The lance was the weapon of choice for many Californios, whose fathers had used it with such devastating effect against U.S. dragoons in 1847. These Mexican American soldiers felt comfortable with lances, which they commonly used for herding cattle in peacetime. They saw nothing unusual in using a weapon long since abandoned by cavalry units in the eastern theater.[28]

The horsemen of the Native Battalion impressed civilians and Anglo volunteers alike when they demonstrated their skill with their obsolescent weapons. But the lance was ill-suited to the broken terrain of Arizona, and the nature of warfare with the Apaches, who relied heavily on ambush and other unconventional tactics, compounded the weapon's ineffectiveness.[29]

Carleton to his credit had had the foresight to arm the teamsters. When the rear guard of Captain T. L. Roberts's command fell under attack at Apache Pass in 1862, Andrew "Shorty" Sawyer, in charge of one of the company wagons, fought off Apache warriors with his heavy .44-caliber revolver, saving his wagon and its precious supply of water in the process. The army continued to arm teamsters during the war years, though usually with second-class Mississippi Rifles.[30]

The infantry regiments serving in Arizona found their Model 1855 Springfield rifle muskets to be far superior to the bows, lances, and antiquated firearms of the Apaches. Firing Minié balls, the rifle muskets were deadly at five hundred yards. On several scouts the soldiers poured destructive fire into their enemies, who were beyond the effective range of their own weapons. Even so, the steel musket barrels posed another problem for the troops. The sun reflected off the polished metal, betraying the soldiers'

27. For Carleton, a dyed-in-the-wool dragoon, the *arme blanche* was the very symbol of the horse soldier. Maj. Edwin V. Sumner's dragoons had used sabers with success against the Cheyennes on the plains in 1858. Perhaps Carleton believed he could emulate this feat in combat with Arizona's Apaches—if so, he was sadly mistaken. Ordnance Returns, Office of the Chief of Ordnance, 1861–65, RG 156, NARA; Orton, *California Men,* 879–900.

28. *San Francisco Evening Bulletin,* July 8, 1865, 5. An excellent summary of the formation and campaigns of the Native Battalion (officially the First Battalion of Native California Cavalry) is Prezelski, "Californio Lancers."

29. Although French lancer units served in Mexico while the Native Battalion patrolled the border, there are no documented clashes between these troops. *San Francisco Evening Bulletin,* Oct. 20, 23, 1865; Hunt, *Army of the Pacific,* 180–81.

30. *Alta,* Aug. 16, 1862, 1; SO 3, July 28, 1864, Dept. of the Pacific, General, Special, and Post Orders, vol. 1, RG 393.

From time to time the desert yields up evidence of the California soldiers.
(*above*)
—shrapnel from an exploded 12-pounder case-shot round and .58-caliber Minié ball found in Apache Pass.
—steel-toed mule shoes, uniform button, infantry horn hat device, knapsack hook, and soldier's stencil found near Stanwix Station.
(*below*)
—Native Battalion lance head and ferrule from Tubac and Ft. Mason.
—1840 pattern cavalry saber found in Picacho Pass.
—1855 Sharps carbine barrel (ser. no. 18467) discovered near Fort Buchannan.
Courtesy of the Arizona Historical Society, Tucson.

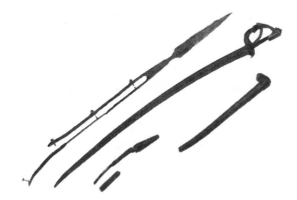

positions to the enemy. The men remedied this on at least one scout by blackening their barrels.[31]

The California soldiers found a variety of uses for their triangular bayonets. Although designed to be fixed to the rifle musket, these stabbing weapons may have seen service more often as picks, candleholders, and

31. Rigg to Cutler, Sept. 14, 1864, *OR*, 50(1):368. See also Capt. James H. Whitlock to Capt. C. A. Smith, Apr. 13, 1864, *OR*, 50(2):828. Whitlock's men, armed with long-ranged rifled muskets, kept Chiricahua warriors from approaching closer than eight hundred yards, preventing a counterattack against his outnumbered command.

roasting spits; there are no recorded instances of their use in combat in Arizona. Like the lance, the bayonet was ineffective against an enemy that rarely fought in the open or at close quarters.

Unexpectedly the mountain howitzers manned by California Volunteer infantrymen played a major role in battle with the Apaches. In fact these guns turned the tide in the Apache Pass fight. The warriors had fortified the heights of the narrow canyon and blocked both the advance to the springs and the retreat. A shower of arrows and small-arms fire rained down on the troops, bunched in the sandy wash. The mule-drawn artillery did not get into action quickly; one of the guns overturned in the panic, and most of the gunners, who had been allowed to keep their rifle muskets, were too busy firing their individual weapons to man the howitzers.[32]

Two cavalrymen used their lariats to right the overturned piece, and Lieutenant Thompson finally got his "Jackass Battery" into action. The howitzers threw round after round of spherical case shot (hollow 4.5-inch iron balls filled with lead musket balls and a bursting charge) into the Apache positions. The explosive shells killed or wounded many warriors, which along with the psychological effect of the big guns shifted the momentum of battle in favor of the Californians. An Apache survivor later observed, "We would have done well enough if you had not fired wagons at us."[33]

Both of the mountain howitzers were damaged in Apache Pass. Firing at extreme elevation had broken the wooden trails. The gunners had been forced to dig holes in the sand during the battle in order to angle the muzzles high enough to reach the Apache positions on the bluffs. Afterward Lieutenant Thompson designed a modification that would lessen this difficulty in the future. The Apache Pass engagement was the first and last time U.S. troops effectively deployed artillery against Indians in Arizona.[34]

32. Albert J. Fountain, a corporal in Company E, First California Infantry, contended years later that the soldiers fixed bayonets and charged the Indian positions in Apache Pass. Although the bayonets may have boosted the morale of the besieged Californians, most agree the Chiricahuas never felt cold steel. *Rio Grande Republican,* Jan. 2, 1891. See also Fountain, *Life and Death;* W. A. Thompson to West, July 18, 1862, *OR,* 50(2):26–27.

33. *Alta,* Aug. 16, 1862, 1. George Hand confirms that the Californians referred to Thompson's howitzers as the "Jackass Battery," even though they were not packed on mules like Lt. Jeremiah Phelan's guns. George Hand Diary, Sept. 10, 1862, Arizona Historical Society, Tucson. Captain Cremony observes, "the howitzers being on wheels, were deemed a species of wagon by the Apaches." *Life among the Apaches,* 164.

34. Cremony, *Life among the Apaches,* 164; W. A. Thompson to West, July 18, 1862, *OR,* 50(2):26–27.

Isolated instances of ammunition shortages occasionally threatened the success of expeditions against Apaches in Arizona. This was not a supply problem, though, but a matter of improper cartridge boxes and poorly designed ammunition. In 1865 several companies of the First California Cavalry received the tall tin-lined infantry cartridge box instead of the shorter box intended for mounted soldiers. When looped on the troopers' waist belts, the taller boxes banged against the cantles of the saddles, breaking the paper and cloth cartridges. Captain John Merriam requested permission to cut down the boxes in an effort to save both the ammunition and the saddles from excessive wear.[35]

The linen cartridges for the Sharps carbine proved more durable than those made of paper. Major C. E. Bennett reported that on one Apache scout his men each lost from one to four cartridges per day, necessitating frequent stops to replenish broken rounds and consequently shortening the length of the campaign. The metallic cartridges used with the Maynard carbine eventually eliminated the problem caused by fragile, combustible cartridges.[36]

When the California Column first arrived in Arizona, Colonel West took no chances that he would run low on ammunition. He issued a general order requiring camp guards at the end of their shift to draw the loads from their rifle muskets rather than unloading by firing at a target, as was common practice. The men threaded a ball screw, or worm, onto the ends of their ramrods and labored to pull the bullets from the muzzle, carefully preserving the lead and powder for reuse. When West discovered that illegal trading with civilians (eight rifle cartridges would buy a beer in any Tucson saloon) was wasting even more ammunition, he ordered supply officers to issue guards only five rounds per man rather than filling their forty-round boxes. As a further precaution against theft and accidental breakage, infantry companies had their ammunition allotments cut in half.[37]

The clothing of the California Volunteers occasionally meant the difference between success and failure on campaigns in Arizona. From hats to bootees, the kind and quality of attire became a factor. Carleton had ordered the foot soldiers to wear the broad-brimmed uniform hat without trimmings,

35. J. L. Merriam to J. Green, June 10, 1865, Regimental Letter Book, First California Cavalry, Co. L, RG 94.
36. C. E. Bennett to Greene, July 6, 1865, *OR*, 50(1):418.
37. GO 8, Tucson, June 13, 1862, Dept. of the Pacific, General, Special, and Post Orders, vol. 1, RG 393.

feeling that the men would need protection from the sun and that distinctive unit insignia was unnecessary. But the volunteers would not be denied their gaudy trimmings, and there is evidence that they sometimes wore them in the field. An eyewitness to the skirmish at Picacho Pass noted that when the Californians charged the Rebel position, chance spared one cavalryman's life when a musket ball glanced off his "hat brasses." Generally the California soldiers in Arizona followed Carleton's instructions and wore stripped-down versions of the regulation hat, even after his promotion to commander of the Department of New Mexico.[38] They wore the army hat with the brim folded down rather than looped up on the side as specified in the *Regulations*, with the distinctive colored cord and tassels of worsted wool indicating the branch of service (blue for infantry, yellow for cavalry, and red for artillery). The men also acquired a variety of sombreros and other practical civilian headgear. Sensible officers allowed these deviations, especially when the men were actively campaigning or laboring on fatigue duty. The soldiers liked the natty French-style forage cap worn in garrison or on fatigue, but because of its small bill and lack of ear and neck protection, the cap saw limited use when campaigning in the field.

The Californians wore lined or unlined versions of the four-button fatigue blouse, depending upon the time of year and availability. The wool blouses, when soaked with sweat, acted like a second skin, the evaporating moisture cooling the wearer. By 1863 the infantry regiments on garrison duty in Arizona also had nine-button frockcoats for formal occasions. These uniforms, complete with decorative brass shoulder scales, were fine for dress parades and Tucson fandangos but did not see active service in the field. Some by-the-book officers even required their men to wear regulation leather neck stocks, also known as "dog collars," or cravats for morning inspections. Infantrymen and cavalrymen wore sky-blue woolen greatcoats with attached capes. These were popular pieces of apparel during the winter, when even two five-pound woolen bed blankets seemed insufficient to combat the cold desert nights.[39]

38. Carleton to Canby, Aug. 2, 1862, *OR*, 50(1):94; Clothing Account Books of CV Regiments, 1861–66, California State Library, Sacramento. *Sacramento Union*, May 23, 1862, 1. See also D'Heureuse's photographs taken at Fort Mojave in 1863. D'Heureuse Photograph Collection, Bancroft Library, University of California, Berkeley. Men of the Fourth California Infantry wear the uniform hat without trimmings, other than the sky blue worsted-wool hat cords.

39. Clothing Account Books. For illustrations of California troops wearing forage caps on garrison duty in Tucson, see Browne, *Adventures*.

The troops quickly wore out their pants in Arizona. Frequently the sky blue kersey trousers lasted but one month. A civilian prospector commented that the men of Company A, First California Cavalry, returning from an Apache scout, "were surely the raggedest set of men I ever saw in one body, up to that time. There were hardly one of the soldiers who had any pants on at all from the knee down." The infantrymen suffered similarly from clothing worn to tatters due to campaigning in the rough chaparral and rocky terrain. One recalled the deplorable state of his company's clothing: "Most of the boys who had lost the base of their pants had repaired the wreck with pieces of flour sack and when the order to 'front face' was given, the men on the other side could not tell whether he was witnessing the inspection of a body of troops or amusing himself by reading the advertisements of a California flouring mill. The lenient regards for nudity here [Tucson] in those days saved the boys a good deal of trouble, and there were, as a consequence, few municipal arrests." In an attempt to extend the life of their garments, the foot soldiers occasionally drew issues of cavalry trousers with reinforced seats, especially when required to perform mounted escort or vedette service. One embarrassed soldier was forced to wear his knapsack slung low over his backside when walking the streets of Tucson because the seat of his trousers had entirely worn through.[40]

Shoddy workmanship contributed to the rapid deterioration of government-issued clothing. Overworked and corrupt inspectors approved much clothing that might have been condemned during peacetime. In May 1862 Carleton insisted that the army find another clothing contractor when he discovered a "wretchedly poor" shipment of uniforms. Whenever the quartermaster had ample supplies, experienced soldiers drew multiple issues of important items, namely trousers and shoes, in anticipation of future shortages.[41]

Just before launching the Arizona campaign, Carleton admonished Captain Roberts, commanding the San Diego garrison, to "be careful of your clothing; have it carefully mended, particularly the men's shoes." Footgear became as important to the success of an operation as weapons. On several occasions the Californians suspended their hot pursuit of Apache raiders because the shoes of the infantrymen gave out. In 1865 Colonel Charles H. Lewis, with a cavalry detachment, and Captain Calderwood, with thirty men

---

40. Conner, *Joseph Reddeford Walker*, 53–54; *Tucson Citizen*, May 17, 1884.
41. Carleton to Drum, May 10, 1862, *OR*, 50(1):1060.

of the Seventh California Infantry, pursued the Chiricahuas responsible for the killings at Spanish Ranch. After forty miles the foot soldiers were forced to turn back after their shoes fell apart. One volunteer officer wrote in disgust, "frequently a pair of shoes are worn out in a single scout of ten days."[42]

Carleton's request for shoes with sewn soles could not be filled. The men drew bootees and cavalry boots from available supplies, including many with pegged soles. Some of Colonel Oscar M. Brown's First California Cavalry had to resole their shoes with wood and even sang a comic song about their tattered clothing and "shoes made of pine." In 1866 a combined force of California and Arizona volunteers—Pimas and Maricopas—had to make moccasins from a bearskin after their double-soled shoes wore out during a scouting expedition lasting only two weeks.[43]

Army shoes exhibited distinctive characteristics that allowed easy recognition. Shoemakers fashioned civilian styles on a straight last, while army brogans were made for right and left feet. When the charred remains of several victims of Apache torture were discovered near Apache Pass in 1862, the only means of identifying the bodies was by their soldier shoes. The distinctiveness of army clothing also served to discourage illicit trafficking in government clothing.[44]

Arizona citizens suffered almost as much as the soldiers from the lack of good clothing. A prosperous but illegal trade prompted Major Fergusson, commanding the Tucson garrison, to issue orders in Spanish and English that "any civilians caught wearing Army clothing or with military goods in their possession will be arrested by the Provost Marshal." Officers warned repeatedly that, according to the Articles of War, the military would punish soldiers selling government property. These measures did not seem to prevent clothing "condemned" by corrupt quartermaster sergeants from falling into private hands.[45]

---

42. Carleton to Roberts, Dec. 19, 1861, *OR*, 50(1):773; Post Returns, Tubac, Ariz. Terr., June 1865, RG 393 NARA, M1652, reel 1297; Report of W. S. R. Taylor, Sept. 19, 1863, *OR*, 50(1):237.

43. Underhill, "Arizona Volunteers," 79.

44. Brinckerhoff, *Boots and Shoes*, 2–3.

45. GO 21, Tucson, Aug. 10, 1862, Dept. of the Pacific, General, Special, and Post Orders, vol. 1, RG 393; Conner, *Joseph Reddeford Walker*, 307–8; The Apaches were also eager to obtain clothing and went to extraordinary lengths to salvage military and civilian apparel from the bodies of enemies slain in raids and skirmishes. On at least one occasion, soldiers discovered bodies from which the Indians had broken off their arrow shafts in order to strip off clothing. *Alta*, May 15, 1865.

One piece of equipment, universally despised by foot soldiers, had threatened to stall the advance of the Arizona expedition almost before it began. The regulation knapsack was a waterproof, tarred canvas-and-leather affair capable of holding clothing, bedding, and other personal items. Its poor design made it uncomfortable even when packed lightly. On February 11, 1862, Carleton issued general orders requiring the men of the First California Infantry to wear their knapsacks while performing all drills.[46] These backbreaking drills caused Company A to mutiny. Threats by Colonel West and an appeal by Carleton himself finally convinced the men that the success of the campaign rested on their ability to carry the necessary supplies on their backs. Drilling with the knapsacks was the only way they could prepare themselves for the journey. Still, thirteen recalcitrant privates were shackled hand and foot and imprisoned at Fort Yuma.

When the First California Infantry crossed the Colorado River and marched up the Gila in the spring of 1862, they wore their knapsacks. One soldier wrote that when the column halted for a rest "to recruit our failing powers of locomotion . . . , we became aware of aching all over and stiffness everywhere as the result of the weight of our knapsacks. I have often heard the groans of the heavily loaded pack mules moving past on their way to the mountains, but never did I sympathize with those animals until I threw the burden off my back and rolled in the desert sand after a twenty-mile march from Fort Yuma."[47] By the time the California Column reached Tucson, Carleton reconsidered the knapsack order. His General Orders No. 10 declared, "every soldier may move forward with a light, free step, now that we approach the enemy, he will no longer be required to carry his knapsack."[48] Company wagons carried the hated knapsacks the rest of the way to the Rio Grande.

The lack of horses almost precipitated another rebellion, this time among the cavalry. While en route to Fort Yuma in October 1861, Major Eyre of the First California Cavalry wrote in desperation for Carleton to "send the saddles left by the three companies now with me, as whispers are already circulated among the men that they are to be turned into infantry. That is the only thing I fear for a serious breach of discipline. . . . For God's sake do not leave me long with this only cause of danger hanging over my

46. GO 3, Hdqrs. Dist. of Southern Calif., Feb. 11, 1862, *OR,* 50(1):858.
47. *Sacramento Union,* May 23, 1862.
48. West to Carleton, Feb. 19, 1862, *OR,* 50(1):886; West to Carleton, Feb. 24, 1862, ibid., 888; GO 10, Hdqrs. Column from California, July 17, 1862, ibid., 90–91.

head." Fortunately the troopers got their horses in time to prevent a riot, but the animals themselves created some problems.[49]

The horses available in California were not trained cavalry mounts. Carleton had hoped that the army would provide his troopers good "American" horses turned over by departing regulars, which he believed would be better than the California "half breeds" for big men loaded down with equipment. He also felt that it was important for the horses to be accustomed to the noise of firearms and slashing saber exercises. He advised Colonel West that "cavalry recently mounted on California horses cannot use any kind of firearms with success." The only hope would be to use the saber, which must be kept sharp, and to kill the enemy's horses as quickly as possible. The Confederates in Arizona were well mounted, as Carleton had suspected. When the advance guard of the California Column first encountered Captain Hunter's Rebels some eighty miles east of Fort Yuma, the gray riders retreated and soon outdistanced their pursuers.[50]

Although most of the Californians who volunteered for mounted service had experience with horses, they were not accomplished horse soldiers. One volunteer recalled that disaster ensued the first time his battalion received the order to mount up. The men, encumbered by saber, revolver, carbine, bedroll, greatcoat, saddlebags, and other equipage, could barely control their skittish mounts. The rattling sabers spooked the horses and caused a stampede. Only seventy-five of the three hundred men maintained their seats, and it took an hour to round up all of the terrified animals. During the march from Fort Yuma to Tucson, the cavalrymen performed saber exercises—cuts, points, and circular *moulinets,* according to Cooke's manual—while mounted in order to accustom the horses to the noise and movement of arms. After the first hundred miles, men and horses settled into a routine and for the rest of the journey moved as one.[51]

Maintaining the health and safety of the horses became one of the principal duties of the cavalrymen. The troopers used their sheath knives to cut grass for the animals and brought it to the picket line piled in blankets. They also carried tubular bags of grain, when it was available, slung over their cantles and offered it to their mounts in nosebags or hats after taking

49. Eyre to Carleton, Oct. 21, 1861, *OR,* 50(1):670.

50. Carleton to Drum, Dec. 21, 1861, ibid., 775; Cutler to Rigg, Mar. 15, 1862, ibid., 930.

51. Edward E. Ayer, "Reminiscences of the Far West and Other Trips, 1861–1918," manuscript, Bancroft Library, University of California, Berkeley, 1–16.

care to soak it first in water to aid digestion. Guards stayed constantly on the alert for Apaches, who relied on stolen stock to trade for food and other supplies. In September 1863, Chiricahua warriors ran off all of the horses at Fort Bowie, rendering the garrison completely ineffective. The sergeant in charge of the grazing detail attributed the loss to a shortage of hobbles and picket ropes to secure the animals.[52]

The men knew that their lives often depended on their horses. Early in the war officers enforced standing orders that "no enlisted man will be permitted to ride his horse faster than a trot except by order, or in the case of urgent necessity." On the march across Arizona, cavalrymen walked half the time in order to spare their animals. Mounted soldiers paid particular attention to the care of their horses' backs and hooves, quickly learning to treat sores and fit proper shoes. One private had to cut the leather *mochila* of his Ranger saddle in order to make "moccasins" for his horse, which suffered foot trouble while on a scout.[53]

Yet even the best of intentions could not make up for the harsh conditions in Arizona. In 1865 Major Davis, then acting inspector general of the department, noted that the lack of forage, excessive field service, and overexposure had rendered most of the horses in the Arizona District unserviceable, even for mounted drill. He considered only 160 of the animals that he inspected to be of any use. Some thirty-five cavalry mounts, as well as four quartermaster horses and four mules, had died in the last three months. Mounted scouts and pursuit of raiders were virtually impossible.[54]

Even when the horses were healthy, saddles continued to be a problem in Arizona. California officers relegated the old Grimsley dragoon saddle to the artillery, which ended up with the broad-backed American horses. The cavalry companies received either the 1859 McClellan saddle or the Mexican-style Ranger saddle. The men preferred the latter for several reasons. It was better suited for the narrow-withered California horses, and the volunteers felt more comfortable with the familiar western-style Ranger saddle as

52. Report of Sgt. Charles Kuhl, Sept. 1, 1863, *OR*, 50(1):233–34.

53. Carleton to David Fergusson, Mar. 23, 1862, ibid., 949; T. A. Stombs to Commanding Officer, Fort Bowie, Ariz. Terr., July 11, 1864, U.S. Army Commands, Fort Bowie Letters Received, 1862–71, RG 98, NARA. California soldiers at Fort Whipple were authorized to cut up log chains in order to fashion mule shoes—iron had become a rare and valuable commodity at frontier army posts. N. H. Davis to Carleton, Mar. 20, 1864, *OR*, 34(3):204.

54. Report of Nelson H. Davis, acting inspector general, Dept. of New Mexico, Feb. 1865, Office of the Inspector General, Extracts of Inspection Reports, 1864–65, RG 156, NARA, 575–76.

opposed to the lightweight, rawhide-seated McClellan. The Californians complained that the eastern-manufactured McClellans exhibited inferior workmanship and rapidly deteriorated in the Arizona elements.[55]

Major Bennett reported that the rawhide on his rain-soaked McClellan saddles softened sufficiently to allow the wooden trees, or frames, to spread out and gall the horses' backs. When the rawhide dried rapidly in the hot sun, it split and curled, creating sharp edges that injured the men. The resourceful Bennett remedied this problem by covering the rawhide seats with supple bridle leather. Commanding officers usually left such field modifications to the discretion of company commanders, but in 1865 Inspector General Davis recommended that this become standard practice. Although California officers typically requested Ranger saddles, ordnance officers supplied the cavalry with whichever saddle they had the most of, striving for uniformity within a company.[56]

In June 1862, while in pursuit of retreating Rebels, the California Column halted in Tucson while two shops worked day and night repairing rolling stock. Carleton reported, "The tires of the wagons get loose, and the sand working in the joints of the wheels soon grinds them into an utterly unserviceable condition." Sherod Hunter had hidden the smithies' anvils before departing, causing still more delay until they could be found and returned to service. The volunteers had to cut and re-weld the iron tires to fit the shrunken wooden wagon wheels. This lengthy layover enabled the Confederates to escape a full-scale battle with the Californians.[57] Not only had the Rebels gotten away, but the California troops arriving in Tucson also had to subsist on reduced rations because of the shortage of rolling stock to haul commissary stores. To boost morale, officers assured the men that they would receive additional pay for the difference of the ration reduction. When they discovered that many men were too weak to perform their work on short rations, officers had to restore teamsters, farriers, and men working extra duty in the Commissary Department to full rations.[58]

As Carleton had predicted, the war in Arizona was a monumental logistical challenge and a battle against the unrelenting desert. The arms and

55. McAllister to G. D. Ramsay, Aug. 1, 1864, Letters Received, 1864, Office of the Chief of Ordnance, RG 156.
56. Report of Nelson H. Davis, Feb. 1865, Office of the Inspector General, Extracts of Inspection Reports, 575–76; Bennett to Green, July 6, 1865, *OR*, 50(1):418.
57. Carleton to Drum, June 18, 1862, *OR*, 50(1):1146–47.
58. GO 10, June 19, 1862, Dept. of the Pacific, General, Special, and Post Orders, vol. 1, RG 393.

equipage used by the Californians in Arizona between 1862 and 1866 played a significant role in their effectiveness. Available supplies often determined what was issued, but the preferences expressed by officers and men influenced such decisions too. Carleton carefully selected equipment to meet the special demands of military service in the territory's arid climate. The arms and equipage influenced operations; so too, desert campaigning necessitated nonregulation equipment and field modifications. Although supply deficiencies occasionally reduced the effectiveness of the volunteers, the men and matériel proved equal to the demands of operations in Arizona.[59]

59. Even in 1864, as commander of the Department of New Mexico, Carleton bombarded his subordinates with orders stressing the importance of maintaining equipment to ensure success in the field. No detail seemed too small: "Pray get all your cavalry in the best possible order for the field—shoes set, others fitted, equipments carefully repaired and oiled, haversacks and canteens in good repair, hobbles or lariats and pins got in readiness, and all camp equipage in your district put in perfect repair and got ready to put into wagons without an hour's delay." Carleton to Bowie, Apr. 15, 1864, *OR*, 50(2):820.

CHAPTER 4

Occupation Duty

As the Civil War dragged on, so too did the occupation of Arizona. In 1864 the thinly spread garrisons of California Volunteers had much to do. The troops provided protection and essential services for the civil government and the young territory's growing population, explored and improved roads, and prepared the first accurate maps of Arizona's interior. They also took advantage of their situation to mine, explore, and fraternize with the locals. The soldiers also provided the only source of law and order in the territory, though occasionally they engaged in criminal activity themselves.

When not engaged in active campaigns against the Apaches and Navajos, the volunteers escorted politicians, surveyors, and journalists, as well as miners and other travelers. In the fall of 1863, a contingent of Californians accompanied Arizona territorial governor John Goodwin's party from the East, by way of New Mexico, to the new territorial capital of Prescott. Volunteers also escorted those Federal officials who traveled the long way from Washington by sea and entered Arizona from California. During the war years the soldiers provided food, supplies, and protection for starving refugees from the Pinos Altos mines and other victims of Apache raids.[1]

When Superintendent of Indian Affairs Charles D. Poston reached Tucson in January 1864, he demanded fresh mules and a thirty-man cavalry escort for himself and J. Ross Browne, the noted journalist and illustrator for *Harpers Magazine*. Poston took his party on a sightseeing and mineral-

---

1. GO 27, Hdqrs. Dept. of New Mexico, Oct. 23, 1863, *OR*, 50(2):653–64; Browne, *Adventures*, 139.

exploring adventure throughout southern Arizona, much to the annoyance of the short-handed California officers. Inspector General Nelson Davis complained, "all come upon the military for every d——d thing they want," and Colonel Poston "is cross as a bear, and terribly down on me and others." When "Especial Indian Agent" Abraham Lyon arrived one month later, he received a smaller escort—this time officers would spare only eleven infantrymen and three mules.[2]

The California troops also guarded the Colorado River steamers, the key to provisioning the territory. Army officers considered the supply shipments from the Gulf of California to Fort Yuma and Fort Mojave especially vulnerable to attack or sabotage. Early in the war Carleton had ordered the commander at Fort Yuma to keep all boats secured on the California side of the river. Every vessel had a guard with instructions to be especially vigilant on downriver runs to the gulf. If the steamboat pilots were found to be in league with secessionists or even suspected of betrayal, the soldiers had orders to shoot them and disable or burn their boats. An attack on Fort Yuma by river would mean disaster for the entire District of Arizona, and possibly California as well.[3]

Some Arizona entrepreneurs unfairly accused Carleton of restricting business in Arizona Territory, when in fact his troops enabled the resumption of commerce and the establishment of new enterprises. The general believed that only a firm hand would preserve military security, public health, and safety. Concern for private-property rights and individual liberties did not deter him. He ordered his soldiers to destroy five Colorado River ferryboats, including one in Mexico thirty miles below Yuma, and to move three others to the crossing near the fort. The Mexican ferry owner who lost his boat, a man named Gonzales, never received compensation from the U.S. government.

Carleton maintained rigid military discipline wherever he went. In Tucson he closed the dram shops and gambling halls; those that remained open faced heavy taxation. Desperados charged with crimes committed as many as four years earlier stood trial before a military commission composed entirely of California Volunteer officers. The commission sent Palatine Robinson,

2. SO 9, Jan. 17, 1864; and SO 16, Feb. 16, 1864, Hdqrs., Tucson, Commands of J. R. West, Special, General and Post Orders, RG 393, NARA; Davis to Carleton, Apr. 5, 1864, *OR*, 24(3):209–10.

3. Drum to Commanding Officer, Fort Yuma, Apr. 11, 1863, *OR*, 50(2):390; Carleton to West, Nov. 5, 1861, *OR*, 50(1):704–5; Carleton to Rigg, Feb. 5, 1862, ibid., 847–48.

accused of murder and kidnapping, to Fort Yuma for confinement, along with other known criminals and secessionists. In a controversial move Carleton had ordered the seizure of Sylvester Mowry and his Patagonia Mine. Mowry, though an avowed Rebel sympathizer, filed a damage claim in December 1862 totaling $1,029,000 for the loss of his property, naming Carleton and other officers involved in his arrest in the suit. The well-connected Mowry did manage to get Arizona's first territorial legislature to pass a concurrent resolution condemning Carleton's actions, but even after a congressional investigation the government never paid damages. Military authorities also seized and sold at public auction property abandoned in Tucson by secessionists who fled with Sherod Hunter's ranger company in 1862.[4]

Most loyal citizens considered Carleton's heavy-handed tactics justified. The presence of his troops encouraged the return of citizens to the territory and promoted Arizona's nascent mining industry. In Tucson troops repaired William S. Grant's flour mill, which the departing regulars had disabled to deprive the Rebels of its use. Law-abiding citizens and those who had escaped Carleton's justice generally believed that the law-and-order campaign served the interests of the territory. Fair elections continued only because of military supervision. In August 1862 the Tucson depot commander announced that Francisco S. Leon had been confirmed as "Commissioner of Streets, Roads, and Bridges" and Francisco Romero as "Mayordomo de Acequias," or head of Tucson's water department, under Carleton's authority as Arizona military governor.[5]

Since 1857, Arizona residents had petitioned the U.S. government repeatedly for separation from New Mexico. They believed that officials at Mesilla ignored the needs of the sparsely populated western portion of Doña Ana County. John R. Baylor recognized the need for separating Arizona from New Mexico Territory when his Texas command invaded in the winter of 1861. Confederate president Jefferson Davis issued a proclamation in support of Baylor's plan in February 1862. The Confederate Arizona Territory Organic Act also named Baylor as military governor.[6]

---

4. Lockwood, *Life in Old Tucson*, 132–33; Hunt, *James Henry Carleton*, 265–67; Colton, *Civil War in the Western Territories*, 110. Carleton took advantage of the opportunity to relieve his command of deadwood and made certain that the escort destined for Fort Yuma with the Tucson prisoners was made up of hard cases and outcasts from the California Column. See Pettis, *California Column*, 15.

5. Gilbert J. Pedersen, "A Yankee in Arizona: The Misfortunes of William S. Grant, 1860–61," *Journal of Arizona History* 16 (Summer 1975): 141; Proclamation, Aug. 2, 1862, Hdqrs. Tucson, Commands of J. R. West, RG 393.

6. Executive Dept., Ariz. Terr., Proclamation, June 11, 1862, *OR*, 9:692.

But it was Carleton's proclamation on June 8, 1862, that provisionally established Arizona as a U.S. territory, and as military governor he became the first federally recognized executive of Arizona. Governor Carleton moved quickly to define the territorial boundaries and to establish mail, legal, and police services. He ordered maps made, property disputes settled, and a census taken. Accordingly, Major Fergusson commissioned Tucson pioneer William S. Oury to survey property in an attempt to settle land-ownership claims. This became no small task as irate citizens besieged the military government with requests for clear titles to disputed properties. In September 1862 Fergusson wrote Governor Pesqueira of Sonora requesting his aid in settling Tucson land claims based on old Spanish and Mexican grants. The frustrated major even asked that Pesqueira forward to him the Mexican government documents taken when Mexican troops abandoned Tucson in 1856, two years after the United States ratified the Gadsden Purchase.[7]

Following the arrival of the newly appointed Arizona territorial officials in December 1863, military authorities gradually turned over the reins of government to these civilians. Although the military government was no longer needed, Governor Goodwin did rely on the California cavalry for protection and assistance in making an inspection tour of the territory, establishing a capital, and defining three temporary judicial districts. On July 18, 1864, voters in Arizona held a general election and selected Charles D. Poston as their delegate to Congress. Citizens also elected the twenty-seven members of the legislative assembly. Several of these legislators were California Volunteer officers who took leaves of absence to serve the new territory.[8]

During and immediately following the Civil War, a number of California soldiers became civil officials in Arizona Territory. Captain Converse C. Rowell, Fourth Infantry; Colonel Charles W. Lewis, Seventh Infantry; Lieutenant Edward D. Tuttle, Fourth Infantry; and Sergeant Alonzo E. Davis, Fourth Infantry, all served in the Arizona legislature. Rowell also served as U.S. district attorney for Arizona and later became district attorney for Yuma County. Davis's commanding officer had allowed him to "read law" in a darkened commissary building at Fort Mojave after taps. The ambitious

---

7. James H. Carleton, Proclamation, June 8, 1862, *OR*, 50(1):96–7; Hunt, *James Henry Carleton*, 220–21; Fergusson to Ignacio Pesqueira, Sept. 15, 1862, Sonora, in "Fergusson," Hayden Arizona Pioneer Biography Files, Arizona Historical Society, Tucson. Fergusson commissioned John B. Mills to make an accurate map of Tucson. Sonnichsen, *Tucson*, 66.

8. Bancroft, *Arizona and New Mexico*, 522.

sergeant later received an appointment as Mohave County attorney after serving several terms in the territorial legislature. Discharged from the Second California Infantry at Fort Yuma in 1864, Private George E. Young received appointment as public administrator and examiner of schools for Mohave County. In short, California Volunteers provided the young territory with a corps of educated and energetic men to draw on for political leadership during and soon after the war.

Citizens and territorial officials agreed that the extermination or subjugation of the Apaches constituted the most important contribution the soldiers could make to aid the development of Arizona. They firmly believed that these Indians prevented the full exploitation of Arizona's mineral wealth by limiting the movement of miners, supplies, and ore. It mattered little that the Apache bands had occupied the territory for more than a hundred years prior to settlement by U.S. citizens. Miners petitioned to have soldiers stationed at their mines and escort freight wagons hauling supplies and machinery. In 1864, Arizonans pressured the governor to request permanent garrisons for mines in the booming Lynx Creek and Randall districts of Yavapai County.[9]

In February 1864 a detachment of volunteers, commanded by Major E. B. Willis, located a new fort in the center of the territory. Some seventy-five miners, as well as the territorial governor, accompanied this scouting party. Willis reported, "we propose to afford them all facilities possible in prospecting the country over which we pass, and at the same time, if possible, to strike a blow at the Indians." When the major selected a site for Fort Whipple on Granite Creek, the governor and the miners established Prescott, the new capital, one and a half miles farther upstream.[10]

On at least two occasions in 1863, California officers ordered their men to prospect in the Arizona gold fields. In April Major Fergusson instructed Captain James Whitlock, commanding Fort Bowie, to explore and prospect: "[T]ake advantage of your own experience, and that of so many members of your company as possess it, to prospect the vicinity of Fort Bowie for minerals. I am under the impression that very rich deposits of gold and silver can be found in the Chiricahua Mountains in the vicinity of Fort Bowie. . . . When you can spare the men let them have leave to go hunting and prospecting in sufficient numbers to make it safe. . . . It is our duty to do all

9. Davis to Carleton, Mar. 2, 1864, OR, 34(2):595; Underhill, "Arizona Volunteers," 7–8.
10. E. B. Willis to Cutler, Feb. 11, 1864, OR, 34(1):121–22.

First Lt. Edward D. Tuttle served with Company H, Fourth California Infantry at the Colorado River and Fort Yuma. After the war he worked at the Yuma Quartermaster Depot and for the Colorado Steam Navigation Company. He established himself as a post trader and later became a successful Arizona merchant. Courtesy of the Arizona Historical Society, Yuma.

we can to develop the rich mineral resources of this country." In June Carleton ordered Captain Nathaniel Pishon's company of the First California Cavalry to the new diggings near Lynx Creek in central Arizona. He instructed Pishon to have his men "prospect and wash," record the time each soldier worked, and carefully note the amount of gold obtained. Carleton stressed that citizens relied upon such statistics, which would also determine whether the army would establish a post in that area. Carleton's tests proved that the diggings were indeed rich, and he ordered Fort Whipple built in the "heart of the gold region."[11]

The general understood the importance of discovering new mineral wealth, not only for the development of the territory but also to aid the war effort. He believed it "providential that the practical miners of California should have come here to assist" in the discovery and development of Arizona's riches and pleaded with superiors in Washington to sanction his

11. Carleton to Nathaniel Pishon, June 22, 1863, in Orton, *California Men,* 72; Hdqrs. Dept. of New Mexico, GO 27, Oct. 23, 1863, *OR,* 50(2):654; Fergusson to James Whitlock, Apr. 23, 1863, ibid., 413.

Alonzo E. Davis enlisted in Company I, Fourth California Infantry. Stationed at Fort Mojave, Arizona Territory, he attained the rank of sergeant while prospecting for gold and studying law in his spare time. A tireless Arizona booster, Davis returned after the Civil War, practiced law, and served in the territorial legislature. From *Mohave County Lawmakers.*

prospecting plan: "I beg to ask authority to let, say, one-fourth of the command at a time have one month's furlough to work in the gold mines and the country will become developed, while the troops will become contented to remain in service where the temptation to leave is very great."[12]

Apparently the War Department saw wisdom in Carleton's request, and the men prospected whenever they had the chance. Many soldiers whose enlistments expired in 1864 began successful placer operations in southern Arizona. California Volunteers in central Arizona filed 828 claims between 1864 and 1866. These men led the way for others who came with capital and equipment to work the rich gold and silver deposits. The entire Seventh California Infantry, raised in January 1865, became known as the "gold diggers" regiment of Arizona. Many had journeyed to California during the rush of 1849 and never lost hope that one day they might strike it rich in the Far West.[13]

On May 19, 1863, two companies of the Fourth California Infantry crossed the Colorado River and reestablished Fort Mojave. The regulars had abandoned the post two years earlier, but miners drawn by the rich Col-

12. Senate Rep. 156, 39th Cong., 2nd sess., 1866, 110, 114–15, 135–37, 140; Farish, *History of Arizona,* 3:153.
13. Dunning and Peplow, *Rock to Riches,* 73; Yavapai County Book of Claims No. 1, 1864–66, Yavapai County Courthouse, Prescott.

orado River gold deposits coexisted uneasily with the Mojave Indians, prompting the Department of the Pacific to reoccupy the place. The Mojaves remained peaceful, and the volunteers played a significant role in the development of the upper Colorado region. Glowing accounts of the richness of the area sent home by the soldiers encouraged many more Californians to prospect along the Colorado and its tributaries. The men of the Fourth California Infantry alone established several mining districts. In fact they dominated the mining in the Cerbat Mountains near Fort Mojave to the extent that the citizen prospectors complained of a soldier monopoly.

Alonzo E. Davis, then a corporal in Company I, Fourth California Infantry, understated the amount of soldier prospecting around Fort Mojave when he wrote, "a few of us boys went out on prospecting trips into the mountains. We would get a pass and, taking ten days rations of hardtack, pork and beans, we would explore the region for mining wealth." The volunteers controlled several of the mining districts, modeling their organizations after districts in northern California. In 1864 they filed 22 percent of the claims in the Sacramento and San Francisco mining districts of Mohave County.

Many of the soldiers stationed at Fort Mojave did not want to return to Drum Barracks, near Los Angeles, for their discharges because they hoped to remain with their profitable claims. Some had purchased lots in Mohave City, situated on a bluff overlooking the river about a mile north of the fort. Discharged soldiers of the Fourth Infantry soon returned and began constructing houses. Even the soldiers on active duty found time for prospecting and mining, recording their discoveries and working their claims. They established the Iretaba District near Fort Mojave and competed with civilian miners, who continued to criticize the soldiers for holding all the best claims. Most of these soldier-miners returned to Arizona after mustering out, determined to develop their claims.[14]

The Californians also participated in a number of other extramilitary activities during their stay in Arizona. These included hunting, fishing, and sightseeing, not to mention the carousing and gambling that inevitably occurred when men in garrison towns had the opportunity. Commanders occasionally sanctioned hunting for the subsistence of the troops; foragers ventured out in small detachments to hunt the bear and antelope that

14. Davis, "Pioneer Days in Arizona," Arizona State University Library, Tempe, 53; *Alta*, Jan. 26, Mar. 26, 1864, Jan. 15, Apr. 3, 1865; Mohave County Book of Claims, 1864–66, Office of the Mohave County Historian, Kingman.

abounded in the rugged mountains and grassy river valleys. The men hunted and fished individually for recreation and to add variety to their dismal diet of salted or dried meat and hard bread. The soldiers wondered not only at the abundance of the game but also the incredible strength and tenacity of the Arizona fauna. One volunteer private swore on his honor as a gentleman that "he had shot a hare four times and carried away a leg every time, so that the body of the poor animal had nothing left on it but the ears and the tail; yet with even such limited means of locomotion it actually escaped by whirling over on its ears and tail, though he ran after it as fast as he could." Wherever they went the soldiers wrote of the sights they saw. They marveled at Arizona's giant saguaro cactus and other desert flora. Ancient Indian ruins, such as the abandoned earthen city of Casa Grande north of Tucson, captured the imagination of many of the scholars in the ranks.[15]

Some of the educated men among the California Volunteers recorded and attempted to preserve knowledge of Arizona's rapidly vanishing Indian cultures and artifacts. It is sadly ironic that the same troops engaged in bloody and relentless combat with native peoples took the time and had the interest to study and carefully preserve evidence of their cultures. Perhaps the strange circumstances surrounding the death of Mangas Coloradas offer the best illustration of this moral dilemma.

Mangas had suffered a serious gunshot wound during the Apache Pass fight in 1862 but survived thanks to treatment by a Mexican doctor, who tended the war leader under extreme duress. Repeated raids by warriors loyal to Mangas had made him the most feared Apache in the territories. On January 17, 1863, Company C, First California Cavalry, commanded by Captain E. D. Shirland, captured the Apache leader not far from Fort McLane near the Arizona–New Mexico border. No one knows with certainty the details of his death, but most accounts agree that the Californians tormented the bound chief with heated bayonets. When he tried to make a run for it, the guards shot him down. Then in a macabre twist, the soldiers boiled and defleshed his head, which was said to be extraordinarily large, and sent the skull to the American Museum of Natural History in New York for study.[16]

15. Farish, *History of Arizona*, 3:153; Brown, *Adventures*, 280; William Addison Bushnell Diary, Oct. 11, 1865, typescript in possession of author.

16. Orton, *California Men*, 71; Conner, *Joseph Reddeford Walker*, 39–41. No charges were leveled against Mangas's murderers, and General West evaded censure for his role in the affair. *OR*, 50(2):296–97; Josephy, *Civil War in the American West*, 279–81. See also Sweeney, *Mangas Coloradas*, 441–49.

Casa Grande, 1864. By J. Ross Browne, from *Adventures in the Apache Country.*

San Xavier del Bac, 1864. By J. Ross Browne, from *Adventures in the Apache Country.*

Some enlisted men kept daily journals, recording detailed accounts of prehistoric sites, early Spanish *visitas,* churches, and landmarks. Many described Indian artifacts, noting with wonder the variety of polychromed shards found near Casa Grande and other ruins. Private Thomas Keam became fascinated with the Navajo culture. He learned the language, married a member of that tribe, and collected ancient ceramics and other objects near Fort Defiance. He shipped these to museums in the East, including Harvard's venerable Peabody Museum.[17]

A California officer traveling with Joseph R. Walker's mining and exploring party in 1863 asked superiors if he could send the cremated remains of an Indian, discovered in a cave, back to New York for analysis. The burial practices of the natives intrigued the men, who wrote home about them and published stories in their hometown newspapers. A number of soldiers noted in their journals that the Maricopas practiced cremation as did the Yumas, while the Pimas buried their dead.[18]

Some of the volunteer officers demonstrated a talent for ethnography and included observations of native customs and lore in their reports and letters. Lieutenant E. D. Tuttle wrote a detailed description of the bark skirts worn by the women of the Colorado River tribes. Captain John C. Cremony actually compiled a dictionary of Apache words, while other volunteers recorded Piman and Navajo dialects for the first time.[19]

Arizona's natural resources also intrigued some of the soldiers. Carleton himself took time from his busy schedule to inspect a meteorite used as an anvil by Tucson blacksmith Ramon Pacheco. The "aerolite," a 632-pound chunk of iron and nickel, so impressed the general that he succeeded in wresting it from the reluctant smithy. The "Carleton Meteorite" received a great deal of attention from geologists and others in San Francisco; eventually it became part of the Smithsonian's collections. Sergeant Alonzo E. Davis, stationed at Fort Mojave, also reported seeing meteors flash across Arizona's night sky and hunting for the aerolites that fell to earth.[20]

17. A soldier in the Seventh California Infantry wrote that his company (E) stopped to admire the Spanish mission San Xavier, "the inside of which beggars all description. It contains some fine paintings and some of the most beautiful plaster statues I have ever seen." *Calaveras (Calif.) Chronicle,* July 1, 1865; Bailey, "Thomas Varker Keam," 18.

18. Conner, *Joseph Reddeford Walker,* 47; Cremony, *Life among the Apaches,* 102–3; *Alta,* June 29, July 9, 1862.

19. Tuttle, "River Colorado," 59.

20. Hunt, *James Henry Carleton,* 326; *Alta,* Apr. 3, 1865.

While it might be expected that the officers would keep detailed journals, the men also recorded temperatures and made scientific observations. Whether driven by curiosity, scholarly zeal, or boredom, the soldiers continued to send specimens to academicians and museums. Seeds, flora, and fauna received much attention. Even the exorbitant freight rates did not deter them from shipping their discoveries back home to California or to the East. One item particularly treasured by the Smithsonian was the skull of a two-headed rattlesnake found by a California soldier.

The troops stationed in Arizona during the Civil War became the territory's most ardent boosters. Their letters home to newspapers kept Arizona on the front page in California for four years. Soldier correspondents touted the rich mines and wrote descriptions of climate, natural wonders, people, politics, towns, and events. The first accounts of Arizona sent back to California stressed the harshness of the land. Stories of "Plutonian" heat, rugged terrain, and gagging alkali dust riveted eager readers. But the soldiers developed a new appreciation for Arizona after they settled into the routine of garrison life. California newspapers began featuring accounts of sparkling rivers, picturesque mountains, antelope herds, and abundant fish. Correspondents soon dispelled rumors of 142-degree temperatures as "humbug."[21]

Some volunteer columnists attempted to lure capitalists and immigrants to the territory in order to develop the mines. Thousands of letters reached California postage due; soldiers, unlike citizens, did not have to pay postage in advance. Many proud relations of volunteers willingly turned over their private correspondence for publication in local newspapers, which touted the efforts of the California soldiers in checking the hostile Indians, considered a necessary first step in exploiting Arizona's vast mineral wealth. The soldiers also submitted articles to mining journals praising the richness of the mines and encouraging investment by capitalists. Although it is difficult to accurately gauge the influence of these correspondents, Arizona's population exploded between 1863 and 1866. The territory also experienced an unprecedented boom in mining claims located and recorded during this same period.[22]

21. See *Alta* and other California newspapers for letters written home by soldier-correspondents, many of which are compiled in Masich, "Columnists with the California Column."

22. There were more claims filed in central Arizona between 1864 and 1866 than during the next two decades combined. Yavapai County Book of Claims No. 1.

At least five volunteer soldiers had previous newspaper experience, while others learned the trade during their enlistments. Alonzo E. Davis wrote under several pseudonyms during the war, including "SIVAD" and the less imaginative "California Volunteer." Davis also wrote a chapter in J. Ross Browne's highly regarded book *Mineral Resources of the Pacific Slope,* published in 1866. After mustering out of the service, Davis returned to Arizona and continued as an "occasional correspondent" for California's most popular daily, the *San Francisco Daily Alta California.* Invariably his articles cast Arizona in a favorable light, pointing out investment opportunities for capitalists and promising prospects for miners. In 1864, as many soldiers' enlistments expired, he wrote that most of the men "intend to stick to the country, for they feel confident they have got their 'golden-egged goose' cooped, sure." At the same time, the California soldiers increased "outside" awareness of the territory, providing information-hungry Arizonans with news from the States by sharing their incoming letters and newspaper subscriptions.[23]

The presence of a large military force resulted in increased business and profits for Arizona entrepreneurs. Lucrative contracts encouraged new businesses and alleviated the territory's chronic currency shortage. Government contractors stood to gain the most, but all of the citizens of the rapidly growing territory reaped the benefits of access to commodities, currency, and improved transportation. A number of energetic men saw the profit potential in the contracts for delivering subsistence stores to the military garrisons; George F. Hooper, F. Hinton, Louis Iager, and J. M. Redondo made small fortunes supplying cattle and other stores. These men employed hundreds—teamsters, herders, butchers, farmers, smiths, mechanics, and laborers—to prepare food for men and animals and to haul massive quantities of supplies. The citizens of Arizona City, on the banks of the Colorado across from Fort Yuma, enjoyed a boom period as their town became the jumping-off point for freight destined for the interior.

Steamboating on the Colorado River also flourished during the war years. Entrepreneurs supplied the military posts and mines for nearly three hundred miles above Fort Yuma. George Alonzo Johnson, who began his career as a Colorado River ferryman in the early 1850s, monopolized the river trade until 1864. Johnson secured so many contracts that supplies

23. Browne, *Mineral Resources,* 443–81; *Alta,* July 19, 1864. In May 1862 some of the printers among the Californian Volunteers attempted to publish their own newspaper in Tucson and cranked up the old Washington hand press that had once issued the *Arizonian.* After the war California officer Sidney R. DeLong purchased the press and started a new paper in Tucson. Soon after, DeLong became the city's first elected mayor. See *Arizona Daily Star,* Nov. 29, 1879; Sonnichsen, *Tucson,* 82, 91.

stockpiled in Arizona City sat for months before he could ship them upriver on his overburdened boats.

In 1861 George A. Johnson and Company operated two sternwheelers, the *Colorado* and the *Cocopah*. Big government contracts prompted Johnson to dismantle the *Colorado* under the protection of the guns of Fort Yuma in 1862 and cannibalize its parts to construct a larger boat. By 1864 miners and officers upriver clamored for supplies, so Johnson built a third boat, the *Mohave*, a twin-engine vessel capable of beating against the mighty Colorado River even in flood stage. Before the *Mohave* launched, however, Thomas E. Trueworthy of San Francisco successfully established the Union Line to break Johnson's monopoly. Trueworthy commissioned Captain George B. Gorman to pilot the company's only boat, the *Esmeralda*, which towed a barge for increased capacity.[24]

Another boat, the *Nina Tilden*, entered the Colorado River trade competition in September 1864. Alphonzo F. Tilden, managing director of the Philadelphia Silver and Copper Mining Company, soon found the going too tough, and in the summer of 1865 he sold out to yet another new company that also bought Trueworthy's *Esmeralda*. The fierce competition for river trade continued until the late 1860s, when Johnson and his newly organized Colorado Steam Navigation Company once again controlled river traffic. Reduced shipping rates and more frequent service made possible the development of many mining towns along the lower Colorado and as far as six hundred miles upriver from the mouth. The army, which was largely responsible for the boom, also benefited from the regular shipments and lower prices.

Surprisingly, several of the Indian tribes in Arizona also benefited from military occupation. In Tucson Major Fergusson issued a circular requiring citizens to reward Papago Indians who recovered stolen stock from the Apaches. The Papagos received four dollars per head for stock returned or one-third of the herd. Yuma and Mojave Indians regularly gathered and stacked wood at designated points along the Colorado River for use by the steamboats carrying government supplies. The Pimas and Maricopas also profited directly by providing food crops and forage to the army.[25]

Since the arrival of the California Column in 1862, the Gila River tribes provided wheat and corn for military consumption. The army, however, rarely paid the natives in cash. Carleton planned from the start to supply his

---

24. For the steamboat industry on the Colorado, see Lingenfelter, *Steamboats on the Colorado*.
25. Circular, July 27, 1862, Hdqrs. Dist. of Western Ariz., Tucson, Commands of J. R. West, RG 393; Tuttle, "River Colorado," 57.

command with the surplus crops produced by these farming tribes. Before the Californians even entered the territory, the army commissioned Ammi White to trade for wheat. Later volunteer quartermaster and commissary officers dealt directly with the Pimas and Maricopas. In April 1863 James H. Toole, acting assistant quartermaster, with the assistance of Pima subagent Abraham Lyon, distributed fifty-eight "old pattern dragoon coats and jackets, and 415 pompons" to the Indians. Major Fergusson had suggested that Toole use these obsolete items for barter, adding that "two fanegas [three bushels] of wheat can be got for each coat and jacket." Carleton also requested that the army ship ten thousand yards of manta (cheap cotton cloth) and five thousand pounds of other "presents" to Arizona to trade for Pima and Maricopa grain and fodder.[26]

Arizona's white population showed less trust in the army than Indian contractors did. Citizens disliked government scrip, but specie was in short supply. In the gold-based economy of the Far West, lenders and merchants discounted paper money as much as 60 percent during the war years. General Wright requested that the army pay California troops in hard currency, for greenbacks "can only be converted at a ruinous discount." The soldiers accused the army of favoritism, particularly when rumors circulated that the few regulars still remaining in California received payment in specie. Whenever possible, the paymaster counted out hard cash to the volunteers in Arizona.[27]

The government payroll benefited Arizona by providing a steady supply of money into the region. In the southern part of the territory, gold bars, some as small as two dollars in value, had served as currency. Volunteer officers repeatedly asked headquarters for hard money, saying beef contractors and Sonoran farmers would not accept paper money. They demanded U.S. gold dollars or Mexican silver reales. Lieutenant Colonel Davis wrote Carleton in 1864 that "coin is the currency which makes the mare go." Payday was erratic for the California Volunteers in Arizona. When the men did get their money, they often received six months or even a year in back pay.[28]

Officers in garrison towns had to be especially vigilant after paydays. Some soldiers went on drinking or gambling sprees and others, with money

26. Fergusson to George A. Burkett, Apr. 17, 1863, OR, 50(2):405–6; Cutler to West, Mar. 31, 1862, OR, 50(1):970; Carleton to Drum, Dec. 21, 1861, ibid., 773–80.

27. Young, *Journalism in California*, 61; Wright to Thomas, adjutant general, Feb. 4, 1863, OR, 50(2):303.

28. Altshuler, "Case of Sylvester Mowry, the Mowry Mine," 160; Davis to Carleton, Mar. 2, 1864, OR, 34(2):595.

in their pockets, thought the time right for deserting. Thieves and conmen, who seemed to be in no short supply in Tucson and other towns, stalked recently paid volunteers. In 1862 Carleton ordered his officers not to pay the men until they left Fort Yuma, and then only two months' worth, in order to avoid the temptations of Arizona City. One officer wrote, "there are no local diseases to be feared here, except such as arise from bad whiskey and diseased women." But a majority of the soldiers were stationed at isolated posts far from towns and never had a chance to carouse.[29]

By 1864 Tucson boasted a population of some fifteen hundred people. The census had trebled since the arrival of the Californians in 1862. Despite the efforts of local commanders Fergusson and Coult, Tucson still had a reputation as a lawless resort of thieves and unsavory characters, whom Carleton referred to as the "red sash, bowie-knife-and-pistol, card-playing Americans who will be found swaggering about all frontier towns." To curb crime he ordered the town's provost marshal to issue passes to all travelers. Local citizens had to prove they were gainfully employed and loyal to the Union.[30] Carleton attempted to clean up Tucson and provide some semblance of order and justice "so that when a man does have his throat cut, his house robbed, or his fields ravaged, he may at least have the consolation of knowing there is some law that will reach him who does the injury."[31]

A soldier correspondent for the *San Francisco Evening Bulletin* contended that many of the depredations attributed to Apaches were actually the work of Tucson "cut-throats," and he went on to say, "I am forced to the conclusion that all the Indians and greasers and White men feel privileged to murder whoever has money or stock enough to make it worth the trouble to cut short the thread of his existence." Captain Cremony firmly believed that of the forty-seven graves in the local cemetery, only two of the interred had died of natural causes. Major Coult wrote that border-jumping Mexican desperadoes contributed to Tucson's high crime rate. This opinion seemed born out when, on December 31, 1862, Captain Fritz pursued a group of thieves responsible for stealing government horses, saddles, and carbines into Sonora. The relentless Fritz recovered the stolen property at Hermosillo, Mexico, 350 miles south of Tucson.[32]

29. Carleton to Drum, Dec. 21, 1861, *OR,* 50(1):772–74; West to Cutler, Nov. 12, 1861, ibid., 719–20; Browne, *Adventures,* 135–36.

30. SO 142, Sept. 10, 1863, Hdqrs. Tucson, Commands of J. R. West, RG 393.

31. Carleton to Drum, June 10, 1862, *OR,* 50(1):52–53; Hunt, *James Henry Carleton,* 222.

32. *San Francisco Evening Bulletin,* Mar. 11, 1863, July 9, 1864; Coult to Drum, Dec. 31, 1862, *OR,* 50(2):270–71.

In 1863 Major Fergusson announced that gambling was "absolutely prohibited in the town of Tucson. . . . No more licenses for such a villainous
trade shall be issued." The military would deal harshly with transgressors;
they would be required to leave town in twenty-four hours and suffer their
money, monte tables, and other implements confiscated. Fergusson's successor, Major Coult, took a more relaxed stance. On January 1, 1864, Coult
ordered the provost marshal to restrict the sale of liquor by the glass to the
saloons of J. B. Allen, Juan Fernandez, and Fernando Urrquides but
allowed for the purchase of liquor by the bottle at the establishments of
Warner & Stevens and John Gleason. Coult also tolerated fair gaming
houses with relatively good reputations. Two other gambling halls received
similar privileges later that month.[33]

J. Ross Browne noticed that the saloons attracted soldiers too: "Volunteer
soldiers are stationed all over the town—at the mescal-shops, the monte-
tables, and houses of ill-fame—for the preservation of public order, or go
there of their own accord for that purpose, which amounts to the same
thing." A garrison court-martial conducted in June 1862 found that the
number of men drunk on duty or parade increased drastically soon after
the troops arrived in Tucson. The situation was not much better at Fort
Yuma. A private in the Fifth California Infantry recorded in his diary that
Captain Joseph Tuttle, "while in charge of the Parade at Fort Yuma was so
drunk as to fall his whole length on his face and actually had to be carried
off by his men." The officers at Fort Yuma, an observer noted, are "too
much engaged (or at least the majority of them) consuming whiskey."[34]

The soldiers at the Tucson garrison had occasional run-ins with citizens,
and orders appeared from time to time to safeguard the rights of the town's
inhabitants. In General Orders No. 35, dated September 1862, the local
commander prohibited all soldiers "from trespassing upon, or crossing cultivated fields, or gardens, of the citizens of this place, without permission."
Another order admonished soldiers not to destroy "fences or enclosures in
this town or vicinity when procuring brush or other building materials for
quarters."[35] On August 28, 1862, a court-martial found Sergeant George

33. GO 5, Apr. 18, 1863, Hdqrs. Tucson, Commands of J. R. West, R 393; SO 2, Jan. 1, 1864,
ibid.

34. Browne, *Adventures*, 134–35; George O. Hand Diary, Sept. 30–Oct. 4, 1862, Arizona Historical Society, Tucson; Fergusson to J. F. Bennett, Apr. 14, 1863, *OR*, 50(2):396. See also Bushnell Diary, Nov. 10, 1865.

35. GO 35, Sept. 14, 1862, Hdqrs. Tucson, Commands of J. R. West, RG 393; GO 13, June
28, 1862, ibid.

Tucson's saloons were either regulated and taxed or closed by the military government imposed by General Carleton's "Column from California" in 1862.
Carleton had little patience for the "red sash, bowie-knife-and-pistol, cardplayng Americans who will be found swaggering about all frontier towns," and
he required them to provide proof of loyalty and gainful employment. Courtesy
of the Arizona Historical Society, Tucson, B 74.

Hand, Company G, First California Infantry, guilty of neglect in a case
involving a citizen. The sergeant failed to turn out the guard when a man
named Levi Aldrich reported Apaches killing stock near Tucson. The court
reduced Hand to the ranks and deducted ten dollars per month from his
pay for six months. But Fergusson could not spare good noncommissioned
officers and took it upon himself to reverse the ruling of the court.[36]

Illegal trade in army goods plagued all the posts situated near population centers in Arizona. Corrupt soldiers in the Quartermaster Department
sold civilians everything from government mules, wrongfully branded "C"
for condemned, to army clothing. Inspector General Davis informed Carleton that "grave and discreditable accusations . . . of fraudulent and unauthorized transactions [had surfaced at Fort Yuma and elsewhere] with

36. GO 29, Aug. 28, 1862, Hdqrs. Tucson, Commands of J. R. West, RG 393; Hand Diary,
Aug. 27, 1862; Senate, *Federal Census—Territory of New Mexico and Territory of Arizona*, 19 (1860).

REAR VIEW OF TUCSON.

Rear view of Tucson. In 1864 *Harpers Weekly* satirist J. Ross Browne depicted California Volunteers carousing in Tucson, but he said of the soldier escort that protected him in Apache country, "a better set of men I never travelled with. They are good-humored, obliging, and sober, and not one of them stole a pig or a chicken during the entire trip." By J. Ross Browne, from *Adventures in the Apache Country.*

regard to supplies purchases of horses, etc." Apparently the California officers were not among those caught up in this illicit trade. Boards of survey, convened routinely to inspect quartermaster accounts and inventories, found no misconduct among the officers assigned to supply duties.[37]

Morale and discipline suffered most during extended periods of tedious garrison duty. Charges at courts-martial ranged from sitting down on guard to outright insubordination. The judges found most offenders guilty of minor infractions, such as refusing to police the camp or straying from the post boundaries. Many of the enlisted men believed themselves to be their officers' equals. Sergeant Hand commented that Captain H. A. "Humpy" Greene of Company G, First California Infantry could not command his

37. Conner, *Joseph Reddeford Walker,* 307–8; Davis to Carleton, Apr. 4, 1864, *OR,* 34(3):207; SO 14, June 13, 1862, Hdqrs. Tucson, Commands of J. R. West, RG 393.

men because he did not have their respect. They mocked him and called him "Right Face" and "Shoulder Arms" behind his back.[38]

A Tucson court-martial convicted one private of "conduct to the prejudice of good order and military discipline." He received a sentence of thirty days at hard labor and forfeited ten dollars of his pay for addressing a second lieutenant "with words too obscene to repeat." Private Frederick Franklin of Company D, Fifth California Infantry allegedly remarked while on duty at the Tucson depot on January 21, 1864, that "he would be damned if he would turn out the Guard for Coult or French." The court sentenced the defiant soldier to carry a forty-pound log on his shoulder in front of the guardhouse for three days.[39]

Of course officers charged with violating the Articles of War also found themselves standing before a court-martial. Lieutenant Colonel Clarence E. Bennett presided over one such affair at Maricopa Wells. Lieutenant William J. Perkins of the Seventh California Infantry had gotten disgracefully drunk while in charge of a wagon train en route to Fort Yuma during the final days of the war in April 1865. The lieutenant's wife had accompanied the train, and Perkins accused her of dallying with an enlisted man. The enraged officer threatened to "shoot any damned son of a bitch" who attempted to interfere and then aimed his cocked pistol at the head of Private Henry A. Howard of Company K while screaming at his wife, "if you want some beef, I'll shoot it for you." Mrs. Perkins and Private Howard both survived the assault, which took place in front of the entire command. Lieutenant Perkins was cashiered for drunkenness and conduct unbecoming an officer.[40]

Most discipline problems stemmed from frustration and boredom. Some of the citizen-soldiers had difficulty adjusting to the seemingly arbitrary system of military discipline. Others developed personality conflicts with commissioned and noncommissioned officers, but these problems were common in the volunteer service in the East as well. Generally the morale and discipline

---

38. Results of Garrison Court-Martial, May 12, 1862, Tucson, Commands of J. R. West, RG 393; Results of Garrison Court-Martial, June 19, 1862, ibid.; Hand Diary, Sept. 30, 1862; Orton, *California Men,* 363.

39. GO 4, Jan. 21, 1864, Hdqrs. Tucson, Commands of J. R. West, RG 393.

40. Perkins clearly violated Article of War 45 ("Any commissioned officer who shall be found drunk on his guard, party, or other duty, shall be cashiered"), for he admitted at his court-martial to being "so drunk that he did not know his ass from a hole in the ground." William J. Perkins Court-Martial, GO 2, Jan. 5, 1866, Hdqrs. Dept. of California, C. E. Bennett Papers, Arizona Historical Society, Tucson; Orton, *California Men,* 767; *Revised U.S. Army Regulations of 1861,* 494; *Alta,* Jan. 16, 1866.

of the Californians was good. Even J. Ross Browne admitted of his California cavalry escort, "a better set of men I have never traveled with. They are good-humored, obliging, and sober, and not one of them stole a pig or a chicken on the entire trip."[41]

Carleton demanded strict discipline when his column marched into Arizona in the spring of 1862. His General Orders No. 1 prohibited any man from leaving ranks without permission from his company commander. The other soldiers of the company were required to carry the musket and knapsack of any man on leave until his return. When in camp, General Orders No. 6 specified, "No soldier will be allowed to go more than five hundred yards from his quarters, without permission from his company commander." Men who strayed from the camp, it was reasoned, might fall prey to Apaches. Those caught off limits by the camp guard or provost marshal received the punishment meted out by courts-martial.[42]

The monotonous camp routine varied little from post to post. Foot soldiers followed a demanding daily regimen. The cavalrymen had to care for their horses as well as the usual fatigues and drills. Bugle calls or drumbeats sounded the daily duties of camp. In 1862 a typical day included:

Reveille	Immediately after daybreak
Stable Call	Immediately after Reveille
Fatigue Call	Ten minutes after Reveille
Drill Call—Infantry	5:30
Recall from Stables	6:00
Boots and Saddles	6:00
To Horse	6:15
Recall from Drill—Infantry	7:00
Recall from Drill—Cavalry	7:15
Sick Call	7:15
Breakfast Call	7:30
Guard Mounting	8:30
Dinner Call	12:00
Orderly Call	1:00
Stable Call	5:00
Recall from Stable	5:45
Dress Parade	Thirty Minutes before Sunset

41. Browne, *Adventures,* 139.
42. GO 1, Apr. 7, 1862, Commands of J. R. West, RG 393; GO 6, May 22, 1862, ibid.

Tattoo	8:30
Taps	8:45[43]

In May 1863 the Tucson garrison performed one extra hour of drill and dispensed with dress parade. Similarly, at Fort Yuma, Major Clarence Bennett believed that more drill markedly improved the morale and discipline of the troops. A year before, the volunteers of the California Column marshaling at Fort Yuma had practiced the manual of arms and marched with a will, causing Major R. C. Drum to remark that their drill "would have done credit to regular troops." At Fort Mojave the Fourth California Infantry did not have a rigorous drill schedule but discipline did not appear to suffer. Captain Charles Atchisson was a spit-and-polish officer, and his men competed for the privilege of serving as their commander's orderly. The man with the cleanest outfit won the easy job.[44]

Camp Tucson and other large posts required officers, commissioned and noncommissioned, to attend "School Call" at 6:00 P.M. Monday, Wednesday, and Friday evenings were set aside for officers to study from Hardee's *Infantry Tactics*, including the "School of the Soldier," "School of the Company," and "School of the Battalion." Noncommissioned officers and privates with special aptitude attended classes on Tuesday and Thursday. Major Coult hosted school for the officers of the Tucson garrison in his own quarters.[45]

Surgeon McNulty, medical director of the California Column, kept close watch on the health of the men during their march across the desert in 1862. Some of the regiments stationed in Arizona later in the war did not enjoy such good care or health. The camps at Tucson, Tubac, and Fort Mason in southern Arizona were notorious for malaria. In July 1863 Captain William Ffrench requested to be relieved of his duties at Tucson for disabilities caused by malarial fevers. Unfortunately he reported his other officers and Assistant Surgeon Cox sick as well, and headquarters decided that it could not spare the captain at that time. In September 1866 the California companies at Tubac could only muster one-tenth of their numbers at roll call due to sickness.[46]

Contaminated water contributed significantly to the poor health at the permanent posts. Poor hygiene and rations made the situation worse,

43. GO 30, Sept. 1, 1862, Hdqrs. Tucson, Commands of J. R. West, RG 393.

44. GO 11, May 26, 1863, ibid.; Clarence E. Bennett Diary, May 1863, Arizona Historical Society, Tucson; Drum to AAG, May 30, 1862, *OR*, 50(1):1110–16; Davis, "Pioneer Days in Arizona," Arizona State University Library, 40.

45. GO 40, Nov. 9, 1862, Hdqrs. Tucson, Commands of J. R. West, RG 393.

46. Ffrench to West, July 15, 1863, *OR*, 50(2):25; Farish, *History of Arizona*, 4:4, 100.

Capt. Charles Atchisson, Company I, Fourth California Infantry, stands outside his quarters at Fort Mojave with his company clerk and orderly. Atchisson was a spit-and-polish officer. The enlisted men competed for the honor of serving as the captain's orderly—the man with the cleanest outfit won the easy job. Atchisson returned to Mohave City after the war, serving as postmaster and later as probate judge. Courtesy of the Bancroft Library, University of California, Berkeley.

resulting in dysentery and other ailments. One officer prohibited the "washing of clothes, utensils, or persons in the ditch that supplies the command with water." At large posts the soldiers "messed" by company, and the officer of the day supervised the meals, tasted the food, and saw that a non-commissioned officer ran the kitchen.[47]

Deficiencies in rolling stock, low water in the Colorado River, and the shortage of horses and mules hindered the regular flow of provisions and

47. GO 2, May 6, 1862, Hdqrs. Advance Guard, California Column, Commands of J. R. West, RG 393; GO 1, Apr. 7, 1862, ibid.

frequently forced volunteer officers to order reductions in rations. Negligent contractors and a chronic shortage of supplies from Arizona and Sonora contributed to the problem as well. In September 1862 the Tucson garrison received reduced flour rations. At the same time, Major Fergusson cut the daily pork ration to only once every ten days. Troops on the march with the California Column subsisted on "pemmican," a concoction of pounded dried beef and lard, much despised by the men. Unable to identify the meat, the soldiers called it "pelican" and complained that it would serve better as rat poison; others suggested that fresh mule meat would be a vast improvement. Regardless, commissary sergeants continued to issue this indigestible article from ten-pound cans at the rate of ten ounces per man every day until all available stores were expended.[48]

Before the men of Company I, Fourth California Infantry left Drum Barracks for Arizona, they had protested the quality of their beef ration. The soldiers arranged a public funeral for one of the beeves and erected a headboard over the grave that read:

> Why should we mourn for this old ox
> or grieve for his poor beef?
> When he has caused us pain and woe
> and worn out all our teeth?
> His spirit has gone to other lands;
> we trust it's for the best
> For when we had his bones to gnaw
> we were more cursed than blessed.[49]

Little did they know that beef of any description would be a luxury once they crossed the Colorado River into Arizona.

A soldier stationed at Fort Mojave summed up his desert life as a "scarcity of water, plenty of hard-tack and 'sow-belly,' and [an] abundance of torrid weather." An officer with the Native Battalion, stationed at Fort Yuma in August 1865, wrote home: "For heaven's sake, never come out this way if you can help it. You will surely melt. The thermometer is 112 in the shade every day, with no wind. Scorpions thick as molasses and flies still more.

48. GO 33, Sept. 6, 1862, Hdqrs. Tucson, Commands of J. R. West, RG 393; Carleton to Drum, Dec. 21, 1861, *OR*, 50(1):774, 779; James P. Newcomb, draft letter, July 8, 1862, James P. Newcomb Papers, CAH. The editors of the *Alta* omitted Newcomb's description of pemmican as "pelican" in the final printed version of N.'s letter published on August 10, 1862.
49. Davis, "Pioneer Days in Arizona," Arizona State University Library, 47.

When we want to drink cool water we have to boil it and drink it immediately or else it gets hotter."[50]

When subsistence stores did get through, the troops ate fresh beef, salt pork and horse, rice, desiccated potatoes, coffee, tea, sugar, and *pinole* (sweetened gruel of corn and mesquite flour). Fresh vegetables were rare. Many soldiers supplemented their diet with purchases from the post sutler, if they had one, or grew their own vegetables in camp gardens. Although the food and climate took their toll, health among the volunteer regiments was generally good, especially when compared to conditions in the eastern armies.

Corporal William A. Bushnell, Company K, Second California Infantry, opined that the shortage of "grub" at Fort Goodwin (a.k.a. Camp Starvation) was not the worst part of garrison life, "but it is of another deficiency that we must speak now, namely the scarcity of intellectual food . . . , of reading matter, we are living on less than one-fourth rations." One copy of *Robinson Crusoe* and a few other novels available had "gone from company to company and from hand to hand until with such perpetual thumbing the text is threatened with oblivion." With books and newspapers in such short supply, Bushnell reported that some of the soldiers turned to reading the Bible, to the amazement of their comrades.[51]

The soldiers entertained themselves with theatrical performances of Shakespeare, and they were always on the lookout for fresh talent among casual newcomers and freight-wagon escorts. But the men were most starved for female companionship. Competition for the affections of an attractive *señorita* at a Tucson fandango resulted in a riot followed by arrests and a guardhouse full of bruised and battered soldiers. Corporal Bushnell observed that a shooting at Fort Goodwin resulted from jealousy over a "mujere [woman] who holds forth in the lower part of the garrison." At isolated posts even women of ill-fame were a rarity.[52]

50. Ibid., 48; Porfirio Jimenez to Pablo de la Guerra, Aug. 3, 1865, De la Guerra Papers, Owen Coy Room, University of Southern California, Los Angeles.

51. Hand Diary, July 23, 1862; Bushnell Diary, May 17, 1865. One soldier lamented in print over the scarcity of newspapers: "Oh! For a *Bulletin*, a *Union*, or an *Alta!*" *San Francisco Evening Bulletin*, Dec. 6, 1862. A California lieutenant begged his wife to cut out and mail "scraps" from newspapers. When he received them he exclaimed that the men of his company passed them around "until there was not a piece left bigger than your finger." George H. Pettis to Annie (wife), Sept. 26, 1862, George H. Pettis Papers, Western Americana Collection, Beinecke Library, Yale, New Haven, Conn.

52. Bushnell Diary, Feb. 19, 24, 1865; Hand Diary, Oct. 26, Nov. 2, 1862. Women rarely accompanied the California soldiers to Arizona, but occasionally exceptions were made for surgeons and officers. The army frowned on such arrangements, however, because the

Some of the California soldiers did meet and marry Arizona girls. One of the express riders at Fort Mojave wed the youngest daughter of Bio-oo-hoot, a Mojave chief, in a service performed by the enlisted men in the presence of Captain Atchisson. Other volunteer soldiers married Indian women shortly after their enlistments expired. J. D. Walker married and settled with the Pimas at Sacaton after his discharge from the Fifth California Infantry; he later commanded a company of Pima Arizona Volunteers. Thomas V. Keam, a veteran of the First California Cavalry, married Astan Lipai (Gray Woman) and lived with the Salt Clan of the Navajo. These "squawmen" suffered discrimination from fellow whites but were generally held in high regard as interpreters and Indian agents.[53]

At least five marriages of California soldiers and Mexican American women took place at the Cathedral of San Augustin in Tucson between 1864 and 1867. These men received permission to wed from their company commanders, who generally preferred that their men avoid local entanglements. The army had a longstanding tradition of noncommissioned officers marrying company laundresses, but marriages between California soldiers and the daughters of Tucson's most prominent families could create political complications. Yet in a garrison town, the opportunities for fraternization increased the chances of meeting and marrying. Some of the soldiers eschewed convention, and there is no way to determine the incidence of cohabitation or common-law marriages. In Yavapai County four volunteers married local women soon after discharge, and along the Colorado River Alonzo E. Davis married Emily W. Mathews, the daughter of a Hardyville businessman, whom he had met at the Fort Mojave New Year's

practice undermined morale and discipline. See Perkins Court-Martial, GO 2, Hdqrs. Dept. of California, Jan. 5, 1866, Bennett Papers; and *Alta,* Jan. 16, 1866.

Many California soldiers wrote home with titillating tales of licentious local women. Some disparaged the virtue of Hispanic and Indian women who fraternized with the volunteers, though in truth the camp followers that inevitably hovered around army posts—from California to Washington, D.C.—were not representative of the general population. Invidious racism pervaded the ranks, and while contact with people of the territories enlightened some soldiers, others continued to harbor deep-seated prejudices: "The whole race of natives of this country are no better [than "*peones* (slaves)"] neither do they look any more enlightened than the dirty Greasers of Cal. The women here are nearly all prostitutes, never work but all smoke, drink, and gamble. There is some exceptions but they are few and far between. The diggers of Cal. will compare better with the natives of Mexico than anything I know of." Cpl. Aaron Cory Hitchcock to Thomas and Naomi Hitchcock, July 20, 1864, Hitchcock Letters.

53. Farish, *History of Arizona,* 4:117–18; Bailey, "Thomas Varker Keam," 15–19; *Alta,* July 15, 1864.

Soldiers of the Fourth California Infantry with Mojave women and children on the banks of the Colorado River near Fort Mojave, 1863. The soldiers enjoyed good relations with the Mojaves and when off duty spent time prospecting for gold and hunting. Courtesy of the Bancroft Library, University of California, Berkeley.

Eve Ball in 1864–65. Other veterans wed in later years when they returned to settle in Arizona.[54]

Supply deficiencies continued at the Tucson depot. In the spring of 1864, army officials attempted to reroute the garrison's supply line through the Sonora towns of Libertad and Guaymas, on the Gulf of California, bypassing Fort Yuma entirely. As early as September 1862, Carleton had instructed Fergusson to survey a wagon road to these important coastal ports; the Guaymas route particularly offered advantages in freighting time and expense. The major reported that the route was "smooth or even all the way; and the largest stretch without water at any time is forty-five miles." But the French blockade of Mexican ports, mutual distrust between the

54. Marriage Registry, 1864–67, San Augustin Cathedral, Tucson; Marriage Records, Yavapai County, 1865–75, Arizona Historical Society, Tucson; Davis, "Pioneer Days in Arizona," Arizona State University Library, 83, 114. Some of the Californians expressed revulsion at the thought of marrying outside their race. Soon after leaving Tucson for New Mexico, Cpl. Aaron Hitchcock wrote his parents, "Once and awhile we hear of a Soldier marrying a Spanish Girl. I tell you what it is I will die single before I will disgrace the whites so much as to marry one of those that live in this country." Hitchcock to Thomas and Naomi Hitchcock, July 20, 1864, Hitchcock Letters.

Captain Atchisson's cook, a private in Company I, Fourth California Infantry, poses with "Topsy" and other Mojave women at Fort Mojave, 1863. California Volunteer soldiers fraternized with and married native women, even though officers attempted to discourage such liaisons. Courtesy of the Bancroft Library, University of California, Berkeley.

United States and Mexico, and government red tape doomed the Sonora route to failure during the war years. Nevertheless, General Wright, commanding the Department of the Pacific, was so pleased with Fergusson's report that he recommended him for the colonelcy of the First California Cavalry. And Fergusson's map of the Tucson–Lobos Bay route became a standard source for cartographers and travelers in southern Arizona.[55]

55. Henry Walker, "Freighting from Guaymas to Tucson," 294; GO 20, Sept. 5, 1862, Hdqrs. Las Cruces, *OR*, 50(1):115.

California Volunteers contributed greatly to the exploration and mapping of Arizona's uncharted wilderness. A detailed map of Tucson commissioned by Fergusson in 1862 depicted the layout of the "Old Pueblo" for the first time since the Spanish occupation nearly one hundred years earlier. Military surveyors also made a map of the District of Arizona, showing practical wagon roads. The most spectacular chart of the Southwest produced during the war was drawn by Captain Allen L. Anderson, on detached service from the Fifth U.S. Infantry. General Carleton ordered him to draft a map of Arizona and New Mexico. With an escort of Californians, Anderson explored the virgin territory. He also relied upon the reports of officers who had made forays deep into uncharted Indian territory. The result, Carleton proudly proclaimed, was "much more correct than any other map of this country hither to published." Volunteer officers also provided the miners flooding into the Arizona gold fields with reports of wells, grazing conditions, and intelligence regarding Indian tribes.[56]

Captain Cremony accurately summarized "the gigantic labors performed by the Column from California, in making roads; digging and restoring wells in desert places; constructing bridges; establishing depots; [and] escorting trains" as they occupied Arizona Territory.[57] During the five years of their service in the territory, California troops blazed or improved hundreds of miles of trails and, more importantly, wagon roads. They gave early attention to the ferry landing at Fort Yuma, where for years wagon masters had to double-team their wagons to haul loads up the steep grade from the river to the Gila Trail. Under Major Rigg's direction the Californians cut through the bank and regraded the approach from the Colorado, facilitating travel for military and civilian trains alike. Along the Gila route itself, troops removed obstacles, graded roads, and dug wells.[58]

Projects undertaken in the later years of the war included work on the Mohave Trail across southern Nevada to the Colorado River. Besides making this route passable for wagons destined for central and northern Arizona, the volunteers built fortified way stations to guard against Indian attacks. The California troops also explored a new wagon road from Las Vegas to Fort Mojave. In October 1863 a detachment under Captain Herbert M. Enos blazed a practicable wagon road between Fort Whipple (near

56. Wheat, *Mapping the Trans-Mississippi*, 5:127–28, 381; Carleton to Drum, Sept. 15, 1865, *OR*, 48(2):1230.

57. Cremony, *Life among the Apaches*, 145.

58. Charles D. Poston, "Military Roads in Arizona," *American Railroad Journal* 38 (Jan. 14, 1865), 54.

Prescott) and the Colorado River. The Californians generally strengthened the lines of communication between the northern Arizona outposts, Las Cruces, and other points east.

Interior trails also received attention. In addition to improving the route from Fort Whipple to the La Paz placers along the Colorado, Major Thomas J. Blakeney opened a road between Fort Goodwin and the Salt River near the Pinal Mountains in the summer of 1864. In July 1865 Brigadier General John S. Mason directed Lieutenant Colonel Bennett to lead a small mounted force on a reconnaissance from Fort Bowie to Fort Barrett via old Fort Breckenridge. Bennett reported on the feasibility of a new, shorter wagon road. He also led a combined force of Arizona Volunteers and Californians to clear a road between Maricopa Wells, on the Gila, north to Fort McDowell, a new post on the Verde River in Tonto Apache territory. As a result of these efforts, a network of easily traveled roads now linked the forts and population centers of Arizona Territory.[59]

Civilians and soldiers alike came to rely on California vedettes to carry the mail. In the eastern theater vedettes were mounted scouts or sentinels, but in Arizona the term became synonymous with "express rider." Only picked troopers with the best horses rode the routes between posts and to points outside the territory. The men traveled singly or in pairs; only rarely did they enjoy the safety of an escort. A late express often meant that an Apache war party had ambushed a vedette.[60]

The riders faced other challenges too, from worn-out horses to the desert itself. The cavalry mounts suffered terribly from the lack of grain and forage. The army pressed animals of every color, size, and description into service, but by April 1863 Major Fergusson at Tucson asked that the men of Company B, Second California Cavalry be relieved—both men and horses were "used up." Private William Hollister, a member of Company I, Fourth California Infantry, rode the express to Fort Mojave. During the summer of 1865, the *Wilmington Journal* reported that the private was "sunstruck, and never recovered from the effects of it."[61] Civilian contractors and infantrymen sometimes carried the expresses when government mounts and cavalrymen were not available.

59. Report of Thomas J. Blakeney, Aug. 8, 1865, *OR*, 41(1):81–86; Clarence E. Bennett to Green, AAG, Hdqrs. District of Arizona, July 21, 1865, *OR*, 50(1):421–23; Underhill, "Arizona Volunteers," 38.

60. Hunt, *Army of the Pacific*, 133; GO 9, May 15, 1862, Fort Yuma, *OR*, 50(1):1075.

61. Fergusson to J. F. Bennett, Apr. 14, 1863, *OR*, 50(2):396; *Wilmington (Calif.) Journal*, July 29, 1865.

On January 31, 1864, Major Coult posted arrival and departure times for the Tucson "Government Express":

1. Arrivals from Mesilla on the 9th and 24th of each month.
2. Arrivals from Ft. Yuma on the 5th and 17th of each month.
3. Leaves Tucson for Mesilla on the 5th and 20th of each month.
4. Leaves Tucson for Ft. Yuma on the 11th and 26th of each month.

All letters not mailed before 6 o'clock A.M. on the day prior to the departure of the Express will lay in this office until the departure of the next one.

Fergusson had two new mailbags, fitted with small padlocks, made in Tucson to reduce the risk of tampering. Evidently, bored vedettes between Fort Yuma and Tucson had taken to reading newspapers and, occasionally, private letters from California.

Late in 1864 shortages of men and horses put a stop to the vedette service for a time. Then in the spring of 1865, the fresh recruits of the Seventh California Infantry resumed the Arizona mail service. One soldier commented: "Yesterday the expressman left with the first mail consisting of 350 letters showing conclusively that the seventh, besides being *hungry*, is literary. If we keep on sending letters in that manner, California will be overrun with them." The Californians provided communication between Arizona and the "outside" until late 1865, when civil authorities once again accepted responsibility for the mail service.[62]

California Volunteers provided other basic services required by Arizona citizens until the establishment of the civilian territorial government. Besides blazing trails, developing roads, and making maps, army supply contracts for forts along the Colorado River and isolated interior posts bolstered the economy of the fledgling territory. The military occupation also kept criminals and Apache raiders at bay, encouraging settlement and resulting in a population boom during the war years. Both officers and enlisted men publicized the territory's mineral wealth as well as its climate, geography, and cultures. The Californians took an active role in the establishment of the new territory, and many would return after their military service to settle and further shape Arizona's future.

62. SO 12, Jan. 31, 1864, Hdqrs. Tucson, Commands of J. R. West, RG 393; Fergusson to J. F. Bennett, Apr. 14, 1863, *OR*, 50(2):396–97; Hunt, *Army of the Pacific*, 143, *Calaveras (Calif.) Chronicle*, Aug. 12, 1865.

Border Patrol and Mustering Out

The First Battalion of California Veteran Volunteer Infantry organized in November and December 1864, just as the three-year enlistments of the original California Volunteer regiments began to expire. The consolidation of reenlisted veterans of the First California Infantry into two companies, A and B, and the Fifth California Infantry into five companies, C, D, E, F, and G, resulted in a battalion of experienced frontier troops. The Californians, however, did not join in numbers sufficient to fill these companies to their full one-hundred-man strength, so by drawing lots, commanding officers chose Company F to have its members distributed among the understrength companies of the battalion. In March 1865 General Carleton directed Lieutenant Colonel Rigg to assume command of the veteran volunteers and establish his headquarters at Fort Craig, New Mexico. Soon thereafter the veteran companies left for active duty in Colorado, New Mexico, and Texas, leaving Arizona's forts and depots in the care of newly raised California regiments and a handful of New Mexico and Arizona volunteers.[1]

In July 1864 dwindling manpower and supplies forced Carleton to order the evacuation of the Tucson depot. He instructed Major Coult to distribute the limited commissary stores remaining at the post to the garrisons at Tubac, Goodwin, and Bowie. Carleton urged him to be discreet in his withdrawal to avoid alarming the locals, who might feel that they were being abandoned. As the enlistments of the men stationed at Forts Whipple and Bowie began to expire, New Mexico Volunteers and one company of the

1. Orton, *California Men*, 381.

Fifth U.S. Infantry, the first unit of regulars stationed in Arizona since 1861, took their places. Carleton withdrew the California vedettes on the Yuma road, severely curtailing communication with the Pacific coast, and by December 1864 the District of Arizona ceased to exist.[2]

When the three-year enlistments of the volunteers who composed the original California Column expired in the fall of 1864, most marched to Las Cruces or Mesilla, New Mexico, to be mustered out. These men had mixed feelings about their service. Some griped about the lack of recognition for their hard years in Arizona. Throughout their terms of enlistment they had constantly asked, "When are we going to be ordered to the seat of the war?" only to be disappointed that the orders never came. Others complained about being discharged in the territories, knowing there would be a long, costly, and dangerous journey home to California. Still others declared that they would have preferred that the army muster them out in Arizona, where they had staked mining claims. But many of the men had grown accustomed to army life and, seeing no better alternative, reenlisted in one of the five companies of veteran volunteers and continued service in the Southwest.[3]

California troops in Arizona remained alert for Confederate reinvasion attempts until the war ended, but in 1865 the morale of the Californians on duty in the territories began to deteriorate. Newspapers brought reports of the grand reviews of the victorious armies in Washington, D.C., following the surrender of the Confederates in the eastern and western theaters. The last spark of rebellion had been crushed, and the California Volunteers remaining in Arizona were eager for discharge and home. Since the beginning of the war, volunteer officers stationed in Arizona felt their primary responsibility was to guard against another Confederate invasion of the territory. Rumors of Rebel troop buildups and occasional confrontations with Confederate sympathizers fueled their fears of attack from Texas or Mexico.[4]

Sympathy for the Rebel cause ran high in southern California in the months following the fall of Fort Sumter in 1861. Those first shots had signaled an exodus from California of heavily armed secessionists, who traveled via Arizona or Mexico to the East. Federal authorities diverted the first California Volunteers mustered to quell civil unrest in Los Angeles and the southern counties. In November 1861 these troops surrounded and captured eighteen men traveling with the notorious secessionist Dan Showal-

2. Carleton to Coult, July 19, 1864, *OR*, 41(2):277–78; SO 46, Dec. 8, 1864, Dept. of New Mexico, *OR*, 41(4):803.

3. Orton, *California Men*, 5.

4. Pettis, *California Column*, 18; Orton, *California Men*, 669–70.

ter, on his way east by way of Fort Yuma and the Gila Trail. Rebel secret societies and unrest continued in southern California throughout the war, and
the troops in Arizona remained constantly on alert for rumors of uprisings.[5]

In 1862 Carleton ordered suspected secessionists in Arizona arrested
and imprisoned at Fort Yuma. The general's firm hand quickly closed the
Arizona route to California to the rebellious South. The political prisoners
at Yuma were eventually released after they signed loyalty oaths. But one
diehard Rebel sympathizer, captured with the Showalter party, launched an
attack that became Arizona's westernmost Civil War confrontation. William
"Frog" Edwards ambushed three soldiers belonging to the Fourth California Infantry at La Paz, Arizona, on May 20, 1863. Edwards seethed with
resentment for his rough treatment and waited for an opportunity to strike
a blow for the Confederacy in the Far West. When news of General Robert
E. Lee's victory at Chancellorsville, Virginia, reached the Colorado River,
Edwards saw his chance. Soldiers escorting military cargo on the steamer
Cocopah disembarked to purchase supplies. The men had gathered in front
of Cohn's Store when gunshots shattered the darkness, killing Private Ferdinand Behn of Company H. Two others, Privates Truston Wentworth,
Company K, and Thomas Gainor, Company H, also received severe
wounds. Wentworth died the next day aboard the *Cocopah* as it steamed to
Fort Yuma. Lieutenant James A. Hale quickly organized a search of the
town, but to no avail. A month-long search by a forty-man detachment from
Fort Mojave under Captain Charles Atchisson failed to bring the "Frog" to
justice, but soon afterward soldiers found a body in the desert that authorities identified as that of Edwards. On the run and alone, he had died of
exposure in the waterless waste while attempting to elude his pursuers.[6]

The La Paz incident alerted California troops to other Confederate
movements. On May 28 Captain Joseph Tuttle received orders in Tucson to
intercept a party of fifteen to twenty secessionists intending to join Confederate forces in Texas. Intelligence reports indicated that it might be possible to head off the Rebels, along with the cattle and horses they had stolen
in San Bernardino County, California, before they went east. Tuttle commanded twenty men of the Fifth California Infantry and a "spy party,"

5. Rigg to Carleton, Nov. 30, 1861, *OR*, 50(1):33. See also Finch, "Arizona in Exile," 57–84;
Robert J. Chandler, "California's 1863 Loyalty Oaths: Another Look," *Arizona and the West* 21
(Autumn 1979): 215–34; and "The Velvet Glove: The Army during the Secession Crisis in California, 1860–1865," *Journal of the West* 20 (Oct. 1981): 35–42.
6. Tuttle, "River Colorado," 57; C. E. Bennett to Drum, May 28, 1863, *OR*, 50(2):459–61;
Fireman, "Extending the Civil War Westward." Orton, 652, 653, 667, 872, 883.

Lt. James A. Hale was in charge of the guard assigned to protect the Colorado River steamer *Cocopah* when it docked at La Paz for supplies on May 20, 1863. Secessionist William "Frog" Edwards shot down three of Hale's men during Arizona's westernmost Civil War skirmish. Courtesy of the Los Angeles Public Library, Security Pacific Collection.

including Jackson H. Martin, deputy sheriff of San Bernardino County; Joseph Bridges; and a Mexican *vaquero* named Prefetto. The captain had authority to enlist any other citizens deemed necessary to intercept the Rebels. Tuttle tracked the raiders into Mexico and finally apprehended them in the Sonora village of Altar. The volunteers recovered the stolen livestock and prevented the California secessionists from uniting with Texas Confederates. Mission accomplished, Tuttle's exhausted command returned to Tucson nearly a month after the pursuit began.[7]

Arizonans occasionally alerted authorities to Rebel activity. On November 29, 1864, Major General Irvin McDowell, commanding the Department of the Pacific, which then included Arizona, received an alarming letter from M. O. Davidson, a mine superintendent:

Dear Sir: Mr. Elihu Baker, a major-domo of the Arizona Mining Company, has just come down [to Guaymas] from Arizona to escort me to the Territory. He informs me that a band of Confederates are

7. Orton, *California Men,* 669–70; Pettis, *California Column,* 18; Ffrench to Joseph Tuttle, May 28, 1863, *OR,* 50(2):461.

encamped in Sonora, between Magdalena and the boundary, awaiting re-enforcements from Texas, Chihuahua, and Durango, to make an attack upon the advanced military posts of Calaba[sas], Tubac, and Tucson. If they are successful in such a raid, for a while they will have the southern portion of Arizona at their mercy. Although you may not be the military commander of that department, I think it proper to give you this information, as it may be in your power to communicate with those who have the power to re-enforce speedily the limited garrisons of the posts so seriously threatened.[8]

Perhaps there was something to the rumors after all. Earlier, on October 16, a Los Angeles "Government Detective" named Gustav Brown reported that a party of thirty-two heavily armed members of the Knights of the Golden Circle, an active Copperhead club, had left San Diego for Texas on August 12. Brown cautioned that King S. Woolsey, the noted Arizona "Apache hunter," was waiting for a chance to spring into action with his armed band as soon as he could get assistance from Texas. The detective added that men were leaving "daily from Los Angeles by twos and threes who represent themselves as miners going to the Colorado." These California Rebels believed that, in the event Abraham Lincoln defeated General George McClellan in the November presidential election, they would be ready to grab Arizona.[9]

Judge Lansford W. Hastings had proposed this same plan to President Jefferson Davis in January 1864. Hastings outlined an elaborate scheme to capture "the most valuable agricultural and grazing lands, and the richest mineral region in the known world." He would send men disguised as miners to the Colorado mines above Fort Yuma and to Guaymas as well. These agents would then capture the vast quantities of military stores stockpiled at Yuma and use them to launch a campaign to recover the territories. Hastings believed the Knights of the Golden Circle and other secret societies would spring to the call and help carry out his plan.[10]

High-ranking Confederates had a genuine interest in retaking Arizona. In February 1863 Major General John Bankhead Magruder busied himself with the organization of an Arizona Brigade, "having been directed by the [Confederate] Secretary of War to take steps to recover Arizona." Colonel

8. M. O. Davidson to Irvin McDowell, Nov. 29, 1864, *OR*, 50(2):1080.
9. Gustav Brown to A. Jones Jackson, Oct. 16, 1864, ibid., 1018–19.
10. Lansford W. Hasting to Jefferson Davis, Dec. 16, 1863, ibid., 700–701.

Baylor's removal from command had stalled the planning effort; President Davis disliked Baylor and found his exterminationist Indian policy repugnant. Consequently the Confederate campaign never got out of the planning stage, and Judge Hastings's clandestine approach never received approval by the War Department. James A. Seddon, Confederate secretary of war, agreed that "the overthrow of Federal domination in Arizona and the repossession of that country through the instrumentality of forces to be drawn from California [was] an end important to be accomplished," but he had no confidence in Hastings. General E. Kirby Smith, commanding the Confederate Trans-Mississippi West, concurred, and so ended officially sanctioned Southern operations in Arizona. Unaware of the Confederate strategy shift and command difficulties, the California Volunteers remained vigilant for any renewal of the Rebel threat.[11]

Morale among the Californians in Arizona reached a low point in late 1865 and early 1866. As the war wound down in the East so did the zeal of the volunteer troops. Manning forts, patrolling the Mexican border, and remaining on the lookout for diehard Rebels became the tasks of the fresh regiments. But most of these men could not wait until the day came for their final discharge from service.

In January 1865 General McDowell annexed the Arizona Territory to his Department of the Pacific. Carleton had suffered much criticism from military men and civilians alike for neglecting Arizona during his administration. Actually the troops and transportation at his disposal allowed him to do little more than maintain the garrisons at only a few key forts in the territory.[12]

The same problems plagued General John S. Mason, who commanded the newly recruited California units sent to the territory in 1865. These troops included the First Battalion of Native Cavalry, the Second California Infantry, and the Seventh California Infantry. Federal officials chose the Native Battalion, composed almost entirely of Californians of Mexican descent, for service in Arizona because of the extraordinary horsemanship displayed by the Californios. Mason, however, worried about using these troops so close to the border, fearing their sympathies for the plight of Benito Juárez's Republic of

11. John B. Magruder to S. Cooper, Mar. 2, 1863, ibid., 332; Baylor to Thomas Helm, Mar. 20, 1862, OR, 50(1):942; Colton, Civil War in Western Territories, 123; James A. Seddon to E. Kirby Smith, Oct. 15, 1863, OR, 50(2):648–49; Smith to Seddon, Nov. 22, 1863, ibid., 681.

12. GO 9, AGO, Jan. 10, 1865, OR, 50(2):1121; GO 10, Hdqrs. Dept. of the Pacific, Feb. 20, 1865, ibid., 1137.

Mexico might result in conflicted loyalties. Although the liberal Juárez had been duly elected president in 1858, France's Napoleon III installed Austrian archduke Maximilian, backed by Mexico's conservative landed aristocracy, as emperor of Imperial Mexico in 1864. During the Civil War, California officers exercised diplomacy rather than military strength along the border in an effort to avoid open conflict with the French. The pressing need for mounted troops for border patrol soon overruled Mason's concerns about loyalty. The Native Battalion proudly rode into Arizona with red pennons snapping from their nine-foot lances.[13]

Although Paragraph 1642 of the army's 1861 *Revised Regulations* specifically stated that no volunteer "will be mustered into the service who is unable to speak the English language," most of the men of the Native Battalion spoke only Spanish. The *San Francisco Evening Bulletin* reported: "The battalion is truly a mixture of colors and tongues, the men very rugged and hearty—more than half being native Californians, and the remainder Mexicans, Chilenos, Sonorians, California and Yaqui Indians, Germans, Americans, etc. Those of them, however, who are not American speak more or less English, the English tongue crowd understanding Spanish—the officers being adept in both languages."[14]

Both the Native Battalion, commanded by Major Cremony, and parts of the Seventh California Infantry, commanded by Colonel Charles W. Lewis, served along the Arizona-Mexico border. Fort Mason, so named in honor of the new district commander, became the principal post in southern Arizona in 1865–66. Its importance stemmed from its location near Calabasas on the main road from Arizona to Sonora. Union officers no longer feared Mexico as a possible route for a Confederate invasion, but they believed that French troops guarding Maximilian's puppet government posed an imminent danger. The presence of these foreign soldiers irritated American politicians and military men, requiring border commanders to exercise considerable restraint and diplomacy.

In 1862 Carleton had opened correspondence with Ignacio Pesqueira, the Republican governor of Sonora. He acted on orders from the Department of the Pacific commander at the time, General George Wright, who

13. Anderson and Cayton, *Dominion of War,* 305–7. See also Brinckerhoff, "Last of the Lancers," manuscript, Arizona Historical Society, Tucson, 6–7; and Prezelski, "California Lancers," 29–52.

14. Paragraph 1642, *Revised U.S. Army Regulations of 1861,* 496; *San Francisco Evening Bulletin,* July 8, 1865.

José Ramón Pico (*right*) and Antonio Maria de la Guerra (*left*), captains of Companies A and C, First Battalion of Native Cavalry (Native Battalion). Armed with lances, these "Californio" volunteers saw service along Arizona's border with Mexico during Maximilian's reign and French occupation in 1865. Courtesy of the Los Angeles Public Library, Security Pacific Collection.

wanted to stay on the Sonoran's good side and hoped to purchase supplies and gain trade concessions at the Mexican port of Guaymas. Carleton tactfully warned Pesqueira against recognizing or agreeing to supply the Confederates in Arizona. The Mexican governor found himself in an embarrassing situation after his interpreter gave copies of his correspondence with Confederate ambassador James Reily to a correspondent from the *San Francisco Bulletin*. In truth Pesqueira never really trusted the Texans, and relations between the Sonoran government and the Californians remained cordial. In May Carleton lifted his ban against Mexican citizens crossing the border into Arizona to work the rich Colorado River placer fields, much to Pesqueira's benefit and satisfaction.[15]

At the same time the United States struggled to preserve its fragile union, Mexico found itself in a desperate fight against foreign invaders. British, French, and Spanish claims for loans incurred by Antonio Lopez de Santa Ana and other past presidents could not be paid by current president

15. Hunt, *Army of the Pacific*, 58; Carleton, Report 2, May 25, 1862, *OR*, 50(1):89.

Juárez's beleaguered government. The European nations sent warships to Vera Cruz to demand payment, but the British and Spanish withdrew when it became evident that Napoleon III had imperialistic designs on Mexico. On May 5, 1862—as Carleton's column closed in on Tucson and Hunter's Rebels rode east to the Rio Grande—a French army of six thousand smashed itself against the fortified town of Puebla, midway between Vera Cruz and Mexico City. While the Mexicans celebrated their *cinco de Mayo* victory, the French resolved to return with a larger force of men and siege guns that would eventually batter its way to the Mexican capital in 1863.

By 1864 some thirty thousand French troops occupied Mexico. The California officers in Arizona had grown so friendly with the Sonorans that high-ranking officials in the War Department considered the relationship dangerous to the maintenance of France's neutrality. In the fall of 1865, Franco-Mexican imperial troops forced Governor Pesqueira—with his family, servants, livestock, and valuables—to cross the border and take refuge with the Californians stationed at Fort Mason. Sympathetic officers and men entertained the governor's party. The Americans had allowed Pesqueira to cross into Arizona in pursuit of Apaches a year earlier, and they respected the Sonoran's capability as an Indian fighter and his defiance of the French invaders.

Colonel Davis wrote General Carleton on March 22, 1864: "Pesqueira is friendly to the United States and says, *entre nous,* that in case of necessity or trouble in his State from the French, he will raise the United States flag and ask our assistance. If our Government will only allow our people to act in the matter, Sonora will soon be ours. Colonel Coult is anxious to go down with the troops here, when the proper opportunity arrives. I cautioned him to do nothing to complicate our international affairs with Mexico, or take any hasty steps in this matter. . . . Sonora must and is bound to be ours; it is well to have the question considered, and be prepared for whatever may turn up. It is essential to this Territory. We want the ports on the Gulf of California."[16]

Carleton agreed that the California troops ought to be ready to seize Guaymas. He wrote General Henry Halleck that "a naval station on the Gulf of California" would be the answer to the problems of developing Arizona's mineral resources. But the response from Washington quickly reined in the enthusiasm of the California officers. The Lincoln administration did not

16. Robert Miller, "Californians against the Emperor," 193–212; Davis to Carleton, Mar. 2, 1864, *OR,* 50(2):842.

even want to discuss the possibility of conflict with French forces in Mexico while the rebellion still raged. Carleton reluctantly cautioned his subordinates: "It is required by the War Department that no steps be taken by the military forces within this department [New Mexico] which will at all complicate us in the matter growing out of the occupation of any of the States of Mexico by the French. Our relations with France are of the most friendly character, and it is desirable that they remain so. You will be careful not to jeopardize those relations by act, or word, or letter."[17]

Of course Lincoln and Secretary of State William Seward seethed at Napoleon's brazen disregard for the Monroe Doctrine. So they turned a blind eye to supplies of arms and ammunition sent from the United States to Juárez while publicly professing neutrality. California Volunteers did cross the international border when the necessity arose, despite the official warnings to avoid contact with the French. On several occasions detachments pursued Rebels, Apache raiders, bandits, or deserters into Mexico. The Californians conducted most of these forays quickly and without incident. But rounding up deserters in French-occupied Mexico proved difficult.

In September 1865 Captain José Ramón Pico, with a mounted force comprising two junior officers and thirty men, crossed the Mexican border in pursuit of sixteen deserters from Companies A and B of the Native Battalion. The men bolted from Camp Mason with all of their arms and equipment and thirty good army horses. Pico followed the deserters to Magdalena, ninety miles south of Fort Mason. There his party encountered about 250 poorly armed Mexican soldiers fighting under Maximilian's imperial flag. Wishing to avoid armed confrontation, Pico entered the town with only six soldiers and Lieutenant William Emery, Seventh California Infantry, sent by Colonel Lewis at Fort Mason to record any negotiations with Mexican or French officials.[18]

At Magdalena, Mexican prefect José Moreno refused Pico's demand for the return of the deserters unless the volunteer officer agreed to recognize Maximilian's government. Pico replied that his government would recognize only President Juárez, Mexico's legitimate ruler. As tension mounted, Pico ordered the twenty-four troopers under Captain Porfirio Jimeno to return to Fort Mason while Moreno received instructions from the French officials at Hermosillo. It took eight days for the orders to arrive from Hermosillo, during which time adherents of the two factions vying for control

17. Carleton to Halleck, Mar. 13, 1864, *OR*, 34(2):591–92; Carleton to Coult, May 10, 1864, *OR*, 50(2):842.

18. *San Francisco Bulletin*, Oct. 23, 1865.

of the country alternately lauded and threatened the California Volunteers. Finally Moreno sent word that he would not turn over the deserters and that the Californians had eight hours to leave Magdalena and forty-eight hours to get out of the country. Pico's party had no choice but to depart emptyhanded.[19]

When imperial commanders posted guards near the border, Colonel Lewis strengthened his own border sentinels. In late September six more Native Battalion deserters crossed into Mexico, taking fourteen pistols and fifteen horses with equipment. Lewis, fearing the consequences of another border crossing, mounted no pursuit. His men, however, chafed at this restraint. Lieutenant Emery wrote: "If we could only have a little fight with the French, it would be something worthwhile stopping here; but as it is, it is very dry. Fighting Indians is dangerous enough, but we do so little of that that the time drags." When rumors reached Fort Mason that Prefect Moreno was massing three hundred to four hundred men for an attack designed to capture Governor Pesqueira, the usually restrained Lewis exclaimed, "Let him come and try it."[20]

A Mexican imperial force did make an abortive raid across the border at San Rafael, Arizona, opposite Santa Cruz, Sonora. On November 4, 1865, Colonel Refugio Tánori, an Opata chief, attacked the border town with a force of nearly five hundred men. They fired on American citizens, wounding one in the skirmish. Major Cremony, who had recently arrived at Fort Mason with Company C of the Native Battalion, chased after the invaders, hoping to obtain a truce and a parley. Tánori fled, however, outdistancing a detachment under Lieutenant Edward Codington assigned to head off the Mexicans at Ures, Sonora. Cremony later learned that the imperial troops, most of whom were infantry, made the forty-three-mile retreat from Santa Cruz to Imuris in a record time of nine hours.[21]

The Native Battalion and the Seventh California Infantry served in Arizona until the summer of 1866. The battalion spent almost its entire tour of duty in southeastern Arizona at the posts of Tubac, Reventon Ranch, and Fort Mason, the latter noted for its malarial fevers and high desertion rate. Companies of the Second and Seventh Infantry regiments were scattered about the territory, with detachments at Fort Goodwin, Fort Grant, Fort Mojave, Fort McDowell, Fort Whipple, Fort Yuma, Tucson, and Fort Mason.

19. Ibid., Oct. 20, 1865; Orton, *California Men*, 5.
20. *San Francisco Bulletin*, Oct. 20, 23, 1865; Prezelski, "California Lancers," 43–45.
21. Brinckerhoff, "Last of the Lancers," 11–12; Cremony, "How and Why We Took Santa Cruz," 335–40.

The principal duties of these troops involved campaigning against Indians and protecting the military mail.[22]

Colonel Thomas F. Wright, son of the former commander of the Department of the Pacific, led eight companies of the Second California Infantry to Arizona in the summer of 1865. Charged with hunting down Gila Apaches, the men of the Second had little stomach for combat once they learned that the Civil War was indeed over. Pressed by Carleton and Mason, however, the officers of the Second launched numerous scouts from Forts Goodwin and Grant. Corporal William A. Bushnell summed up the spirit of the men in a diary entry written on December 11, 1865, following a seventeen-day scout:

> At this season of the year, carrying one blanket, your overcoat, half a shelter tent, your gun accoutrements and 210 rounds of ammunition, is not very desirable pastime, especially when you are out seventeen days without finding an Indian. If Jomini [author of *The Art of War*] could peruse a detailed account of our expedition, he would, no doubt, see fit to change his definition of military terms considerably. Thus the term Scouting (in an Indian country, at least) as our experience proves, is to start out and travel 8 or 10 miles a day, camping about noon and keeping good fires burning all night so as to warn all Indians of your whereabouts. In the morning a large fire should be built so as to make smoke so that the enemy can see it and flee your approach. It is also well to take precaution a few days before leaving the garrison to post all guides and interpreters so that they can easily go out into the mountains and intimate the coming danger to their savage brother. Thus you will easily avoid coming into collision with the noble red man. An appropriate report to send to Headquarters would be something like this:
>
> "Deserted Rancheria, December 1865
>
> General:
>
> We are at the camp of the enemy and they are ours (hours ahead of us)."[23]

The regiments that served in Arizona from 1863 to 1866 suffered from poor morale, especially when contrasted with Carleton's 1862 command.

22. Orton, *California Men,* 763–65.
23. William Addison Bushnell Diary, Dec. 11, 1865, typescript in possession of author.

The men of the California Column enlisted to fight Confederates and save the Union, marching to war with a will. General Wright marveled at their training and discipline, declaring that he had never seen a finer body of troops. The First California Infantry earned an enviable record. Five companies of this regiment had not one desertion during their four years of service. In contrast the Fifth California Infantry and the Native Battalion, which followed the California Column, had some companies that suffered desertions totaling 30–40 percent of their total strength.[24]

There are several explanations for the desertions and relatively low morale during the last two years of the war. The overall desertion rate for California troops reached 10 percent, slightly higher than the national average for volunteer soldiers but well below that of the regular army. Reduced rations, isolation, and the practice of mustering out soldiers in the territories may have caused men of the Fifth Infantry to desert in larger numbers. Company D, which garrisoned Tucson, suffered an incredible 39 percent desertion rate. This hard-luck company, recruited primarily from Sacramento and Marysville, had three men die in post hospitals and a fourth shot to death by a noncommissioned officer of the provost guard. Ten other men received dishonorable discharges.[25]

General Carleton felt strongly that the volunteers should be mustered out in the territories where they served. This, he believed, would be an excellent way to populate Arizona and provide a good class of citizens to develop the mines and establish the institutions required to civilize the territory. In this he misjudged his men. Many veterans wanted to return home when their enlistments expired. Some felt misused and cheated, even though soldiers discharged in the territories received a travel allowance. The unhappy volunteers circulated petitions seeking redress, and Carleton, who had once been admired and respected by the men, became the principal target of their displeasure. California Volunteer newspaper columnists now openly criticized him.[26]

The Fifth Infantry and the Native Battalion compiled dismal records during their service in Arizona. The war had already ended in the East when most of these soldiers arrived for garrison and patrol duty. Malarial fevers and poor living conditions at Fort Mason frequently left only one-third of the command fit for duty. Sympathy for the Mexican loyalists fighting

24. Hunt, *James Henry Carleton*, 202; Orton, *California Men*, 5.
25. Lonn, *Desertion*, 219.
26. *Alta*, Oct. 17, 1864; Cremony, *Life among the Apaches*, 198.

against the French-backed imperial forces probably precipitated some of the desertions. Many ex-volunteers, officers and enlisted men, offered their services to the Republic of Mexico upon discharge.[27]

Leadership at both the regimental and company level made a big difference in troop morale. The Seventh California Infantry served at various posts in Arizona at the same time the Native Battalion patrolled the border. The "hungry Seventh" experienced only a 5 percent desertion rate, and most occurred at the Presidio in San Francisco just prior to discharge. Once home many volunteers could not understand the delay in formal mustering out, especially when the war was over and their job done.[28]

The state of California never drafted soldiers to meet the quotas imposed by the U.S. government, but enlistments began to decline as the war began its fourth year. On April 4, 1864, the legislature passed an act authorizing the payment of $160 for enlistment bounties, $40 payable at the time of enlistment and $20 at the end of each successive six-month period of service. In addition to these incentives, the U.S. government also began paying bounties to encourage reenlistment. Veterans received $50 for one-year extensions and $100 for two years. Of course these bounties also had time-payment provisions designed to discourage desertion. Some of the California Volunteers wanted nothing more than a chance to fight the Rebels. A few actually deserted in order to reenlist in eastern regiments and engage organized Confederate forces in the bloody battles that would determine the outcome of the war. One volunteer wrote: "There would be glory and honor in being a soldier if we were where we could distinguish ourselves in any way, but to be kept in this out of the way place doing nothing, there is but little fame in it that I can see."[29]

Most of the volunteer companies serving in Arizona in 1865 and 1866 formally mustered out on the West Coast or at one of the military posts in New Mexico. Individual soldiers occasionally received their discharges in Arizona, but as a rule commanders sent troops to the large military installations in California, which made provisions for paying the troops, issuing

27. *Santa Fe New Mexican,* Apr. 7, 1865; *Alta,* Sept. 26, 1866; Orton, *California Men,* 76, 151. See also Hunt, *Army of the Pacific,* 182–83; Darlis Miller, *California Column,* 43; and *OR,* 50(2):788–89.

28. Orton, *California Men,* 776–87.

29. Hunt, *Army of the Pacific,* 140–41; Davis, "Pioneer Days in Arizona," Arizona State University Library, Tempe, 52; Ryan, *News from Fort Craig,* 65.

In June 1865 a California Volunteer infantry regiment, with field musicians (*left*) playing, company officers (*front rank*) in position, and the regimental colors unfurled, stands for a photographer prior to final mustering out at San Francisco. Reproduced by permission of the Huntington Library, San Marino, California.

discharge papers, and turning in arms and accoutrements at permanent forts and arsenals. Although Carleton's decision to discharge troops in New Mexico angered many of the soldiers, the order had a positive influence on the development of the territories.[30]

By 1866 the government had shifted the burden of the military duties in Arizona from the California Volunteers to other troops. Four companies of native Mexican American and Indian soldiers continued to wage a bloody campaign against defiant Apache raiders. These Arizonans had endured decades of warfare with the Apaches. They knew the ways of their elusive enemies and took the field with a will. An enlisted man in the Second California Infantry noted that "the Pimas and Maricopas are allies against the Apaches, between which there seems to be a hereditary hatred," and he conceded, "they fight the Apaches in their own way and in this respect are

30. For the Californians' influence on New Mexico, see Darlis Miller, *California Column.*

superior to our own soldiers, perhaps." The army also began filtering regular troops back to the frontier after four years of hard service against the Rebels in the East.[31]

In the spring of 1866, regulars of the Fourteenth U.S. Infantry and First U.S. Cavalry began marching into Arizona Territory. More than once California units returning home to be mustered out rescued these inexperienced soldiers in the Arizona desert. John Spring, an enlisted man in Company E, Fourteenth Infantry, wrote that on one occasion his company became lost in the desert east of Yuma. Fortunately a homeward-bound company of the First California Cavalry saw their signal fire and came to their relief. The Californians buried one man, who had died from exposure, and provided the others with food and water. The regulars marched the roads and trails blazed by the volunteers. The new companies often rested at Picacho Peak and wondered who lay buried beneath the bleached and nearly illegible headboards marking the graves of the first Californians to fall in the struggle for Arizona. Reoccupying the camps and forts recently turned over by the Californians, the regulars appreciated the comfortable quarters at Fort Bowie and other posts, though they little understood the effort, hardship, and sacrifice that had gone into building these places in the Arizona desert.[32]

The men of the Second California Infantry turned over their quarters at Fort Goodwin to U.S. regulars on May 10, 1866. A seven-day march brought the volunteers to Tucson, where Corporal Bushnell observed, "the boys indulged themselves to their heart's content drinking Tucson poison, Tarantula juice, Arizona lightening & & &. Many of the boys deprived for so long a time of the beverage they favored, got unconsciously drunk and in this state many were robbed of what few greenbacks they possessed by a set of harpies in the shape of regular soldiers belonging to the 14th U.S. Inf. stationed in the town." By the time the regiment reached Picacho Peak, most of the intoxicated men had rejoined the command, completing the 462-mile march from Fort Goodwin to Yuma in twenty-six days. A Colorado River steamer took the weary soldiers to Port Isabel, where the muddy river joined the blue water of the Gulf of California, and the men, singing and cheering, boarded an oceangoing vessel bound for San Francisco.[33]

31. Farish, *History of Arizona*, 3:96; H. S. Washburn, Company E, Arizona Volunteers, to Goodwin, August 15, 1865, in *Arizona Graphic*, Mar. 24, 1900, 6–7; Bushnell Diary, Oct. 23, 1865.

32. Gustafson, *John Spring's Arizona*, 38–39, 49.

33. Bushnell Diary, May 10–June 10, 1865.

The California Volunteers stationed in Arizona during the Civil War had accomplished much. They marched in good order across the desert and helped roll back the Confederate threat in the Far West. Foreign invaders south of the border were held in check while the Californians spurred the growth of the territory and provided protection for the settlers and prospectors who came to build homes and open mines. Prospecting boomed as the soldiers announced new discoveries and established military posts in mining districts, making travel and living conditions safe and profitable once again. The Californians opened and worked entire mining districts, and many returned to continue prospecting after they left the service. The volunteers also dealt the Indians in the territory a serious blow, particularly the Navajos, who lost their ability to wage war. Establishing precedents for warfare against the Apaches in Arizona, the volunteers inaugurated a system of military-civilian cooperation and a policy of total war against groups considered hostile. Other tribes, however, flourished during the Californian occupation: the agricultural Pimas and Maricopas benefited from army contracts and the military alliance against their traditional Apache enemies.

Carleton had declared Arizona a separate territory when he organized his military government in 1862. In February 1863 President Lincoln approved an act of Congress officially creating the Arizona Territory, and the presence of the Californians made possible the establishment of a civil government. Carleton also used his troops to clear out thieves and scoundrels from Tucson and the rough camps of the new mining districts. During their service the volunteers policed the territory and instituted a military mail system—the only means of communication with the outside world during the war. Following their discharge from the army, many veterans played prominent roles in the social, political, and economic development of the new territory.[34]

Perhaps the greatest contribution made by the Californians in Arizona occurred after the war. Hundreds of former soldiers settled in the territory, providing energy and leadership. Although Carleton's mustering-out plan stirred controversy and heated debate in the press, the army actually discharged few volunteers in Arizona. Some ended their service at Arizona posts due to resignation, health problems, or personal reasons, but these were exceptions. Most of the California veterans marched with their companies or

34. Although some artistic license has been taken, the best account of the Camp Grant Massacre is Schellie, *Vast Domain of Blood.*

regiments to New Mexico or went to the Presidio in San Francisco for their release from the service.

More than six thousand Californians had gotten a good look at Arizona during the war and liked what they saw. Many soon returned to seek their fortunes, believing the new territory to be a land of opportunity. Most came back to work in the mines or to prospect for new ones, particularly in the lower Colorado River region and central Arizona. Others found the more sedentary existence of hotelkeeper, shopkeeper, or military-post sutler to their liking. Still others raised cattle or worked on Colorado River steamers. A number of those returning were former officers and well-educated men. Several became prominent lawyers and territorial legislators, while others obtained government appointments. Some accepted the dangerous duties of town marshal or sheriff. Two veterans worked as educators, one serving as Mohave County school superintendent.

Some of the Californians demonstrated an aptitude and liking for the military. Two enlisted men became officers with the Arizona Volunteers, leading these native companies on successful campaigns against the Apaches. Others accepted commissions in the regular army and returned to Arizona for continued service during the vicious fighting with Apaches in the years following the Civil War. Some had developed Indian-language skills and served as interpreters and guides for the postwar army. The Californians returned in numbers equaling nearly 10 percent of Arizona's population and provided a healthy boost to the growth of the newly organized territory.[35]

In September 1865 Lieutenant Colonel Clarence E. Bennett, First California Cavalry, established Fort McDowell along the Verde River, just above its junction with the Salt River in central Arizona. Strategically located to deter Yavapai and Western Apache raiders, Fort McDowell became the key to unlocking the riches of the Salt River valley. This fertile yet uninhabited land lay fallow for centuries. Situated as it was between the sedentary Pimas and Maricopas of the Gila River and the nomadic Yavapais and Western Apache bands to the north and east, the valley had become a no man's land between warring tribes. White miners and settlers also steered clear of the place until John Y. T. Smith discovered the abundant native galleta grass in the river bottoms.

35. More than five hundred California Volunteers settled in Arizona after the Civil War. See U.S. censuses for Arizona and New Mexico territories, 1864, 1870, 1880, 1890, 1900, 1910; and Hayden Arizona Pioneer Biography Files, Arizona State University Library, Tempe.

Lieutenant Smith had come to Arizona in 1863 with Company H, Fourth California Infantry. Soon after mustering out, the entrepreneurial officer secured the sutler's contract at Fort McDowell. He successfully bid on other lucrative government contracts to supply provisions for the hungry garrison, composed of three Seventh California Infantry companies, and hay for the horses and mules. The hay, it turned out, was the easy part. Seasonal rains caused the Salt to overflow its banks and flood the bottoms, yielding tons of forage—free for the taking.

By 1867 Smith needed help and enlisted former Confederate ranger, and later scout for the California Volunteers, Jack Swilling. Although Swilling spent more time fighting Apaches than mining or ranching, he knew a good opportunity and almost immediately organized the Swilling Irrigation and Canal Company. Beneath the fields of grass, the valley was crisscrossed with ancient canals abandoned by the Hohokam people nearly five hundred years earlier. Smith encouraged Swilling to cut new connections to the river and flush out the prehistoric ditches in order to grow the produce needed to fill the army's contracts. Within months Swilling's crew had shoveled and scraped canals enough to flood fields of vegetables, corn, and grain. An agricultural boom resulted, which provided the economic base for a thriving new settlement—appropriately dubbed Phoenix, for it had miraculously emerged from the ruins of an earlier civilization.[36]

Carleton himself eventually became disenchanted with the territories he had helped save for the Union. Stung by criticism from his own California soldiers and hounded mercilessly by territorial leaders, newspapermen, and business interests opposed to his "military despotism," the general seemed incapable of making friends or political allies. Most felt him unapproachable and imperious in his dealings with citizens and soldiers alike. "Behold him!" wrote the editor of the Santa Fe *New Mexican*, "his martial

36. Early in the twentieth century, Phoenix took its place as Arizona's largest and most prosperous city. The three men most often honored with the title "Father of Phoenix" all have a California Volunteer connection. William A. Hancock, Seventh California Infantry, built the first store; served in every imaginable elected office, including first sheriff; and surveyed the canals that provided the desert town with its vital water supply. In 1866 John Y. T. Smith, Fourth California Infantry, established his hay camp and recognized the agricultural potential of what became the Phoenix town site. Jack Swilling served the Confederacy for only eleven months before defecting and working as a scout and government contractor with the California Volunteers. To Swilling goes the credit of renewing the ancient Hohokam canals and beginning large-scale irrigation in the Salt River Valley. Farish, *History of Arizona*, 6:70–74; Finch, "Sherod Hunter," 194–97; Orton, *California Men*, 651, 794.

cloak thrown gracefully around him like a Roman toga." Carleton's efficiency and self-reliance made him a favorite of his superiors, up to and
including General U. S. Grant, who saw fit to bestow upon him the brevet
rank of major general of volunteers in October 1865. But during the
months following the end of the war, Carleton's Bosque Redondo reservation for relocated Navajos and Mescaleros proved a disaster. Even under the
watchful eye of the loyal Major William McCleave, many of the Indian
internees died of disease and malnutrition.[37]

The 1866 election of Carleton's chief political adversary, J. Francisco
Chaves, as congressional delegate from the territory sent the War Department a clear message—the people of New Mexico had lost confidence in
the general's leadership. Later that year Secretary of War Edwin M. Stanton
informed the beleaguered Carleton that he had been transferred to military oblivion in Texas, as lieutenant colonel of the Fourth U.S. Cavalry.

Although the tumultuous events of the Civil War in the eastern theater
had overshadowed the achievements of the soldiers from California, Carleton remembered with pride the singular accomplishments of his men.
On the eve of accepting the command of the Department of New Mexico,
the hard-bitten dragoon wrote: "[T]he march of the Column from California across the Great Desert in the summer months, in the driest season that
has been known for thirty years, is a military achievement creditable to the
Soldiers of the American Army. However, it would not be just to attribute
the success of this march to any ability on my part. That success was gained
only by the high physical and moral energies of that particular class of officers and men who compose the Column from California. With any other
troops, I am sure I should have failed."[38]

37. Carleton died in 1873, still on active duty but embittered by the treatment he received
from the country he had served for more than thirty years. News of his death, at age fifty-eight,
was received with expressions of sorrow in the territories. Even his critics seemed willing to recognize his accomplishments. The citizens of Santa Fe drew up resolutions honoring Carleton's
memory, which they asked to be published in territorial newspapers, the San Antonio *Herald*,
the *Army and Navy Journal*, and the *Alta. Santa Fe New Mexican*, Sept. 23, Dec. 16, 1864, Feb. 4,
11, 1873; Hunt, *James Henry Carleton*, 348–49; Darlis Miller, *California Column*, 210; Thompson,
Army and the Navajo, 121–28; Arrell Morgan Gibson, "James H. Carleton," in Hutton, *Soldiers
West*, 59–74.

38. Carleton to Drum, Sept. 20, 1862, in Orton, *California Men*, 64–67.

Bold and resourceful, Confederate Lt. Jack Swilling of Captain Helm's Arizona Guards escorted captured California Volunteer captain William McCleave from Tucson to Mesilla. Swilling then deserted from Gen. H. H. Sibley's retreating army and offered to scout for the California troops fighting Apaches. Courtesy of the Arizona Historical Society, Tucson, AHS 18127.

First Lt. Robert P. Nason, Company I, Fourth California Infantry, poses on the parade ground at Fort Mojave. The photographer, R. D'Heureuse, included some Mojave men and women for local color. Nason displays the 1840 light-artillery saber he purchased when supplies of the regulation foot-officer's sword ran out. Courtesy of the Bancroft Library, University of California, Berkeley.

Indian Scouting in Arizona, by George Holbrook Baker. California Volunteers became expert in campaigning against Arizona Indians, attacking rancherias and tracking raiding parties with deadly efficiency. During the Civil War the Californians deployed infantry, cavalry, and even artillery more effectively than the regular-army units they replaced. Courtesy of the Bancroft Library, University of California, Berkeley.

Just as the Civil War generation passed, the 1940 Columbia Pictures classic *Arizona* captured the arrival of the California Volunteers in Tucson, with flags snapping in the wind, fifes and drums playing—just as described by the soldiers who made the desert trek with the California Column. *Arizona*, © 1940, renewed 1968 Columbia Pictures Industries, Inc. All rights reserved. Courtesy of Columbia Pictures.

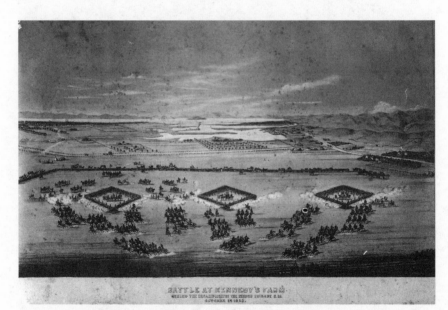

MEN WANTED
FOR
FIRST CAVALRY

CALIFORNIA VOLUNTEERS.

For Active Service in Lower Cal. and Arizona.

The following is the pay of Non Commissioned Off ers, Artificers and Privates:

Sergeant Major	$26 00
Orderly Sergeant	25.00
Quarter Master's Sergeant	22.00
Comnissary Sergeant	22.00
Duty Sergeant	22.00
Corporals	19.00
Saddlers	19.00
Blacksm'ths and Farriers	19.00
Privates	18.00

In addition to the above

**$402 PAID TO VETERANS REENLISTING
AND $302 PAID TO RECRUITS.**

Clothing and Subsistence will be furnished as soon as accepted.

Apply at once, to &c.

1st Lieut **L. F. SAMBURN,**

Regimental Recruiting Officer.

After the patriotic zeal that prompted many California men to enlist in 1861 had passed, recruiters offered financial incentives to fill the ranks and meet federal quotas for volunteers. By 1864 a private's monthly pay had risen from eleven dollars to eighteen dollars, and cash bounties induced many to join up. But desertion rates were high in some of the regiments sent to Arizona late in the war. Courtesy of the Hayden Library, Arizona State University.

Battle at Kennedy's Farm, 1863, by Gen. H. Bakee. The "battle" was a mock battle conducted by the California Militia. During the Civil War, the reassuring presence of California's large and well-regulated militia allowed the state to export its volunteer troops for service in Arizona and other western territories. The militia companies also provided a training ground for officers and men who eventually served with the volunteers. Courtesy of the Society of California Pioneers, San Francisco. Bequest of Charles B. Turrill.

Confederate Alfred B. Peticolas marched up the Rio Grande with Sibley's Texas Brigade only to retreat before advancing Union troops from Colorado and California. Courtesy of the Arizona Historical Society, Tucson.

Capt. Benjamin C. Cutler served on Gen. James H. Carleton's staff as adjutant general and as secretary of the Arizona territorial government established by the California Volunteers in 1862. Courtesy of the New Mexico Historical Society.

In April 1865 California Volunteers and militia companies mourned the death of Abraham Lincoln in San Francisco, but the war was not over for hundreds of California soldiers who remained on duty in Arizona until 1866. Courtesy of the California History Room, California State Library, Sacramento, California.

Picacho, a volcanic plug of red rock rising nearly one thousand feet from the floor of the pass midway between the Pima Villages at the Gila River and Tucson, marks the best remembered of Arizona's Civil War sites. On April 15, 1862, Lt. James Barrett and two enlisted men of the First California Cavalry died in a skirmish with Confederates here. Courtesy of the Arizona Historical Society, Tucson, AHS 20825.

California Volunteer captain and historian Richard H. Orton wrote after the war, "the graves of the Union Lieutenant and his men may now be seen within twenty feet of the Southern Pacific Railroad, as it goes through Picacho Pass." On April 3, 1928, with pioneers of 1860s Arizona looking on, the Southern Pacific and the Arizona Historical Society dedicated this monument at the place believed to be the burial site of Lt. James Barrett. Photo by Norman Wallace.

Officers of the Fourth California Infantry stationed at Drum Barracks, near Los Angeles, posed for this photograph in 1865: (*left to right*) Lt. Col. Edgar W. Hillyer, Lt. Orlando H. Lee (adjutant), Col. James F. Curtis, Capt. Matthew Sherman (quartermaster), Maj. Vincent Gelcich (surgeon). Courtesy of the Drum Barracks Historical Society.

Maj. Clarence E. Bennett graduated from West Point in 1855 but resigned his commission in 1860. He served briefly as a California Militia officer before Gov. Leland Stanford confirmed his appointment as a major of California cavalry in 1862. Many officers serving with the California Volunteers in Arizona rose from the ranks of the regulars and militia. Bennett returned to Arizona and the regular army in 1866. Courtesy of Art Woodward.

Pvt. William A. Hancock, Company K, Seventh California Infantry, posed for this portrait in December 1864 just before marching for Arizona Territory. Hancock epitomized the contributions of the California Volunteers—while stationed at Fort McDowell, he accepted a lieutenant's commission with Company C, Arizona Volunteer Infantry, which was composed entirely of Pima Indians. After mustering out in 1866, Hancock returned to Arizona, was one of the founders of Phoenix, and erected the first store there. He served as the first sheriff of Maricopa County, Phoenix postmaster, county surveyor, district attorney, coroner, probate judge, and school superintendent. He also surveyed and located the canals that enabled the growth of Phoenix and neighboring cities in the Salt River valley. Courtesy of Herb McLaughlin.

Cpl. Aaron Cory Hitchcock, Company M, First California Cavalry, posed for this portrait in 1863 before his company left for Arizona. He wrote home, "the Capt. has ordered me to put a stripe of ½ inch yellow tape down on the outside of each pantaloon leg also two half diamonds on each jacket sleeve." Here he wears his dress uniform, including the 1858 uniform jacket trimmed with yellow lace, brass shoulder scales, and regulation hat with its brass ornaments and ostrich feather. Hitchcock was issued a Colt Army Revolver and an 1860 Light Cavalry Saber. Courtesy of the El Dorado County Historical Museum.

Two

Dispatches from the California
Volunteers, 1862–65

CHAPTER 6

California's Soldier-Correspondents to the San Francisco Daily Alta California

The annotated articles that follow have been selected from the pages of the *San Francisco Daily Alta California* issued during 1862–65. They deal with a variety of themes centering on the experiences of the California Volunteers in Arizona. Written by soldier-correspondents, the articles provide insight into what the volunteers believed to be newsworthy. They penned their letters on the march or while stationed at isolated Arizona posts, providing news fresh from the front. These articles are a valuable primary source of information concerning characters and events that shaped the history of Arizona and the Southwest.

In 1862 the *San Francisco Daily Alta California* was the oldest and most influential newspaper in the state. Pioneer editor E. C. Kemble wrote that the *Alta,* as it was popularly known, "has become something of a monument among our political institutions, and its files contain the only complete transcript of California past life and events to be found in the State—the only material from which the future historian will be able to collate a reliable and unbroken volume." The *Alta* is the logical choice for a study of California Volunteers in Arizona because the complete run of the Civil War years is still available and the paper provided the most consistent reporting from the territory.[1]

Although the *Alta* did not have the largest circulation in California, being second only to the *San Francisco Evening Bulletin,* its columns reached

1. Karolevitz, *Newspapering,* 51; Kemble and Bretnor, *California Newspapers,* 98. The complete run of the *Alta* was microfilmed by the Bancroft Library.

readers around the world. The *Alta* boasted a handsome 32 x 46 inch "blanket sheet" format, and subscriptions sold for only fifty cents a week. Besides the daily version, the *Alta* was issued as a weekly, reprinting the matter published in the *Daily Alta* and intended for circulation along the Pacific coast. There was also a semimonthly *Steamer Alta*, which provided a condensed version of the news for readers in the Atlantic states and Europe.

The articles selected here deal with those parts of Arizona and New Mexico territories that are included within the present boundaries of the state of Arizona. California Volunteers in Arizona or special correspondents traveling with these troops authored all of the articles. The letters have been organized by the date they were written, rather than the publication date, in order to preserve a logical series. The correspondence dealing with Arizona during the years 1861 and 1866 was not included in the final selection because it was meager and inconsistent.

The microfilmed *Alta* was examined page by page. All items pertaining to the volunteers were noted, and all the signed correspondence was copied. The articles written by soldier-correspondents or special correspondents with the troops were then transcribed, preserving as much as possible the original format, spelling, sentence structure, and punctuation.

Most of the articles included here were penned by soldiers. Unlike their counterparts in the eastern theater, the majority of the Californian correspondents were not professional newspapermen. They tended to be enlisted men, though officers and civilians traveling with the troops contributed as well. All of the *Alta*'s "Special," "Occasional," and "Army" correspondents signed their letters only with pseudonyms or initials.

Although the trend in Europe and America during the middle and late nineteenth century was moving away from the use of pseudonyms, army correspondents preferred to maintain their anonymity. Just before launching his expedition into Arizona, James Carleton noted with concern the amount of information the newspapers were printing concerning troop movements, especially after having taken extraordinary precautions himself to ensure secrecy. On February 8, 1862, he wrote to Major E. A. Rigg in an attempt to quiet the army correspondents in the ranks: "Stop all newspaper writers in your camp from commenting on the movement of troops in this district. Quiet, implicit, and prompt obedience to orders must take the place of so much of this debating society system now in vogue."[2]

2. Salmon, *Newspaper and the Historian,* 68–71; Carleton to Rigg, Feb. 8, 1862, *OR,* 50(1):851. Carleton had gone so far as to write dispatches in Greek and secret code.

Several days later Carleton felt compelled to issue a general order on the subject: "The colonel commanding has observed that there has grown up a habit of writing for the press about military matters and movements by persons in the volunteer service in this district. This is not only unprofessional, but is strictly prohibited. There must be neither discussions among military men nor any but official letters written for publication, which have for their object the purpose of giving either censure or praise to any person belonging to the profession."[3]

Carleton's order did little to stem the flood of letters. But the problem was not unique to the Californians. From Washington, President Lincoln ordered a stop to all newspaper correspondence concerning military movements or "respecting the troops, camps, arsenals, intrenchments, or military affairs." General Joseph Hooker combated newspaper speculation, inaccuracy, and criticism by requiring all correspondents to sign their true names to their articles. In the South the Confederate War Department simply advised field commanders not to let correspondents into their lines.[4]

Army regulations stipulated that anyone convicted of "giving intelligence to the enemy, either directly or indirectly, shall suffer death, or such punishment as shall be ordered by the sentence of a court-martial." This and the prospect of incurring their commander's wrath induced most soldier-correspondents to cover their tracks well.[5]

Occasionally the editors of the *Alta* and the correspondents themselves revealed subtle clues to the identities of the columnists. Four types of signatures are found on the *Alta* articles. Most often the soldiers employed pseudonyms or *noms de guerre*. These names cleverly reflected the writer's association with the military; thus "Vedette" (a mounted scout or courier), "Dragoon" (the obsolescent equivalent of cavalryman or horse soldier), and the rather unimaginative "California Volunteer." Initials, both single

3. GO 3, Dist. of Southern Calif., Feb. 11, 1862, *OR,* 50(1):858–59.

4. A. Lincoln, Aug. 7, 1861, *OR,* ser. 3, 1:390; Knightley, *First Casualty,* 28; J. P. Benjamin to J. E. Johnston, Jan. 5, 1862, *OR,* 5:1020–21. See also Dary, *Red Blood and Black Ink;* and Perry, *Bohemian Brigade.*

5. See Article 57, Articles of War, *Revised Regulations,* 508; Even Department of the Pacific commander Gen. George Wright seem incapable of stopping the flow of letters from soldier correspondents. He complained that "the invitation held out by a certain paper in San Francisco for soldiers to make known their grievances through its columns without fear of a disclosure of their names has not only had a tendency to discourage enlistments, but is directly encouraging conduct among the soldiers subversive of good order and military discipline. . . . I am determined to put a stop to this resort to disaffected newspapers, whose only aim is to make the soldier dissatisfied with the service and to cast reflections on the military administration of this department." G. Wright to R. C. Drum, Feb. 20, 1865, *OR,* 50(2):1137.

and multiple, were also used to sign off letters. In two instances the authors used their true names, and on several occasions private letters were reprinted with the permission of the recipients.

Only a handful of authors can be identified with certainty. (A brief biographical sketch of each correspondent will be included in the annotations accompanying the letters.) These men were William Curry ("Corporal Curry"), Company D, Fifth California Infantry; Alonzo E. Davis ("California Volunteer" and "SIVAD"), Company I, Fourth Infantry; William B. Holmes ("W.B.H."), Company I, Fifth Infantry; James P. Newcomb ("N."), scout and interpreter with the California Column; Captain John C. Cremony ("Vedette"), Company B, Second Cavalry; and the twenty-two enlisted men who signed their names to a petition urging fair treatment for discharged California Volunteers in December 1865.

The modern reader should be prepared for the pedantry and verbosity found in many of the articles. Most of the authors were obviously well read, though the amount of their formal education, or lack thereof, is reflected in their writings. Latin, French, and Spanish words often spice the narratives, and classical references are common. Allusions to literary characters such as Münchausen, Don César de Bazan, and Grimwig are sure indicators of the popular literature that the soldiers carried in their haversacks. The drawn-out descriptions of exotic people and places are typical of the writing style then in vogue, but since the *Alta* sometimes paid correspondents by the line, padding was not uncommon. One wonders at Vedette's motives for his article of June 1862: "The whole air was filled with corruscating brilliancy, as lightnings' rapid glances cleft the clouds asunder, and lavish their aqueous burdens upon the parched bosom of the earth. Down came the rain in perfect Niagras; flash, flash, flash hissed the electric fluid as it lighted up the scene; boom, boom, boom; bang, bang, bang; roar, roar; crash, crash thundered the columbiads of the skies."[6]

The letters are often opinionated. It must be remembered that newspapers made little attempt to separate news from editorial opinion and propaganda during this period. The insidious racism of nineteenth-century America shows through clearly. Talk of exterminating the "hostile" Apaches may seem ludicrous today, but the Californians espousing this philosophy were merely expressing the opinion of whites in Arizona in the 1860s. So too, disparaging comments about "blood-thirsty savages" and simple "Greasers"

6. *Alta*, June 29, 1862.

are common and express the superiority the largely Anglo and Germanic invaders felt toward the people they encountered in Arizona.[7]

The practice of heaping excessive praise on officers and politicians, especially good Union men, is also evident. Sylvester Mowry, a Southern sympathizer and Carleton's avowed enemy, scolded the soldier-correspondents: "The letters from the California Column, published in several of the California newspapers, are mostly written to inflate some balloon reputation that will get a woeful collapse some day, or to accomplish some private end. . . . [T]hey are certainly not intended to enlighten the public."[8]

Some of the soldiers may have been bucking for promotions, but this puffery was also a means of expressing one's patriotism. It was dangerous to be labeled "Secesh" during this period of Rebel witch hunting. Soldiers learned to criticize their officers in such a way that would not offend Union men at home or in the ranks. The correspondents rarely mentioned desertion, a chronic problem that in some cases drained companies of their manpower. Most felt it their duty to help bolster the morale of civilians and soldiers alike. In short, patriotic propaganda will be found as a matter of course in the articles.[9]

In general the soldier-correspondents submitted reliable and accurate accounts for publication in the *Alta,* especially considering the word-of-mouth information gathering done by the enlisted reporters. It is true that the correspondents occasionally exaggerated and at times passed judgment on their superiors too quickly. It must have been difficult for the young men to maintain a measure of objectivity while marching through dust and intense heat, worrying about water, weather, and elusive enemies. Even so the correspondents and their comrades in arms seemed to sense the fact that they were shaping the nation's destiny and making history.

The Apache Pass fight of 1862 and the Tidball expedition a year later made the *Alta*'s front page. Vedette astutely noted that Apache Pass was the first battle in which the Apaches faced artillery. The correspondent who accompanied Captain T. T. Tidball on his expedition to Arivaipa Canyon accurately reported that it was "the most successful expedition ever sent out against the Apaches by the United States authorities in Arizona." Both

7. An extreme example of racist writing may be found in the diary of California Volunteer George Hand, who cast his intolerant eye upon "niggers" (especially General Carleton's slave, who dared to dance with Tucson *señoritas*), "greasers," Indians, and officers (of any ethnicity). Carmony, *Civil War in Apacheland,* 84–86.

8. Mowry, *Geography and Resources of Arizona and Sonora,* 50.

9. Knightley, *First Casualty,* 22.

California Volunteer and N. correctly predicted that the march of the California troops, with ranks filled with miners from the gold fields of the Pacific coast, would be the means of locating, advertising, and developing much of Arizona's mineral wealth.[10]

While the *Alta* correspondents sometimes exaggerated to drive home a point, there was little of the sensationalism found in the eastern papers, written by professional reporters vying to outdo one another. Vedette might be forgiven his tongue-in-cheek account of Apache dexterity in the art of stealing when he writes, "Lieut.-Colonel Eyre, in order to attract the Apaches into camp, caused a white flag to be hoisted on a prominent height, and to such good purpose that they stole the flag."[11] Alonzo E. Davis (California Volunteer) could have tempered his glowing accounts of the mining districts around Fort Mojave to provide a more accurate picture of the frontier for the home folks. But he had staked time and money on the Arizona mines. Davis firmly believed that no one would realize a profit until capitalists moved in with needed equipment and supplies. His personal ambition to cash in on Arizona's mineral wealth no doubt fueled his hyperbolic rhapsodies.

In most cases the army correspondents did not need to stretch the truth in order to hold the interest of California readers hungry for Arizona news. Information from the territory could almost always be found on the front page. Gold discoveries and mining news often prompted editors to issue a supplement, the *Alta Junior*. The popularity of the *Alta* with the men in the ranks served to keep the soldier-correspondents honest, peer pressure being more persuasive than officers and editors.

One soldier called to account Alonzo E. Davis for an article he wrote concerning the harsh and counterproductive Indian policy espoused by many whites in the Fort Mojave area. Davis defended his views with his fists. Luckily some coolheaded friends disarmed the critic when he resorted to his pistols to settle the argument. When a writer was proven wrong or when he later discovered himself to be in error, he usually attempted to make amends in hope of preserving his reputation. Anxious to mitigate any harm done by his letters concerning Captain Calloway's conduct at Picacho Pass, Vedette wrote: "I exceedingly regret that I should have been imposed upon to the extent of injuring, even in the slightest degree, any gentleman; but the positive manner and repeated affirmations of my informants were such

10. *Alta*, Aug. 16, Sept. 11, 1862.
11. Ibid., July 23, 1862.

as to induce any one to credit their assertions. I, however, take the earliest moment to make the *amende,* and will be particularly careful for the future as to the reliability of others."[12]

Of course the correspondents all relied on the army grapevine and local gossip for information. Vedette assured his readers that he would avail himself "of every opportunity to let you know all that transpires and I believe to be true, but cannot venture upon surmises which have little or no foundation." Still rumors continued to find their way into the *Alta*'s columns. The better correspondents either identified their sources or frankly stated that their information was unsubstantiated.[13]

Most correspondents gathered their news by personal observation and by word of mouth. In one instance Vedette thanked General Carleton for providing him with a list of names of men killed near Apache Pass. Since most of the writers were enlisted men, this sort of reporting would have to be considered an exception, unless the correspondent happened to be a company clerk with access to official documents.[14] Word-of-mouth intelligence gathering had some inherent drawbacks. Corruptions of personal and place names were common. The phonetic spellings are not too difficult to decipher if they represent English words, but Spanish names can be more troublesome, especially when the writer had little or no knowledge of this tongue, the *lingua franca* of the Southwest.

One must remember too that mistakes were sometimes made by deadline-driven typesetters who struggled to read the scribbles of the soldier-correspondents, themselves forced to write under trying circumstances. A comparison of an original letter written by James P. Newcomb (N.) shows that the author was not to blame for the misidentification of "Fort Thomas" for Fort Thorn and "Lieutenant Hudson" for Lieutenant Haden. These typos are the result of a bleary-eyed compositor trying to make out unfamiliar words written in an unfamiliar hand by a correspondent rushing to finish a letter before the mail carrier rode off.[15]

The articles compiled herein tell the story of the march of the California Column through Arizona and subsequent campaign and the garrison duty performed by other California regiments. There are some gaps in the story,

12. Davis, "Pioneer Days in Arizona," Arizona State University Library, Tempe, 65; *Alta,* July 23, 1862.

13. *Alta,* June 7, 1862.

14. Ibid., Aug. 31, 1862.

15. James P. Newcomb letter, July 7, 1862, James P. Newcomb Papers, CAH; *Alta,* Aug. 10, 1862.

however. The editors of the *Alta* solved this problem in the later war years by supplementing their Arizona correspondence with general- and special-orders issued from the Department of the Pacific headquarters in San Francisco. Since these official records have, for the most part, been published in the *War of the Rebellion,* they have not been duplicated here.

Several distinct threads of continuity can be traced as the reader peruses the *Alta* articles. The six major themes, in order of their significance to the correspondents, are: troop movements, Arizona sights and developments, Indians, mining, Confederates, and commanding officers.

Despite Carleton's efforts to discourage the publication of military intelligence, discussions of troop movements, activities, and health are invariably a part of the correspondents' letters. In the early years of the war, California citizens feared a Confederate invasion and eagerly sought information on the whereabouts of Federal troops that might offer protection. Later, families relied on the *Alta* to provide them with news of their menfolk on garrison duty, Indian campaigns, or patrols for secessionists in Arizona. The correspondents generally provided accurate reports on the movement of troops in their vicinity or military district. As a rule, the farther the writer was from the troops he referred to, the less accurate his information was likely to be. Regiments consisted of ten to twelve companies of one hundred men each. The reporters rarely mentioned the letter designation of their own company in order to preserve their anonymity, but knowledge of the regimental number and the location usually enables us to identify the company.

Although army documents such as orders, post returns, and company returns mention troop movements, additional details can be gleaned from the *Alta* articles. The letter writers recorded place names that are sometimes missing in official correspondence. The articles also provide additional information on troop strength, morale, and events that cannot be found in other sources. For example, the best account of the troops engaged at the battle of Apache Pass is found among the *Alta* articles.

The soldier-reporters described Arizona Territory for eager California readers. Many volunteer soldiers saw the territory as a land of opportunity while others found only misery in the Arizona desert. Regardless of the correspondents' feelings toward the country, their letters contained descriptions of the flora and fauna, climate, people, politics, towns, and events.

The soldiers' first accounts of Arizona stressed the harshness of the land. All of the correspondents wrote of the "Plutonian" heat, rugged terrain, and gagging alkali dust. But after the men finally became accustomed to the routine of garrison life and inured to the hardships, a new appreciation for Arizona began to develop. Soon glowing accounts of picturesque mountains and sparkling rivers appeared on the *Alta*'s pages. Prehistoric ruins captured the imaginations of the soldiers. They wrote of herds of antelope and the good fishing in the Gila River. The correspondents soon dispelled rumors of 142 degree temperatures and myths of desert dangers. Although the summer temperatures soared, the soldiers touted the dry climate as the healthiest possible.

The men composing the occupation force that remained in Arizona after the California Column passed through to New Mexico and Texas developed a keen interest in local affairs. At Fort Mojave, California Volunteer reported on the development of the territorial government, the founding of the *Arizona Miner,* and the election of public officials. In Tucson W.B.H. described the marked difference in the behavior of the population since General Carleton had declared martial law and cleaned out the secessionists and undesirables. Direct courts, he wrote, were soon established, and "law and order was all the rage."

Some of the soldier correspondents liked Arizona enough to stay or return after their enlistments expired. Alonzo E. Davis was determined to stay on the Colorado River near Fort Mojave. His letters to the *Alta* reflect a deep interest in the affairs of the young territory, including accounts of exploring expeditions in search of wood and coal, steam navigation on the Colorado, wagon roads, and descriptions of the territory's mineral wealth.

Tales of the Arizona Indians fascinated both the California Volunteers and the *Alta*'s readers at home. Some correspondents wrote of the origins, customs, and dress of the "friendly" tribes, the Pimas, Maricopas, and Mojaves. Some of the soldiers displayed remarkable objectivity and tolerance in their letters; their descriptions of Indian cultures approximated a modern ethnographic approach. Other writers confined themselves to accounts of enemy tribes, describing Apache depredations and failed attempts to treat with those "murderous brutes." The Californians also boasted of their prowess in the art of Indian fighting. Without question they saw more success in armed encounters with Indians in Arizona than any troops before or after the Civil War.

The *Alta* articles reflect the tension caused by rumors of Indian uprisings and the disappointment felt by soldiers sent in response to these false alarms. They show the exhilaration of victory over an elusive and skillful enemy as well as the frustration of not being able to effectively strike back against a foe that did not fight by the rules of "civilized warfare." Almost without exception, the volunteer correspondents favored arming friendly tribes with guns and exterminating hostile tribes, unless they unconditionally surrendered. Carleton advocated this course, as did the majority of Arizona's citizens.

News of Arizona's mineral wealth and mines was a recurring theme in the *Alta* articles. The Californians panned, sampled, and tested their way across Arizona's deserts. They wrote home of their discoveries and claims, encouraging others to follow in their footsteps. The influence of these enthusiastic letters on the *Alta*'s readership is difficult to gauge accurately, but Arizona experienced unprecedented growth when the Californians mustered out at the end of the war. Many returned to seek their fortunes. Alonzo E. Davis wrote in 1864 that most of the soldiers "intend to stick to the country, for they feel confident they have got their 'golden-egged goose' cooped, sure." Davis's pleas for capitalists to invest in the mines inspired considerable interest in the upper Colorado region.[16] Reporters with the California Column sent accounts of established mines to the editors of the *Alta*. The fate of the Patagonia (Mowry's) Mine, seized by Carleton's troops in 1862, merited considerable column space. The attempted confiscation of the Heintzelman Mine near Tubac by Palatine Robinson in the name of the Confederacy also made news in California.

Some skeptics believed the reports of rich mines to be a "humbug," and most of the soldiers stationed near the mining districts of central Arizona felt neglected and resented being mustered out in the territories. A letter by "Vide" charged that the military establishment was trying to make the public believe that the soldiers wanted to stay in Arizona to prospect in order to save the cost of transporting the men back to California. Indeed Carleton himself was convinced of the richness of Arizona's mines and even ordered his men to prospect and record their findings so they could be publicized in Washington. In any event the positive reaction of the Californians to Arizona's mineral wealth far outweighed the cynicism expressed by some.[17]

The composition and disposition of the Confederate troops in Arizona, New Mexico, and Texas also concerned the army correspondents of the

16. *Alta*, Aug. 6, 1864. Many discharged California soldiers returned to Arizona after the war. Several listed their occupation as miner, capitalist, or a trade related to mining, such as machinist, freighter, or laborer. Sen. Carl Hayden documented hundreds of such early Arizona pioneers. See Hayden Arizona Pioneer Biography Files, Arizona State University Library, Tempe.

17. Carleton to N. Pishon, First Cavalry, CV, June 22, 1863, Orton, *California Men*, 72.

Alta. In 1862 the letters from the California Column frequently referred to Sibley, Baylor, and Van Dorn, the leading Rebels in the Southwest. Rumors and eyewitness accounts gleaned from informants along the Yuma-Tucson road were quickly sent back to eager California readers. Descriptions were printed of the California secessionists who had passed over the road ahead of Carleton's Column. Speculation about Sherod Hunter's force in Tucson and the seemingly inevitable confrontation filled the correspondents' letters.

It seemed certain that the Rebels would entrench and make a stand at Tucson. The first reliable intelligence, however, came from the paroled Californians who had been captured with Captain McCleave at White's Mill. Hunter was not prepared for a showdown and had withdrawn from Tucson soon after the survivors of the Picacho Pass skirmish announced the approach of the California Column.

News of covert Confederate activity in Arizona and New Mexico continued to appear in the *Alta*'s columns after 1862, but this later coverage was scanty compared to the early reports. Some volunteers tried to rationalize the importance of their duty in Arizona by playing up the threat of another Rebel invasion, but most resignedly set about the tasks at hand: Indian fighting, escorting mail and supply wagons, and garrison duty.

Commanding officers, quite expectedly, often found themselves the subjects of the correspondents' scrutiny. In 1862 Carleton could do no wrong in the eyes of his men. The *Alta*'s columns bristled with strong words in defense of the commander of the California Column. The soldier correspondents felt duty bound to include testimonials of his loyalty and ability in almost every letter. This staunch support contrasts sharply with articles submitted in 1864 and 1865. By the time the volunteers' enlistments had expired, so had their devotion to James Carleton. Vide wrote from Fort Goodwin that "Carleton & Co." had misrepresented the plight of the volunteer troops being mustered out of service in the territories. He insisted that "our worst fears are realized" and that "we are well aware that the leading officers in this Department are responsible for this outrage." Personal attacks of this kind would have been court-martial offenses in 1862.[18]

Other officers, including Calloway, Eyre, and West, suffered the criticism of soldier-correspondents. In general only specific actions, or lack of action, on the part of superior officers elicited comment. For example, Colonel Eyre's decision not to attack the Apaches who killed three of Captain Fritz's

18. *Alta*, Oct. 17, 1864.

cavalrymen in Apache Pass drew considerable condemnation from both N. and Vedette.

General John Mason did not command the District of Arizona long enough to provoke much criticism from the volunteer newspapermen. W.C.W. did note that the general's Apache campaign had stalled because of the lack of transportation for the troops and supplies. He assigned no blame for this oversight, however.

Several generalizations can be made about the number and content of the California Volunteer articles that appeared in the *Alta*. The correspondents submitted more letters in 1862 because there was so much to write about: the Confederates had pressed dangerously close to California itself; hostile Indians, it seemed, had the run of the territory; new mining districts were being located; not to mention that in 1862 thousands of California men got their first taste of military life and the adventure of travel into a strange new land. It is no wonder that the correspondents penned most of the letters in 1862.

The three subsequent years saw a drastic reduction of troops in Arizona. The ever-changing commanders established small garrisons to keep supplies moving to the front and to launch sporadic Indian expeditions and scouts. Troop strength reached a low in 1863, which is reflected in the small number of letters submitted for publication.

Regularity of correspondence by a writer also influenced the number of articles in any one year. The years 1862 and 1864 are especially well covered because Vedette and California Volunteer consistently submitted letters for publication. Regular correspondents afforded the *Alta*'s readers continuity and allowed for less repetition than would have been expected had many correspondents been employed.

Some soldier-correspondents sent their letters to hometown newspapers. For example, men of the Fifth California Infantry, raised largely in Sacramento, sent letters back to their home city. Consequently, little correspondence from Fifth Infantry garrisons, such as Tucson and Fort Bowie, is found in the *Alta*.

Finally the location of a garrison in Arizona tended to affect the subject matter of the letters. The men of the Fourth California Infantry stationed at Fort Mojave were fortunate to have a company commander who encouraged them to prospect and mine. Hence much of California Volunteer's news deals with mining. Men stationed at Tucson, Tubac, or Fort Bowie may have had only tales of Indian campaigning to report. So too, population centers provided the correspondents with more to write about than the more isolated posts.

The *Alta* articles that follow are a valuable research source. They provide eyewitness accounts of the campaigning, occupation duty, people, and places in Arizona Territory from its creation through the turbulent years of the Civil War and the clash of Indian and white cultures. What follows is the story of the California Volunteers in their own words.

CHAPTER 7

Arizona Dispatches, 1862

ALTA, MAY 14, 1862

Letter from Our Army Correspondent
Cariso [Carrizo] Creek,[1] April 27th, 1862

EDS. ALTA: I arrived at this place on the 25th inst., en route for Fort Yuma, and thence to meet the foe in Arizona, or wherever else he is to be found. Cariso Creek is located on the western edge of the Colorado desert, and is 112 miles from Yuma,[2] the whole distance being one unbroken waste of blinding white sand, which reflects the rays of the sun with terrible lustre and withering effect. Men, mules and horses sink under its power, as if suddenly blighted, losing all energy, and relaxing every fibre to absolute flaccidness. In consequence of the very small quantity of water to be obtained in this desert, the force under Colonel Carleton[3] is sent forward in detachments, con-

1. Carrizo Creek, a stage station on the abandoned Butterfield Overland Mail route, was used as a forage depot and water stop by the California Column. It was located 106 miles west of Fort Yuma and 167 miles from Los Angeles. Conkling and Conkling, *Butterfield Overland Mail*, 2:227–28, 363.

2. Fort Yuma was established on the west bank of the Colorado River near the confluence of the Gila by a detachment of U.S. dragoons on October 2, 1849. Occupied intermittently until the Civil War, it became the jumping-off point for Carleton's Arizona expedition and the major distribution center for supplies and reserves for the territory. Brandes, *Frontier Military Posts*, 81–86.

3. Maine-born James H. Carleton was major of the First U.S. Dragoons when the war began. A slaveowner, he was nevertheless a staunch Union man. Appointed colonel of the First California Infantry, Carleton later won the honor of leading the Arizona expedition. He was a brevet major general and commander of the Department of New Mexico by the war's end. A diehard regular since 1839 with a reputation as a martinet, Carleton was a veteran of the

centrating again at Yuma, and going forward, up the Gila, in larger detachments, until Tucson is reached, where another concentration is effected.

MILITARY MOVEMENTS

Some time since, Capt. Calloway[4] was sent forward from Yuma toward Tucson, in command of three Companies, to obtain reliable intelligence of the enemy, who are known to be in possession of Tucson, Imores [Imuris],[5] and other places, and if possible, to rout them from their positions. This service is so well performed, that Capt. Calloway's command reached the Pimo [Pima] villages without his approach being known even to those Indians,[6] and then moved forward toward Tucson. Capt. Calloway was followed by Lieut. Col. West,[7] on the arrival of that officer at Fort Yuma, Col. W. taking with him a force of seven Companies, cavalry and infantry, which is now making rapid marches toward Tucson. The battery, commanded by Lieut. Shinn,[8]

Mexican War and numerous Indian campaigns on the frontier. During his volunteer service Carleton proved himself well suited for command. Tactful in his dealings with officers and men and exhibiting a flair for diplomacy in international politics, he was above all a superb logistician. For a complete biography, see Hunt, *James Henry Carleton.*

4. William P. Calloway enrolled as captain, Company I, First California Infantry in San Francisco, August 16, 1861. He mustered out with his company at Fort Union, New Mexico, on September 30, 1864. A veteran of the Mexican War, Calloway was a capable company commander. An investigation of his retreat and conduct following the Picacho affair determined that the captain was motivated by an excess of caution but that his actions were not cowardly or criminal. Orton, *California Men,* 372; Hunt, *Army of the Pacific,* 86.

5. Imuris, Sonora, boasted a population of around one thousand people in 1862 and was located fifteen miles north of Magdalena. Fergusson to West, June 25, 1862, *OR,* 50(1):1159.

6. The Pimo (Pima) Villages, or simply Pimos, were located along the Butterfield Overland Mail route twelve miles east of Maricopa Wells and two hundred miles east of Fort Yuma. J. Ross Browne notes that there were ten Pimo and two Maricopa villages in this group. Barnes, "Arizona Place Names," 332–33.

7. Joseph Rodman West (1822–98) was enrolled as the lieutenant colonel of the First California Infantry on August 5, 1861. Upon his promotion to colonel, the rank-and-file took to calling him "the Bald Eagle" because of his distinctive bald head. George Hand Diary, June 24, 1862, Arizona Historical Society, Tucson. At the beginning of the Civil War, West was one of Carleton's confidants and served as his second in command during the expedition to the Rio Grande. The two ambitious officers became competitive, then adversarial. West succeeded Carleton to the command of the District of Arizona until being transferred to the Department of Arkansas in the spring of 1864. A Mexican War veteran and California businessman before the Civil War, West returned to his native state of Louisiana after being mustered out a brevet major general in 1866. He held several political offices, including that of senator from Louisiana. Boatner, *Civil War Dictionary,* 902; Orton, *California Men,* 335.

8. Lt. John B. Shinn commanded Battery A, Third U.S. Artillery, which was the only unit of the regular army to accompany the Column from California. A West Point graduate (1856), Shinn was promoted to captain in 1864. The next year he was brevetted major for successfully marching his battery across Arizona and New Mexico. Shinn's military career ended in 1870, when he was honorably discharged at his own request. Heitman, *Historical Register,* 1:883.

3d Artillery U.S.A., is now at San Felipe,[9] thirty-two miles westerly from this place, and will push forward for Yuma as soon as Capt. John C. Cremony's[10] Company of the 2d Cavalry C.V. shall have vacated Cariso Creek, so as to give room to Judge Winstan's [Winston][11] train of wagons now at Vallecito.[12]

I may as well here add that Capt. Cremony's company will be the only one of the Second Cavalry that will have the opportunity to meet the enemy in the field. It is in admirable condition—the men eager to distinguish themselves, and the horses fat, strong, and capable of enduring great fatigue. Major Wood[s],[13] Paymaster, U.S.A., selected his escort of twenty men from this company, and is probably now at the Pimo villages, where he will commence to pay off the troops, and pay them all as fast as he meets the several detachments on his return. Major Wood is accompanied by Major

9. San Felipe station, on the Overland Stage route, was situated in the San Felipe Valley, California, 142 miles west of Fort Yuma. The adobe station and creek there lay between Warner's Ranch, 16 miles to the west, and Vallecito, 18 miles southeast. Conkling and Conkling, *Butterfield Overland Mail*, 2:236, 363.

10. John C. Cremony (1830–79) enlisted as a captain of Company B, Second California Cavalry on September 14, 1861. He is probably "Vedette," the author of this letter. After nearly four years of service in Arizona and New Mexico, Cremony accepted a commission as major in the Native Battalion. He was mustered out of the volunteer service on March 16, 1866, in San Francisco. A born adventurer, as a boy Cremony ran away to sea. He saw something of piracy and slave trading during this period. He claimed to have lived as a captive among the Patagonian Indians of South America before making it back to the United States in time to serve as a Massachusetts volunteer during the Mexican War. Afterward he served as an interpreter for the U.S. Boundary Commission in the Southwest. Later he established himself as a rancher in California. In the late 1850s he edited two San Francisco newspapers. During the Civil War Cremony compiled a dictionary of the Apache language and took notes for his book *Life among the Apaches*, published in 1868. After the war he returned to newspaper work and was one of the founders of the Bohemian Club in San Francisco. Cremony, *Life among the Apaches*; Orton, *California Men*, 209, 307; Franklin Walker, *San Francisco's Literary Frontier*, 114, 352.

11. "Judge" Joseph Winston was one of four wagon masters who led Carleton's supply trains across the desert. Each wagon master selected three assistants from among the teamsters. Each train consisted of fifty six-mule teams and wagons. The other wagon masters for the Rio Grande expedition were Gabriel Allen, N. L. Roundtree, and William S. Veck. Carleton to T. Moore, assistant quartermaster, Feb. 9, 1862, *OR*, 50(1):853; Cutler to W. G. Morris, Second Cavalry, CV, April 27, 1862, ibid., 1034.

12. Vallecito was the Butterfield station eighteen miles east of San Felipe and nine miles west of Palm Springs. Its good grass and sulfurous but potable water had made it a stopping place since the Spanish first entered the area. The site had been used as a station for a semimonthly military mail established between San Diego and Fort Yuma in 1854. Conkling and Conkling, *Butterfield Overland Mail*, 2:229.

13. On April 9, 1862, Maj. Samuel Woods left Los Angeles for Fort Yuma to pay off the troops. Woods had been an officer since his graduation from West Point in 1837. He served with the Sixth and Fifteenth U.S. Infantry regiments until he transferred to the Paymaster Department in 1848, remaining there until his retirement in 1881. Carleton to R. W. Kirkham, acting AAG, San Francisco, Apr. 11, 1862, *OR*, 1(1):1000; Heitman, *Historical Register*, 1:1058.

R. C. Drumm [Drum],[14] Assistant Adjutant General of Gen. Wright's Staff,[15] who is here to see that all of the troops are in fighting condition and properly equipped for the field.

Col. Carleton also selected his private escort of twelve men and a sergeant from Capt. Cremony's company, which is expected to reach Fort Yuma on or about the 1st of May. No grazing of any description is to be had at either San Felipe, Vallecito, or Cariso Creek, and the horses suffered much for want of it, but Capt. Cremony found some ten or twelve Digueño [Diegueño] Indians at the last-named place,[16] and for a blanket or two, employed them to go into the mountains and cut him a quantity of hay in places known to them. By this means he has been enabled to obtain some five or six hundred pounds, which has proved of inestimable benefit to his horses. For the past two months not a man of this company has been on the sick list, or so unwell as to be excused from duty. They are armed with Sharp's carbines, army revolvers, and sabres, in the use of which they have become quite dexterous.[17] It is also worthy of note that there has been no occasion to punish a single man for more than two months past.

THE ENEMY

I learn here, from an old sergeant named McLagan,[18] who resides in an adobe house, and is the only white inhabitant, (barring a small detachment of the 1st Infantry,

14. Maj. Richard Coulter Drum was dispatched by Carleton to inspect the troops en route to Arizona. A veteran of the Mexican War, Drum was a captain and assistant adjutant general of the Department of the Pacific at the beginning of the Civil War. Promoted to major on August 3, 1861, and to lieutenant colonel on July 17, 1862, he attained the rank of brigadier general before retiring in 1889. Carleton to Rigg, *OR*, 50(1):999; Heitman, *Historical Register*, 1:384; SO 54, Hdqrs. Dept. of the Pacific, Apr. 5, 1862, *OR*, 50(1):985.

15. George Wright (1803–65) commanded the Department of the Pacific from October 20, 1861, to July 1, 1864. A graduate of the West Point class of 1822, he saw action in the Seminole War, Mexican War, and Indian fighting in the Pacific Northwest. He was the colonel of the Ninth U.S. Infantry when the war began and was appointed brigadier general of volunteers on September 28, 1861. While traveling north to assume command of the Department of the Columbia, Wright drowned during the wreck of the *Brother Jonathan* on July 30, 1865. Boatner, *Civil War Dictionary*, 949; Heitman, *Historical Register*, 1:1062.

16. The Diegueños, a Yuman tribe, occupied southwestern California and the northwestern part of Baja California. "Diegueño" is derived from the name of the Mission of San Diego. Swanton, *Indian Tribes*, 488, 620.

17. Cremony's company was probably issued Model 1859 Sharps carbines, the old 1840 pattern saber (which Carleton insisted be ground sharp enough to cut through clothing and reins), and Colt's heavy Model 1847 .44-caliber "Dragoon" revolver. Carleton did not consider this last weapon suitable for cavalry—he preferred Colt's lighter .36-caliber "Navy" revolver but was unable to procure enough to outfit all of his cavalry companies. The men were required to practice their saber drill one hour each day while marching across the desert.

18. Sergeant McClaggan, formerly of San Diego, is identified by J. J. Warner as living at Carrizo Creek. Warner to Carleton, Dec. 23, 1861, *OR*, 50 (1):784–85.

Lieut. Burkett,[19] retained here to guard train and provisions,) that no less than from three to four hundred Secessionists have gone by this place on their way to join their brother rebels. They moved before the capture of the Showalter party;[20] but since the establishment of the force at Yuma, they have adopted the Mojave crossing.[21] The reports that we obtain go to show that Sibley[22] is still in New Mexico and Arizona, with a force of from sixteen to eighteen hundred Texans, and three to four, or perhaps five hundred Californians, a great many of whom are known to be escaped convicts.

19. George A. Burkett enrolled as first lieutenant of Company F, Fifth California Infantry at Camp Union, California, on October 25, 1861. Promoted to captain, Company I, Fifty Infantry, on November 24, 1864, Burkett played a prominent role in Davis's and Whitlock's actions against the Apaches that year. Transferred first to Company F, then to Company G, First California Veteran Infantry, he was finally mustered out with his company at Los Pinos, New Mexico, on September 20, 1866. Burkett was a brevet major when he left the volunteer service. N. H. Davis to Cutler, June 5, 1864, *OR*, 50(2):872; Orton, *California Men*, 699; Whitlock to C. A. Smith, Apr. 13, 1864, *OR*, 50(2):827–29.

20. Dan Showalter organized a large party of secessionists who planned to travel east to proffer their services to the Confederacy. Carleton wanted to take a hard line with these men in order to show that the time was past in which secessionists in southern California could openly give their support to the Confederacy. A combined force of the First California Cavalry and the First California Infantry captured Showalter and fifteen of his heavily armed men at John Winter's ranch in the San José Valley on November 29, 1861; two others had already been caught on the twenty-seventh. Intercepted dispatches confirmed that several of the men had received commissions in the Confederate service. All were imprisoned at Fort Yuma until each took an oath of allegiance. The following men composed the party: Charles Benbrook, F. N. Chum, Henry Cromwell, William "Frog" Edwards, A. King, J. Lawrence, T. L. Roberts, Levi Rogers, S. A. Rogers, J. M. Sampson, William Sands, Dan Showalter, E. B. Sumner, William Turner, R. H. Ward, T. A. Wilson, T. W. Woods, and W. Woods. Orton, *California Men*, 15; Rigg to Carleton, Nov. 30, 1861, *OR*, 50(1):33. See also Clendenen, "Dan Showalter," 309–25.

21. The ferry crossing the Colorado River at Fort Mojave was commonly called Mohave Crossing.

22. Henry Hopkins Sibley (1816–86) was a major in the U.S. Army when the war began. His plan to drive Federal troops from New Mexico was endorsed by the Confederate government, and he was commissioned as a brigadier general in July 1861. In December Sibley created the Army of New Mexico, but he was ill suited for command. A poor strategist with a chronic drinking problem, Sibley lacked many essential qualities of a leader. These factors, coupled with poor health, doomed his efforts in New Mexico from the start. He was relieved of command in 1863. Graduating from West Point in 1838, Sibley had served in the Seminole War, Mexican War, and frontier Indian campaigns before the Civil War. After the war he became a general of artillery in Egypt until 1874. Probably the most outstanding of his military accomplishments was the invention of a teepee-style army tent in 1856, which saw extensive use until the turn of the century. Boatner, *Civil War Dictionary*, 759; Jefferson Davis to Sibley, July 8, 1861, *OR*, 4:93; Hall and Long, *Army of New Mexico*, 25.

The enemy are armed with revolvers, knives, and Mississippi rifles,[23] many of them having shotguns in place of the rifle. They have no sabres, and their guns are not calculated to kill at long range. I imagine they will find a very great difference between encountering half-armed, half-clad and starving New Mexicans, and fighting with the energetic, well-drilled, well-disciplined and splendidly armed troops of California.

THE FIRST ENCOUNTER

News has reached us of the first encounter between our soldiers and the Texans. It appears that Capt. Calloway was advised of the fact that the enemy had posted a picket guard to watch the road leading to Tucson, and he accordingly, on or about the 16th or 17th [15th] inst., sent Lieut. Barrett,[24] of Co. A, 1st Cavalry California Volunteers, with twelve men, to cut off or drive in the enemy's picket. Lieut. Barrett managed to get between Tucson and the picket, which was posted in the chaparral, and then attempted to drive the picket forward on Capt. Calloway's command. In endeavoring to execute this manoeuvre he unwisely entered the chaparral mounted, whilst the enemy watched his advance from their covert. At the first discharge the gallant Barrett was killed, with one of his men, and another was mortally wounded. Nevertheless, the brave fellows who remained dismounted and gave the enemy a taste of their quality, killing three, wounding three and taking three prisoners, besides capturing all the enemy's stores, camp and garrison equipage, etc. The rebels numbered sixteen, and our force but twelve men. Our loss was three killed, including Barrett, and three

23. Although the Mississippi, or Model 1841, Rifle was no longer considered a "first class" weapon by 1862, it was one of the finest and most accurate weapons in service. Made famous by Jefferson Davis's Mississippi troops during the Mexican War, it was a .54-caliber rifle with a short, heavy barrel. Many of these arms were bored out and re-rifled to .58-caliber just before the Civil War and were valued by frontiersmen. Army tests proved this altered weapon quite deadly at long range: propelled by sixty grains of black powder, the five-hundred-grain bullet could pass through three inches of seasoned white pine at one thousand yards. Hicks, *United States Ordnance*, 1:70; Scott, *Military Dictionary*, 30–31.

24. James Barrett was the second lieutenant of Company A, First California Cavalry. To Barrett goes the unfortunate distinction of being the first California Volunteer to be killed in action against the Rebels. An eyewitness reported that "a ball took him in the neck and broke it, killing him instantly." Pvts. George Johnson, Company A, and William S. Leonard, Company D, were the other two Union fatalities in the skirmish. *Sacramento Union*, May 23, 1862; Orton, *California Men*, 89, 94,120; Julius Hall, "Wild West." The actual date of the Picacho skirmish is controversial. Sherod Hunter reported that the fight took place on April 16, while California officers consistently held that it occurred on the fifteenth, and the graves of the slain were marked with that date. Leonard died early the morning after the fight, and his headboard was carefully marked April 16, 1862. Hunter's pickets did not make it back to Tucson until early on the morning of the sixteenth, probably contributing to the Confederates' confusion. See Finch, *Confederate Pathway*, 268; and "Sanctified by Myth," 251–66.

A Union officer sketched one of Baylor's Texas Rangers, noting that each Rebel was mounted on a mustang and carried a rifle, tomahawk, bowie knife, two Colt revolvers, and a "lasso for catching and throwing the horses of a flying foe." From *Harper's Weekly*, 1861.

wounded. This is the first conflict that has occurred between California troops proper and the rebels. There is every reason to believe that we shall have hot work, sharp work and plenty of it, before long. The California troops will probably do the best fighting in the contest, as the rebels are being gradually driven southward upon the position they must sooner or later occupy.

MILITARY COURIERS

Col. Carleton has very wisely established a regular line of military couriers from Fort Yuma to Los Angeles, under the superintendence of Lieut. W. G. Morris,[25] Co. I, 2d Cavalry California Volunteers, who is now engaged in selecting his posts, and supplying them with the requisite number of men and horses, with the provisions necessary for their subsistence. It is probable that a courier will be dispatched regularly from Fort Yuma for Los Angeles twice or three times a week, perhaps oftener, and in like manner from Los Angeles for Fort Yuma, by which means regular and rapid communication and correspondence will be established.

COL. CARLETON

The more I see of Col. Carleton, the more confident I feel of his entire fitness and ability to command the force now under him, and conduct the important campaign entrusted to his charge. His vigilance is sleepless, and his energy untiring. With all the attention to detail and even minutiae, which characterizes the thorough disciplinarian, he possesses the ability to elaborate and carry out operations on an extensive scale, and with remarkable accuracy and timeliness. I venture to assert that no officer in the service has performed so great an amount of labor in the same time as Col. Carleton. The troops under his command have attained a degree of perfection in discipline, drill and military organization, never before equaled by any volunteer force, all of which is immediately referable to his personal attention and zeal; while he has projected and is rapidly accomplishing an important movement which is to be extended over 1,800 miles of territory, a large portion of which is a perfect barren waste, an uninhabitable desert.

In the meantime the lower counties have been deterred from open revolt;[26] rebellion has been strangled before it could mature; our frontiers protected from the red skinned foe, by detachments marched to long distances to punish their offences and insure peace

25. William Gouverneur Morris enrolled as adjutant on the regimental staff of the Second California Cavalry on October 2, 1861; he soon transferred to Company I of the same regiment as first lieutenant. On May 22, 1862, he transferred back to the regimental staff. Morris then resigned in order to accept a commission as captain and assistant quartermaster, U.S. Volunteers. In San Francisco on April 25, 1866, Morris delivered the keynote address to the first meeting of California veterans, the Society of California Volunteers. Orton, *California Men*, 197, 267; Morris, *Address*.

26. Occasional shows of force were necessary to avert open hostilities in the southern California counties, especially Los Angeles and San Bernardino. The presence of volunteer troops and the capture of the Showalter party served to drive most secessionists underground. Secret societies such as the Knights of the Golden Circle and the Knights of the Columbian Star became the only outlet for staunch Confederate sympathizers. See Robinson, *Los Angeles in Civil War Days*.

and quiet; roads repaired and others made; depots of provisions for men and animals established; camps of instruction formed; supplies obtained for present and prospective requirements, and California placed in perfect repose and security; and all this in the face of the most terrible winter ever experienced since the occupation of the State by the American people. I cannot but think that Col. Carleton's merits have been strangely overlooked by the proper authorities, owing, perhaps, to the fact that his operations have not taken place under the immediate agency of the powers that be. I believe that every officer of the regular army, who served with the Colonel at the battle of Buena Vista,[27] is now a Brigadier General, while he is but a Major of Cavalry and Colonel of Volunteer Infantry, although he ranked many of them during the Mexican war. It is not my province to find fault, nor intimate to the authorities what they ought to do, but it is my province to state well known facts, which I leave to your readers to digest at their leisure and according to the capacities of their several stomachs.[28]

My next will be dated from Fort Yuma, and I will omit no opportunity to keep you posted on the events of the campaign now commenced unless I should "lose the number of my mess," but depend upon it I have no pressing desire to "shuffle off this mortal coil," and for the present would sooner "bear the ills I have, than fly to those I know not of " in the next world.

27. In 1848 Carleton's book *The Battle of Buena Vista, With the Operations of the "Army of Occupation" for One Month* was published by Harper Brothers, New York. It proved to be very popular and remained in print for twenty years. It is likely that many members of the California Column had read this work and, as a result, had a heightened awareness of his presence at Buena Vista—his actual role was minor. It is true, however, that many of Carleton's regular-army comrades were attaining high rank rapidly in the critical eastern theater of the war. Carleton himself was concerned with the delay in his promotion. He wrote General Wright that "a score of others junior to myself are brigadier-generals. I feel that I am not thought worthy of advancement by those in authority." Carleton to Wright, Mar. 22, 1862, *OR*, 50(1):945.

28. Evidently "the powers that be" also thought Carleton's work deserving. On April 28, 1862 (one day after this letter was written), he was promoted to brigadier general of volunteers. Orton, *California Men*, 321.

It is now certain that Captain McCleave,[29] Co. A, First Cavalry California Volunteers, has been captured by the enemy. He was sent to Texas by them from Tucson, on the 19th of this month.

VIDETTE.[30]

ALTA, MAY 24, 1862

Letter from Our Army Correspondent
Camp at Antelope Peak,[31] *New Mexico, May 10*

EDITORS ALTA—Thus far we have marched into the bowels of the land without impediment, being some 45 miles east of Fort Yuma, and 150 west of Pimo Villages, at which point our whole force is to be concentrated, preparatory to our expected clash with the rebels at Tucson, which place is being fortified for a sanguinary resistance to our further progress, if the reports from there are to be credited, and I think they are.

OUR STRENGTH

The forces under command of Colonel James H. Carleton, for the repossession of New Mexico, consist, so far, of the First Regiment of California Volunteers Infantry,

29. William McCleave was captain of Company A, First California Cavalry when he was taken prisoner at White's Mill by Sherod Hunter's Rebels on March 18, 1862. After his exchange four months later, he returned to his company and was subsequently promoted to major and brevet lieutenant colonel before being mustered out at Fort Union, New Mexico, on October 19, 1866. A native of Ireland, McCleave had served with Carleton in the First U.S. Dragoons from 1850 to 1860. After the war he returned to the regular army and retired a captain in 1879. Heitman, *Historical Register,* 1:655; Hunt, *Army of the Pacific,* 85–92.

30. "Vidette" was the well-chosen pseudonym of one of Captain Cremony's men (Company B, Second California Cavalry). Military manuals of the period define a "vidette" (or "vedette") as a mounted sentinel placed to best observe the movements of the enemy and able to communicate with others by signaling. Unfortunately Vidette's identity remains a mystery. There is a remarkable similarity, however, between his writing style and that of John C. Cremony. Indeed Vidette always seemed to be where Cremony was, which was unusual since Company B was often broken up for vidette and escort duty. Another factor suggesting that Cremony and Vidette may be one and the same is Vidette's reliance on information "derived from the officers in this command" or "current among the officers of this command." These repeated assertions indicate that Vidette was either an enlisted man privy to the conversations of his officers, an eavesdropper, or, most probably, Cremony himself. Scott, *Military Dictionary,* 639; *U.S. Infantry Tactics,* 431; Cremony, *Life among the Apaches,* passim; *Alta,* May 24, 1862.

31. Antelope Peak, or Hill, was located about forty-three miles east of Fort Yuma along the Southern Overland route. It was added to the Butterfield itinerary in 1859, and the California Volunteers used it as a forage drop as well as a stopping place. The adobe station buildings were situated on the west side of the peak, south of the Gila. Barnes, "Arizona Place Names," 19; Conkling and Conkling, *Butterfield Overland Mail,* 2:185–86, 363.

ten companies; the Battalion of the First Cavalry, Lieut.-Col. Eyre,[32] five companies; Capt. Cremony's Company, B, of the Second Cavalry, Cal. Vols.; and Lieut. Shinn's Company, A, Light Artillery, U.S. Army. Besides, there are two 12-pounder mountain howitzers[33] now at the Pimo Villages, and two more at Fort Yuma to be sent forward, together with some five or six companies, perhaps more, of Colonel Bowie's Fifth Regiment California Volunteers Infantry,[34] making an aggregate of sixteen infantry companies, six of cavalry, one of light artillery, four pieces and four mountain howitzers, comprising a force of 1,800 men.

These troops are all admirably drilled and disciplined; perfectly armed, equipped, and provisioned, with abundance of transportation, and unbounded faith in their leaders. Many of them have seen active service in the field, and are no chickens in a "bar fight." All are keenly anxious to get a sight of the adobe buildings of Tucson, where the enemy is said to await our coming, and where we hope to give a good account of him.

THE ENEMY

Late intelligence from Tucson gives us to understand that the rebels are mustering at that place. Some five or six hundred are reported to be already there, and awaiting reinforcements from the San Pedro River, where they appear to have encamped, and as many more with some pieces of artillery. The place is being entrenched, the houses crenelled for musketry,[35] ditches dug and earth works thrown up; but we hope to be on the other side of them ere long.

32. Edward E. Eyre enrolled as a major in the First California Cavalry on August 24, 1861. Promoted to lieutenant colonel on November 1, 1861, he was chosen by Carleton to lead the advance guard of the California Column on a "forced reconnaissance" to the Rio Grande. Although Carleton pushed for Eyre's promotion and considered him "eminently fitted for the profession of arms," Eyre resigned on November 30, 1862. Carleton to Eyre, June 17, 1862, *OR*, 50(1):98; Carleton to Canby, Sept. 20, 1862, ibid., 101, 104; Orton, *California Men*, 87.

33. Four twelve-pounder mountain howitzers accompanied Carleton's column. The two at the Pima Villages were under the command of 2nd Lt. Jeremiah Phelan, Company K, First California Infantry, while those at Fort Yuma were assigned to 2nd Lt. William A. Thompson, Company E, First California Infantry. Phelan's howitzers were packed on mules for use in mountainous and broken terrain, while Thompson's guns were mounted on prairie carriages and pulled by horses or mules. These lightweight guns could throw a twelve-pound ball, shell, case shot, or canister charge. *Ordnance Manual*, 20, 74; SO 57, May 8, 1862, Hdqrs. Dist. of Southern Calif., *OR*, 50(1):1058; Julius Hall, "Wild West."

34. Col. George Washington Bowie enlisted in the Fifth California Infantry on September 12, 1861. Some of his companies accompanied the California Column, others followed in 1863 and 1864, while still others remained in California throughout the war. Bowie himself was a Mexican War veteran and well liked by the men. He was honorably discharged at Franklin, Texas, on December 14, 1864. Hand Diary, Sept. 30, 1862; Heitman, *Historical Register*, 1:234.

35. Crenellated: loopholed. Scott, *Military Dictionary*, 212.

THEIR DEMORALIZATION

The enemy are evidently much demoralized, judging from the tone of the prisoners captured in the affair that cost Lieutenant Barrett, 1st Cavalry, his life. They appear to have no confidence in each other, and complain bitterly about being betrayed by the very men who first induced them to join the ranks of secessiondom. As a general rule, the Texans scout [scoff] at the rigid discipline and regular movements trained soldiery, depending mainly on the guerrilla mode of warfare they have been accustomed to in their conflicts with Mexicans and Indians; but there are not lacking those among them who feel and appreciate the vast inferiority of undisciplined troops, however brave personally, when arrayed against those which are disciplined, and such men have great fear for the result to their faction.

The conversation and remarks of the prisoners lead one to infer that many of the Secessionists of New Mexico have taken up arms against the Union, not from any feelings or convictions of their own, but through the pleadings and intercession of others, who wielded some influence, and the fear of a clan of desperadoes who have fled into this territory to escape well-merited punishment, and who have nothing to lose but a worthless life, and as much to gain from anarchy, war, and its concomitants. It is easy to comprehend that no great moral principle can exist and bind together over such a miserable brigandage or ill-assorted crew, their only tie being the hope of plunder and unbounded license. I have not been a good deal in New Mexico, and particularly in that portion known as Arizona, and "speak the words of soberness and truth," acquired by personal observation of its white inhabitants. Of course, there are numbers of honorable exceptions; but one has to go far and search closely to find them.

THE BARRETT AFFAIR

It is current among the officers of this command that the untimely death of poor Barrett, of Company A, 1st Cavalry, was caused by a total misapprehension of orders by Capt. Calloway, 1st Infantry. It seems that Calloway was ordered to move rapidly and silently on Tucson, with his company of infantry, and Captains McCleave's and Pickon's [Pishon's][36] companies of the 1st Cavalry, to occupy Tucson and retake Capt. McCleave and some ten of his men, who had been surprised or surrounded and captured by the enemy while on a scout. Calloway succeeded in reaching the Pimos so

36. Nathaniel J. Pishon served as an enlisted man in the First U.S. Dragoons for twenty years, including active duty in Arizona, prior to the Civil War. Carleton saw that he received a commission as captain of Company D, First California Cavalry, on February 24, 1862, succeeding William Singer. Pishon mustered out with his company on November 23, 1864, at Fort Whipple, Arizona Territory. Orton, *California Men*, 72–73, 117; Carleton to McCleave, March 15, 1862, OR 50(1): 931.

successfully that these wary Indians were ignorant of his approach until he was really among their villages.

At that place he received information of a scouting party of the enemy, or a picket guard of 16 men, and he detached Barrett and 12 men to attack them, whereas his orders were to send Barrett to get between them and Tucson, so as to intercept their retreat, then advance upon them, surround and make them all prisoners. The result was that Barrett charged as soon he saw them, when they abandoned their horses and fled to a chaparral, where they made a stand. Barrett pursued on horseback, very unwisely, and was shot, together with two others, at the first fire. Our brave men, however, rushed in, wounded three, and took three prisoners; the rest escaped to Tucson and gave notice of Calloway's approach, upon which Capt. McCleave and his men were immediately forwarded to Mesilla, over 300 miles distant.

Calloway, instead of making a forced march on Tucson, then only forty-five miles distant, and arriving there, with his two cavalry companies, as soon as the runaways, or, at least, soon enough to rescue McCleave and hold Tucson, deliberately fell back to the Pimos, (45 miles) and abandoned the expedition, to leave which he had advanced 240 miles beyond Fort Yuma. The above account is derived from the conversation of the officers in this command, and is probably true, although I do not vouch for its entire correctness. Captain Calloway has the reputation of being an excellent gentle-men—but more is required to make an efficient officer. I learn that he has been placed under arrest.

THE GILA RIVER

As you know, the Gila is the southernmost tributary of the Colorado, joining that river at Fort Yuma, or rather half a mile above. It is between 450 and 500 miles in length, flowing, for the most part, through a sandy, wild and broken country, with iso-lated mountain peaks and small ranges scattered here and there over its surface, and composed mainly of granite rock, friable and easily disintegrated. The bed of the Gila is sandy, quicksand abounding, and during the dry season it is dry for much of its course, although just at this time it contains a great abundance of water; at this place, Antelope Peak, it is 150 yards wide, with an average depth of four or five feet.

Forty miles beyond this point the traveler arrives at Grinnell's rancho,[37] which is cultivated. Grinnell is the man who distinguished himself by procuring the release of

37. Grinnell's Station, or Texas Hill, was named for the first stage-station keeper there, Henry Grinnell. It was located about seventy miles east of Fort Yuma. The first armed con-frontation between the Californians and the Confederates occurred nearby. On March 29 or 30, 1862, two pickets were driven in, one (Pvt. William Semmilrogge) received a flesh wound through his right shoulder. Conkling and Conkling, *Butterfield Overland Mail*, 2:183; *Sacramento Union*, May 23, 1862; Hayden Arizona Pioneer Biography Files, Arizona State University Library Tempe.

the Oatman girl.[38] His loyalty is regarded as somewhat uncertain, and the prisoners captured in the Barrett affair openly brand him as being a "secesh" at bottom, at the same time they affirm that he is not to be trusted by either side. After leaving Grinnell's, the traveler continues along the river until he arrives at Gila Bend,[39] where he leaves it to the left, and does not see it again until he arrives at the Pimos, forty-five miles further on, when he again leaves it for the last time, on his road into Arizona.

FUTURE MOVEMENTS

We learn here that Gen. Heintzelman,[40] at the head of a considerable force, is about to enter New Mexico from Independence, Mo., and if so, it is not at all probably that the rebels can raise anything like men enough in that territory to resist the attacks of Heintzelman and Carleton, either of whose forces, aided by the Union men in the Territory, would prove more than a match for them. Should there be such a movement on the tapis it is certain that our troops will not be allowed to remain inactive, but will be pushed vigorously forward to create a diversion either in Arkansas or Texas. But this is more speculation which time and circumstances will determine.

THE REBELS AND PESQUEIRA

I have been reliably informed that Col. Reilly [Reily],[41] of the rebel forces, has made an ineffectual attempt to enlist the aid and sympathy of Pesqueira, Governor of

38. Olive Oatman was rescued from the Mojave Indians by a Quechan man named Francisco and Henry Grinnell in 1856. Grinnell had been a carpenter at Fort Yuma since 1851. In that year the Mormon emigrant family of Roys Oatman, bound for Yuma, was surprised by a band of Yavapais or possibly Tonto Apaches some eighty miles west of the Pima Villages. Oatman, his wife, daughter Lucy (eighteen), son Roys Jr. (five), daughter Charity and infant son Roland were killed. Their son Lorenzo (fifteen) was left for dead. Olive (thirteen) and her sister, Mary Ann (eight), were taken captive and later traded to the Mojaves. Mary Ann died in captivity, but Olive was rescued with Grinnell's help after he heard the story of the massacre from Lorenzo, who had survived the ordeal and never lost hope of recovering his sisters. Stratton, *Life among the Indians*. See also Conkling and Conkling, *Butterfield Overland Mail*, 2:178–80, 183; and McGinty, *Oatman Massacre*.

39. Gila Bend, so-called because of the big turn to the north the river makes at this point, is located midway between Fort Yuma and Tucson. The stage station at the east end of the bend, where the town of Gila Bend is today, was known as Gila Ranch station. Conkling and Conkling, *Butterfield Overland Mail*, 2:364.

40. Samuel Peter Heintzelman had served in Arizona during the 1850s. He was appointed brigadier general of volunteers on May 17, 1861. A West Point graduate (1826) and career officer, Heintzelman spent the Civil War years with the Army of the Potomac in the eastern theater. In May 1862 he was busy capturing Alexandria, Virginia, and was not involved in any attempt to retake New Mexico. He retired a major general in 1869. Boatner, *Civil War Dictionary*, 392; North, *Samuel Peter Heintzelman*.

41. James Reily was commissioned colonel of the Fourth Regiment Texas Mounted Volunteers on August 20, 1861, and selected by Sibley as special agent to the Mexican states of Chihuahua and Sonora. He accompanied Sherod Hunter's company to Tucson in February 1862

Sonora.[42] He went to Ures,[43] the capital, and made the three following propositions: 1st. That Pesqueira should throw off his allegiance to the Mexican Government, or in other words, secede, and join the Southern Confederacy as an independent State. 2d. That Pesqueira should furnish supplies from Sonora, for the use of the rebel troops along the southern border of New Mexico. And 3d. That he should allow the rebels to land a force at the mouth of the Colorado River. All of which were most respectfully, but absolutely refused.

When a man thinks all other persons fools but himself, it is a pretty clear evidence that his own brain is softening. Such seems to be the mental condition of Col. Reilly, who evidently thought that the presence of the Allied powers in Mexico would induce Pesqueira to desert his country and wed himself to the now asphyxiated Southern Confederacy. But Pesqueira knows full well that the Confederacy is in its last throes, and any affiliation with it would at once prove his overthrow from California. It is boldly asserted by Sonorians of weight and standing that the ill-fated Crabb expeditions[44] was but the forerunner and intimate connection of our present rebellion, and that Pesqueira invited Crabb into Sonora with the view of actually joining the Confederate States when the rebellion should break out; and placing Guaymas in their hands as a naval station in the Pacific, besides furnishing all the resources of Sonora

---

and soon left for Mexico with a twenty-man escort under Lt. James H. Tevis. Reily was supposed to learn of any Federal troop activity south of the border, seek permission to purchase supplies, and reach an agreement allowing Confederate troops to cross the border when in pursuit of hostile Indians. He was also directed to secure shipping rights at Guaymas. Greeted cordially, but cautiously, by the Mexican governors, Reily was only able to obtain permission for Confederate agents to purchase supplies. Finch, "Sherod Hunter," 173; Hall and Long, *Army of New Mexico,* 51–53.

42. Ygnacio Pesqueira (1828–86) became the governor of Sonora after deposing Manuel Gándara in 1856. In 1865 he arrived at Fort Mason, Arizona, seeking refuge from French troops in Mexico; Col. C. W. Lewis, Seventh California Infantry, granted him asylum. The governor established his residence at Tubac for several months until it was safe to return to Sonora. Altshuler, *Latest from Arizona,* 272; Robert Forbes, *Crabb's Filibustering Expedition,* 13.

43. Ures, the capital of Sonora, was situated in the Sonora River valley forty-seven miles "by the post road" from Hermosillo. It was an agricultural center of about 3,500 people. In 1860 it was observed that the town was "poorly built, and, for a capital city, is singularly destitute of public buildings." Stone, *State of Sonora,* 9–10.

44. In the spring of 1857, Henry Alexander Crabb, a California lawyer and politician, embarked on a Sonoran filibuster with a motley company of ninety men. Crabb had married into the prominent Aiensa family of Sonora, and in 1856 he made an agreement to help Ignacio Pesqueira defeat rival Manuel Gándara in return for land concessions along the U.S. border. A second wing of Crabb's expedition was supposed to land at Guaymas and effect a rendezvous at Altar. The sea wing never arrived, however, and Pesqueira turned against the filibusters after defeating Gándara before the Americans arrived. All of Crabb's men, save one, were slain at Caborca. For details see Robert Forbes, *Crabb's Filibustering Expedition.*

to be used in subjugating California—his return for all this being the perpetual Governorship of Sonora and an immense bounty.

Unfortunately for this fine scheme, the populace of Sonora either did not understand or did not relish the idea, and Pesqueira found himself in a most delicate fix. He either would be driven from Sonora with ignominy, and perhaps lose his life, or he must victimize Crabb—and so chose the latter; hence the massacre at Cavorca;[45] and so fearful was Pesqueira lest a single American should escape to betray his agency in the matter, that he secretly gave orders for the execution of every soul connected with the expedition.

But a little while ago the rebels boastingly sought, nay, even demanded, the alliance of England and France; but now they humbly beseech that of Sonora, and are refused. "Now are the mighty fallen!" The idea of purchasing supplies in Sonora for Confederate shinplasters,[46] is so absurd, that one wonders at Col. Reilly's hardihood in making propositions; while that of landing a force at the mouth of the Colorado, where it could be immolated in less than three weeks by any number of troops from San Francisco, apart from the fact that the concession by Pesqueira would of itself be a declaration of war, go to show that Col. Reilly is at least no diplomat.

VIDETTE

ALTA, JUNE 7, 1862

Letter from Our Army Correspondent
Antelope Peak New Mexico, May 16, 1862

EDITORS ALTA: The news received here, in this almost terra incognita,[47] relative to the capture of New Orleans, has been accepted with exceedingly great joy. A national salute[48] was fired from Lieutenant Shinn's battery, and other evidences of satisfaction displayed by the ardent soldiery, and their no less ardent officers. A rumor reached me, two days ago, that the enemy was evacuating Tucson, and hastening toward the Texan

45. Caborca was several miles south of Altar, Sonora, in the Asuncion Valley. Crabb's filibusters were ambushed just north of the town. Outnumbered, they took refuge in an adobe house in the town and were besieged for six days. They finally surrendered after being guaranteed safe passage to the border. The next day all but sixteen-year-old Charles Evans were executed, their bodies left for the hogs. Ibid., 17, 29.

46. "Shinplaster" commonly referred to paper money of a denomination less than one dollar. During this period any paper money of little value, especially Confederate, was awarded this sobriquet.

47. Terra incognita (Latin): an unknown or unexplored land, region, or subject.

48. The national salute was determined by the number of states in the Union (including the disaffected Southern states), one gun fired for each. *Revised U.S. Army Regulations of 1861*, 42.

frontier. This is probably correct, as your telegraphic reports announce the retreat of Sibley before the combined forces of Slough[49] and Canby,[50] and neither Baylor,[51] the horse thief, nor Reilly, the unfortunate diplomat, would relish being caught between Canby's forces and those of Gen. Carleton. Still, it may be a ruse to lull us into indiscreet carelessness; but time will tell, and *nous verrons*.[52] Under any circumstances, the presence of our force in New Mexico, and its advance upon Texas or Arkansas, cannot fail to produce a desirable diversion in our favor, by compelling the troops of those States to return home and defend their own soil.

Lieutenant W. G. Morris, of Company I, 2d Cavalry California Volunteers, has been promoted, and is now a Captain in the Sixth Regiment Cavalry, U.S.A. So much

49. John P. Slough (1829–67) was appointed captain in the First Colorado Volunteer Infantry on June 24, 1861. He was soon promoted to colonel and led the Coloradans in the victory over Sibley's Texans at Glorieta Pass, New Mexico, forcing the Rebels to retreat to Texas. A man of fiery temperament, Slough had been dismissed from the Ohio legislature years earlier for striking a fellow member. Although his advance at Glorieta was contrary to Canby's orders, Slough received a brigadier general's star and served out the rest of the war in the eastern theater. He became chief justice of the New Mexico Supreme Court after the war. Slough was killed in a gunfight on December 17, 1867, by W. L. Rynerson, who had come to New Mexico with the California Column. Keleher, *Turmoil in New Mexico*, 204 n. 43. See also Roberts, *Death Comes for the Chief Justice.*

50. Edward Richard Sprigg Canby (1817–72) was a major in the Tenth U.S. Infantry at Fort Defiance, New Mexico Territory, when the Civil War began. He was soon promoted to colonel as commander of the Department of New Mexico. Although he immediately undertook the consolidation of troops in the department, the resignations of Southern officers and desertions among the ranks hampered his administration. John Baylor's incredible capture of regular troops retreating from Fort Fillmore further crippled Canby's defensive efforts. On February 21–22 Sibley's brigade defeated his forces at Val Verde, but Canby maintained control of his troops, forcing Sibley to sidestep and continue northward. He correctly predicted that Sibley's downfall would be a result of an inability to supply an invading army in sparsely populated New Mexico. After the Confederate defeat at Glorieta and their hasty retreat to Texas, Canby was replaced by Carleton and ordered to Washington. He commanded the troops in New York City during the draft riots of 1863 and, later, the Division of West Mississippi. Canby received the surrender of the last Confederate armies in the field, under Gens. Richard Taylor and Edmund Kirby Smith. After the war he commanded the Department of the Columbia. He was murdered during a peace conference with Modoc Indian leaders in northern California on April 10, 1872. Keleher, *Turmoil in New Mexico*, 194–95; Heitman, *Historical Register,* 1:279.

51. John Robert Baylor (1822–94) was elected lieutenant colonel of the Second Texas Mounted Rifles and mustered into the Confederate service on May 23, 1861. He led three hundred men up the Rio Grande in June 1861 and captured Fort Fillmore, New Mexico, on July 27. Proclaiming himself governor of Arizona in August (later confirmed in Richmond), Baylor was promoted colonel on December 15, 1861. His commission was later revoked because of his Indian extermination policy. He served as a private during the Galveston campaign of 1863 and was later elected to the Confederate Congress. Baylor advocated for the reinvasion of Arizona and was actually commissioned to raise troops for that purpose only days before Lee's surrender in April 1865. Boatner, *Civil War Dictionary,* 52; Baylor, *John Robert Baylor;* Hall and Long, *Army of New Mexico,* 299.

52. *Nous verrons* (French): we shall see.

for having friends at home to look after one's interests. Captain Morris had been detailed by Gen. Carleton to take charge of military couriers or videttes, established between Fort Yuma and Los Angeles, but since his promotion, St. [Lieutenant] James P. Bennett,[53] of Capt. Cremony's Company B, Second Cavalry, California Volunteers, has been assigned to that responsible duty, and from my knowledge of this officer I am persuaded that the duty will be well done. He leaves us this afternoon at 5 o'clock, and will at once enter upon the discharge of his duties. Everybody is satisfied at the richly-merited promotion of our commander, who has been untiring in his efforts, and whose capacity is beyond all question. If all our military appointment and promotions tallied with this, it would be well for the country. Carleton's promotion has been fairly earned, and not obtained by political preference or intrigue, and it is gratifying to know that pure merit is not altogether overlooked.

Our detachment, consisting of Lieut. Shin[n]'s Battery, U.S.A., two companies of the First Infantry, (Captain Willis[54] and Roberts,[55]), and Capt. Ford's,[56] of the Fifth, together with Capt. Cremony's company of the Second Cavalry, will probably proceed on their winding way by the 19th or 20th inst., to form a junction at the Pimos with the forces under Lieut. Col. West (probably now Colonel) of the First Infantry. The retreat of Sibley would appear to visably diminish our chances for a fair stand up fight with the enemy; but it cannot be denied that we have traveled far to find one, and shall have traveled a great deal farther before we again behold the "Queen City of the West."[57] The hardships endured on a march like ours, over vast and consecutive deserts, under broiling sun and amidst withering, blighting sand storms, will compare with anything suffered

53. James P. Bennett enlisted as a private in Company B, Second California Cavalry on September 14, 1861. He was promoted to second lieutenant and placed in charge of vedettes carrying the mail between Fort Yuma and Los Angeles. He resigned at Fort Sumter, New Mexico, on May 29, 1863. Orton, *California Men,* 209; *San Francisco Call,* June 4, 1862.

54. Edward Banker Willis (1831–79) enlisted as a first lieutenant in Company A, First California Infantry on August 15, 1861. He was promoted to captain on September 5 and led Company A across Arizona to the Rio Grande. Promoted to major on May 5, 1863, Willis mustered out of the California Volunteers at Santa Fe on September 5, 1864; he was appointed major in the First New Mexico Infantry the following day. Promoted lieutenant colonel on February 3, 1865, he was honorably discharged on October 1, 1866. "Edward Banker Willis," Hayden Arizona Pioneer Biography Files, Arizona Historical Society; Orton, *California Men,* 335–36.

55. Thomas L. Roberts was enrolled as captain of Company E, First California Infantry at the Presidio in San Francisco on August 26, 1861. He was mustered out at Los Pinos, New Mexico, on September 13, 1864, upon the expiration of his term of service. Orton, *California Men,* 354.

56. Silas P. Ford raised Company E, Fifth California Infantry in Sacramento, California, and became its captain in October 1861. He resigned his commission on November 11, 1862, and was succeeded by Benjamin F. Harrover as company commander. Orton, *California Men,* 673, 694, 703.

57. Although Cincinnati, Ohio, was referred to as the Queen City of the West as early as 1835, this reference must be to San Francisco, which has been called the Queen City of the Pacific. Mathews, *Dictionary of Americanisms,* 1341.

by our brethren at the East, where every convenience exists, towns and villages abound, and railroads and steamers perform much of the labor of traveling. Although on the march, the duties of camp life are rigidly performed. The regular guard mountings, fatigue and drill calls responded to; even parades &c., all gone through with the same as if in a permanent camp, if the troops only halt for a single day.

Dr. David Wooster and his amiable lady are with this command, the doctor having been ordered to the front.[58] He understood, as did Mrs. Wooster, that he was to be permanently located at Fort Yuma, and it was because of this understanding that the lady came so far; but on arriving at the Fort he found his destination to be further forward, and as she could not return over the deserts alone and unprotected, she was fain to come on also.

There are two or three kinds of fish caught in this portion of the Gila River, the finest being a species of pike, weighing from four to ten pounds each; but they are by no means plentiful. Yesterday, I caught a noble fellow of six pounds weight, and presented him to Mrs. Wooster, who has a charming little child with her, aged about two years. Fresh fish is quite a treat in these regions of sand and rock.

I shall avail myself of every opportunity to let you know all that transpires and I believe to be true, but cannot venture upon surmises which have little or no foundation.

VIDETTE

ALTA, JUNE 8, 1862

Letter from Our Army Correspondent
Progress of the Column from California—Probable Occupation of Tucson
—Attacks upon General Carleton—Intense Heat—The Roads—Rivers—
Rattlesnakes—Hard Marches—Soldiers' Idea of Luxury, Etc., Etc.
Grinnell's Station, May 21, 1862

EDITORS ALTA:—Since my last, dated from Antelope Peak, we have advanced forty-five miles further on our way, and are now a little over one hundred miles distant from the Pimo villages, and about 195 from Tucson, the first village of any consequence in New Mexico, on the southern route from California. We have already marched or progressed nearly eight hundred miles from San Francisco, in search of a

58. A graduate of Western Reserve class of 1849, Dr. David Wooster was enrolled as surgeon of the Fifth California Infantry at Camp Union, California, on September 28, 1861. Wooster, his wife, and child accompanied the California Column on the Arizona campaign, but by October 1862 he had returned to Fort Yuma; his family had been escorted back the month before. He resigned on March 10, 1863. Orton, *California Men,* 676; Quebbeman, *Medicine in Territorial Arizona,* 49, 381.

conflict with the rebels, and chances now are that we shall be obliged to go much farther before they can be met with in organized bodies of any considerable force. Concentrated at this point, and under marching orders, are the infantry companies of
Captains Roberts, Willis and Parvine[59] of the 1st, and Ford of the 5th, part of Lieut.
Shinn's Battery, U.S.A., part of Capt. Shirland's Company,[60] 1st Cavalry, and part of
Capt. Cremony's Company, Second Cavalry, and other part serving as body guard or
escort to Gen. Carleton, who has gone forward to the Pimos, and will probably reach
the villages by the 23d inst. Lieut. Col. West has been ordered forward with the force
concentrated at the Pimos, and, no doubt, entered Tucson several days ago. Information from that point is to the effect that the "secesh" have followed the rule laid down
for them by [Gideon] Pillow,[61] of Camargo [Mexico] celebrity, and others of their
leaders, and "absquatulated" from Tucson without gratifying our soldiers even with a
sight of their coat tails. This report being pretty well founded, Col. West will meet
with no opposition at that place, and will advance straightforward to Fort Buchanan.[62]
Capt. Calloway's disobedience of orders has proved a serious impediment to our
advance, as it is asserted by persons direct from Tucson that at the time he fell back
upon the Pimo villages, with a command of three hundred men, there were not more
than thirty rebels at that place, which might easily have been surprised, and Capt.
McCleave, of the First Cavalry, rescued from his captors. This is positively asserted
by McCleave's men, who were taken prisoners with him, but have lately been released
by the rebels because they had no more subsistence to give. Two of these men have
rejoined their company at the Pimos, and seven others are reported to have remained

59. Washington L. Parvin enrolled at San Francisco on August 16, 1861, and commissioned
as captain, Company F, First California Volunteer Infantry. His resignation dates November 26,
1862. Orton, *California Men*, 359.

60. Edmond D. Shirland enrolled at Camp Merchant, California, on August 16, 1861, and
was commissioned captain, Company C, First California Cavalry. Under Shirland's command
this company raised the U.S. flag over Fort Davis, Texas, and later was responsible for capturing
the famous Mimbres Apache chief Mangas Coloradas. Shirland's resignation took effect on
October 21, 1863. *OR*, 1(2):11, 296; Orton, *California Men*, 108.

61. Gideon J. Pillow (1806–78) was an influential Democratic politician and lawyer before
and after the Mexican War. He served as a brigadier general of volunteers at Camargo, Mexico, infamously known by his men as a disease-ridden deathtrap. Although initially opposed to
the secessionist movement, he accepted a Confederate commission as brigadier general. At
Fort Donelson, Tennessee, in February 1862, Pillow turned his command over to a junior officer and then made good his escape as U. S. Grant's Union forces attacked and captured the
place. Reprimanded for his cowardly conduct, Pillow never received another command. *Webster's American Military Biographies*, 324.

62. Fort Buchanan was established by the First U.S. Dragoons on November 17, 1856. Originally called Camp Moore, it was renamed in May 1857 in honor of Pres. James Buchanan.
Located along Sonoita Creek some twenty-five miles east of Tubac, the post was ordered
destroyed when the garrison of regular troops under Isaiah N. Moore departed on July 23,
1861. Brandes, *Frontier Military Posts*, 21; Prucha, *Military Posts*, 62.

at Tucson; Capt. McCleave and a man named White,[63] who had a mill at the Pimos and had sold us supplies, were carried off to Mesilla, and will, undoubtedly, be retained by the enemy until exchanged.

ATTACKS ON GEN. CARLETON

A very large number of the officers attached to this command—indeed all with whom I have spoken without an exception, express themselves deeply pained and insulted at the malicious attack of some writer or writers, who have singled out Gen. Carleton as the present special object of their venom, accusing him of disloyalty and treason, and even going so far as to intimate a comparison between Carleton and that wretched Judas, Gen. Twiggs.[64] It is certainly not my province to defend Gen. Carleton, whose untiring zeal for the service of his country, and whose military skill have been so eminently displayed in organizing this expedition, arranging and carrying out its movements and marching so large a body of men over a vast stretch of country, heretofore held impracticable for a greater number than 100 or 150 at a time; foreseeing and providing for all contingencies, amassing and stationing stores of provisions and other necessities, and giving so great personal attention, night and day, to perfect all its appointment; but, it is my province to defend myself and my associates in this expedition for the covert slander, and implied charges of the writers alluded to. Were the statements reliable, the unavoidable inference would be, that all the officers and men of this command were either fools or traitors; either unsuspecting sheep that were being led to the slaughter with their eyes wide open, or traitors dyed in the wool, for it must be evident to even men of feeble comprehension, that no villainy, such as is charged against Gen. Carleton, could have been perpetrated by him without the knowledge of officers in his command, through whom, and by whose direct agency all of his orders are and were executed. Now, as almost every officer in this region, has been more or less employed by Carleton in this way, and as they are all particularly well informed about matters and men in the Southern District [District of Southern California], it follows that either they have willingly lent themselves to Carleton's

63. Ammi M. White had owned the trading post at Casa Blanca since 1860 or 1861 and had erected the first flour mill in the territory. He was arrested by the Rebels but was later released. Appointed agent for the Pimas in 1864, White finally left Arizona in 1867. J. Ross Browne describes him as "quaint . . . long, lank, and leathery, . . . slow of speech he may be, and prejudiced against the luxuries of civilization." *Adventures*, 29.

64. David E. Twiggs (1790–1862) served as a regular-army officer during the War of 1812, the Black Hawk War, and the Mexican War. Twiggs distinguished himself and emerged from the latter conflict as a brevet major general and military governor of Vera Cruz. He commanded the Department of the West until 1857 and then the Department of Texas. Twiggs surrendered his entire command to the Confederates on February 16, 1861, and accepted a commission as a major general in their service. *Webster's American Military Biographies*, 444.

alleged turpitude and treason, and are equally guilty with himself, or that they are natural fools, if the charges against the General be well based. To suppose either of these
positions, would be to suppose the grossest absurdity, and the conclusion is, that the
charges are slanderous and fearfully unjust to one of the most loyal men and best officers in the army. They are evidently the bilious excretions of persons who have failed
to secure any contracts, and they failed simply because their excess Union sentiment
and loyalty led them to tack on a corresponding excess in the prices they asked for
their chattels. I have no doubt that some parties of doubtful loyalty are interested in
one or two Government contracts; but they did not appear so openly and their goods
were better and cheaper than those of others, while the security for the faithful per-
formance of those contracts was ample and unexceptionable. The hue and cry set up
against the General, on the ground of associating in the Southern District only with
men and women of secession proclivities, is quite unfounded. The fact is simply, that
society is extremely limited in and about Los Angeles, and nearly all that can be had is
more or less tinctured with disloyalty, so that if an officer goes into society at all he
must expect to meet those who are opposed to his principles. Dr. Griffin,[65] as you
may know, was for many years a surgeon of the U.S. Army, and for a long time the
family physician and probable friend of General, then Captain, Carleton; and it is
very likely that a mutual regard exists between them and their families to this day. But,
Dr. Griffin is also the brother-in-law of the late Gen. Albert Sidney Johnston,[66]
whose family still remains in Los Angeles under his care, and the Doctor himself is a
secessionist; hence, in the opinion of the illiberal and bigoted, it is a high crime and

65. Dr. John Strother Griffin was born in Virginia and graduated from the University of
Pennsylvania's medical school. He was appointed assistant surgeon on June 18, 1840, and
served in the army until his resignation on June 14, 1854. His sister married Albert Sidney
Johnston, and the doctor's Southern sympathies were well known, though he remained a
highly respected member of the Los Angeles community. Griffin died on August 23, 1911.
Heitman, *Historical Register*, 1:478. Carleton was very upset by the allegations made against himself by witch-hunting California loyalists. When he heard that a petition had been sent to the
secretary of war requesting his removal from command for showing "undue favors to secessionists," he wrote to Maj. R. C. Drum, the assistant adjutant general, requesting help in clearing his name. Carleton felt that "a man can do his duty and be true to his colors, and not
proclaim it from house tops or from the corners of the streets." *OR*, 50(1):1066.
66. Albert Sidney Johnston (1803–62) graduated from West Point in 1826 and served in the
Black Hawk War. He led volunteer troops during the Texas Revolution and commanded the
First Texas Rifles during the Mexican War. Johnston rejoined the regular army in 1849. He was
colonel of the Second U.S. Cavalry by 1855 and in 1857 led a successful—and bloodless—campaign against the Mormons in Utah. Johnston commanded the Department of the Pacific but
resigned his commission when Texas seceded in April 1861. He successfully made his way east
with other Southern sympathizers and was appointed the second-ranking general in the Confederate States Army. Johnston was killed during the first day of the battle of Shiloh, Tennessee. *Webster's American Military Biographies*, 203–4.

misdemeanor on the part of Gen. Carleton to employ the services of his friend and physician, Dr. Griffin, for his sick wife and child or himself; he must neither visit nor be visited by him; must violently sunder all personal and private relationships, and give him the absolute go-by or be deemed a downright and unconditional traitor; an Arnold, a Twiggs, the vilest of wretches whose object is to lead into captivity or to the slaughter some two thousand of his fellow citizens. Certes! I envy not the thing in human form who possesses a heart so profoundly dead to all kindly sentiment as must be his who would so act. Do our officers who are making a glorious advance southward abjure all society because they can find only that which is composed of disloyal persons? And are they traitors because they avail themselves of the opportunities which may offer to enjoy the companionship of well bred ladies and gentlemen, although nationally their opponents? Certainly not; and how much less when the association is with old and well tried friends! But enough of this. Gen. Carleton needs no defender; his acts speak for themselves, and they are such as will shine brighter the closer they are scrutinized.

THE WEATHER—ROADS, RIVERS, &C, &C

The weather is decidedly Plutonian, the thermometer (one of the Smithsonian standard) marking 119° in the shade. When I say "shade," I mean inside of a brush house, perfectly sheltered from the sun by green boughs, and all sides open to the air. I do not know what you good people of San Francisco may think, but marching through such fearful heat for six or seven consecutive hours is no child's play. This is bad enough in all conscience, yet it is only a trifle by itself, for the roads are covered with a fine, almost impalpable alkaline dust, of light brown color, to the depth of six inches; and at every step it rises in immense and blinding clouds two or three hundred feet above our heads, completely hiding all things from sight—filling the eyes, ears and nose, getting into the mouth and choking the traveler, penetrating the clothing and fastening upon the person in the shape of a thin, sticky plaster, which is terribly irritating and uncomfortable. The infantry have it hard enough, but the cavalry, when dismounted, suffer a great deal more, as they are compelled to pack a carbine, a saber and a heavy Colt's dragoon pistol (which alone weighs four pounds and three-quarters,) besides ammunition for the two sorts of firearms, and the additional care of their horses. Capt. Cremony makes his men walk about half the time, he dismounting and mounting when they do, and marching at the head of his column.

We are supplied with canteens, which hold about a quart and a half each, but we generally empty these in the first six or eight miles of a march, and the remainder of it sometimes sixteen or eighteen more, has to be made without a drop of water, our tongues hanging out, and thickly covered with this infernal dust, and our bodies encrusted with it and perspiration. If we never have the fortune to meet the enemy, we shall at least have deserved well at the hands of our fellow loyal citizens, for verily our march is full of severe trials and privations.

The Gila River is falling rapidly, the waters having subsided some three feet since we crossed the Colorado, while those of that river have risen nearly six feet, caused by the melting of the snow in the mountains, at or near its source. Nearly the whole of this country, so far, is a barren and worthless waste, perfectly incapable of cultivation, and inhabited principally by millions of rattlesnakes, scorpions, centipedes, and similar pests. On two occasions, recently, soldiers have found their blankets occupied by rattlesnakes, and yesterday a corporal of Captain Ford's company had the pleasure of finding one in his boot, just as he was about to haul it on. Agreeable this, and certainly piquant!

"We know not the value of a friend until we lose him" is an old proverb, and there never was a truer—so we know not how to prize little comforts we may possess at home until we find ourselves where there are none. I can imagine the intense luxury of a crystal vase, (half gallon size,) filled with the right royal "sherry cobbler," having a glittering prism of ice in its centre, crowned with fragrant strawberries and golden hued orange, the whole suspended above one's head, in some cool spot, with a sparkling fountain, while the beatified recipient reclines at length in a hammock, or on a lounge, and with a long curved macaroni conveys the grateful beverage from the vase to his glowing, eager lips. Add to this a choice Havanna, and a perfect absence of all annoying cares, *et voila de vrais plaisir.*[67]

ALTA, JUNE 11, 1862

Letter from Our Army Correspondent
Grinnel's Rancho, Gila River, New Mexico, May 20, 1862

EDITORS ALTA: The total absence of letter paper compels me take refuge in a blank book, whose pages I now inscribe, *seriatim,*[68] for the benefit of all who have any desire to know how the California column progresses on its hostile errand. The company to which I am attached[69] will probably resume its march by the 1st of June, having been delayed here for the arrival of transportation and forage; but as the expresses, up and down, have come in here to report to Captain Cremony, and be forwarded by

67. *Et voilá de vrais plaisir* (French): and that would be the life.
68. *Seriatim* (Latin): in a series; one after another.
69. Vidette was attached to Company B, Second California Cavalry. He may have been J. C. Cremony, the company commander.

him until his command moves forward, I manage to learn more or less of what is transpiring all along the line.

ARMY MOVEMENTS

Brigadier General Carleton is now at the Pimos, and will move to the head of the column without delay. Colonel West is in command of the advance, which has probably reached Fort Buchanan by this time, and perhaps engaged the enemy if he is to be met with this side of Texas. From 500 to 700 rebels are reported to be in the occupation of Mesilla, immediately across the Rio Grande from Doña Ana,[70] and it is possible that they will show fight, but West's command is fully able to cope with a still greater number, unless supplied with artillery. Capt. Shirland's Company C, 1st Cav., Cal. Vols., left this camp ground for the Pimos, on the 27th, and will reach its destination by the 31st. Co. F [D], 1st Infantry, Lieut. Martin,[71] commanding, and Lieut. Vestal[72] left here this morning for the same place. Major Ferguson,[73] with a detachment of Co. E., 1st Cav., C.V., has just arrived from below, the Fort Yuma side, en route for the Pimos, and will go on to-morrow morning. Major Rigg,[74] with another detachment of troops, infantry, is expected in a day or two; and Capt. Cremony's Company, B, 2d Cav., C.V., will proceed as soon as forage and transportation can be had, say in three days from this date. The chase through Missouri after Price[75] is nothing to that we are having after the rebel Texans in New Mexico.

70. Doña Ana, New Mexico, was a farming community five miles north of Las Cruces and fifteen miles west of the Organ Mountains. It became the county seat when Doña Ana County was created in 1852. Pearce, *New Mexico Place Names*, 48.

71. John Martin was mustered in as first lieutenant of Company D, First California Infantry at San Francisco on August 29, 1861. He was mustered out at Las Cruces, New Mexico, on August 31, 1864. Orton, *California Men*, 350.

72. Dewitt C. Vestal was enrolled as second lieutenant of Company D, First California Infantry on August 29, 1861. He resigned his commission on February 28, 1863. Orton, *California Men*, 350.

73. David Fergusson was commissioned as major of the First California Cavalry. He explored a supply route between the Sonora ports of Libertad and Lobos and served creditably as commander of the California troops at Tucson. Promoted colonel of the regiment on February 9, 1863, he was dismissed from the service per War Department SO 323 on November 6, 1863, for deserting his post to attend to personal matters in California. Orton, *California Men*, 87.

74. Edwin A. Rigg raised Company A, First California Volunteer Infantry in San Francisco and became its first captain on August 15, 1861. He was trusted by Carleton and advanced rapidly. Rigg was promoted to major on September 5, 1861, lieutenant colonel on April 28, 1862, and colonel of the First California Infantry on February 7, 1863. He was mustered out at Santa Fe, New Mexico, in September 1864 but soon received a commission as lieutenant colonel of the First California Veteran Infantry, the position he held when mustered out on October 13, 1866. Orton, *California Men*, 335–36, 385.

75. Sterling Price (1809–67) was a Missouri lawyer and legislator before the Mexican War. He had served as a brigadier general of volunteers in Kearny's Army of the West during that conflict. Price afterward served as governor of Missouri, which he later sought to secure for the

INDIAN RUMORS

Two of Capt. Cremony's men arrived here on the 26th direct from the Pimos, one hundred miles distant, having made the trip in 30 hours, and they report being "bounced" by a large body of Apache Indians (Gontos) [Tontos],[76] some 200 or 300 in number, who were lying in wait at the Maricopa Wells,[77] 12 miles this side of the Pimos. Some time ago these Apaches killed two Pimos,[78] and these latter, together with their allies, the Maricopas,[79] have taken the war path to revenge the death of their people, and it is probable that the Apaches, met by the express riders, were a war party intended to operate against the allied Indians. In all their conflicts the Pimos come off victorious; but in the matter of horse stealing and villany they are no match for the Apaches. It is possible that some of our messengers or even trains may be cut off by these savages, who are the veritable Ishmaelites of this country; but every precaution will be taken to guard against such an untoward event.

ENCOUNTER WITH AN APACHE

A solider named Carver,[80] a member of Company B, 2d Cavalry, California Volunteers, and attached to the body escort of Gen. Carleton, was ordered by him to ride off toward the river, and report the distance from the road to water; and was also instructed not to fire upon any Apache unless first attacked. Carver proceeded for

---

Confederacy throughout the Civil War. Although driven into Arkansas in February 1862 by Gens. John C. Frémont and Samuel R. Curtis, Price remained a significant figure in the struggle for the Trans-Mississippi West. After the war he attempted to establish a colony of Confederate veterans in Mexico. *Webster's American Military Biographies,* 333.

76. The Tonto Apaches, or Tontos, constituted the greater part of the Western Apaches, inhabiting the Tonto Basin and the Mogollon Rim country as far north as present-day Flagstaff, Arizona. Spicer, *Cycles of Conquest,* 244. "Bounced" was an expression of the time meaning "jumped."

77. Maricopa Wells was a stage station and Indian trading post located near the confluence of the Santa Cruz and Gila rivers some twenty-five miles south of present-day Phoenix. Barnes, "Arizona Place Names," 265.

78. The Pima Indians of the Gila and Salt river valleys were invariably referred to as "Pimos" during the 1860s. The word itself is a Spanish corruption of *pi-nyi-match* (Pima for "I don't know," the answer usually given a Spanish interrogator). Pimas called themselves "Ah-kee-mult-o-o-tom" (river people). They were inveterate enemies of the Apaches and early allies of white men. Dutton, *Indians of the American Southwest,* 209.

79. The Maricopas are a Yuman tribe living with and below the Pimas along the Gila River. They warred incessantly with the Yuman tribes of the lower Colorado River until an alliance with the Pimas resulted in the defeat of the Yumas (Quechans) in 1857. An act of Congress set aside a reservation for the Maricopas and Pimas in February 1859, though no formal treaty was ever made with the tribe. Swanton, *Indian Tribes,* 354, 356.

80. David Carver enlisted as a private in Company B, Second California Cavalry at San Francisco on September 14, 1861. He was mustered out on November 7, 1864. Orton, *California Men,* 212.

some miles in a northerly direction, and at last arrived at the river, taking the precaution to carry his six-shooter cocked in his right hand. Just as he reached the river, an Apache sprang from the bushes, gun in hand, and the muzzle directed full upon Carver, who, fortunately, saw him at the same moment, and brought his colt to bear upon the savage. The latter stood ready for a few seconds, Carver likewise, both with weapons levelled, and both, doubtless, anxious to fire; but the Indian seemed to think the odds too great, at the short distance between them, some twelve feet, and Carver had positive orders not to fire first. The savage, who was in full panoply of war paint, then dropped his muzzle and said, "How de do?" "How do you do?" replied Carver. "You Captain?" asked the Indian. "No," answered Carver; "Are you a Chief?" "No," growled the ring-streaked and spotted Apache, and without further parley he plunged into the river and swam across, bearing his gun up out of the water as he went. The temptation to shoot was a sore one for Carver, but he would not disobey his orders.

There is nothing of importance to communicate just now, but will soon have a batch of general items.

VIDETTE

ALTA, JUNE 29, 1862

Letter from the Column from California
Maricopa Wells, New Mexico, June 4

EDITORS ALTA: We reached this place yesterday morning, having made a march of eighty miles in forty-eight hours. The Maricopa Wells, as the camp ground is called, are located on an extensive alkaline plain, covered with short, horny, saltish grass, with a few mesquit trees here and there, just enough to furnish scanty shade from the scorching heat of mid-day. The nearest Maricopa village is about three miles distant, and is the first of the line of villages inhabited by the Maricopa and Pimo races, of whom I will give you a short sketch, premising that my authority is Juan José,[81] the "Second Chief" of the Maricopas, who is a bright and intelligent Indian, and speaks Spanish well.

---

81. The name Juan José was well known in Arizona during the Civil War as the Apache chief treacherously killed by American mountain men in the late 1830s. It is possible that there was a Maricopa chief by the same name or that the correspondent was confused. Captain Cremony noted in his book after the war that Juan José was a Maricopa chief "of some importance in former times." A Papago (Tohono O'odham [Desert People] is preferred today) chief who served the Californians as interpreter and guide went by the name of Captain José or José Victoriana Solarse. Browne, *Adventures*, 256–57; Cremony, *Life among the Apaches*, 90; Farish, *History of Arizona*, 3:162–63; Spicer, *Cycles of Conquest*, 244–45.

THE PIMO AND MARICOPA INDIANS

"A hundred years ago," the Yumas, Cocopas,[82] and Maricopas were all one people, inhabiting the country from the mouth of the Colorado to its junction with the Gila; but, on account of some serious difficulty, the branch or tribe now known as the Cocopas "seceshed" and set up on their own hook, occupying the region at the mouth of the Colorado. This division was effected peaceably, and with the consent of all parties. But the matter was altogether different when the Maricopa branch split off, for a most furious and never-ending war, waged with the bitterest hostility, was the immediate consequence. In the series of conflicts which ensued, the Maricopas were worsted and driven up the Gila year after year, until they reached the Pimos, who had been partly civilized by those irrepressible planters of civilization, the Jesuit fathers.

On arriving here, a treaty was made between the two tribes, which has been most faithfully kept to the present day. By the terms of this treaty, the Maricopas were allowed to settle on Pimo territory, provided they cultivated the land enough to insure the subsistence of their people, and the consequent safety of Pimo property. They furthermore bound themselves to assist the Pimos in their wars, and hold themselves responsible for the good conduct and faith of their people, with full liberty to preserve their own laws, customs, and habits, intermarry with the Pimos, and regulate their own internal policy. On concluding a peace after a war in which both nations have been engaged as allies, the terms are arranged by an equal number of Pimo and Maricopa chiefs, after whose decision, should there be a disagreement, a grand council is held by an equal number of delegates from each, and the matter in dispute left to them for final adjudication. The Yumas and Apaches are the inveterate enemies of these two peoples, but they never meet in open warfare without being worsted. Neverthless, the Apaches, who are really the Ishmaelites of this country, manage to harass and disturb them a great deal by frequent inroads, and no less frequent plunderings. The Jesuit Fathers who first visited the Pimos, and, as was their invariable custom, established a Mission among them,[83] taught them to cultivate the earth and depend mainly upon it for their subsistence; to spin and weave, and several other valuable arts, the benefits of which they are reaping to this day. They are honest and quite industrious, but are also

82. The Yumas (who today prefer their traditional name, Quechans) and the Cocopas are both Yuman speaking tribes of Hokan stock. The Cocopas traditionally dwelled near the mouth of the Colorado River, warring against and intermarrying with the Yumas at the confluence of the Gila and Colorado rivers. Both tribes were relatively peaceful after Maj. Samuel P. Heintzelman's war of attrition against them in the early 1850s. For more information on the Yumas, see Jack Forbes, *Warriors of the Colorado*.

83. Fr. Eusebio Kino began missionary work among the Pimas in 1687. Although a formal mission was not established along the lower Gila, the Jesuits established *visitas* and attempted to Christianize and "civilize" these people. Spicer, *Cycles of Conquest*, 118–19.

great beggars, and somewhat filthy in their persons. The Pimos retain considerable of the simpler forms of Christianity, but the Maricopas are Pagans. The former bury their dead with much ceremony, with great lamentation and feasting, very much like an old-fashioned Irish wake; but the Maricopas resort to incremation, and with very little pomp. The case is widely different, however, when they return from a successful expedition against their enemies, on which occasions the greatest rejoicings are had for several successive days. Although these two tribes have dwelt together for a hundred years or more, they seldom intermarry, and have to employ interpreters on all public occasions. The virtue of the Pimo women is beyond question, while that of the Maricopas is somewhat relax, although by no means so much so as that of the Yumas, and other Indian tribes. Adultery is punished by burning at the stake, it being a fundamental principle to keep Pimo blood as pure as possible. Their villages are compactly built for the distance of some thirteen or fifteen miles, alternating with each other, so that the traveler from California meets first with a Maricopa village on the right-hand side of the road, and then, about a mile further, with a Pimo village on the left-hand side, and so on, the last being Pimo. They have several thousand acres under cultivation, raising large quantities of wheat, corn, pears, melons, pumpkins, etc., etc., much of which they are now disposing of for the subsistence of the California column. The two tribes probably number seven thousand, and can, jointly, raise an effective force of from twelve to fifteen hundred warriors. Their weapons consist almost wholly of the bow and arrow, which they use with great dexterity, and a very few old and almost worthless escopetes.[84] The Pimos have several times applied to the Government for arms to "clear out" the rascally Apaches; but so far without success. I, however, learn that Gen. Carleton has taken a more comprehensive and practical view of the case, and ordered a couple of hundred muskets (old style altered to percussion locks,) to be furnished them.[85] The Apaches are, doubtless, the most accursed scourge that our California immigrants have to contend with, and hundreds of them have fallen victims to the perfidy of those merciless and blood-thirsty savages, while nothing but kindness and assistance have been met with from the Pimos and Maricopas. It is therefore eminently an act of justice as well as of sound policy, to give those people the means to effectually protect themselves and our way worn immigrants from the ceaseless assaults of the Apaches. On the arrival of General Carleton, the Chief of each tribe

84. An *escopeta* is a short Spanish musket with a firing mechanism similar to a flintlock. The weapons were obsolete by the 1860s.
85. On April 17, 1863, Lt. G. A. Burkett was ordered to distribute "100 stand of old arms, ammunition, &c ... to the Pima and Coca-Maricopa Indians." Burkett was also directed to take fifty-eight "old-pattern dragoon coats and jackets, and 415 pompons" for barter with these Indians. Fergusson to Burkett, Apr. 17, 1863, *OR*, 50(2):405.

placed himself at the head of an hundred mounted warriors, in full feather and paint, and gave him a regular military reception in the best style of their art. It was quite a novel and curious spectacle. In my next I will give you some of the religious traditions of these singular and interesting tribes, as well as a description of their marriage and funeral ceremonies, both of which I have had an opportunity of witnessing.

ARMY MOVEMENTS

The 1st Cavalry, with the exception of a small detachment from Capt. Shirland's company, have gone to Fort Stanford, formerly Fort Breckenridge.[86] They will remain at that Fort for a short time until their horses are perfectly recruited and restored to their original strength and flesh. What their future operations will be, it is now quite impossible to say. Colonel West, with a portion of his command, has pushed on to occupy Fort Buchanan, which is about 80 miles southeast from Tucson. Gen. Carleton is now in Tucson with the battery and six companies of Infantry. Companies A and E, Capts. Joseph Smith[87] and Ford, will occupy the Pimo Villages, where they are constructing a very respectable fort, under the superintendence and command of Major Coult.[88] Capt. Cremony's Company B, of the 2d Cavalry, is now at this place, awaiting further orders, and recruiting their horses. Several of the vidette stations between the Pimo Villages and Fort Yuma are garrisoned from this Company, while Gen. Carleton's body-guard, or escort, is also composed of its members. It may, and probably will be, sent into Sonora, for the purpose of making arrangements for the supply of forage and fresh provisions from that State, or, rather, acting as an escort to the Quarter Master who may be sent on such duty. Fort Yuma is garrisoned by several Companies

86. Fort Breckenridge was established at the confluence of Arivaypa Creek and the San Pedro River in May 1860. It was originally called Fort Arivaypa but was soon renamed for Vice Pres. John C. Breckinridge. The garrison of regular troops destroyed and abandoned the post on July 10, 1861. It was reestablished by California Volunteers on May 18, 1862, and renamed in honor of California's governor, Leland Stanford. In October 1863 the name was changed back to Fort Breckenridge, the incorrect spelling presumably preferred because Breckinridge himself served as a Confederate general and, in 1865, as Jefferson Davis's secretary of war. The post was finally renamed Fort Grant on November 1, 1865. Brandes, *Frontier Military Posts*, 35–39; Prucha, *Military Posts*, 62; Altshuler, *Starting with Defiance*, 18.

87. Joseph Smith was enrolled as captain, Company A, Fifth California Infantry on October 30, 1861. He was promoted to major of the regiment on October 31, 1862, at Fort Stanton, New Mexico. On November 28, 1864, he became the major of the First California Veteran Infantry. Smith was mustered out at Franklin, Texas, on April 8, 1865. Orton, *California Men*, 676–77, 385.

88. Theodore A. Coult enrolled at Sacramento, California, on September 12, 1861. He was appointed major of the Fifth California Infantry and was promoted to lieutenant colonel on October 31, 1862. Coult was mustered out with his regiment on November 27, 1864, at Las Cruces, New Mexico. Orton, *California Men*, 676.

of the 5th Infantry, under command of Col. Bowie,[89] while Col. Forman's[90] regiment is in Los Angeles, San Bernardino, and other southern counties. Gen. Carleton will effect a junction with Col. Canby at the earliest possible moment, and New Mexico will have completely passed out of the hands of rebels and traitors. Shin's Battery came through to Tucson in splendid condition, owing to the extreme care bestowed upon it by Gen. Carleton and the officers of the battery; the horses were fed full rations the whole way; and every possible chance given them to recruit on the road, there being animals enough to afford occasional spells from labor.

MCCLEAVE'S CAPTURE

A piquant story is told of the manner in which Capt. McCleave, of the 1st Cavalry, was made prisoner by the rebels, and although I will not vouch positively for its truth, yet it is nearly correct, according to the account given by his own men who were captured with him. It appears that McCleave reached the Maricopa Wells, from which place this letter is dated, with ten men, and leaving seven of them here, proceeded as far as Casa Blanca,[91] a large adobe mill, owned by a Mr. White, who traded with the Indians for wheat, and converted it into flour, which he sold back to them, the [Butterfield] Overland Mail Company, while in operation, the people of Tucson, and other near Mexican towns, and emigrants along the road. Just then, White had sold a large quantity of wheat to the United States, and being a loyal citizen, was holding it for the use of our troops. The rebels, however, heard of it, and at the time of McCleave's visit, were in possession of the mill, and he held White a prisoner in his own house. McCleave, innocent of this fact, and without making suitable inquiry, pushed on to White's with three men, and on arriving, after dark, rode into the corral, dismounted, and knocked at the door, which was open—by one of the rebels, a member of Capt. Hunter's company of Texas Rangers.[92]

89. George Washington Bowie succeeded John Kellogg as colonel of the Fifth California Infantry on November 8, 1861. Bowie had seen service during the Mexican War as a lieutenant and captain of infantry, receiving a brevet for his part in the battles of Contreras and Churubusco. He was a lawyer and a capable officer, well liked by the men, though some of his troops lacked discipline. Bowie was mustered out at Franklin, Texas, on December 14, 1864. Orton, *California Men,* 676; Heitman, *Historical Register,* 1:234; Hand Diary, Sept. 30, 1862.

90. Ferris Forman succeeded Henry M. Judah as colonel of the Fourth California Infantry on November 9, 1861. He commanded that regiment until his resignation on August 20, 1863. Orton, *California Men,* 595, 599.

91. Casa Blanca (literally "White House") was the trading post run by Ammi White south of the Gila River between the Pima Villages and Maricopa Wells. Barnes, "Arizona Place Names," 78.

92. Sherod Hunter was commissioned captain of Company A, Second Texas Mounted Rifles, formerly the Arizona Rangers. Hunter had been elected first lieutenant of Capt. George Frazer's Rangers at Pinos Altos. Before the war he had farmed at Mowry City along the Mimbres River.

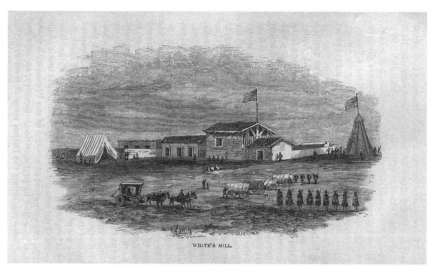

White's Mill, 1864. By J. Ross Browne, from *Adventures in the Apache Country.*

"Does Misthur White live here?" asked McCleave, with a broad brogue.

"Yes," replied the sentinel.

"Arrah! then give him Capt. McCleave's compliments, and say I want to see him."

Upon this the rebel departed into another room, and informed Capt. Hunter, who was there with thirty-five of his company. At Capt. Hunter's appearance, McCleave said:

"Are you Misthur White?"

"Yes," answered Hunter, "what do you want, and who are you?"

"I am Captain McCleave of the 1st Regiment Cavalry, California Volunteers; I am here with three men, and I require supper for myself and men, and forage for my horses."

"Very well, Capt. McCleave, you can have what you require; take off your sword and pistol, dismount your men, and make yourself at home, I am glad to meet you," replied Hunter.

McCleave did as he was desired, settled himself in an arm chair, filled and lighted his pipe, and commenced a conversation, in which he imparted a good deal of valuable information to the supposed Mr. White.

Hunter and his company of picked men, both Texans and former Arizonans, were chosen to occupy Tucson, enlist Southern sympathizers from California, and establish amicable relations with the Sonorans, Papagos, and Pimas. For details on Hunter's career, see Finch, "Sherod Hunter," 139–206; and *Confederate Pathway.*

As soon as Hunter had extracted all the intelligence he required, he quietly remarked, after the manner of Don Caesar de Bazan:[93] "If you are Captain McCleave of the 1st regiment of cavalry, California Volunteers, I am Captain Hunter of the Confederate army, and you are my prisoner;" at the same time, the doors all opened from the various apartments, and the room was filled with his men. Of course, McCleave quietly submitted; and the next morning Hunter rode to Casa Blanca, and captured the seven men left there by McCleave.

MEXICAN WOMEN IN TUCSON

Since the occupation of Tucson by our troops, crowds of Mexican women have flocked thither, and the "cry is, still they come." They do not deign to compliment the rebels with their society, probably being under the conviction that Texas and Arkansas shinplasters were subject to too great a discount; and their presence could be readily dispensed with by our soldiers. As you may suppose, gambling, vice, and the grossest immoralities attend the march of so considerable a column, but are not allowed to interfere with military discipline.

"IN THUNDER, LIGHTING AND IN RAIN"

Start not at the caption above, for I assure you Macbeth's witches really spoke truth when they mentioned the existence of such things as thunder, lighting and rain; the last of which Californians were made extremely sensible of last winter. What do you think of a real old-fashioned thunder storm? Last night we were treated to a splendid visitation of the kind, and right gloriously did I relish the brilliant scene although exposed to its full fury. Huge masses of snow-white clouds had piled themselves upon each other until the whole vault of heaven was filled with their grotesque forms. Not a breath stirred the leaves of the mesquite, and the air stood collected, as if awaiting the shock of an assailing host. Presently it came: a distant, lurid flash, and a long, loud, hoarse roar announced the first gun of heaven's artillery, and the huge columns put their masses into rapid motion at the signal. As they neared our field, whole parks were discharged with a dreadful crashing, booming sound, which seemed as if it would rend the solid earth and shake the mountains from their granite foundations. The whole air was filled with corruscating brilliancy, as the lightnings' rapid glances cleft the clouds asunder, and lavished their aqueous burdens upon the parched bosom of the earth. Down came the rain in perfect Niagras; flash, flash, flash hissed the electric fluid as it lighted up the scene; boom, boom, boom; bang, bang, bang; roar, roar;

93. Don César de Bazan was the chivalrous bandit chief in Victor Hugo's 1838 novel *Ruy Blas*. A French comedy entitled *Don César de Bazan* was written in 1844. Benét, *Reader's Encyclopedia*, 308, 960.

crash, crash thundered the columbiads[94] of the skies, while the frightened wind fled shrieking along the reverberating plain and through the mountain gorges as if undergoing a terrific scourging. It was the first thunder storm I had seen in nearly twelve years, and the effect was grand beyond expression. True, I was exposed to all its fury, being entirely without a tent or other shelter; but who cared for that? The fact never occurred to me until it was all over, and a drenched person warned me that I was but human, and required the less romantic comforts of food, fire, and rest.

VIDETTE

ALTA, JUNE 23, 1862

The Movements of the Column from California En Route to New Mexico

The following letter from Gen. Carleton's Column from California, was received per Senator[95] on the 21st, and although it treats occasionally on matters already mentioned, we give it place in our columns entire—EDS. ALTA

Fort Barrett,[96] *Pimo Villages, May 31st*

EDITORS ALTA:—Thinking you would like a few lines from this out-of-the-way portion of our great Republic, I undertake the task, surrounded by a bevy of wondering Indians, annoyed by a swarm of persevering flies, and enveloped in a cloud of alkali dust. Before saying anything of our march over, the hundred and eighty-odd miles from Fort Yuma to this place, you would, doubtless, like to hear all the news, if news it be.

REVERSES OF THE REBEL TEXANS IN NEW MEXICO

All our news from New Mexico consists of rumors and flying reports. It is evident, however, that the rebel Texans under Sibley have encountered disasters. It is said that while in the act of sacking Albuquerque the Texans were surprised by Canby's forces and fled precipitately, and were so hotly pursued as to be compelled to abandon

---

94. A columbiad was an American cannon of large caliber (up to twenty inches) generally used in seacoast fortifications. Scott, *Military Dictionary*, 164–65.

95. *Senator* was a wooden side-wheel steamer built by William H. Brown of New York in 1848. In 1854 she was purchased by the California Steam Navigation Company and from 1855 to 1882 plied between San Francisco and San Diego. Kemble, *Panama Route*, 246, 247.

96. Fort Barrett was an earthen fortification near White's Mill at the Gila River established by California Volunteers on April 19, 1862. Named for 2nd Lt. James Barrett, First California Cavalry, who died in the Picacho Pass skirmish on April 15, it was abandoned on June 22 because it was no longer useful as a forward outpost. Barnes, "Arizona Place Names," 38; J. R. West, GO 3, May 7, 1862, Command of J. R. West, RG 393, NARA.

much of their ill-gotten booty. I hope to be where I can give you some reliable items from that section before a great while.

BAYLOR AND HIS COMMAND

It is said that at the battle of Fort Craig,[97] Baylor's command, consisting of some three or four hundred men, fought with considerable bravery and were badly cut up; after the battle, Baylor was arrested for some cause or other and sent to Richmond, and his command disbanded in consequence of their time being up and their thinned ranks. All the rebel forces are said to be concentrated at Mesilla and Fort Fillmore,[98] and expect to make a stand. It is evident that their reverses, the want of money, clothing, and provisions, and still more, success, has dispirited them.

THE FLIGHT OF HUNTER, AND ENTRANCE OF COL. WEST INTO TUCSON

Capt. Hunter, in command of some one hundred and fifty Texans, who has been lording it over this whole region of the country for several months, and tyrannizing over Tucson and its inhabitants for two months past, taking whatever he wanted to supply his needy followers, and causing many of the people to fly from their homes— hearing that a superior U.S. force was advancing upon Tucson, and no reinforcements coming to his aid, became so alarmed that on the 14th, one of his lookouts seeing a train of Mexican carts coming upon the road, he and his braves saddled up in double quick time, and fled, imagining that they were pursued. Col. West, with a force of five companies of infantry and one of cavalry, entered Tucson on the 20th, one week after the flight of Hunter, to the great joy and relief of its citizens, who expressed their feelings not only in words but in actions.

CAPTURE OF CAPT. MCCLEAVE'S PARTY

You heard some time since of the capture of Capt. McCleave and party, but I doubt if the particulars or true statement was ever given to the public. From some of the men who were released when Hunter fled from Tucson, I gather the following particulars: Some two months since Capt. McCleave, with a party of nine men, being out

97. Fort Craig was established on March 31, 1854, on the west bank of the Rio Grande at the entrance of the Jornada del Muerto to protect the region from Apache raids. It was abandoned in September 1884. For a complete history of Fort Craig, see Grinstead, *Life and Death of a Frontier Fort.*

98. Fort Fillmore was established on the east bank of the Rio Grande near Mesilla some forty miles above El Paso on September 23, 1851. Abandoned by U.S. troops on July 26, 1861, it was briefly regarrisoned by California Volunteers from August to November 1862. Prucha, *Military Posts,* 74.

upon a reconnoitering expedition to learn something of the whereabouts of a Mr. Jones,[99] out as a scout for reaching the Tank,[100] some 33 miles from here on the Fort Yuma road, got out of provisions; Capt. McCleave, with three men proceeded to this place, where a man by the name of White lived, to procure the necessary supplies to last them back to Fort Yuma. As the Captain and his three men rode up to White's, they were hailed by a sentinel, the Captain answering "Americans;" he was politely invited in; his questions as to his getting forage for his animals and provisions for his men, answered in the affirmative, and his horses unsaddled and taken care of by the *polite* gentlemen he found in charge; the Captain protested against so much politeness, and it is said never suspected the character of his obliging entertainers until requested to give up his arms. The other six at the Tanks, were surprised while eating their last dinner by eleven of Hunter's men, and made prisoners. The Captain and his nine men, and also Mr. White, were taken to Tucson, where they fared as well as their captors, which, to say the least of it, was anything but well. Capt. McCleave and White were finally removed from Tucson to Mesilla, and have the liberty of that place on parole. The returned prisoners speak very well of the conduct of Hunter towards them, and give a deplorable picture of the destitution of the Texans. We also learn of these prisoners that the Apaches made an attack upon Hunter, and succeeded in running off his beef cattle and a portion of his riding animals. They say that his men seemed to evince very little enthusiasm for their cause, and many of them pray for the success of the Union. Two of the prisoners on being released went to the mines.

THE MARCH FROM FORT YUMA TO FORT BARRETT

Now for a few words about our tramp from Fort Yuma to this place.

Gen. Carleton left Fort Yuma on the 16th, and arrived here on the 24th. As the details of our march would be tedious, I will merely run over the road. Our course lay to the eastward, directly up the south bank of the Gila river; the intervening stations are Gila City, Mission Station, Fillibuster Camp, Antelope Peak, Mohawk Station,

99. John W. Jones is one of early Arizona's most interesting and enigmatic characters. A native of New York, Jones arrived in Arizona around 1860 and worked as a farmer, carpenter, and liquor dealer. During the war he served Carleton as a spy and expressman. He was a principal in Arizona City's vigilance committee of 1866. His saloon, the Yuma Exchange, on Main Street was a well-known meeting place. His funeral, following an untimely death by blood poisoning in 1871, was said to have been the most imposing ever witnessed in Yuma. Senate, *Federal Census—Territory of New Mexico and Territory of Arizona*, 3 (1860), 88 (1864), 239 (1870); *Arizona Citizen*, Feb. 25, Mar. 4, 1871. See also "John W. Jones," Hayden Arizona Pioneer Biography Files.

100. Col. J. R. West's itinerary from Fort Yuma to the Pima Villages shows the "Tanks" to be located between Desert Station and Maricopa Wells some 22.5 miles west of the Pima Villages. *OR*, 50(1):1056.

Lagoon Camp, Texas Hill, Grinnel's Ranch, Grassy Camp, Berk's Station, Oatman Flat, Kenyon Station, Shady Camp, Gila Bend, Desert Station, the Tank and Maricopa Wells.[101]

Gila City is a collection of deserted huts, seventeen and a-half miles from Fort Yuma. The mines in the immediate vicinity have been abandoned in consequence of better digging being found on the Colorado, about one hundred miles above. At this point, persons bound for the Colorado mines, cross the Gila.

At Antelope Peak we found several companies of Infantry, Shinn's Battery, and one company of Cavalry, temporarily encamped. Shinn's Battery fired a salute of eleven guns on the arrival of the General. I ascended the Peak, and had an extensive, and I might say, splendid view of the surrounding country. I could trace the bright sheen of the Gila, in its winding course, for many miles above and below, coming, as it were, from the same source as the rising sun, and dispensing its blessings as it forces its way through the barren desert, making glad the heart of the traveler who chances to rest upon its banks and quench his thirst from its clear waters; out from the immediate banks of the river which are fringed with green willows and cottonwoods, stretches the bleak desert, and in the distance, broken ranges of mountains and solitary peaks, looking like immense pyramids.

At the foot of the Peak and along the river is the encampment, the green bowers built by the soldiers to protect them against the sun's heat, running in regular rows and looking like booths of a fair, alive with military life. This mountain produces a fine echo, and the sound of a bugle or report of a gun is perfectly charming.

At Grinnel's ranch the General and staff were treated to a fine dinner, by the gentlemanly proprietor. While lying at this point Company B of the First Infantry threw up a very good fortification.

At Grassy Camp we found Capt. Shirland encamped, recruiting his horses on the fine wild millet found on the adjoining river flats.

A DRIED INDIAN

Eight or ten miles this side of Grassy Camp we came to where a body of an Indian was hanging to the limb of a dead tree.[102] He was one of three killed out of a party, by

101. The places listed on "Dragoon's" itinerary were all well-known stops on the Butterfield route. Some were changing stations with corrals and adobe buildings, while others were merely wells or hay stations with rude shelters. Most were from fifteen to twenty miles apart. For details on each station, see Conkling and Conkling, *Butterfield Overland Mail*.

102. Nearly every California Volunteer who wrote home or kept a journal mentioned this mummified body. Pimas, Maricopas, and white frontiersmen often resorted to terror tactics to discourage Apache raiding parties. Suspending the corpse of a slain enemy was a common practice. Sgt. Daniel Robinson, Seventh U.S. Infantry, observed, "the Apaches have a

Apache Hanging, 1864. By J. Ross Browne, from *Adventures in the Apache Country.*

a white man whom they had attacked. This body had been hanging over a year, and is in quite a state of preservation, the flesh having dried upon the face and body and legs as far down as the knee, showing the character of the climate; the rope by which it is suspended has nearly rotted off. As this ghastly figure swayed to and fro in the morning wind, I thought it a truly sad episode on the "human form divine."

OATMAN FLAT

Oatman Flat derives its name from the Oatman family who were murdered there in 1851. A solitary grave, nicely enclosed with a rude head-board, bearing this simple inscription, "The Oatman Family, 1851," marks the spot where their remains were laid, imprinting a tale of horror on the mind of the traveler as he looks upon the desolate flat and dark hills which encompass it.

---

superstitious dread of dying by hanging, nothing could induce them to touch or go near these bodies, their worse enemies were perfectly safe within a certain radius." It seems incredible that the same Indian could still be a landmark on the Gila route two years later, but in 1864 J. Ross Browne described a mummified Indian missing one foot and both hands, bristling with arrows, and hanging in a mesquite tree not far from Burke's Station. Browne wrote that King Woolsey had killed the Indian "more than two years ago." *Adventures*, 99–102; "King S. Woolsey," Hayden Arizona Pioneer Biography Files; McChristian and Ludwig, "Eyewitness to the Bascom Affair," 293; Julius Hall, "Wild West." See also George H. Pettis to Annie [wife], Apr. 30, 1862, George H. Pettis Papers, Western Americana Collection, Beinecke Library, Yale, New Haven, Conn.

SCENE OF THE OATMAN MASSACRE.

Scene of the Oatman Massacre, 1864. By J. Ross Browne from *Adventures in the Apache Country*.

GILA BEND

Up to Gila Bend, our road lay, for the most part, along the river flats, and although not heavy for wagons, it is a most disagreeable one to the traveler, on account of the alkali dust. Here the river makes a sharp bend, and the roads strike out across the *mesa* forty miles to Maricopa Wells, without water, but a fine road. At the bend, the valley widens, and it is certainly one of the lovliest valleys and richest tracts of land I ever saw. At one time, the Overland Stage Company had a station there, but the last person who kept the station (Capt. Sutton,[103] an old frontiersman, with his family) was so annoyed and harassed by the Apaches, that he was finally compelled to leave, having been attacked three times, his house set on fire, and stock driven off. In the last attack his son killed the chief. Quite a numerous tribe of the Apaches live in the mountain range, on the opposite side of the river, and seem to guard this valley with jealous care, as it is a passage way on their route to Sonora. It is said that the Maricopas once attempted to settle there, but were so harassed by the Apaches that they had to give it up.

103. Jesse Sutton, aged fifty-four, is listed on the 1860 census as a farmer along the San Pedro near Fort Breckenridge. He was born in Tennessee, but his children were all born in Texas. His family included his wife, Frances, and four children, Abel (aged sixteen), Francis E. (twelve), Jepe (eight), and Eliza A. (six). Senate, *Federal Census—Territory of New Mexico and Territory of Arizona*, 28 (1860); Bancroft, *Arizona and New Mexico*, 320, 322.

TALK WITH THE INDIANS

At Maricopa Wells, the principal Chief of the Maricopas,[104] accompanied by a score of warriors, came to pay the General a visit. They presented a comical appearance, half civilized, half barbarous, as they rode up to our camp on their raw boned ponies, dressed off in some United States uniforms, given them by order of the General, brass buttons, and red paint, infantry dress coats and bare legs, military caps and long hair. Through a Spanish interpreter, they made known the burden of their story. The Chief wished an explanation of our political troubles, spoke of the friendship of his people to the whites, of the late raid of the Apaches, in which two Pimos were killed, and of their having rifles, and wound up by asking a gift from the General. The General expressed his great pleasure at seeing them, acknowledged their constant friendship, explained, as best he could, the nature of our political affairs, said he had heard of their late misfortune by the attack of the Apaches, and that he had written to San Francisco to see if he could procure one hundred rifles for them and the Pimos, and told them that he had also sent for manta, flannel, and agricultural implements, part of which he would give them, and part exchange for wheat, corn, etc., and advised them to plant abundantly. The General invited them to see him next day at the Fort. Next day, there was a general friendly talk with the combined Indian dignitaries—Pimo and Maricopa—virtually one and the same tribe, living and intermixing with each other.

FORT BARRETT

Is so named after the gallant Lieutenant who was the first to fall in defence of the Union, in this part of our rebel infested Republic. It is situated in the heart of the Pimo Villages, two miles from the river, out upon an open and barren plain, without a tree to shade or adorn the ground. Some adobe buildings, once occupied by White, serve as hospital and commissary, while fronting the parade ground are several sheds for the accommodation of passing troops. Around the building occupied as a hospital, a fortification is being erected by the troops, and promises to be a very substantial work when completed.

THE PIMOS

When first visited by the white men, the Pimos were found in possession of nearly all the arts of civilization practiced by the ancient Aztecs; they spun, wove, and had planted fields of grain. They once acknowledged the universal sway of the great

104. Juan Chivaria was the principal chief of the Maricopas in the 1860s. Browne, *Adventures*, 121; Cremony, *Life among the Apaches*, 90.

Montezuma, and to this day, in a manner, look for the coming of the same agricultural deity whom the Aztecs worshipped. They have always been a good friend to the white man, and it seems that God has so placed them to furnish bread for the desert. As a people, they are brave, honest, and virtuous. They are more than a match for the skulking Apaches, and wage an offensive warfare upon that numerous and warlike tribe, who have always been a trouble to the white emigrant, and the scourge of northern Mexico. In appearance the men are tall and fine looking; the women are generally pleasing in features, straight as arrows, and some of them quite pretty. As to costume, the Pimos wear very little clothing; the men putting on every article of dress they acquire from the whites, without regard to taste, having an inordinate love for red. The women might well plead the complaint of our modern belles, "Nothing to wear," their dress hardly furnishing a description, consisting of a simple piece of manta or calico wrapped about them, extending up as far as the waist and down to the knees. We might say that two modern fashions—low-necked dresses and the bloomer—come near meeting on the Pimo beauty. In speaking of the Pimos, I include the Maricopas, whose villages, collectively, extend for twenty miles along the river. The Pimos seem not to have suffered the same demoralizing effects as other tribes, from contacts with the white man. Their villages are a promiscuous collection of huts, which resemble in appearance the huts of the Esquimaux, built in the open plain, off from the river. In manners they are gentle and lively, and seem on the whole to be a happy and contented people, with few wants and less cares. Their fields extend for twenty miles along the river, and are irrigated by a perfect system of ditches. From an eminence, they present one vast sea of waving grain, truly delightful to view. It is now harvest time, and it is quite interesting to ride along the fields and witness the harvesting, which is done entirely by the squaws. They do not mow the wheat, but go through the fields, and whenever they find a ripe patch they clip off the heads with a knife, and thus the crop is gathered as it ripens. These heads are then carried to where they are threshed out by main strength, with a stick. You can imagine the labor expended in harvesting so large a crop of wheat, and all performed by the squaws, while their lords lay in the shade or strut about the fort. After the wheat has been beheaded, the straw is set fire to and burned down; then a crop of corn is put in. They also plant considerable cotton, which does finely. It is said that the men attend to the irrigation and planting, but I am much of the impression that all the work, except the care of the stock, (of which they have considerable,) the keeping up of a continual vigilance day and night, and the campaign against the Apaches, is performed by the women.

THE GILA VALLEY

The Valley of the Gila is certainly one of the richest for its extent in the world; it is true that it extends through a desert, and has very little that is attractive to the traveler, still the soil is exceedingly rich and will bear irrigation better than any other, and as to its capability, the success of the Pimos, with their rude cultivation, abundantly proves. All the cereal and every fruit of the temperates and tropics can be successfully cultivated, and the barren flats, shaded with fine trees. Under the care of Yankee farmers, this desert would truly "blossom as the rose." Besides, the mountain ranges are rich with mineral; should a railroad be built through to the Pacific, the valley of the Gila will be found to be worth all the United States paid for it.

MOVEMENT OF TROOPS

Upon the arrival of the General, Colonel Eyre was sent on to Fort Stanford in command of two companies of cavalry. Major Coult arrived with his command this evening accompanied by Shinn's Battery. The General will, no doubt, move in a day or two. We will all be on the Rio Grande in July at the farthest. Our troops chafe, under restraint, fearing that they will never get a chance at the rebels.

DIFFICULTIES AHEAD

We are now in the midst of the dry season, and the road between here and Tucson is very destitute of water. The well at Blue Water Station[105] had been rendered useless in consequence of a man by the name of Ware,[106] who had been murdered by a Mexican, some time since, and thrown into the well. Ware had considerable money with him and was once engaged in the service of the Overland Stage Company. Lieut. Hary [Harvey][107] has been sent forward with a detachment to bail out the wells and dig them deeper.

DRAGOON

105. Blue Water Station was established as an intermediate change-and-water station by the Butterfield Overland Company in late 1858. It was fourteen miles northwest of Picacho Station on the east side of the north branch of Santa Cruz Wash. The deep well there provided water even during the driest months. Barnes, "Arizona Place Names," 56; Conkling and Conkling, *Butterfield Overland Mail*, 2:164–65.

106. Ammi White wrote to Maj. Edwin Rigg on February 9, 1862, "An old and respected resident of Tucson, Major Ware, was murdered and robbed, and his body thrown in a well at Blue Water Station, by a notorious Mexican, Juan Robles." *OR*, 50(1):867. Pvt. Julius C. Hall, accompanying Captain Calloway's advance guard in April 1862, remembered that "water here [Blue Water] was only procured from a well, and we were forbidden to use any of it, as it was said the dead body of a man was lying at the bottom. A man's skull and other indications we found went to show that this was true." Hall, "Wild West."

107. Benjamin F. Harvey was commissioned first lieutenant of Company A, First California Cavalry. Although he commanded the company after Captain McCleave's capture, he seemed plagued by ill health since the expedition began. Harvey was mustered out for disability on December 31, 1862. *OR*, 50(1):869, 871, 939; Orton, *California Men*, 89.

ALTA, JULY 9, 1862

Letter from the Volunteer Column from California
Maricopa Wells, New Mexico, June 12, 1862

EDITORS ALTA: The Express surprised me last night, at 12 o'clock, during one of the finest lunar eclipses I have ever witnessed; but as another Express will leave to-morrow for your region, I avail myself of it to give you an account of passing events in and about New Mexico. First in point of immediate interest is the condition and loca-tion of our little Californian army. Scarcely any change whatever has occurred in the relative disposition of our troops since my last. The General has taken up his head-quarters at Tucson for the present; but how long he will remain there is a mere matter of conjecture, his movements depending much on those of the enemy as well as of the Federal forces under Colonel Slough. I believe the latter has effected a communica-tion with Canby, and they will act in concert for the public good and safety. Several companies of infantry are still at the Pimos, making adobes for the construction of a very considerable fort, the walls of which are already four feet above the surface of the earth, and about twelve feet in thickness. This fort [Barrett] will accommodate from four to five companies, and will be permanently established.

The health of the troops is good—remarkably so, indeed—and it is fortunate that such is the case; for through the negligence of somebody, a very limited and insuffi-cient supply of medicines is on hand at this post; in fact, the scarcity is so great as almost to amount to destitution. No doubt the oversight will be remedied as soon as it is made known to the medical director of the column, who, I am satisfied, is not cognizant thereof.

MISSING EXPRESSMEN

It is reported that two expressmen, cavalry soldiers, running on the route between Tucson and the Pimos, are missing, and as they were not men who would desert, it is feared that they have either been murdered by rebels or Apaches. Major Coult, com-manding Fort Barrett, at the Pimos, sent for a detachment of six men and a Sergeant from Capt. Cremony's company, last Tuesday, the 10th inst., and for another of a cor-poral and five men yesterday, all well mounted and thoroughly armed for "any emer-gency." These detachments will probably scour the surrounding country in search of the missing expressmen, and if possible, discover their fate. Since they were missing, two of Capt. Cremony's men have been to Tucson and brought through an express, which has been forwarded to California. The Apaches between the Pimos and the Rio Grande are a most merciless set of savages, never losing an opportunity to attack small parties of any other people, and it would be as well, now that the proper force is here, to wipe them out as much as possible. The idea of making treaties with them is, to use a California expression, "played out." They hold no faith whatever; will make a treaty and solemnize it with great eclat one day, and deliberately break it the next, laughing at you for your trust in their honesty. Nothing but the most dreadful lesson will bring them to their senses, and it cannot be given too soon. Our own internal difficulties have emboldened them to a much greater degree than before, rendering the roads altogether unsafe for fewer than six or eight well mounted men.

THE PIMOS AND MARICOPAS

In glaring contrast with the Apaches are the Indian tribes whose names adorn the heading of this paragraph. In my former letter I gave you an account of the separation between the Maricopas and the Yumas; their reception by the Pimos, and some other facts of note, and will now redeem my promise by describing a courting match and a marriage, and a funeral ceremony, together with such other matters as may prove interesting to your readers.

When a Maricopa brave is inclined to become a Benedict,[108] he paints his face to the most killing manner he knows how, dresses himself in all his finery, and promenades the village in quest of a wife. All the marriageable girls take due notice and govern themselves accordingly, likewise painting their faces, and casting the most coquettish, glances at the lonely savage. Having selected one of the young offerers, he "shines up to her," which is immediately perceived by the shrewd old squaws who happen to be her relatives, and when the evening comes, at which time he is expected to call on the lady of his choice, the house is well filled with her male and female relatives and immediate friends. Not at all abashed, and expecting this sort of thing, the lover enters carefully, stepping clear of the prostrate dusky forms which line his path, and takes his seat near the object of his attachment, who sits in a remote corner, looking as sheepish as possible. There they sit, cheek by jowl, talking and whispering to each other, while all the rest in the room pretend not to see them, until past midnight, when, if she concludes to accept him, he either remains all night, or she leaves the house in his company, but if she declines, he goes out alone. The next day the accepted lover hides himself all day from the gaze of everybody, and that night he receives his wife alone. The marriage is thus completed without any fuss or feathers, and no one but the parties immediately interested have a word to say in the matter. Little or no difference exists between the Maricopa and Pimo usages in this respect, although there is a material discrepancy in their funeral ceremonies.

---

108. "Benedict" alludes to a Shakespearean character by the name of Benedick. In this context it means a married man.

When a Maricopa dies a large funeral pyre is made, and every article the deceased possessed while living, is placed upon it with the corpse. All his clothing of every description; his horse or horses; all his poultry, all his wheat or other crops; his bow and arrows; in fine, every article of any kind whatsoever—the fire is put and all reduced to ashes, which is then cast to the winds, amidst howlings and lamentations, which last one day and one night. You may suppose the death of a man is the signal for the complete impoverishment of his family, which insures their deepest and most unfeigned grief, while it destroys that pleasurable anticipation said to be common in England among elder sons, who impatiently wait to "step into the shoes of their father."

The Pimos do not burn, but bury their dead, taking care, however, to bury all their worldly goods with them. The reason for this marked difference in their respective religious beliefs, an account of which I will now endeavor to give:

The Pimos believe in a strange mixture of Christianity, after the Roman form, and paganism; the mixture being attributable to the fact that the Jesuit Fathers, to whom they are indebted for their Christian teachings, as well as their semi-civilizations, never broke rudely upon the existing superstitions of the savage tribes among whom they planted missions; but endeavored to wear them away by degrees; and to this end, allowed them to retain a few of their more appreciated paganisms, which were singularly blended with Christian teachings. Thus, it is not uncommon to find the history of the crucifixion connected and mixed up with some of their own traditions, leaving a strangely chaotic jumble of religious ideas and notions among the people, which have not been improved by the lapse of a century without religious instruction of any kind. The Pimos believe in two separate and distinct external issues—a God and a devil; the Spirit of Good and the Spirit of Evil; each of which is equally just toward, but at desperate enmity with each other. The former of these spirits lives in heaven, among the clouds in some unknown expanse beyond their comprehension, and troubles himself but little with the affairs of this world; although receiving those who die, after having led just lives, and locating them in happy hunting grounds, the soul being accompanied by the body after its total disintegration in the earth. The Spirit of Evil is supposed to dwell here among men, and to take note of all their acts, but without interfering in any way. They believe, if a body is suitably buried, it will go to heaven; but if left disinterred, it will remain like the ghost of Hamlet's father, restless and unhappy until its crimes shall have been expiated.

The Maricopas also believe in two essences, but with some modifications. They say that God created the earth, peopled it and came here to live among men. He took up his residence on top of a high hill in Mexico, surrounded by a chosen people whom he named "Moctezuma" or "Montezuma," while the devil had possession of a considerable portion of the earth. That after a long time, the devil and his people prevailed and killed God, whose hands and feet they cut off and pierced to his sides with a spear; but that after some days he arose from the dead and ascended into heaven where he now dwells; while his chosen people were scattered into fragments and dispersed all over the earth; but that the time will come when all will be reunited and God again take possession of the earth, driving out the devil into an unknown and trackless region. They also aver that if a body be buried it will go to heaven and wander there homeless until the reorganization of the people of God; but that if it be burned it will remain upon this earth with the devil, doing pretty much as it did in the flesh, until the return of God when it will be again gathered to its people. On account of this belief they resort to incremation and worship the devil, paying him all their adorations as the immediate Divinity upon whose bounty they are dependent and whose chastisement they dread. You will perceive what a strange melange this is of Judaism, Christianity, and Paganism. They claim to be of the family of the "Moctezumas," and say the Pimos are another branch of the same. They also name several Indian tribes, some of them in California, who they declare to be "Moctezumas."

The limits of a letter will scarcely permit a more extended notice of the religious persuasions of these singular peoples, and I will rest at this point. Your readers can form some estimate of the vast differences between these two tribes by the differences in their language, which I shall exemplify by means of their numerals.

MARICOPA	PIMO
One-Shendigk.	One-Hermaco.
Two-Havick.	Two-Coke.
Three-Hamock.	Three-Vike.
Four-Shoompapa.	Four-Keek.
Five-Sarapk.	Five-Hertas.
Six-Hamhook.	Six-Jusse.
Seven-Pahkeak.	Seven-Huerco.
Eight-Sephoogk.	Eight-Keek-keek.
Nine-Ham-ham-hook.	Nine-Humukh.
Ten-Sahock.	Ten-Westemar.

Their languages are totally dissimilar, and as I said before, although they intermarry and have lived together for a century, are obliged to employ interpreters in their intercourse with each other.

OUR RELATIONS WITH MEXICO

No doubt, it was intended to supply the California Column operating in New Mexico and along the Mexican frontier, through the port of Guaymas and from the state of Sonora, rather than from Fort Yuma; but the existing difficulty between France and Mexico seems to have seriously interfered with any such arrangement for the present.[109] That our supplies must be obtained either in part from Sonora, or be brought through that State from the port of Guaymas, is apparent to all on the line.

FURTHER MOVEMENTS

I had written so far when I received an order "to report without delay" to Major Coult, 5th Infantry, commanding Fort Barrett, and the pen was immediately dropped for the sword and pistol. On arriving at Fort Barrett, with fifteen others of Capt. Cremony's company, we were ordered to take charge of nine prisoners, captured in Tucson, by order of Gen. Carleton, and to be sent to Fort Yuma for safe keeping.[110] They were recognized here by the Indians as belonging to Capt. Hunter's company, when he took Capt. McCleave and Mr. White. One of them, a short, dark complexioned man, was formerly employed under Major Solomon, in the United States Marshal's office, San Francisco.[111] I did not learn his name, as all intercourse with them was strictly prohibited. They have been sent to Fort Yuma, in charge of Lieut. Mitchell,[112] 1st Infantry, who was supplied with a detachment of 16 men of Capt. Cremony's Company, Second Cavalry. Maj. Ferguson, First Cavalry, is reported as preparing to go into Sonora for the purpose of procuring forage for the public animals. He is to take two or three companies of the First Cavalry with him, and will probably be gone a month or six weeks. Fort Breckenridge, or rather, Fort Stanford, has been abandoned; neither its

109. Both the army and citizens of Arizona saw advantages in supplying Tucson via the Sonora ports of Guaymas, Libertad, or Lobos on the Gulf of California. Although the roads were good, red tape in dealing with the Mexicans and the unrest caused by French intervention resulted in limited use of the supply route during the Civil War. For a complete discussion of this topic, see Henry Walker, "Freighting from Guaymas to Tucson," 291–304.

110. The nine prisoners sent to Fort Yuma were Nelson Van Alstine, J. S. Douglass, Fritz Constance, Thomas Venable, Robert L. Ward, J. W. Davis, J. S. Bratton, James McDurfey, and Agapito Pacho. Carleton would have some twenty men rounded up before his law-and-order campaign ended. Orton, *California Men*, 52; Post Return, Fort Barrett, Ariz. Terr., June 1862, Returns from U.S. Military Posts, RG 393, NARA, M617, roll 1494.

111. Major Solomon was a San Francisco lawman and involved in purchasing horses for the Pony Express just before the Civil War. *Sacramento Union*, Mar. 17, 1860; O. P. Fitzgerald, *California Sketches* (Nashville: Southern Methodist Publishing House, 1880), 10.

112. Francis S. Mitchell began his short military career as first lieutenant, Company B, First California Infantry. On June 23, 1862, he was promoted to captain of Company D. Following months of tracking Apache raiders, he deserted his command near Fort West, New Mexico, and was cashiered on October 26, 1863. Orton, *California Men*, 324, 341, 350.

strategic location, nor its salubrity, rendering it of importance. Fort Buchanan has also been abandoned. Col. West went there, raised the Stars and Stripes over the fort, saluted them, and abandoned the place for the same reasons that Fort Stanford was left in loneliness. These two places were only valued as striking points from which to reach the Apaches, but only weaken the available strength of the column in a war like that in which we are embarked, as they require the presence of troops to man them, who would be completely isolated and out of the line of operations.

YOURS SINCERELY, VEDETTE[113]

ALTA, JULY 10, 1862

Letter from the Volunteer Column from California
Tucson, Arizona T., June 16, 1862

EDS. ALTA: We left Pimo Villages, or Fort Barrett, on the 16th [1st] inst., and arrived here on the 7th. The General marched by way of the Fort Stanford [formerly Breckenridge] road as far as Cottonwood Spring,[114] then turned off to the right over a new route, again coming into the Fort Stanford road at the Cañada del Oro.[115] I judge this to be some twenty-five or thirty miles longer route than the regular traveled road between Fort Barrett and Tucson, and portions of it quite bad—especially one day's march of thirty-five miles, without water; and through a heavy sandy cañon of several miles. The General took this route, I believe, in order to let Lieut. Shinn, with his battery, pass over the other at the same time. Lieut. Shinn arrived here two days in advance, and, upon the General's arrival, gave him a salute. For the first two days, our road kept along the Gila, and then we left it for good. The second day out, some of our party saw a few Apaches, but, further than this, these American Arabs never troubled us.

"ARE RUINS, THEN, ALREADY HERE?"

About twenty-seven miles from Fort Barrett, our road passed over the ruins of an old city, supposed by some to have been built and occupied by the Aztecs.[116] However

113. The spellings "vedette" and "vidette" were both in common usage during the Civil War. It is unknown if the author, editor, or typesetter decided to change the spelling of the pseudonym from "Vidette" to "Vedette," but beginning with this issue of the *Alta,* the latter spelling is invariably used.

114. Cottonwood Springs was about forty miles southeast of present-day Florence on what became the San Pedro stage road between Florence and Fort Breckenridge. Barnes, "Arizona Place Names," 114.

115. The Cañada del Oro is a stream originating in the Catalina Mountains north of Tucson. The stream (or wash) joins the Santa Cruz River several miles above the town. Barnes, "Arizona Place Names," 75.

116. These are probably the ancient Hohokam ruins of Casa Grande.

this may be, it is evident time has made a desert place of what was once no doubt a populous city. Old foundations, mounds, and pieces of broken pottery, scattered for miles over the plain, are all the evidence that now remain to tell the tale of a past people.

CANADA DEL ORO—PROSPECTING

The Canada del Oro is situated about twenty-eight miles, in a northerly direction, from Tucson, and behind a high, broken range of mountains. In the bed of the cañon is a beautiful, bold, mountain stream, and the scenery is quite romantic—the mountains, forming the back ground, running up to curiously shaped summits, suggesting the idea of old castles. One or two years since, considerable gold fever existed in the Territory, by gold being found there, and several parties worked in the banks of the stream with success; but the Apaches have always been too strong and troublesome for small parties, and consequently it has never been worked to any great extent. As we did not leave camp until 11 o'clock on the morning following our arrival in the Cañada, our whole party turned out prospecting with tin pans, buckets, etc—the fever running pretty high for two or three hours; all got "color," and all come to the conclusion that rich diggings could be found. I heard old Californians say that it would be as good a thing as they would want; and one waggish fellow, in order to express his idea of its richness, said "the national debt could be paid out of the Canada del Oro." Of course, all the prospecting was on the surface. Arizona is certainly a rich mining district, and I believe that the marching of this expedition, composed for the most part of old Californians and experienced miners, over this country, will eventually be the means of developing it. The entire route has been prospected, and it was quite interesting to witness them examining the ledges and turning over the dirt. The climate is dry and healthy, and the valleys capable of producing abundance of grain. Provisions can be obtained at reasonable rates; and all that is necessary is, that parties shall be large enough to protect themselves against the Apaches.

MORE RUINS

Some eighteen miles from here and near the Rincon,[117] our last camping place, are the traces and ruins of an old walled, stone-built city. In company with an old residen-

117. The "old residenter" was most likely Francisco Romero, who established a ranch on the west side of the Santa Catalina Mountains near Cañada del Oro in 1844. The extensive ruins were the remains of a Hohokam village from around 500–1450 A.D. The fifteen-acre ruin site is now managed by Catalina State Park. Elson and Doelle, *Archaeological Survey*, 5–6, 93–94; Swartz and Doelle, *Archaeology in the Mountain Shadows*, 4–10. The authors note that the earliest mention of this site previously in the historical record was in 1875, thirteen years *after* the California Volunteers published their observations in the *Alta*.

ter, as guide, I ascended the elevation upon which it was built, to make examinations. The deep silence common to those wilds was unbroken, and I was far from supposing that there had ever been a habited city, so completely did nature seem to be left to her own caprices. But when I had reached the point of the elevation bordering on the banks of a dry stream, I saw walls standing several feet high. Upon closer examination, I found that the town had extended almost to the mountain, and had been surrounded by a strong stone wall. Over the ground was a profusion of broken earthenware. This is said to have been an old Spanish Jesuit Mission and mining town, and stories are told of old silver mines in the mountains adjacent; however, it may be of greater antiquity. The people who built and lived there have disappeared, and their stone city has fallen to indistinct ruins—whether over powered by the wilder tribes, or how they perished, we do not know.

TUCSON

Tucson may be properly described in these few words: A little, old, Mexican town, built of adobe, and capable of containing about fifteen hundred souls. The Santa Cruz runs within a mile of the town, and feeds the numerous ditches that irrigate the beautiful little valley that extends to the high hills to the westward, and which was, a week since, one vast field of fine grain, harvesting having commenced. The climate of Tucson is dry and healthy, and the soil will produce almost anything planted. The peach, quince, fig, and pomegranate grow to perfection.

Upon our arrival in Tucson, we found it lively with U.S. Volunteers, but abandoned by its former population. Since then, however, they have been coming daily, and a better pleased set of people cannot be found. Some who have returned have been required to take the oath of allegiance. The portion of the community which could be best spared left with Hunter, a few weeks since, and will be sure not to come back unless brought.

ARREST OF SUSPICIOUS CHARACTERS

The General, immediately upon his arrival went to work to renovate and straighten out the affairs of the Territory. His first move was the arrest of eight or ten suspicious characters who had been prowling about the place ever since Hunter's departure. Upon the afternoon of the same day we came in, Captain Fritz, at the head of his company, dashed through the town at full speed, and in five minutes it was surrounded, and shortly after the prisoners were marched to the guard-house. So secret had this movement been kept that every one was taken by surprise. These prisoners have been sent to Yuma. They are a portion of a set of bad men who have had things all their own way, scorning all law; but affairs have taken a turn, and I think their jig is up. The General

Tucson, 1864. By J. Ross Browne, from *Adventures in the Apache Country.*

has taken hold with a firm hand and not one of these outlaws against the civil or national authority will escape his vigilance.

DECLARATION OF MARTIAL LAW

General Carleton has declared martial law over the Territory and is now its Governor. His Adjutant, Ben. F. Cutter [Benjamin C. Cutler],[118] Acting Secretary of State, with a Military Board for examining and regulating matters in general.

MUNICIPAL REGULATIONS

Tucson has fallen into strict hands, its municipal affairs have been overhauled and put to rights; ordinances have been passed pertaining to its stores, whisky shops, gaming tables, etc. A license of $100 per month has been placed upon each grog shop, and the same upon every gaming table, and heavy penalties attached. Five hundred dollars have already been collected and turned over to be devoted to the use of the hospital.

118. Benjamin Clarke Cutler enrolled in the First California Infantry at San Francisco on August 15, 1861. He was promoted from first lieutenant to captain and assistant adjutant general of volunteers on August 6, 1862. Earlier, on June 11, Carleton had appointed him secretary of state of the newly proclaimed Arizona Territory after declaring martial law. Cutler was one of Carleton's favorites and was one of only two men the general kept on his personal staff after assuming command of the Department of New Mexico. *OR,* 9:692, 50(2):150; Orton, *California Men,* 335.

CONFISCATION

All property belonging to Secessionists has been taken possession of, much of which comes in very good use, such as forage, etc. Of the amount taken in this way I am unable to State.

OPENING NEGOTIATIONS WITH SONORA

Major Ferguson, now at the head of the Commissary Department in place of Lieut. Hammond,[119] relieved, has gone down into Sonora, for the purpose of seeing if provisions, etc., can be obtained from there, and to open up negotiations. Before the Major's departure, two trains, loaded with corn, arrived and disposed of their cargoes. The Major took an escort. The General is endeavoring to create friendly relations, at the same time taking a firm and independent position, in consequence of reports to the effect that the Governor of Sonora had entered into negotiations with the secessionists, desiring their occupation of this Territory.

MORE PRISONERS

On the 8th inst., Col. Eyre left with a detachment of cavalry upon an expedition, nobody knew where. To-day, Col. Eyre arrived, bringing twenty-one prisoners, among them Sylvester Mowry.[120] They were taken, all together, at the Patagonia mines,[121]

119. Lafayette Hammond was commissioned first lieutenant, First California Infantry on August 15, 1861, and was appointed regimental quartermaster. He impressed Carleton favorably and was promoted to captain of Company H on July 17, 1862. Hammond resigned his commission on August 5, 1863. Orton, *California Men*, 67, 335, 367.

120. Sylvester Mowry, a native of Rhode Island and a West Point graduate, had attained the rank of first lieutenant by the time he resigned his army commission on July 31, 1858. He settled in the "Middle Santa Cruz Settlements" and purchased his Patagonia Mine in April 1860. Besides his mining interests, Mowry was an Arizona booster and represented the unrecognized territory in Congress. It is possible that he made his fortune as a confidence man, selling his mining property after misrepresenting its potential. In 1859 he fought a duel with the editor of the *Tubac Weekly Arizonian*, Edward E. Cross, who had labeled Mowry's claims "humbug." General Carleton confiscated Mowry's property and incarcerated him at Fort Yuma because of his Rebel sympathies. He spent the remainder of his life suing Carleton and the U.S. government for losses, both real and imagined, suffered during his arrest and for the confiscation of supplies (thought to be stockpiled for Confederate use) and property. Mowry never received the compensation he felt he deserved, and in 1871 he died in London, where he had gone to seek treatment for an unknown illness. Senate, *Federal Census—Territory of New Mexico and Territory of Arizona*, 27 (1860); Heitman, *Historical Register,* 1:733. For additional information on Mowry, see Altshuler, "Case of Sylvester Mowry, the Charge of Treason," 63–82; and "Case of Sylvester Mowry, the Mowry Mine," 149–74; and Halaas, *Boom Town Newspapers*, xiii–xvii.

121. Located in the Patagonia Mountains twenty miles east of Calabasas, the Patagonia Mine opened in 1857 after a group of army officers purchased it from a Mexican herder. Elias Brevoort, post sutler at Fort Buchanan, purchased the mine in 1859, and Sylvester Mowry in

some 80 miles from here, although Col. Eyre traveled over 100 miles to reach them. Of course they were surprised, and taken without any trouble. The Patagonia mines are situated just on the American side of the line, and this batch of Secessionists (as they all are, no doubt) thought, upon the slightest alarm, to cross over into Mexico. Capt. Willis was left in charge of all the property, which will amount to considerable. These prisoners will be examined before a Military Board. Mowry takes things quite coolly, puts on a good many airs; had along his mistress, Private Secretary and servant. I think a dose of military treatment will cure him. He has been guilty of writing secessionist letters, and giving shelter to outlaws.

ARMY NEWS

Gen. Carleton has turned over the command of the First Regiment California Volunteers to Col. West, who is now in command at this place. Gen. Carleton returns tomorrow to Pimos, or Fort Barrett, by way of Fort Stanford, on a tour of inspection, and to hasten up supplies. Capt. T. Moore,[122] chief Quartermaster, accompanies him. No troops will move beyond here until the 1st of July; now being the driest season, and the June rains have yet to fall. Troops are moving up to this point as fast as possible. The town is full.

CONDITION OF THE TROOPS

The troops are in the best of health and spirits, and the whole expedition may be said to be in the best of fighting and working condition, notwithstanding they have made the greatest march of the war. As to fighting, most of the men, think they will never have a chance—that Baylor and Sibley are phantoms that will disappear at our

---

turn bought out Brevoort and Henry P. Titus on April 9, 1860, after which it became known as the Mowry Mine. Mowry himself did much to promote its potential before selling out his interest. The Patagonia Mine was known chiefly for lead and silver. Barnes, "Arizona Place Names," 290; 320. For more information on the ownership and operation of this site, as well as the effects of the war, see Altshuler, "Case of Sylvester Mowry, the Mowry Mine."

122. Tredwell Moore graduated from West Point in 1847 and remained in the regular army until his death in 1876. Appointed assistant quartermaster in 1859, he served in this capacity, as a captain, until 1863, when he was transferred to the eastern theater. Moore had attained the rank of lieutenant colonel and brevet brigadier general by 1872. Boatner, *Civil War Dictionary*, 564; Heitman, *Historical Register*, 1:723.

approach, and that peace will come finding us a long ways from anywhere. But *nos veremos.*[123]

N.[124]

ALTA, JULY 12, 1862

Letter from the Column from California in Arizona
Maricopa Wells, June 10

EDITORS ALTA: The English word "comfort" seems to be quite expunged from the vocabulary, at least so far as we are concerned. The heats are so intense, that animate and inanimate creation give evidence of being deeply affected; the very rocks appear to be disintegrating under its withering effects, while the solid earth is rent in many places. There is no lack of breeze, which comes laden with caloric as if from the blast of a furnace, parching the skin and dessicating the whole frame. The advent of night is scarcely a relief to this intolerable withering of everything; the thermometer standing at 104 at one o'clock in the morning for several days in succession. What would we not give for the cool and refreshing breeze of Frisco? But we have made our choice and intend to see it out, particularly as an opportunity may arise, ere the term of our enlistment expires, to measure our strength with the British Lion or the Gallic Eagle, or perhaps with both. It matters little to us who our enemies may be; even the whole world in arms would find that the spirit which animated our fathers of '76 is still rife among us, and that their sons are capable of protecting the inestimable heirloom bequeathed to us by those good and great men.

ARIZONA A TERRITORY

On the 9th inst., Brig. General Carleton issued a proclamation at Tucson in which he proclaimed Arizona a Territory, declared martial law, and announced himself as Military Governor. I presume that this territorial partition has been made purely for the purpose of dividing New Mexico into suitable Military Districts, and giving Carleton

123. *Nos veremos* (Spanish): we shall see.
124. Subsequent letters authored by "N." provide more clues to his identity. He is not an officer but has unusual access to information; travels with the First California Cavalry, especially companies B and C; and is close to Lt. Col. E. E. Eyre. "N." is most likely James Pearson Newcomb (1837–1907), who fled Texas after a secessionist mob destroyed the presses of his pro-Union San Antonio newspaper, the *Alamo Express.* He made his way to California by way of Mexico and joined Carleton's command as a special agent and interpreter. Newcomb traveled back to California in November 1862 and established a newspaper in San Francisco before returning to Texas in 1867. *Alta,* Aug. 10, Nov. 13, 1862; *OR,* 50(1):121. See also James P. Newcomb Papers, CAH.

command of the one nearest to California. Arizona, in my opinion, does not yet possess the means for self-government, and will for some time to come, have to be governed by the strong arm. This Territory has been the refuge and paradise of rascals of every type, who have made it unsafe for them to dwell elsewhere. Escaped convicts from California and desperadoes from Texas and New Mexico compose the majority of its white population, who scruple not at the commission of the most hideous crimes and excesses of iniquity. Dreading each other, for they are ranged in cliques, they make common cause against the native inhabitants, whom they rob and murder without ceremony.

Gen. Carleton has already commenced a vigorous course against these noxious vermin, and seems determined to make a clear sweep. The fellow who fired the hay at Mohawk Station, Texas Hill, Gila Bend, and Oatman's Flat, has been captured in Tucson, and is now at the Pimos in double irons. All civil law has been suspended, and crimes and misdemeanors are brought before a Board of army officers, who try the cases and pronounce sentence, which, together with a complete written statement of the case, is laid before the General for his approval, disapproval, or modification. The arrests made, up to this time, have been of the vilest wretches, and have had a most salutary effect, and has given the vicious to understand that they are under rigid and unbending surveillance. The avenger is on their track, and they will yet feel the weight of his heel on their traitor necks.

ARMY MOVEMENTS

Major Rigg, who, I presume, is now Lieut. Colonel, or ought to be, if he is not, passed here on the 15th, on the way to the fort. The Major is a good soldier and a most excellent hearted man. His able administration at Fort Yuma, the fine discipline and condition of the troops under his charge, and the ready tact with which he manages all matters entrusted in his care, testify his fitness for the responsible office he holds. Few men in the column command the respect and esteem of those with whom they come in contact to so great an extent as Major Rigg. By order of Gen. Carleton, the Major took with him an exact and accurate statement of the strength and condition of every post and station, whether of troops or vedettes, on the route between Fort Yuma and Tucson. This is another proof of Carleton's attention to details. The whereabout, and duties and condition of every man in the column is known to him, and he takes every opportunity to keep himself exactly informed.

I have learned nothing further reliable in relation to Major Ferguson's visit to Sonora; but have no reason to doubt his entire or partial success in the purchase of forage for the use of this command. Abstract reasoners would argue that, in consequence of the difficulty with France, and the active levy of troops now going on in

Sonora to reinforce the armies of the Republic, it would be the policy of Pesqueira to hold fast to all the material requisite for the prosecution of hostilities; but such argument would be wide of the truth. There is nothing so scarce in Sonora as money. Gold and silver are rare curiosities in the eyes of its inhabitants; and for its acquisition they are ready to sell all they possess without reference to future wants. With the ready money in hand, received in payment for forage, such as corn, wheat, hay, etc., and for sheep, beef, fresh pork, they can pass through Sinaloa and the intervening States, to the capital for one-half the expense, and one-tenth the trouble they would incur by carrying their forage and provisions along. Their road being through their own country, which becomes more thickly settled, richer and more productive, as they advance, their march could be made by companies instead of regiments or brigades, and by taking different routes, abundance could easily be found for all the troops Sonora can bring into the field. Neither fear of the French, nor any other reason, will prevent them from parting with produce, if they have any, for money, especially when it is so scarce as at present.

MANUEL GANDARA

I learn upon pretty good authority that Manuel Gandara,[125] the renowned Governor of Sonora, has made his peace with Pesqueira, and returned to his own State; having first secured the beef contract to furnish the California column from Tucson onward to the frontiers of Texas. Whether Pesqueira has been let in for a portion of this contract, as a douceur,[126] I am unable to say; but the impression prevails that such is the case. Unless it prove far different from that which was given to Joseph Beard,[127] it will prove a losing affair. The beef consumed at Fort Barrett, Pimo villages, and along the Gila is furnished to the Government at the remarkably reasonable price of nine cents a pound, exclusive of neck pieces and shin bones. It is driven a distance of four hundred and odd miles, during the passage of which many stampedes occur, and many of the cattle are irretrievably lost to the contractor, absolutely destroying all profit and leaving him a loser. Gandara is a fine, shrewd, and very intelligent looking man, of about fifty years of age; erect, vigorous, and athletic as a man of twenty-five, with a fine, clear, gray eye; broad

125. The Arizona Special Census for 1864 shows that Manuel Gándara had been living in Tucson with his two sons for eighteen months. He had been governor of Sonora until his defeat by Pesqueira's forces in 1856, ending twenty years of political feuding and violence. Senate, *Federal Census—Territory of New Mexico and Territory of Arizona*, 68 (1864); Robert Forbes, *Crabb's Filibustering Expedition*, 13.

126. *Douceur* (French): a conciliatory gift or bribe.

127. Joseph R. Beard was awarded the contract to supply the Column from California with beef. He drove the cattle to the troops and slaughtered the animals as needed. In October 1862 his cattle were sixty days overdue in Tucson. *OR*, 50(2):73, 171.

and high forehead, and clear olive complexion. His father was a "Gachupin," or native of Spain, and his mother was a member of one of the first families of Sonora, (F.F.S.) Gandara possess remarkable natural abilities, but is more cunning than wise, more shrewd than sagacious. Having passed his whole life in the employment of chicanery, political and otherwise, he naturally suspects that all who approach him have some intrinsic design; some ulterior concealed object, toward the completion of which he (Gandara) can render valuable aid. Nevertheless, he is remarkably hospitable and generous, particularly to Americans, many of whom have received timely and much needed service at his hands. Were he less shrewd and cunning, and more sagacious and wise, he would doubtless have long since fallen a victim to his many unscrupulous and vindictive foes; while, on the other hand, had his country and the people been different, Gandara's inferior qualities might have arisen to a higher scale, and rendered him a far superior man. He is rich, and all-powerful in some parts of Sonora, and will undoubtedly fulfill his contract to the letter.

EXODUS FROM SONORA

Three or four months ago no little excitement was occasioned about Fort Yuma, and the lower counties of California, by the discovery of new and reported rich gold diggings, about one hundred miles above Yuma, on the Colorado river. The stories at first related about these mines were of the most Munchausenish description.[128] Diggers were reported to be taking it out at the rate of $1,000 a day to the hand in some parts, while nowhere was the yield less than from $75 to $100. You and I, and many others, know how gullible is the great mass of mankind; but despite the wonders related of the new diggings, comparatively few had the curiosity to go, and nearly all of the first visitors have returned. The placers, as described to me, by one who was three months there, are what are called "dry spot diggings," the gold being found in isolated spots, and no less than miles from the river, the nearest water. The yield in the most lucrative claims has been from $8 to $12, and as high as $15 a day; but the average is from $5 to $6, in good claims. The miners are obliged to pay from two to three "bits" a gallon for drinking water, and never use a drop for cooking purposes; you may therefore imagine the cleanliness of their condition. Provisions are scarce and very dear, so that is a claim which pays six dollars a day, yields the possessor about two or two and a half clear gain, the remainder being expended for the requisites to support life and carry on the work. The result is, that so far as Americans are concerned, these diggings

---

128. "Munchausenish" refers to Baron von Münchausen (1720–97), a German soldier, adventurer, and teller of wildly exaggerated tales. The Colorado River placer deposits discovered by Powell Weaver in 1862 soon played out after thousands of gold seekers from the United States and Mexico rushed to the site.

have fallen into disrepute, and but few are now wending their way thither. American traders, who located at these mines, and were the only ones who made the gold "stick," are getting away as fast as possible, having a wholesome dread of the state of affairs when several hundred starving miners shall be deceived into going there.

On the other hand, the Sonorians have just received the glowing relations above mentioned, and are flocking thither from all parts of the State by thousands. A party of forty, composed of Mexicans and seven Americans, who said they came from Guaymas, passed through here on the 12th, on their way to these mines, and they assured me that not less than three thousand people were getting ready to leave that State for the same destination. At least five hundred have already come through, and I have passed over two hundred on my road up the Gila. Many of these poor wretches were without food of any kind, and very scanty clothing. Quite a number had no cooking utensils, and most of them were without arms of any description. Even should they escape the Apaches, Mojaves, Yumas, and Chimihuahuas, [Chemehuevi][129] their case is desperate. Numbers have perished from thirst upon the long deserts which intervene between the Gila and the populated portions of northern Sonora; and to those who have come thus far, three hundred miles of painful and dangerous travel still remain. It is truly pitiable to contemplate the deplorable condition and infatuation of these starving multitudes, who, with little trouble and expense, and not half the risk, could acquire independence by tilling the ground at their own homes, or working the rich mines near their own firesides. One man, an American at that, assured me that he had passed diggings paying from three to six "bits" to the pan, on his way to the glittering promised land of golden rocks.

PESQUEIRA WANTS SOLDIERS

A few days ago two envoys arrived at these villages, from Pesqueira, to the chiefs of the Pimo and Maricopa tribes, bearing very handsome and gaily variegated Mexican blankets, with balls of different colored wool and worsted. The object of their mission was to engage the services of fifty warriors, forty Pimos and ten Maricopas, for the State of Sonora. In payment for these services, Pesqueira binds himself to feed and clothe the warriors, and furnish blankets to their tribes. As there are from 7,000 to 7,500 souls in these tribes, you may judge whether Pesqueira intended to fulfil his contract, and if he did, the amount it would cost at the rate of ten dollars for each blanket, which is as low as they can be had in Sonora. What particular service was to be

---

129. Chemehuevi is the Yuman name for a tribe most closely related to the Paiute of Uto-Aztecan linguistic stock. By the 1880s these Indians lived in the Chemehuevi Valley and at other points along the Colorado River. Swanton, *Indian Tribes*, 482–83.

required from these warriors, I cannot say; but it is probably they were meant to keep the Apaches in check.

Antonio Azul,[130] the Pimo chief, and Juan Chivaria,[131] the Maricopa chief, returned for answer, after taking the blankets and goods sent as a peace-offering, that "it would require two months for them to make up their minds, at the expiration of which time the envoys could come again, and they would talk with them." The respect they entertain for the Government of Sonora can be estimated by their reply. More anon.

YOURS TRULY, VEDETTE

ALTA, JULY 23, 1862

The Column from California under General Carleton
[From the Army Correspondent of the ALTA CALIFORNIA]

Tucson, Arizona, July 5th, 1862

EDITORS ALTA: After a long and most toilsome march, I have at length reached Tucson, so lately in possession of the rebel forces. The town is of adobe, built in the style of all Mexican places of the kind, and with nothing particular to recommend it to notice beyond the clear stream of water which irrigates the fields in the neighborhood, a quantity of fine shade trees, and a fair amount of valuable land. The native population, when all present, might number about five hundred, but nearly all are now absent, having been driven away by the outrageous acts of the rebels. If credence is to be placed in the statements made by the people of this place, Hunter's command was composed of the most depraved cut-throats and gallows-birds.[132] The advent of the California Column has restored confidence, and the inhabitants are returning by scores. I shall now

130. Antonio Azul was the head chief of the Pimas and is so listed in A. B. Chapman's census of the Pimas and Maricopas. J. Ross Browne noted in 1864 that Antonio Azul had accompanied the Mohave chief Iretaba on his sightseeing tour of San Francisco the year before. *Adventures*, 29; Senate, 35th Cong., 2nd sess., 1857, S. Exec. Doc. 1, pt. 1, Serial 974, 560.

131. J. Ross Browne encountered Juan Chivaria and fourteen of his warriors in 1864, identifying Chivaria as chief of the Maricopas. *Adventures*, 121.

132. Most of Sherod Hunter's men were originally enlisted as Arizona Rangers at the mining settlement of Pinos Altos, New Mexico, and were primarily concerned with protecting lives and property from raiding Apaches. Many deserted the Confederate cause when the opportunity arose. Finch, "Sherod Hunter," 53. Some of the California soldiers did not care much for the government's leniency toward the ex-Confederates who were hired as scouts and teamsters. On February 8, 1863, Manson A. Mesenheimer of Company B, Second California Cavalry wrote from Tucson: "A screw is loose somewhere. A few days ago the three secesh prisoners taken at [Picacho] Pass were turned loose on parole . . . , and one of them is driving a Government team." *San Francisco Evening Bulletin*, Mar. 11, 1863.

endeavor to give your readers a description of matters and things in this region, commencing with [...]

FORT STANFORD AND THE APACHES.

On arriving at Cotton Wood Springs, my captain was sent for by General Carleton, to repair to Fort Stanford [Breckenridge] to hold a talk with the Apaches, a number of whom had been collected at that place by Captain Picton [Pishon], 1st Cavalry, for that purpose, and being relieved by Lieut. [Albert H.] French 1st Cavalry, the Captain repaired thither without delay; but on arriving, not an Apache of any kind was to be seen or heard of. So thorough is their education in the art of stealing, that I will relate two instances in this connection, from which you can judge for yourself. Lieut.-Colonel Eyre, in order to attract the Apaches into camp, caused a white flag to be hoisted on a prominent height, and to such good purpose that they stole the flag. After entering camp at Fort Stanford, they discovered a beef which had been slaughtered that day for the use of the command, and left hanging to a tree in the midst of the camp; but when morning dawned, the beef was gone, while the satisfied expression of the savages proclaimed its fate and their success. Every article at all exposed was sure to be appropriated by them, and after stealing all they could, they left and returned no more. The General had cherished the hope that these pestilent savages could be won over by kindness and firmness; but I am inclined to believe that his views are undergoing a radical change in this respect. What can we expect of a people whose earliest education inculcates address and dexterity in stealing as the most cardinal of the virtues? From earliest infancy, or as soon as it can comprehend anything, the papoose is taught to appropriate the goods of others, and as he grows older, his ambition to excel in this regard is incited by premiums and encomiums heaped upon his dexterity. When of age to have a family of his own, the young girls are sure to cast the tenderest regards upon him who has proved himself the most adroit thief, as holding out the promise of the easiest and most abundant living to the wife. Any effort to innoculate honesty and morality upon so vicious a system must be utterly futile and vain. Nothing remains of Fort Stanford [formerly Fort Breckenridge] but the walls, all the wood work having been burned by order of Lieutenant Ford [Lord],[133] U.S.A., to prevent the fort being useful to the rebels.

133. A native of Ohio, Richard S. C. Lord graduated from the U.S. Military Academy in 1856 and became part owner of the Patagonia Mine in 1857 while stationed at Fort Buchanan. A court of inquiry was convened at Santa Fe on October 2, 1862, at Lord's request. The court determined that charges alleged by the *Santa Fe Gazette* that his company "ingloriously" fled at the battle of Val Verde were unfounded. Exonerated, Lord joined his regiment, the First U.S. Cavalry, in the East, where he served throughout the rest of the war. He died a brevet lieutenant colonel in 1866. Heitman, *Historical Register,* 1:641; GO 92, Hdqrs. Dept. of N.M., October 13, 1862, *OR,* 9:504.

ARMY MOVEMENTS

Over two weeks ago Lieut. Col. Eyre, with Companies B and C of the First Cavalry, was ordered to the Rio Grande, 300 miles distant, to make the reconnoissance of the country; discover the army's position, force and general condition, and report accordingly. It is altogether probable that Gen. Carleton had such advices from that quarter as warranted him in detaching the squadron, I have mentioned, for so long a distance; and he is prepared to send off another detachment at the earliest moment. In fact, the whole column will move forward as soon as the summer rains, which have already commenced, shall have filled the water courses and holes along the route. Our next halting place will therefore be somewhere around Mesilla, or Dina [Doña] Ana, 300 miles further east. Major Ferguson has returned from Mexico, having gone no further than San Francisco de la Magdalena,[134] a small town on the frontier, and the place where the image of San Francisco is said to work miracles yearly, which mainly consists in the easy and sudden transportation of money from the pockets of devout believers, into those of other people, wearing long black gowns and long black hats. I learn that the Major found no difficulty in contracting for all the forage we may require for the use of the column. The force now at Tucson consists of the First Regiment of Infantry, with the exception of Company G, which is now *en route* from Fort Yuma; Capt. Shinn's Battery of Light Artillery, Companies A, D and E of the First Cavalry, Company B of the Second Cavalry, and a small Howitzer battery, commanded by Lieut. Thompson.[135] Tucson is under the military command of Lieut. Col. West, with Major Rigg as Provost Marshal, and no more orderly or decorous place exists anywhere.

COL. LALLY[136] AND LIEUT. MOWRY

The two gentlemen whose names head this caption, and who have figured somewhat in times past, are now here, but under widely different circumstances. Lally, who was Major of the gallant Ninth in Mexico, is here as the agent for the mining interest of

134. Magdalena, Sonora.

135. William A. Thompson was enrolled as first lieutenant, Company E, First California Infantry. In May 1862 he was ordered to take charge of two of the four twelve-pounder mountain howitzers that accompanied the California Column. Enlisted men of the First and Fifth California Infantry regiments were assigned to him as gun crews. This unit played a pivotal role in the Apache Pass battle with the Apaches on July 15. Thompson was promoted to captain of Company D on October 26, 1863, and mustered out with this company at Las Cruces, New Mexico, on August 31, 1864. Orton, *California Men*, 350, 354; *OR*, 50(1):1058, 50(2):26–27.

136. Thornton F. Lally served with the Maine Volunteers as major during the Mexican War. Later, with the Ninth U.S. Infantry in 1847, he was brevetted lieutenant colonel for gallant and meritorious service. Lally was honorably mustered out on August 26, 1848. Heitman, *Historical Register*, 1:612.

the late Col. Samuel Colt,[137] of six-shooter celebrity. I believe that Lally is himself a part proprietor in these mines, which are of silver, and said to be very rich. The company is known as the Sonora Exploring and Mining Company,[138] and during the reign of terror at this place they were confiscated to the Confederate Government by an outlaw named Palatine Robinson,[139] who is also here in durance vile, with sundry of the gravest charges hanging over his head. Col. Lally is much liked, and will probably be named Governor of Arizona if he will accept the place.

Lieut. Mowry was confined to his quarters with a sentinel constantly over him, and not allowed to converse with any person. He is charged with having endeavored to overthrow the U.S. Government and having fomented the rebellion in this place to the utmost of his power. His mine, known as the Patagonia Mine, also very rich in silver, has been seized by order of Colonel West, and a receiver appointed. It rests with Gen. Carleton to approve or disapprove the action of Col. West; but there is no doubt he will adopt the former course.

Since the above was written, Mowry has been sent as a prisoner to Fort Yuma, where he will remain until the pleasure of the Government be known in his regard. He went under charge of Lieut. S. Taylor,[140] First Infantry, California Volunteers. The General has fully approved the action of Col. West in taking possession of Mowry's silver mines and placing a receiver over them. They are said by many to be yielding $500 a day, clear of expenses.

137. Col. Samuel Colt, who made his fortune as an arms manufacturer, was vitally interested in Arizona's mines. He became the major stockholder and president of the Sonora Exploring and Mining Company, developers of the Cerro Colorado (Heintzelman) Mine, in 1859. North, *Samuel Peter Heintzelman*, 171.

138. Maj. Samuel P. Heintzelman and Charles D. Poston founded the Sonora Exploring and Mining Company in March 1856 with hopes of attracting other investors in order to exploit the mines along the Santa Cruz River in Arizona. Ibid., 22.

139. Palatine Robinson was a Virginian by birth but arrived in Arizona in 1856 via Kentucky. He dealt in wet and dry goods, though his occupation is listed as "farmer" in the 1860 census. Robinson killed R. A. Johnson in 1859 following an argument and brawl at a local saloon. He was confined at Fort Yuma while awaiting trial for this incident as well as charges of assault and kidnapping. He dropped out of sight in December 1862 but turned up in Texas after traveling secretly through Mexico with other Rebel sympathizers. In January 1864 he wrote to Confederate authorities from San Antonio urging them to recruit troops in Arizona and California. Altshuler, *Latest from Arizona*, 277–78; Lockwood, *Life in Old Tucson*, 121–37; Senate, *Federal Census—Territory of New Mexico and Territory of Arizona*, 45 (1860).

140. Edward G. Taylor enrolled as second lieutenant of Company F, First California Infantry on August 16, 1861. Promoted to first lieutenant on June 23, 1862, he was mustered out at Pinos Altos, New Mexico, on August 31, 1864. Orton, *California Men*, 359.

218 DISPATCHES FROM THE CALIFORNIA VOLUNTEERS, 1862–65

A NOTED RUFFIAN

Sometime last year, a noted ruffian who resided in this place, and whose name is Palatine Robinson, posted written notices on the premises of royal [loyal] men, confiscating their possessions and converting the same to the use of the Confederate Government, which, at the same time, was concentrated in the person of the said Palatine Robinson. In addition to this he is charged with the murder of R. A. Johnson,[141] whom you may remember as one of Walker's officers, in Nicaragua;[142] he is also charged with shooting, with intent to kill, one Patrick Dunn [Dunne];[143] also with the abduction and sale of a Mexican girl aged ten years, and named Ramona Ortega.[144] Robinson's case is now being examined into by a Military Commission, consisting of Lieutenant-Colonel West, Captain Cremony, and Lieutenant Hargrave,[145] to inquire into the truth of these charges, and find whether there is ground to deprive him of his liberty and bring him to justice. In so far as relates to the killing of Johnson, it appears that Johnson provoked the quarrel and swore to shoot Robinson on sight. He went to Robinson's house at 11 o'clock P.M., and after many threats met his death at the hands of Robinson. The other charges will, no doubt, be brought home to him and place him in a decidedly delicate situation. There seems to be a fatality in the movements of these desperadoes which eventually consigns them to well merited punishment.

141. "Colonel" R. A. Johnson was a lawyer who had once resided in California and associated with William Walker during his Nicaraguan filibuster. Johnson was shot to death by Palatine Robinson when he went armed to the latter's house following an argument at a card game. Lockwood, *Life in Old Tucson*, 132.

142. William Walker (1824–60) was born in Nashville, Tennessee. Precocious, he graduated from the University of Nashville at the age of fourteen and then pursued careers in law, medicine, and journalism. In 1853 he organized an unsuccessful filibuster in Baja California. His Nicaraguan adventure began when he seized that country with a small army and was "elected" president. Walker was soon deposed but not deterred. He returned in 1860 but was captured by the British and executed by Honduran authorities. For more information on the enigmatic Walker, see Greene, *The Filibuster*.

143. Patrick H. Dunne was listed in the 1860 census as a printer from Maine, aged thirty-six. At the hearing by military authorities in Tucson, Robinson admitted to having assaulted Dunne. Senate, *Federal Census—Territory of New Mexico and Territory of Arizona*, 40 (1860); Lockwood, *Life in Old Tucson*, 135.

144. Ramona Ortega was most likely the oldest daughter of Ramón and Jesúsa Ortega. The girl was named for her grandmother Ramona. Ramón was a native Arizonan and worked as a laborer and farmer, while Jesúsa worked as a housekeeper. Senate, *Federal Census—Territory of New Mexico and Territory of Arizona*, 44 (1860), 74 (1864).

145. Joseph P. Hargrave enrolled as first lieutenant of Company F, First California Infantry on August 16, 1861. Promoted to captain of Company C on June 23, 1862, he was mustered out with that company at Pinos Altos, New Mexico, on August 31, 1864. Orton, *California Men*, 346, 359.

Tubac, 1864. By J. Ross Browne, from *Adventures in the Apache Country.*

FURTHER ARMY MOVEMENTS

To-day, the detachment of Co. B, 2nd Cavalry, which was left at the Cañada del Oro, 28 miles from this place, arrived here, and will be stationed for a few days within a mile and a half of Tucson, when they will be moved to the "Revention," [Reventon][146] 40 miles away on the road between San Francisco de la Magdalena, on what is known as Breevoort's Rancho, the most delightful spot in this country, where they will remain to recuperate their horses and reassemble the Company now scattered from "Dan to Bersheeba" as vedettes.[147] Companies A, D and E of the 1st Cavalry, also arrived from the same place, having camped there on their way from Fort Stanford, and will be sent, without delay, to Tubac, distant about fifty miles, or ten miles

146. Elias Brevoort was a native of Michigan. In 1859 he came to Arizona as the sutler at Fort Buchanan and established a ranch called Reventon along the lower Santa Cruz that was valued at $73,500. J. Ross Browne describes his house as "palatial" and "the most imposing private residence in Arizona" during his travels in 1864. *Adventures,* 259. Brevoort later returned to his home in Santa Fe. Senate, *Federal Census—Territory of New Mexico and Territory of Arizona,* 25 (1860); Hinton, *Handbook to Arizona,* 224; Barnes, "Arizona Place Names," 361.

147. During the Civil War cavalry units were used for all sorts of escort, express, and vedette duty, which broke up the regiments and companies and reduced their effectiveness. This kind of service was irksome to regulars and volunteers alike. "Dan to Beersheeba" is a biblical reference from Judges 20:1 meaning from one outermost extreme or limit to the other, as the settlement of Dan was the northernmost city of ancient Palestine and Beersheeba was the southernmost.

beyond the "Revention." Apaches are extremely thick in both places, and it will require extreme caution and watchfulness to prevent the horses and mules from being stolen by them. In all other respects, the two places named are surpassingly excellent for cavalry command.

Capt. Picton [Pishon], in command of companies A, D, and E, of the 1st Cavalry, takes his departure this afternoon for Tubac, fifty miles distant, where he will organize a camp. Company B, of the 2d Cavalry, will be located for the present at the Reventon, six miles this side of Tubac. Jones, the expressman, who left here with Col. Eyre's command for the Rio Grande, is momently expected back with intelligence from that officer. He is now somewhat overdue.

FOURTH OF JULY IN TUCSON

The "glorious Fourth" was celebrated in this place yesterday by the California column, and the people generally, with a good deal of warmth (no play upon the weather is intended; although the thermometer was rising 108 in the shade.) Captain Shinn's battery fired a Federal salute at sunrise, and a National salute at meridian.[148] The usual drills, etc., were dispensed with, and the soldiers enjoyed a holiday, and I am proud to add, that despite the latitude allowed them by the relaxation of military discipline, the best order and regularity prevailed. In the evening there were two *bailes* or dances, one for the officers and another for the men. As I did not visit either, I can give no account of them further than that there were an unusual number of headaches on the day following. At dress parade on the evening of the 3d, the following order of Colonel West's was read:

HEADQUARTERS, TUCSON, ARIZONA
JULY 3, 1862

ORDER NO. 14

The epoch which marks the disenthralment of our Nation, and held forth assurance of personal, civil, religious and political liberty, is one of the most noteworthy in the history of mankind.

The inestimable blessings confirmed to the American people on the 4th of July, 1776, in the *magna charta* of their independence, have been the unfailing source of terror to tyrants, and of hope and promise to the down-trodden of all lands.

---

148. Whereas the national salute is determined by the number of states composing the Union at the rate of one gun per state (the Southern states were included; their secession was not recognized by the U.S. government), the Federal salute was thirteen guns. *Revised U.S. Army Regulations of 1861*, 42, 43.

The sacred fires of patriotism which glowed in the hearts of our fathers, should burn now as brightly in our hearts, and the column from California is here to-day to testify by their support to the Government which was established at such cost, their appreciation of those blessings and their determination to resist all efforts to dissolve the Union.

Deeply impressed with the sanctity and righteousness of the cause which we maintain, and desirous of appropriately commemorating the anniversary of the day of its . . . [original text unreadable] exercises of the morning be omitted, and that only such work as is absolutely necessary at this post be done during the day.

II. The commander of Light Co. A, 3d Artillery, will fire a federal salute at sunrise and a national salute at meridian.

By order of Lieut. Col. West.

LAFAYETTE HAMMOND,
1ST LIEUT. R. Q. M. 1ST INFANTRY C.V.,
ACTING ADJUTANT

GOVERNOR GANDARA

Manuel Gandara, ex-Governor of Sonora, is here, with two of his sons, and quite a number of his peons, who seem inordinately attached to their master. Once more the strong heart of this veteran is bowed down with grief for the loss of the eldest son of those who still remained to him. He died about two weeks ago from the effects of a wound received from the Apaches, some months ago. When I saw the Governor yesterday, he was seated in a chair outside the door of his house, and just after a grand thunder storm, while the earth was still damp with the refreshing moisture, and the air mild, pleasant and balmy. His regards were fixed intently on the ground, and he appeared absorbed in most profound grief. Gandara has not made his peace with Pesqueira, as I wrote on a former occasion, but scorns to make any advance in that direction. It is true that he has secured the beef contract for the Column.

JOHN RAINS

John Rains,[149] the secessionist, whose zeal furnished several members of General A. S. Johnston's party and others with horses and money to expedite their transit into secessiondom, and who is the owner of the celebrated Cocumunga [Cucamonga]

149. John Rains was a wealthy Californian and owner of the Cucamonga Ranch near San Bernardino. He was purported to be a secessionist. Rains supplied the Column from California with beef in the summer of 1862 but was murdered near his ranch in November of that year. *OR*, 50(1):565; *Alta*, Nov. 26, 1862.

Rancho, arrived here last night.[150] Rains is the contractor, in fact, for the beef supply to this point, while Beard is his "man of business." Rains is here to look after his interests, which sadly required his presence.

MISCELLANEOUS

Dr. Wooster, now of the Pimos, has either been ordered, by this time, or will be ordered, to report for duty at Fort Yuma, while Dr. Christian[151] goes to Fort Vancouver, in Oregon. Both of these *medicos* are extremely disgusted with their present abodes or stations; Wooster being anxious to return to Yuma, and Christian just as anxious to get away. Both will be gratified, and the service benefited by the change.

I find that I have unintentionally done wrong to Capt. Calloway, by saying that he disobeyed orders; no orders, so far as I can learn, having been disobeyed by that officer. I exceedingly regret that I should have been imposed upon to the extent of injuring, even in the slightest degree, any gentlemen; but the positive manner and repeated affirmations of my informants were such as to induce any one to credit their assertions. I, however, take the earliest moment to make the *amende*, and will be particularly careful for the future as to the reliability of others.

The weather is now intensely hot; but not nearly so much so as it was at Maricopa Wells. A thunder storm passes near or over the place nearly every afternoon, and when it gives us the benefit of its visit, a notable change for the better is experienced.

VEDETTE

150. Pvt. John Teal of Company B, Second California Cavalry commented in June 1864 that "Cucamonga ranche is the prettiest & most valuable ranche I have seen in the west." At that time the ranch produced grapes, apples, apricots, pears, peaches, cherries, figs, walnuts, and pomegranates on about two hundred acres. Henry Walker, "Soldier in the California Column," 71.

151. Robert A. Christian was brigade surgeon of U.S. Volunteers in 1862. He was ordered to Fort Yuma in April 1862 and then to move forward into Arizona with the Fifth California Infantry. *OR*, 50(1):1017, 1037.

ALTA, AUGUST 10, 1862

Diary of the March to the Rio Grande
(From the Correspondent of the ALTA CALIFORNIA with Gen. Carleton's
Column from California)
Fort Thomas [Thorn, N.Mex.],[152] *July 10, 1862*

TO THE RIO GRANDE

EDITORS ALTA: As an opportunity offers, I will try to give you a hurried account of our expedition to the Rio Grande. We left Tucson on the 21st of June, the expedition being composed of two companies (B and C), 1st Cavalry, Cal. Vol., Capt. Fritz in command of the former, and Lieut. Hudson [Haden][153] in command of the latter—all under command of Lieut. Colonel Eyre—upon a forced reconnoissance to the Rio Grande. Four wagons with six mule teams comprised our transportation, besides which pack saddles were taken along, so that, in case of necessity forcing us to abandon the wagons, provision could be packed on the mules.

Our road was supposed to be destitute of water for long stretches; our animals would have to live upon the grass along the route, as forage could not be taken; and further, we were going into a country made desolate by the Texans, with whom we would be more than likely to have a brush—yet every man bounded into his saddle with a light heart and high spirits.

Our first day's march was a hard one, fifty-five miles without water, to the "Cienega de los Pimos,"[154] where we found a nice, cool stream with abundance of grass. Here was once a settlement of Pimos, who made mescal; the old cow hide vats

152. The reference to Fort Thomas is incorrect and apparently the typesetter's mistake. The author, James P. Newcomb, correctly identified Fort Thorn in a nearly identical draft of this letter dated July 7, 1862. Although Camp Thomas was located along the Gila River in New Mexico, Colonel Eyre's command was still encamped at Fort Thorn at the time this letter was written. Thorn, an active post between 1853 and 1859, was located at the Rio Grande in southwestern New Mexico. Beck and Haase, *Historical Atlas of New Mexico*, 35; Orton, *California Men*, 886; Newcomb Papers.
153. This misidentification is the typesetter's error. The author correctly identified Lieutenant Haden in a letter dated July 7, 1862. Porter Haden enrolled at Camp Merchant, California, as first lieutenant of Company C, First California Cavalry. He left Tucson with Colonel Eyre's "reconnaissance" to the Rio Grande in command of Company C. Promoted to captain of Company H, the lieutenant declined the position. Haden was mustered out with his company at Las Cruces, New Mexico, on September 7, 1864. Orton, *California Men*, 109, 142; *OR*, 50(1):120; Newcomb Papers.
154. Ciénega de los Pimos (or Pinos) lay twenty-five miles east of Tucson. It was also known as Punta de Agua. Barnes, "Arizona Place Names," 96, 262; Report of Lt. Col. Edward E. Eyre, July 6, 1862, *OR*, 50(1):121.

still remain. Several of our horses got bogged in the creek and were with much difficulty taken out. At night our bugles sounded clearly and defiantly, echoing to the hills—no doubt, waking many dusky Apache from his reverie. On the 22d, we marched to San Pedro Creek, and camped at the old Overland stage station.[155] In one of the rooms we found this notice: "Jones, Wheeling, Mexican, N.S. Express, left this place June 15th, 12 M. No Indians."

PEMMICAN

In order to break the monotony of a journal, let me say a word about our *grub*. The command was furnished with pemmican in lieu of pork and beef, a most unpalatable and unhealthy diet, having been made of rotten old dried beef and the refuse of a soap factory.[156] The samples first furnished may have been good, but the lot furnished to our command is certainly the meanest food ever served up to a hungry man; fresh mule meat would be a luxury in comparison. The men evinced their disgust in many ways, and it was amusing to listen to their questions which were answered by "pemmican." For instance: "What will kill rats;" "what's worse punishment than death;" "what made Lieut. H.'s dog turn back?" etc.

DRAGOON SPRINGS

23d.—At Dragoon Springs found water scarce, but sufficient by using care and patience.[157] At night the surrounding mountains were alive with Indian fires. Near the stage station are the [four] graves of Hunter's men, killed by the Apaches. On the graves were these inscriptions, neatly cut in rough stone, executed by one of the Union prisoners they had along: "S. Ford, May 5th, 1862." "Ricardo." Ford was a Sergeant, and Ricardo was a poor Mexican boy the Texans had forced into service at Tucson.[158]

155. San Pedro Creek Station was located on the east bank of the San Pedro River twenty-one miles southwest from Dragoon Springs. The Butterfield Overland Company constructed a bridge there as well as a large adobe station house and corral. San Pedro Station was an important stop since it was located at the junction of the main east-west and north-south traffic routes through the region. Conkling and Conkling, *Butterfield Overland Mail*, 2:149, 150.

156. Carleton ordered pemmican to be produced and packaged in cans as a high-energy food for campaigning. The men hated it and traded it to the Indians and emigrants at every opportunity. Although there were a number of recipes for this concoction, Carleton's was made from "pounded dried beef and beef lard." *OR*, 50(1):774, 947.

157. Dragoon Springs was situated twenty-five miles southwest of Ewell's Station on the Butterfield route. The spring was about a quarter of a mile south of the fortified stone station house, which was designed to withstand Indian attacks. Conkling and Conkling, *Butterfield Overland Mail*, 2:140, 141.

158. S. Ford was Sgt. Sam B. Ford, a resident of Pinos Altos, New Mexico, who had joined Hunter's Arizona Ranger company. Ricardo had been pressed into service as a stock herder. Another of Hunter's men, John Donaldson, was killed in the same fight on May 5, 1862. The

24th.—Made a dry camp at Ewell Station;[159] men were sent four miles to the mountains, for water to drink.

25th.—Reached the station in Apache Pass[160] about 9 o'clock, where water would have been abundant, but for the improvidence of those in advance rushing in and filling up the spring, so that it was late in the day before all our animals had water.

ALARM IN CAMP—THE PEMMICAN TREATY—THREE MEN KILLED BY INDIANS

Fresh Indian signs were seen in the vicinity of camp, and the fact reported to our commander; but no attention was paid to them, as it was thought that the Indians would not dare come near so formidable a force as ours. Horses were scattered over the hills and ravines, and men wandering carelessly everywhere. Presently a horse was reported gone; shortly afterward, in the midst of *our* feeling of security, several shots were heard up the ravine and the cry of "Indians." The camp became a scene of wild excitement and confusion—horses were driven in, and the men rushed promiscuously to the spot whence the alarm proceeded—upon reaching which I saw the Indians dodging about on the hill and rising ground, several hundred yards off, and the men standing about on the heights ready for a fight; but the Colonel arriving, waving a white rag on a sabre, ordered the men not to fire, as he wished to talk with the Indians. At this juncture Corporal Brown[161] came up, very much excited, and reported that the Indians had killed three of our men, and that he had barely saved his own life by flight—that the men were behind him, having been to water their horses at a spring over the ridge—that the horses broke away and ran by him into camp, and that he saw the Indians close in upon them and heard their cries for help. Some one doubted the story, and the Colonel disregarded it and persevered to get a talk with the Indians, who

---

identity of the fourth man buried at Dragoon Springs is unknown. Cochise's Chiricahua Apache warriors also ran off twenty-five horses and thirty mules that had been confiscated from Tucson citizens. Finch, "Sherod Hunter," 190; and *Confederate Pathway*, 152–53.

159. Ewell's Station, fifteen miles west of Apache Pass, was established in 1859. It was named for Capt. Richard S. Ewell of the First Dragoons. A change station, intended to provide a break in the forty-mile trip between Dragoon Springs and Apache Pass, it was supplied with water from Dos Cabezas Spring five miles away. Conkling and Conkling, *Butterfield Overland Mail*, 2:139.

160. Apache Pass is the narrow defile between the Dos Cabezas and Chiricahua mountains. The Butterfield Overland Mail Company considered it to be the most dangerous point on its route and requested that the government establish a military post there in 1858. The site selected by the California Column for Fort Bowie in July 1862 was only half a mile east of the stage station. Ibid., 145.

161. John Brown was a corporal in Company C, First California Cavalry. He died at Camp Miembres, New Mexico, on May 4, 1866. Orton, *California Men*, 110, 872.

were very wary, only allowing the Colonel and his interpreter[162] to come into the ravine alone, immediately under the rising ground, where some sixty Indians could easily be distinguished, their lances flashing in the sun and their bows and rifles sticking above the bushes and rocks. The interpreter approached within pistol shot of this array, the Colonel following in the rear, and succeeded in coaxing down the Indian interpreter, a couple of chiefs following and several Indians, until a party of about a dozen stood around. A talk ensued through the interpreter, between the Colonel and chief, decidedly peaceful, and wound up by the Indians asking for some tobacco, which was sent for—and along with a can of pemmican was given to the Indians— when both parties parted, evidently well pleased with each other, the Indians promising to come back to see us in the evening, a promise which they kept. The Colonel returned well satisfied with the good intentions of the Apaches, and ordered the horse herders further up the ravine, where grass was better. Six of the guards thinking there was something in Brown's story, proceeded to the spot designated by him as where the men were killed and, sure enough, found the body of Keith[163] lying within thirty yards of the place where the peace conference took place, and exactly where the Indians had tried to entice the interpreter. They gave the alarm, and then rushed up the hill to fight the Indians. Others joined them, and on reaching the top they saw the Indians several hundred yards off, and fired into them with their carbines—with what effect it is not known. Now all was mad excitement. Capt. Fritz ordered some of his men to saddle up to pursue the murderers, which order was countermanded by the Colonel. Then the Captain led a party on foot, but it was of no use—the cowardly Indians had fled far out of reach. The bodies of Smith [Schmidt][164] and Maloney[165] were found far beyond Keith's, and it was a sad and horrible sight to seem them borne into camp stripped of every article of clothing, scalped and terribly mutilated with bullet, arrow

162. Eyre's interpreter was James P. Newcomb, the author of this letter. Newcomb's account of this encounter may be contrasted with Eyre's own. The colonel appears bolder and more decisive in his official report, and the Apaches are more numerous (seventy-five to one hundred warriors), but most of the other details of the parley and killings match very well. It is very apparent in this letter that only Eyre and the interpreter could have made the observations recorded by "N." E. E. Eyre to B. C. Cutler, July 6, 1862, Fort Thorn, *OR*, 50(1):120–24.

163. James F. Keith enlisted as a private in Company B, First California Cavalry at San Francisco on September 5, 1861. He was killed while watering his horse in Apache Pass on June 25, 1862. Orton, *California Men*, 62, 104, 876.

164. Albert Schmidt was enrolled at San Francisco on August 12, 1861, as a private in Company B, First California Cavalry. He was killed while watering his horse in Apache Pass on June 25, 1862. Orton, *California Men*, 107, 881.

165. Peter (John) Maloney enlisted as a private in Company B, First California Cavalry and was enrolled at San Francisco on August 29, 1861. He was killed by Apaches on June 25, 1862, in Apache Pass. Orton, *California Men*, 62, 104, 878.

and lance wounds. Keith was not scalped, as it seemed he was too near us for them to do it without discovery. All three belonged to Company B. Their graves were dug, and, after a sorrowful funeral, we marched out of the Pass and camped in the open plain, in the vicinity of the mountains and between some ravines.

MIDNIGHT ALARM

Proper precaution was not taken against attack and surprise; sentries were placed within only a few yards of the picket line, where the horses were tied and men made down their beds. About midnight, a sheet of fire blazed from a ravine within rifle shot, and the camp was alarmed by a volley of about sixty shots, fired in amongst us; fortunately only wounding Dr. Kittrige in the head,[166] and killing a horse from the picket line. Great confusion ensued; the bugles sounded wildly to arms, and the officers were calling the men to *fall into line;* and such orders as "Go out there," "Get out there," intermingled with expressive language, and men rushing everywhere. Finally, Captain Fritz, who was cool, succeeded in extending the pickets. Several shots were fired by our men; in fact, it seemed a regular little battle for a while. All finally quieted down, and half an hour elapsed, when another alarm was given, which proved to be false.

25th.—Left "Surprise Camp" early in the morning, and reached the Cienega San Simon,[167] by way of the Overland stage stand, about 3 o'clock P.M. Before reaching the cienega, the men suffered for water, insomuch that several were placed in the wagons.

ANOTHER ALARM

Alarms became common. Our first night's rest at the Cienega was broken by a false alarm. Three of the pickets saw an object which they took to be an Indian, and fired upon it. The bugles sounded to arms, and the men crawled to their posts without confusion. The object was found out to be a wolf, and in the morning three bullet holes were in the carcass.

166. Dr. William A. Kittridge was a graduate of the Oakland College of Physicians and Surgeons. He was assigned to the Column from California as acting assistant surgeon and accompanied Eyre's command when it left Tucson on June 21, 1862. The wound referred to was made by a bullet that lodged in the doctor's forehead over his left eye; the lead ball was successfully removed, and Kittridge recovered. Quebbeman, *Medicine in Territorial Arizona,* 352; Carleton to Eyre, June 17, 1862, *OR,* 50(1):98; *Sacramento Union,* Aug. 18, 1862.

167. Ciénega San Simon refers to the San Simon Station on the Butterfield route. The adobe station house with its earthen water tank was just twelve miles west of the New Mexico border. *Ciénega* is a Spanish word meaning "marsh" or "marshy place." Ahnert, *Retracing the Butterfield Overland Trail,* 19; Cremony, *Life among the Apaches,* 171.

CIENEGA SAN SIMON

We encamped about nine miles above the Overland stage station, upon the old emigrant road. The Cienega is a narrow, green strip in the midst of a barren, God-forsaken country. No trees shade it; it is simply a bright green spot, watered by a little brook of delicious cold water, which runs for a short distance, and is absorbed or rather spreads out over the little valley, and disappears amidst a mat of flags and grass. We had fine grazing for our animals, and the men caught a mess of small trout, which were quite delicious to our pemmican-sick palates. Near our camps are the remains of an old Apache rancheria.

EXTERMINATION OF THE APACHES

Before leaving Apache Pass too far behind, I wish to say that I am an advocate for the extermination of the Apaches. They have never made and kept a treaty of peace, but have ever been thieves, highwaymen, and murderers; year out and year in, hundreds have perished upon the roads by their hands, and it is estimated that within the past twelve months, at least one hundred white persons have been killed by them on the road between Tucson and the Rio Grande; some of which murders were most horrible, tying up their victims by the heels, and building slow fires under their heads. Let the Pimos be armed and encouraged to make war upon them and every other tribe urged to the same end, and the Government take energetic steps until they are driven from their mountain hiding places, and rendered harmless.

26th.—Left our pleasant camp on the Cienega, in the evening, and made a dry camp some seventeen miles up the road.

29th.—Started early; found water at Lightendoffer's [Leitensdorfer's] Well;[168] halted a few minutes at Soldier's Farewell,[169] found no water for our animals, and very poor and little of it for the men, many of them having suffered severely from thirst, which an be attributed to pemmican and not sun. Without unsaddling, we marched on to Dinsmore or Cow Spring,[170] our animals having traveled sixty miles without water, and the men without eating; thirty-six hours under the most fatiguing circumstances. A couple of the leanest animals gave out, but came up the next day.

168. Eugene Leitensdorfer came to New Mexico with Stephen Watts Kearney in 1846. He served briefly as auditor of public accounts for the U.S. civil government under Gov. Charles Bent. McNitt, *Navajo Wars*, 98.

169. Soldier's Farewell was the site of a fortified stone "time-table" stage station constructed by William Buckley in November 1858. It is located fourteen miles southwest of Ojo de Vaca on the irregular ridge that demarks the Continental Divide. Conkling and Conkling, *Butterfield Overland Mail*, 1:124–25; Pearce, *New Mexico Place Names*, 158.

170. Dinsmore was also known as Ojo de Vaca or Cow Springs.

MEET EXPRESS FROM FORT CRAIG

29th.—Upon arriving at Dinsmore Spring, the guide who was in the advance, ran against a sentinel, when a conversation of questions ensued; and the sentinel, taking the guide to be in the advance of a party of Texans, let him go, so as to allow his party to saddle up and leave. The guide returned and reported some men camped at the Spring; some confusion occurred, the Colonel ordering the companies into line, at the same time men and animals almost famishing for water. The guide was sent again to spy out the party at the Spring, whom he found saddled up and ready to leave; they then disclosed their character, when the guide assured them, by the presence of a body of Union troops, they then accompanied him to Colonel Eyres. They turned out to be a party of men bearing despatches from Colonel Shippington [Chivington] at Fort Craig.[171]

FATE OF EXPRESSMAN JONES AND PARTY

From the scouts we learned that Jones and party had been attacked by the Apaches, this side of the Pass, and that Jones saved his life by flight, while the Mexican and sergeant was killed. Jones was chased for a long way, but succeeded in getting into Mesilla more dead than alive, when he was taken prisoner by the Texans.

PRISONERS

On the night we came in Cow Spring, we captured a German and a Mexican traveling on foot, they said they were going upon an express to Tucson, to procure provisions for the people at the Placer, a small town at the gold mines, about thirty miles from the Spring; and represented the people there in a starving condition. As their mode of traveling, and their poor provisions for so long a trip looked suspicious, the Colonel thought best to take them along; saving them their long and dangerous trip.

ANOTHER ALARM

On the morning of the 1st of July a sentinel, who had accidentally strolled to the top of a hill half a mile from camp, which commanded an extensive view of the country, discovered a large party crossing in the distance, and gave the alarm that forty men

171. John Milton Chivington (1821–94) was a Methodist preacher and took an active role in the border warfare in "bleeding Kansas" during the 1850s. Known as the "Fighting Parson," he merged his peculiar brand of muscular Christianity with a commission as major, and later colonel, of the First Colorado Volunteer Infantry. Chivington fought Sibley's Texans in New Mexico, distinguishing himself at Apache Canyon during the battle of Glorieta on March 27, 1862. In 1863 he was appointed commander of the District of Colorado. Chivington is perhaps best remembered as the perpetrator of the infamous massacre of Black Kettle's Cheyenne village at Sand Creek in November 1864. *Webster's American Military Biographies*, 70. See also Halaas and Masich, *Halfbreed*, 120–49.

were coming. The bugles blew to arms, the horses were driven in, saddled, and forty men mounted and off in a few minutes. This time it was certain we would meet the Texans. The party soon returned, bringing in a most doleful looking set of travelers—about thirty men and boys on foot, variously armed with guns, lances, and bows and arrows; three women, a dilapidated wagon and cart drawn by the poorest animals I ever saw—in fact, it would be prudent to tie knots in their tails to keep them from falling in through the cracks in the ground—some donkeys and a goat, comprised their outfit. They were citizens of Placer, and were going into Sonora to procure provisions, and return to their friends and relatives still behind. For two weeks they said they had eaten no bread. After questioning them the Colonel let them go, or rather we left them at the spring, and marched to the Miembres,[172] where we encamped at a fine spring, in the midst of what was once "Mowry City."[173]

On the 3d we left the pleasant valley of the Miembres and arrived at Cook's [Cooke's] Spring.[174] Near the spring we saw the graves and skulls, scattered along the roadside, of the poor people killed by the Apaches a year since; also where Lieut. Lord had burned Government property, to prevent it falling into the hands of the Texans. The ground is spangled with spread eagles, upon which "E Pluribus Unum" remains plain as ever, in spite of the fiery ordeal.

MORE HUNGRY PEOPLE

During our first night at Mowry City, some fifteen travelers walked into our camp, and before they knew of our presence were prisoners. They turned out to be more hungry people from Placer, going into Mesilla for provisions. These the Colonel thought best to take along—quite a burden considering our limited supply of provisions.

172. "Miembres" was apparently the preferred spelling for "Mimbres" in the 1860s. Miembres Station was located eighteen miles northwest of Cooke's Spring and some three hundred feet from the east bank of the Mimbres River. It was a large station with many impressive cottonwood and willow trees around it. Conkling and Conkling, *Butterfield Overland Mail*, 1:119, 120.

173. Mowry City, located at the Mimbres River one mile north of the Butterfield stage station, was established in 1859 as a result of a short-lived land boom promoted by Sylvester Mowry. Ibid., 120; Pearce, *New Mexico Place Names*, 105–6.

174. The Butterfield Overland Mail established a station at Cooke's Spring, New Mexico, which was named for dragoon captain Philip St. George Cooke, who led the Mormon Battalion through this country and blazed the first practicable wagon road in 1846 during the Mexican War. The California cavalrymen who stopped here were familiar with Cooke's name—he wrote the cavalry-tactics manual that governed every drill they performed. Fort Cummings was established near this site to combat incessant Apache raids against overland travelers. Julyan, *Place Names of New Mexico*, 94; Cooke, *Cavalry Tactics*.

THE FOURTH OF JULY

On the 4th the men were, to a man, for going in and taking Mesilla, but our commander ordered otherwise; so we spent the 4th traveling round an enemy—a hard day's march to the Rio Grande, without water. We encamped two miles above Fort Thorne. Found the river high, or rather on a Fourth of July "bust," caused by the snow melting in the mountains.

OF THE ROUTE

The road between the Rio Grande and Tucson is hard and fine, and clear of dust; grass is abundant, but water, at the particular time we traveled over the route, very scarce, but still sufficient to admit of troops and supplies being moved over it, with judgment, and I anticipate that the troops now concentrated at Tucson will move forward immediately. Our animals came across in very good order.

FORT THORNE [THORN]

On the 5th we moved down to Fort Thorne and run up our colors on the flag staff still standing. The Texans have been here, and left behind them their marks of desecration and desolation—this fort, however, was abandoned by the Government in 1858, on account of its being sickly.

ARRIVAL OF EXPRESS FROM FORT CRAIG
AND CAPTAIN MCCLEAVE

The 6th was a memorable day. The express sent by Col. Eyre from Cow Spring to Fort Craig for reinforcements, arrived bringing intelligence that two companies would be here on the 8th, and rumors that the Texans had evacuated Mesilla. Shortly after the arrival of the express, the sentinel from the house top at the lower end of the fort, announced that three men were coming up the valley. The Colonel ordered out ten men on horseback to catch them, and seeing that they came on he ordered some men out on foot, and mounting the housetop, he imagined he saw others behind, and called for more men to go out. The advancing party stopped a moment, and then a single horseman galloped straight for us. Some one said, "I'll bet it is Captain McCleave." And so it turned out to be. When the Captain met the advancing party sent out by the Colonel, he dismounted and came in on foot. A pistol shot assured his companions that all was right, when they came on. As the Captain came into the parade ground the men gathered around the colors and gave him three hearty cheers, to which he took off his hat and said, "I am much obliged to you. I am glad to see you;" a speech which, from this brave, honest soldier, bore sincerity and meaning. The Captain had just escaped from three months imprisonment and hard treatment with an order for his exchange, and was on his way to Fort Craig when he discovered our flag flying here, which made his breast beat with joyful surprise. He gives a deplorable account of the ravages of the Texans, who are in a destitute condition and preparing to leave for Texas. Mesilla has been evacuated. The people are universal in favor of the Union, and are now at war with the Texans. Three Mexicans volunteered to accompany the Captain to Fort Craig. Captain Fritz was dispatched the same evening down the river, to effect the exchange for Captain McCleave.

PRISONERS RELEASED

The prisoners taken at Miembres were released after the news of the evacuation of Mesilla was received; and allowed to go on their way of rejoicing, after taking the oath of allegiance.

ARRIVAL OF REINFORCEMENTS—SUPPLIES SENT FOR

On the morning of the 9th, two companies of Regulars arrived from Fort Craig;[175] their horses are in very poor condition. At the time of the arrival of the reinforcements, Capt. McCleave left for Fort Craig with an escort of six men and two wagons to bring down supplies.

RETURN OF CAPTAIN FRITZ

A little after retreat on the 9th, Capt. Fritz returned. He had to go twenty-eight miles below Mesilla to catch up with the rear of the retreating Texans, under command of Col. Steel [William Steele],[176] in order to effect the exchange for Capt. McCleave. The people of Mesilla gave the Captain a hearty welcome. He had hardly dismounted before he heard corks popping from champagne bottles. Going into one place to buy something, he threw down a twenty, and the man ran back into the yard with a spade to effect the change. The people have cached everything they could out of the way of the Texans, and the Captain says stores opened up like magic. The people of Mesilla, whom the Texans thought they had eaten out, will resurrect enough to live

---

175. On July 8, 1862, Capt. George W. Howland, Third U.S. Cavalry, arrived at Fort Thorn. The following day his squadron of one hundred men, riding emaciated and broken-down horses, arrived at the fort and reported for duty. E. E. Eyre to B. C. Cutler, July 8, 1862, *OR*, 50(1):124–26; J. Carleton to R. C. Drum, Sept. 30, 1862, ibid., 100–105; Orton, *California Men*, 63.

176. William Steele served in the Southwest as an officer in the Second U.S. Dragoons before being appointed colonel of the Seventh Texas Mounted Regiment by Gen. H. H. Sibley in 1861. Steele succeeded J. R. Baylor as the Confederate military governor of Arizona and managed the rear guard of Sibley's retreat from Arizona and New Mexico. Hall and Long, *Army of New Mexico*, 216–20.

on for some time to come, and have withal to sell to Uncle Sam. The wheat crop will be coming in soon, and we will grind our own flour on some fine mills convenient.

DEPLORABLE CONDITION OF THE RETREATING TEXANS

Capt. Fritz reports the retreating Texans in a deplorable condition. Col. Steel has some 200 men, and a good many sick, with no supplies. While Capt. Fritz was in conference, an express came from Capt. Tell [Trevanion T. Teel][177] to Col. Steel, calling in God's name to send him aid, as the Mexicans had attacked him, and captured two pieces of artillery. Some fifteen hundred Mexicans and pueblo Indians are now following up the Texans, filled with revenge for the wrongs and injuries inflicted on them by the Texans, and it will be a miracle if they escape to Texas. The first outbreak between the people and Texans took place in Mesilla, when twenty Mexicans, citizens of Mesilla, were killed; then other skirmishes occurred in which the Mexicans came out first best. The Texans went to the fields and took the oxen from the plows, and ransacked the country for supplies; the Mexicans, encouraged by the approach of the Californians, and, burning with revenge, are now following them up, and will annihilate them. The Texans would all reach El Paso on the night of the 9th. Desertions are common. One hundred and fifty citizens of Mesilla started on the 8th on foot down the river, swearing they would ride back on the Texans. This is the miserable wind-up of Sibley's expedition, who, after his disastrous retreat from New Mexico, had to fly for his life from the Texans. I see by a San Antonio paper, that some of the Sibley expedition have reached that place. The way of the transgressor is hard. Expressman Jones came up with the Captain.

MCCLEAVE AND PARTY ATTACKED BY INDIANS

We had hardly got through with Captain Fritz, when two men rode up bearing a dispatch from Capt. McCleave, stating that he had been attacked by a large body of Indians. Forty men were dispatched in a few minutes to the rescue under command of Capt. Howland. The expressmen said that before they left, they heard firing above them, and supposed that the Indians were attacking some party coming down the river. From them I learned the circumstances of the attack. Capt. McCleave, with one man, was considerably in advance of the wagons when the Indians rose out of the tall grass around them, and fired at them, fortunately not wounding them. The Captain had a bullet shot through his hat. He retreated to the wagons, which he drew off the road,

177. A native of Pittsburgh, Pennsylvania, Capt. Trevanion T. Teel led Company B, First Artillery in Sibley's Army of New Mexico. A tough and experienced soldier, Teel was promoted to major and assigned to Col. William Steele's command. Teel's men were the last Confederates to withdraw from Arizona, New Mexico, and West Texas. Ibid., 334–37.

and prepared his little party to defend themselves. The Mexicans, some seventy-five in number, retreated to the cover of the hills.

ANOTHER EXPRESSMAN

Our brave men had hardly galloped out of hearing before another expressman arrived, his horse reeking with sweat. He brought news that Captain McCleave was returning with the wagons, and that he was one of a party of five expressmen from Fort Craig who had been attacked near where Captain McCleave was attacked, and two of the party wounded. The Indians getting their horses, they had to fight their way down on foot to where Captain McCleave was holding the Indians at bay. They are supposed to be Navahoes, and to be one hundred and fifty strong. The wounded arrived next morning. One of the men received quite a severe arrow wound, and the other a slight bullet wound in the arm. I should not wonder to hear of our boys catching the red devils yet; and if they do, woe be unto them!

I will leave my letter open until the Express leaves.

EXPRESSMAN JONES

From this venturesome man, who has made himself celebrated by his expressing, I learned the particulars of the encounter with the Apaches, in which his two companions were killed, and he escaped by the skin of his teeth. Fifty or sixty Indians swept down on them like the wind, and they fought them for three-quarters of an hour, when, by accident, the sergeant lost all his caps, and the Mexican was wounded. At this juncture, the Indians began to close in with terrific yells, and Jones calls to the sergeant to mount his mule, as flight was their only chance. Jones mounted and put spurs to his mule; but the sergeant never followed. Jones ran the gauntlet for several miles, with Indians running alongside him, and shooting at him. He shot three of his pursuers, who gradually dwindled down to one Indian, who brushed by him on a swift horse, and wheeled and took deliberate aim at Jones, cutting the rim of his hat with the ball. Jones drew up and fired at him. They then parted, the Indian exclaiming, "*Mucho wano [bueno] mula, bravo Americano.*" [You have a good mule, brave American.] The Indians dogged Jones for sixty miles, and then gave him up.[178] Jones has been trying to get permission to take an express through from here, alone, to Tucson; but I believe the Colonel has refused to grant it.

178. John W. Jones told the tale of his harrowing escape in a statement that Carleton saw fit to include in his own report of the march to the Rio Grande. The expressman said that "the Mexican fired the sergeant's gun, but lost all the caps out of the breech." Jones also said the pursuing Apaches yelled, "Now let's have a race," and, "Mucha *buena* mula; mucho bravo Americano." Jones's statement, July 22, 1862, *OR*, 50(1):119–20.

THE FUTURE

I suppose we are now under the orders of Col. Canby,* and our movements will be governed accordingly. From present appearances, it seems that no movement will be made farther down than Fort Fillmore, which movement awaits the arrival of the supplies from Fort Craig. The Texans have concentrated at Franklin, opposite El Paso, and will there remain until they learn of our pursing them, in hopes of supplying themselves for the long trip between them and the settlements. It is reported that the swarm of Mexicans which have hovered around them ever since they commenced their retreat, have succeeded in getting all their animals; if so, they are now on foot. Made desperate, they will devestate the country around them. It remains a question if our commander will consider it worth while to move down upon them. It is said that Texans await reinforcements and supplies, but this may be merely a story to deceive.

Several of our hearty men have been taken down sick. It is a shame that we have been compelled to lay idle at this point.

N.

*Since been ordered home by the War Department.—EDS. ALTA

ALTA, AUGUST 16, 1862

Vedette's Letters from the California Column for Texas,
under Gen. Carleton
No. V
Station on the San Pedro, July 22, 1862

EDITORS ALTA: After many trials, perils, and fatigue, I find myself in a condition to resume my correspondence from a point of comparative safety. In order to give a clear and connected account of the numerous and interesting events which Fate decurred, it will be necessary to commence with the beginning; and although this letter may prove rather long, I doubt not it will be of sufficient interest to repay a perusal.

JONES, THE EXPRESSMAN, AND HIS COMPANIONS

Immediately after his arrival in Tucson, Col. Carleton dispatched Jones, the well-known expressman, with a sergeant named Wheelan or Wheeler [Wheeling], and a Mexican, to Gen. Canby, at Fort Craig, informing that officer of the arrival of the California column, and requesting instructions as to our future operations. Jones accordingly started, and weeks elapsed without any reply from Gen. Canby, until the persuasion obtained that Jones and his party had been cut off by the Apaches. This impression turns out to have been tolerably well grounded, for Jones was attacked by the savages in Apache Pass, and his two companions killed, and himself saved only by the superior speed of his mule, after a twenty-five mile chase—but not until some ten or twelve of the savages had bitten the dust. Having still several hundred miles to go, and being in a famishing condition, Jones went to the nearest Secession camp, and was there taken prisoner with his dispatches, which, instead of doing us an injury, only served to hasten the retreat of the enemy into Texas.

MARCH OF LIEUT. COL. EYRE

I have now to recount one of the most singular proceedings on military record, one which I believe unparalleled. As I wrote you, Lieut. Col. Eyre, with companies B., Capt. Fritz, and C., Lieut. Haden, commanding in the temporary absence of Capt. Shirland, was sent forward as our advance to form a junction with Canby, and to occupy the town of Mesilla on the Rio Grande. Col. Eyre proceeded without molestation until he reached Apache Pass, where three of his command, belonging to Capt. Fritz' company, were murdered at the springs in the cañon by the Apaches, their bodies horribly mutilated and stripped, and their weapons stolen. In the face of this most damnable act of hostility, Col. Eyre raised the white flag, called in the Apaches, held a peace talk with them, and absolutely fed them with the provisions which had been issued for the subsistence of his command. Let it be distinctly understood that I am giving you the account furnished by persons who have it from the officers and men of Eyre's command, and not on my own personal veracity; but it is the one current here, and universally accepted. Previous to this singular procedure on the part of Col. Eyre, Capt. Fritz, exceedingly irate at the wanton murder of three of his best men, saddled up twenty-five horses and prepared with that number of men to charge and punish the savages; but he was recalled and forbidden to do so by Col. Eyre. Fritz is said to have flung his carbine and sabre as far as he could, and denounced the order as worse than child's play. But the sequel is not yet, for no sooner had Col. Eyre moved his command from the cañon to the prairie at the foot of the mountain, after making a treaty of peace with the savages, than they collected their force that night and poured a volley into Eyre's camp while his men were sleeping, wounding Dr. Kittredge severely over the left eye. This volley was returned in the dark, and hostilities ceased. After this brilliant exploit, Col. Eyre proceeded on his journey, and when last heard from, was at Fort Thorne, near Mesilla, which he was to occupy.

The names of those killed by the Indians in this affair were Peter Maloney, Albert Schmidt and James F. Keith, all of Captain Fritz's company. They were buried in Apache Pass, and headboards put up to mark their resting places; but the ruthless Apaches have violated the graves, and torn up and split the headboards, fragments of which have been found, with the names and dates upon them. These sad murders were committed on the 25th of June, 1862.

RELEASE AND RETURN OF CAPTAIN MCCLEAVE

On the afternoon of the 20th inst., Captain McCleave, 1st Cavalry, C.V., who, you will remember, was captured by Hunter at White's place, Pimo Villages, passed through this station with Jones the expressman, three expressmen of Gen. Canby's command, and three secession deserters,[179] who had got sick of their bargain, and had come through to give themselves up. McCleave was exchanged for two lieutenants, who had been captured by Canby; White was changed off for three secession privates, and Jones for six. Captain McCleave brings the certain intelligence that the Secession forces have all retreated into Texas, having been fairly starved out. He represents them as undergoing remarkable equanimity. Many of the Texans are evidently laboring under the delusion that the Government intends to force emancipation and even amalgamation upon them, and hence their desperate resistance.[180] It is clear to my mind that the head is more erroneous than the heart among the Southern masses who are egregiously misled by the persons they have been accustomed to look up to for guidance and advice. The tortures of the damned must rack the souls of those who, knowing the truth, have advised and fomented this wicked rebellion. You will perceive that a perfect understanding now exists between Generals Carleton and Canby, and as the white foe has retired, we have only the red one to contend against, but that promises to give us our hands full, for a while at least.

SHARP CONFLICT WITH THE APACHES

On the 9th of July, Capt. Thomas Roberts, commanding Company E, First Infantry, was ordered to advance with his company; a small battery of two mountain howitzers, and fifteen men commanded by Lieutenant Thompson, and Capt. Cremony of Company E, Second Cavalry, with twenty-one of his men, to occupy the Overland Mail station at San Simon, 145 miles beyond Tucson. The party consisted of about

179. Among the three deserters was Jack Swilling, a lieutenant in the Arizona Guards, a company of Confederate rangers raised at the Pinos Altos mines by Capt. Thomas Mastin. Swilling, a native of South Carolina, had lived in Arizona for three years when the war broke out. He had been to Tucson with a portion of his company as an escort for Colonel Reily. Later he was charged with escorting McCleave to Mesilla. Swilling and many of his comrades were disenchanted with the Confederates and had only joined them in order to protect their homes from Apache depredations. Senate, *Federal Census—Territory of New Mexico and Territory of Arizona,* 1864; Finch, "Sherod Hunter," 194–95, 197; Hall and Long, *Army of New Mexico,* 367–69.

180. Most Texans feared that the U.S. government sought to force racial equality upon the people, which they believed would inevitably result in miscegenation and the "amalgamation" of the races.

105 men and 25 wagons, all under the command of Capt. Roberts. It left Tucson on the 10th, and reached Dragoon Springs, 76 miles distant, on the 14th instant, without impediment or accident of any kind except the sight of Apaches running about through the midst of a terrific rain storm, with any amount of thunder and lightening, bearing large brands of fire; but taking good care to consult their safety by keeping at a respectful distance. These fire brands at night, I conceive to be their mode of assembling their warriors, as it is quite impossible for them to keep track of each other in their wide and uncertain wanderings. It is the "Speed, Malise, Speed," of the Apaches.[181] At Dragoon Springs Capt. Roberts took a Sergeant and six men from Capt. Cremony's detachment, and left as many infantry in their place, when he proceeded to Apache Pass with his company and Thompson's battery, to see if water enough could be found to supply the command at that place, leaving Capt. Cremony in charge of the train with twenty-one men. The distance is all of forty miles, and no water between the two places. Capt Roberts left Dragoon Springs at 5 o'clock P.M., of the 14th, marched all night and entered Apache Pass about 11 o'clock A.M. of the 15th. The main body of his command had scarcely reached the station in the Pass, when quick firing was heard in their rear, about a half mile off, where three company wagons were toiling through. He immediately hurried his command to the spot, and found that the savages were posting in considerable numbers behind rocky defences on the hills, both sides of the road, completely commanding the passage.

A SHARP ENGAGEMENT

Commenced, which lasted for nearly six hours, during which the Apaches were driven from their defences and forced back toward the watering place, which is commanded on each side by considerable heights, strongly fortified. Here the conflict raged with violence; the Indians evidently determined to keep the troops from obtaining water, and the latter determined to have it at all costs. Lieut. Thompson's battery of two mountain howitzers was ordered into position, and commenced shelling the heights with admirable effect; but one of the pieces was so exposed, and the enemy's fire was so hot, that the men were driven from the gun, and the carriage overturned.

---

181. "Speed, Malise, Speed" is a reference to Sir Walter Scott's *Lady of the Lake:* "Speed! Malise, speed! Such cause of haste, thine active sinews never braced." The phrase was popularized by its inclusion in James Fenimore Cooper's *The Pioneers,* and educated people understood it to mean an alarm signal. Curiously this same expression is found in Capt. John C. Cremony's memoir. Sentence construction and subject also closely match Vedette's letter— still more evidence that Cremony and Vedette are one and the same. Cremony, *Life among the Apaches,* 157.

Lieut. Thompson, seeing sergeant Mitchell and private John Teal,[182] Company B, 2d
Cavalry, near by, called upon them to assist in righting the piece, which they effected
at considerable hazard, and then helped to place it in a better position. The shells drove
the enemy from their works; but night falling on, Captain Roberts withdrew his command to the station, quarter of a mile distant, after the men had quenched their thirst.
He then ordered Sergeant Mitchell, with privates Teal, King,[183] Keim,[184] Young,[185]
and Maynard,[186] to make their way back through the pass to Capt. Cremony—who
was *en route* with the train, and ignorant of these events—and inform him of what had
transpired, with orders to come on as far and fast as possible, and that he (Roberts)
would come out to meet him with a detachment of infantry. The men mentioned
started on their errand, and got safely through the cañon; but on passing a ravine three
miles outside, were waylaid and fired upon from rocks and trees by about forty
mounted Apaches, shooting two horses through the body, and sending an ounce ball
through the right fore arm of Jesse T. Maynard, who turned to the sergeant and
informed him that he was wounded. Sergeant Mitchell deemed it most prudent, and
in conformity with his orders to reach the train and report to Captain Cremony; so he
pursued his way without further molestation. In the meantime [. . .]

182. Originally from New York, Titus B. Mitchell enrolled as sergeant of Company B, Second California Cavalry on September 24, 1861. John W. Teal, a Canadian by birth, enrolled as
a private in Company B, Second California Cavalry on September 24, 1861. Teal had been left
for dead by his comrades after he was surrounded by Apaches. A well-aimed shot from his carbine felled the famed Mimbres war leader Mangas Coloradas, and the Apaches broke off the
attack. Teal's company commander and messmates were surprised when he later trudged into
camp carrying all of his equipment, less his spurs. The thirty-four-year-old was educated and
possessed a good sense of humor; he noted in his journal, along with brief biographical
sketches of his comrades, that his occupation was "Mudsill," a contemptuous expression common in the 1860s. He was mustered out at San Francisco on October 10, 1864. Orton, *California Men*, 217; *OR*, 50(1):133; Henry Walker, "Soldier in the California Column," 82.

183. Bradley W. King, a New Yorker, enlisted as a private in Company B, Second California
Cavalry on September 17, 1861. He was mustered out at San Francisco on October 10, 1864.
Orton, *California Men*, 214; Henry Walker, "Soldier in the California Column," 80.

184. Oliver F. Keim was born in Pennsylvania. He enrolled in Company B, Second California
Cavalry on September 24, 1861, at San Francisco. Private Keim was mustered out on October 10,
1864. Orton, *California Men*, 214; Henry Walker, "Soldier in the California Column," 80.

185. George F. Young was a native of Germany. He enrolled in Company B, Second California Cavalry on November 13, 1861. Private Young was mustered out at San Francisco on
November 15, 1864. Orton, *California Men*, 217; Henry Walker, "Soldier in the California Column," 82.

186. Jesse T. Maynard, born in New Hampshire, enlisted in Company B, Second California
Cavalry on September 16, 1861. He was promoted to commissary sergeant but was discharged
at Santa Fe, New Mexico, for disability resulting from wounds received at Apache Pass on
December 19, 1862. Orton, *California Men*, 210; Henry Walker, "Soldier in the California Column," 81.

PRIVATE JOHN TEAL,

Who had dismounted, and was leading his horse some two hundred yards of Mitchell and others, found himself suddenly cut off by the intervening savages, whereupon he remounted and endeavored to pass round to the left of them; but his design was frustrated by fifteen, who gave him chase and wounded his horse. One savage, armed with an excellent rifle, then got ahead of Teal and deliberately took a rest at him; but not liking this procedure, Teal jumped from his horse, threw himself flat on the ground, and took a rest at the savage, whose bullet whistled past in dangerous proximity to his right ear. The fight between Teal and the fifteen savages (Apaches) continued from half an hour before sundown until half-past eight o'clock that night, at which time he crawled off, and made his way safely into Captain Cremony's camp, about eight miles off. When the savages found that he had a six-shooter and a sabre, as well as his carbine, they did not venture to charge or close upon him.

WHEN SERGEANT MITCHELL

Reached Captain Cremony, who was proceeding with the train very lightly guarded, it was half-past seven o'clock, and quite dark, and as the moon would be up at ten, the Captain did not deem it prudent to expose the train to almost certain capture, and his men to certain destruction, in a cañon where the savages could conceal themselves, and pick the men off at leisure, by moonlight, so he immediately coralled the wagons, and waited the arrival of Captain Roberts and a suitable force to take the train through. About half-past 12 o'clock Captain Roberts reached the train and approved this decision.

At early dawn the train got under way again and entered the Pass about 9 o'clock A.M. when Capt. Roberts threw out a body of skirmishers on either hand, while the cavalry guarded the train which reached the station without further trouble. Captain Cremony then begged Captain Roberts to let him advance with his cavalry and clear the springs of Indians, and his request was seconded by Lieut. Muller,[187] of Co. C., 1st Cav., C.V. who was attached to the command as Quartermaster; but Capt. Roberts refused on the ground that it would be too dangerous an attempt and that he intended to shell the place, being convinced that the Apaches were there in force. He accordingly assembled the greater number of his command, threw skirmishers out on the hills commanding the road and shelled their summits as he advanced, also shelling the

187. Fred Müller was mustered in as second lieutenant of Company C, First California Cavalry on September 22, 1861. John Cremony wrote that he urged Müller to try to convince Captain Roberts to allow the cavalry to charge the Apaches: "Müller argued for half an hour, until Roberts told him either to obey or be placed under arrest." Lieutenant Müller resigned on April 27, 1863. Orton, *California Men,* 109; Cremony, *Life among the Apaches,* 165–67.

springs which are shaded by trees and shrubbery. Some few Indians were seen hurrying off with speed and there were doubtless others who contrived to conceal themselves. The water being gained and the men and animals refreshed, the cavalry force was divided into two equal parties, dismounted and ordered to occupy the two Indian stone works on the top of the hills to the right and left of the springs, and to hold them all night. This they did, and found that the works were skillfully arranged, being made of large rocks piled on each other, with convenient creunels [crenells] for musket practice, and completely commanding the water and all approach to it. Here were the debris of many horses, mules, and cattle, slaughtered and eaten by the savages; here they were undoubtedly in the habit of having their war dances and festivals; here, too, were found remnants of plunder taken from the white man, and also the soft chestnut hair of a white woman. The rocks were splintered on the inside; blood was seen upon one or two of them, and the traces of marks where they had borne off the bodies of their killed and wounded, were distinctly observable, while bits of bombshells and bullets told the accuracy of the battery fire and its destructive effect. It was probably the first time they had ever been driven from those strongholds, and their first experience with shells.

IN THIS ENGAGEMENT

We lost two killed and two wounded. The loss of the enemy is not known, as they carry off their dead and wounded, but five were seen to fall during the small-arm engagement, and the battery must have put more of them *hors de combat*. The names of the killed are: O'Brien,[188] attached to the battery, and formerly Orderly Sergeant of Company G, First Infantry, and John Bar,[189] a private of Company E, First Infantry. The wounded consisted of a teamster named Sawyer,[190] commonly known as "Shorty," and Jesse T. Maynard, of Company B, Second Cavalry. "Shorty" was shot through the thickest part of the right thigh, near the hip bone, but without breaking the bone,

188. Charles M. O'Brien was a private in Company G, First California Infantry. He enlisted at Nevada City, California, on August 10, 1861, and was attached to Thompson's "Jackass Battery." O'Brien died of wounds received at Apache Pass on July 15, 1862. Orton, *California Men*, 366, 879; *OR*, 50(1):131.

189. John Barr was mustered in at Sacramento on August 26, 1861, as a private in Company D, First California Infantry. He was apparently with Company E at the time of the Apache Pass fight, according to official correspondence. Captain Roberts wrote in his report, "Had Private Barr been as cautious as he was warned to be, he probably would not have lost his life." Barr was killed in Roberts's first assault on the springs in Apache Pass on July 15, 1862. Orton, *California Men*, 327, 350; *OR*, 50(1):129, 131.

190. Andrew "Shorty" Sawyer was a teamster with Roberts's contingent. He was wounded while defending his wagon near the rear of the command about a half mile from the stage station. This attack occurred at about 12:30 P.M. on July 15, 1862. *OR*, 50(1):131.

although some important vessels were cut. He was valorously defending his wagon at the time, and after he was wounded, mounted his mule and drove his team safely through the hailstorm of bullets. He is a plucky fellow and deserves much credit. In the cañon we found the head boards of Captain Fritz's men, who had been murdered on the 25th June, as before mentioned, and buried our own dead; but I feel positive their graves will be desecrated.

DEAD BODIES OF APACHES

The day after these events, Capt. Roberts left the Pass with his whole command, taking every precaution against surprise, and emerged on the plain without further trouble. On the plain, three miles outside the canon, we found the bodies of nine Apaches perferated with ball holes, and evidently killed in a running fight with some parties to the writer unknown. The bodies had the appearance of having been killed some three or four weeks previous, and on two of them were soldiers' shoes,[191] probably those rifled from the bodies of Capt. Fritz's men. There were probably more of their dead lying in the bushes, but I did not see them. Capt. Roberts' command then proceeded to the San Simon Station,[192] eighteen miles further, where it established itself for the present. On the 19th inst., Capt. Cremony, with 19 cavalry of his own company, and 20 infantry— 15 of Company E and 5 of the battery—took charge of the train to bring it back safely to the San Pedro. He avoided Apache Pass and Dragoon Springs and took the route opened by Capt. (now Gen.) Stone,[193] which proved far superior in all respects, and only about nine miles longer. The route is, however, fringed with mountains inhabited by Apaches, and they doubtless saw every step he took, but were afraid to attack him on the open plain, although the very object of their cupidity was that same train. He brought it through safely and without accident, a distance of 80 miles, over a country infested by hostile savages.

191. Soldiers' shoes were readily distinguishable from civilian straight-last styles by the fact that they were made for right and left feet. The bootee or brogan was made of rough-out leather and designed to come up over the ankle and to be fastened by laces. The soles were either sewn or pegged.

192. San Simon was a stage station situated thirteen miles southwest of Stein's Peak. It was one of the smaller change stations on the Butterfield route, consisting only of an adobe building and an earthen water-holding tank. Conkling and Conkling, *Butterfield Overland Mail*, 1:130.

193. Charles Pomeroy Stone (1824–87) graduated from the U.S. Military Academy in 1845. He served as an ordnance officer during the Mexican War and later became chief ordnance officer at Benicia Arsenal, California. He resigned in 1856 and headed a private commission that surveyed the state of Sonora, Mexico, from 1857 to 1860; in 1861 he published *Notes on the State of Sonora*. During the Civil War Stone was imprisoned without charge or trial when he became the scapegoat for the Union disaster at Ball's Bluff, Virginia, in 1861. *Webster's American Military Biographies*, 416.

HONORABLE MENTION

Let me indulge in a few comments in reference to the gallant fellows of Captain Roberts' command. They had already marched seventy-six miles to Dragoon Springs, and from there made forty miles without stop or halt to Apache Pass, where they were attached and fought six hours on arriving, they then turned right about, without rest and marched back fifteen miles to the train, where they rested only four hours and returned to the Pass, fifteen miles more, skirmishing over great heights and down deep canons to the station; making seventy miles in thirty-six hours, besides fighting two engagements, for, although the second day's did not amount to much in the way of actual conflict, yet it involved a great deal of toil and painful labor, and for twenty-four hours of the time they had no water. On the other hand, the cavalry men who accompanied Capt. Roberts, had the day previous, ridden to Dragoon Springs with the main command, and from there to Two Springs,[194] eighteen miles off, and back again the same night through a terrific thunder storm; making fifty-seven miles that twenty-four hours. The next day they rode to Apache Pass, forty miles, where they fought for six hours; then rode back to the train, fifteen miles and had another desperate fight, losing three horses killed, and having one man wounded, and thence back again with the command to the Pass, fifteen miles more, making seventy miles in thirty-six hours and one hundred and twelve in sixty hours, besides doing their full share of the fighting. I call this pretty good work for our Volunteers. Our little cavalry command has been in the saddle all night long for the three past days, and have fed, watered, groomed and tended their now broken down horses in the day time, besides standing guard over them and doing their cooking and other needful work. I assure you we are perfectly exhausted.

TROOPS AT THE SAN PEDRO

Just at this time the whole column is in a state of preparation for a forward movement. Assembled at the Overland Mail station on the San Pedro are the following commands: Of the First Infantry, the companies of Captains McMullen,[195] Willis,

194. Two Springs probably refers to Dos Cabezas Springs, located eighteen miles from Dragoon Springs on the Apache Pass road.

195. William McMullen was captain of Company C, First California Infantry. He enrolled in Amador County, California, on August 16, 1861. McMullen was trusted by Carleton and liked by the men. He was promoted to major on June 23, 1863, and was discharged with his regiment at Fort Union on August 31, 1864. Orton, *California Men*, 66, 346, 335; Hand Diary, Sept. 30, 1862.

Cox,[196] Davis,[197] and Hines [Hinds],[198] and Smith[199] of the Fifth Infantry; Captain Pichon's [Pishon] company of the First Cavalry, and part of Captain Cremony's of the Second, and Lieutenant Shinn's battery, all under the command of Colonel West. Here also are Captain Shirland and Lieutenant Guirardo [Guirado],[200] of the First Cavalry, whose companies are in the advance with Lieutenant Colonel Eyre, and are going forward to join them. Doctors McNulty[201] and Prentiss,[202] and Captain Moore, Quartermaster of the column, are also here, with Major Coult and Lieutenant Hammond, Adjutant of the command. General Carleton, with other troops, probably three companies of infantry and two of the First Cavalry, is expected to-morrow or the day after, when the movement in the advance will be ordered. Lieutenant-Colonel Rigg is at Tucson.

HEALTH OF TUCSON

This is the sickly season at Tucson, fevers prevailing to a considerable extent, and the hospital has been unusually patronized. I, however, venture to say, that there has been less sickness in this column than any other of equal numbers in the army. Two

196. Thomas Cox was mustered in as captain of Company H, First California Infantry on November 1, 1861. He resigned his commission on July 10, 1862. Orton, *California Men*, 367.

197. Nicholas S. "Nick" Davis was mustered in as second lieutenant of Company A, First California Infantry in Calaveras County, California, on August 15, 1861. He was well liked by the men and on January 11, 1862, was promoted to captain of Company K. Davis was chief of transportation for the Column from California. He was mustered out at Santa Fe, New Mexico, on October 29, 1864. Ibid., 336, 376; Hand Diary, Sept. 30, 1862; GO 20, Hdqrs. Dist. of Ariz., Dept. of the Pacific, General, Special, and Post Orders, RG 393, NARA.

198. Capt. Hugh L. Hinds raised Company G, Fifth California Infantry in Placerville, California, and mustered into the volunteer service at Camp Union, California, on October 30, 1861. He resigned his commission on September 20, 1863. Orton, *California Men*, 674, 703.

199. Charles A. Smith was mustered in as captain of Company B, Fifth California Infantry at Marysville, California, on October 18, 1861. He was mustered out at Franklin, Texas, on December 14, 1864, upon expiration of his term of service. Ibid., 681; *OR*, 50(2):24.

200. Juan Francis Guirado enrolled at San Francisco and was mustered in as first lieutenant of Company B, First California Cavalry on September 11, 1861. He was mustered out at Fort Union, New Mexico, on September 30, 1864, upon expiration of his term of service. Orton, *California Men*, 98.

201. James M. McNulty was an 1846 graduate of the Geneva Medical College. He was enrolled as surgeon of the First California Infantry at San Francisco on August 15, 1861. McNulty was very popular among the officers and men and was appointed medical director of the Column from California by Carleton. He resigned on February 19, 1863, to accept a commission as surgeon, U.S. Volunteers. Ibid., 66, 335; Cremony, *Life among the Apaches*, 220; Quebbeman, *Medicine in Territorial Arizona*, 356.

202. John H. Prentiss was appointed surgeon, First California Cavalry on August 16, 1861, after enrolling at San Francisco. He was assigned to the second contingent of the Column from California and later succeeded Surgeon McNulty as medical director of the Department of Arizona in September 1862. Prentiss was mustered out on December 1, 1864. Orton, *California Men*, 62, 87; Hunt, *Army of the Pacific*, 273.

deaths, from disease, have occurred within the past month, viz: John McQuade,[203] First Duty Sergeant of Company B, Second Cavalry, C.V., and private Richards,[204] of Company H, First Infantry, C.V. In a column of over 1,200 men, who have undergone such continued toils and hardships, in a climate entirely different from the one they have lived in for years, this must be considered a remarkably small mortality.

JONES' DISPATCHES

It seems that Jones, the expressman, was provided with two sets of dispatches— one for the enemy, in case he fell into their hands, and one for Gen. Canby. The latter was on tissue paper, in a roll about as big as a cigarito, while the other was done up in regular form. Upon being captured, Jones swallowed the Simon Pure,[205] and gave up the bogus, which was worded for effect, and hastened the retreat of the enemy to such an extent, that he left Paso del Norte for San Antonio de Bexar, a distance of 650 miles, with only four day's rations.

Gen. Carleton arrived, to-day, rested two hours, and moved immediately forward with three companies infantry and one of cavalry. To-morrow evening Col. West moves forward with two companies infantry, Capt. Cremony and 20 of his cavalry. Next day Capt. Willis moves forward with three companies infantry and Shinn's battery, and 10 cavalry of B Company, 2d regiment, and the next after, is followed by Lieut. Col. Rigg, with three companies infantry and 15 cavalry composed of Captains Shirland and Cremony's companies, under Shirland.

Some time may elapse before I have another certain opportunity of writing you, but will lose none that may offer.

VEDETTE

203. John McQuade was enrolled as sergeant of Company B, Second California Cavalry at San Francisco on September 14, 1861. He died at Tucson on July 12, 1862. Orton, *California Men*, 210, 879.

204. James L. Richards enlisted as a private in Company H, First California Infantry on August 17, 1861. He succumbed to a fever and died at Tucson on July 12, 1862. Ibid., 371, 880.

205. Simon Pure is short for "the real Simon Pure," alluding to the victim of impersonation in Mrs. S. Centilivre's play *A Bold Stroke for a Wife* (1718).

ALTA, AUGUST 31, 1862

Vedette's Letters from the California Column for Texas
under Gen. Carleton
No. VI.
Ojo de Vaca,[206] *Arizona, Aug. 2, 1862*

EDITORS ALTA:—The march from Tucson toward Mesilla has thus far been prosecuted with vigor, and we are now, or will be to-morrow, within sixty miles of Mesilla,
so lately occupied by the Secession forces under Sibley. By the way, it is asserted by
those who assume to know, that Sibley was forced to flee from his troops, who were
about to hang him for some cause or other; certain it is, that he is not with those who
returned to Texas lately.

ARMY MOVEMENTS

Gen. Carleton, with the advanced detachment, is now at this place, and will proceed
to the Mimbres this afternoon, where he will await the coming up of the whole column. The second detachment, under Col. West, arrived here this morning, and will
proceed to-morrow for the same place, distant about 16 miles. The third detachment,
Captain Willis commanding, is expected here to-morrow morning, and will be followed on the next day by that under Lieut. Col. Rigg, while the last, under Capt.
McCleave, is to leave Tucson today, all *en route* for the Mimbres river.

THOSE DEAD BODIES

Your readers will remember our meeting with a number of dead bodies, about two
miles to the eastward of Apache Pass, which I then supposed to be those Indians
killed by the command under Lieut. Col. Eyre; but a second observation and closer
scrutiny leave but little room to doubt they were the remaining whites who have fallen
victims to the bloodthirsty savages. My reasons for this disagreeable conclusion are
pretty strong. One man, or rather his charred remains, was found bound to a stake in
the midst of a small pile of ashes, showing that he had perished by slow torture; while
fragments of the riata [*reata*, "lariat"] with which he was bound were also discovered
close by. Another's skull was pierced by an arrow, a portion of which projected from
the wound. Two had soldier's shoes on their feet, and when they were removed the skin
was found white and the nails pared, while the soles of the feet were free from cal-
louses. Gen. Carleton also found a number of papers and some clothing near the

206. Ojo de Vaca was also known as Cow Springs and Dinsmore. It was established sixteen
miles southwest of the Mimbres River in December 1858 as a water stop on the Butterfield
route. Conkling and Conkling, *Butterfield Overland Mail*, 2:122–23.

bodies which he caused to be buried. When I first reached the San Pedro, on our route from Tucson, a paper was found in the station house at that place, upon which the following, or something very similar (I do not remember the precise language) was written: "Capt. Larey and nine men arrived here, July 4th, 1862, having dodged the Federal cusses up the Gila and San Pedro rivers, to this place." This paper bore the names of the nine men, and I give you such of them as I now remember: there were James Powell, H. Vining, Webner, Proctor, Mannus, Riddell, Losing and Marion: the others I have forgotten. As soon as I felt satisfied that the bodies we found were those of white men, I dreaded lest the party above alluded to had perished at the hands of the malicious savages, and a universal regret was expressed throughout the column to the same effect. Since reaching this place I find that an expressman named [Jack] Swilling[207] has come to Gen. Carleton from Gen. Canby with dispatches, having met Gen. Carleton *en route*, day before yesterday, and this Snelling [Swilling] says that they must be the bodies of the nine men who had left the Pino Alto gold mine to go to California,[208] where they undoubtedly had friends and acquaintances, and probably relatives. What lends additional strength to this suggestion of Snelling's, is the fact that Gen. Carleton picked up a knife on the ground where the bodies were, which knife was immediately recognized by Snelling as having belonged to one of the party. I am under many obligations to Gen. Carleton for furnishing me with the following list of names of the men who composed it, and whose bodies were probably those we saw. About the 8th of July a party of ten persons[209] left the Pino Alto mines for California, and it consisted of Thomas Buchanan, of Pennsylvania;[210] William Allen, of Illinois;[211]

207. Swilling was charged with escorting the captured Captain McCleave to Mesilla. After Swilling deserted the Confederate cause, he served the California Volunteers as an express rider, and McCleave signed an affidavit attesting to his loyalty. Muster Roll of Capt. Thomas Helm's company of Arizona Cavalry, Oct. 31, 1961, RG 109, NARA; Finch, "Sherod Hunter," 163, 194–97; Senate, *Federal Census—Territory of New Mexico and Territory of Arizona*, 79 (1864).

208. Pinos Altos (High Pines), located seven miles northeast of present-day Silver City, New Mexico, was a mining area rich in copper, silver, and gold. After gold was discovered there in 1860, the settlement was known as Birchville, after one of the discoverers. Apache raids were particularly severe at this isolated outpost. The settlers remaining in 1862 petitioned Carleton and received relief in the form of troops and food in July and August. *OR*, 50(2):36; Pearce, *New Mexico Place Names*, 122.

209. This party consisted of ex-Confederates en route to California. Most were Arizona or New Mexico residents before the war. They had become disillusioned with the Confederates and deserted. "James Ferguson," Hayden Arizona Pioneer Biography Files.

210. Thomas Buchanan was fourth corporal in Mastin's Arizona Guards. He deserted from Mesilla on July 6, 1862, with his musket and was killed by Apaches in Apache Pass. Hall and Long, *Army of New Mexico*, 369.

211. William Allen enlisted as a private in Company I, Fifth Texas Mounted Volunteers on May 25, 1861. He was later transferred to Capt. Joseph D. Sayer's Valverde Battery. Ibid., 201, 290.

Conrad Stark, of Ohio;[212] William Smith, of Pennsylvania;[213] David Berry, of Iowa;[214] James Barnes, of Wisconsin;[215] and an Irishman and an Englishman whose names are not known to me; James Ferguson[216] and a Mexican from Mesilla. These men were all experienced Indian fighters, but were undoubtedly surprised and the majority of them killed at the first fire of the ambushed savages. They are supposed to have perished about the 13th of July; their bodies were seen and passed by the detachment under Capt. Roberts on the 17th of July, under the supposition that they were the remains of Indians, and they were buried by order of Gen. Carleton, who verified them as those of white men, on the 27th of July.

REMARKABLE MARCHES

In my forgoing letter I gave your readers an account of the remarkable marching done by Captain Robert's Company E, First Infantry, and the men attached to the howitzer battery under Lieutenant Thompson, and I now give you an account of the equally remarkable feat performed by the whole column. From the camping place known on the map as "Ojo de Garilan," or in English, Hawk's Springs, they marched to "Liedesdorf's [Leitensdorfer's] Well," a distance of 25 miles, where there was no water for the animals of the train, and only a drink for each man of the detachment. There they rested for a few hours and then proceeded to Burro Cañon, distant 30 2/3 miles, without water, so to speak, and without halt, and in that place they found only just water enough to give a small allowance to each man and animal. There they rested one night and a portion of the day following, and marched up to "Ojo de Vaca," or Cow Springs, where abundance of water exists. The march of 54 miles was made in about 30 hours, under a burning sun and almost without water, yet I did not hear a single expression of murmuring or anything like down-heartedness. Every man seemed

212. Conrad Stark was a private in Mastin's Arizona Guards. He deserted from Fort Fillmore on July 7, 1862, the day after Lt. Jack Swilling deserted. Ibid., 371.

213. William Smith enlisted in Mastin's Arizona Guards at Pinos Altos on August 17, 1861. He was promoted to second sergeant on January 1, 1862. Smith deserted from Fort Fillmore on July 6, 1862, with his musket. Ibid., 371.

214. David Berry may have been related to Cyrus A. Berry, who deserted from Company I, Seventh U.S. Infantry and enlisted in the Confederate service at Fort Fillmore on July 17, 1861. He served with Light Company B, First Regiment of Artillery under Capt. Trevanion Teel and was later transferred to Sherod Hunter's company, serving as quartermaster sergeant. On May 5, 1862, Berry lost his horse in a fight with Apaches. Ibid., 338, 363; Finch, *Confederate Pathway*, 131.

215. Like his companions killed in Apache Pass, James Barnes was probably an ex-Confederate. A John H. Barnes was elected first lieutenant of Company A, Fourth Texas Mounted Volunteers on May 10, 1862. Hall and Long, *Army of New Mexico*, 63.

216. James S. Ferguson was elected sergeant of Company A, Seventh Texas Mounted Volunteers on October 16, 1861. He was appointed sergeant major on November 16 but resigned this position and returned to the ranks on April 13, 1862. Ibid., 222, 228.

anxious to press forward, to get within reach of the enemy, and do something worthy of being engraved upon the historical record of California. All our loyal sister States at the East have borne their part in the brunt of this heart-rending conflict and have added lustre to their escutcheons, but the glory of California seems hidden under a cloud so far. True, they have borne fatigues, privations, and hardships altogether unknown to our Eastern brethren; but these things have no brightness in war, unless varnished in blood. To deserve well of one's country, in time of war, one must kill or be killed. The battlefield alone: the human shambles, toward which all are pressing with anxiety and ill-concealed furor, is the only place in which renown is to be earned or ability rewarded. This is the fault of mankind, whose insatiate appetite for the tragic and the dreadful must be glutted. The attention of the whole world is invited to witness the deepest of tragedies; one like that of "Hamlet," in which all the leading characters bite the dust, only on the most superb scale, and it will not do to put them off with anything less than wholescale butchery. The gallant officer, no matter how eager to shed his own blood in a glorious cause, or lead his column deep into the ranks of the enemy, upon the incarnadined field, although he may have displayed abilities of the highest order, and the most consummate generalship, either in moving a column safely through the most desert regions, or in causing the enemy to decamp at his very approach, can scarcely hope to obtain that meed of commendation and solid acknowledgement from public opinion as he whose only or chief quality consists in the opportunity he may have to lead his column into the fight, and take part in its sanguinary results. I trust that I may not be considered as derogating from the merits of any other corps of volunteers when I say that the "Column from California" will compare favorably, in all respects, with like numbers from any other State in the Union, either with reference to officers or men, from the General down to the most juvenile drummer boy. In all the column of nearly 2,000 men, undergoing almost incredible fatigues, I have not heard a single murmur; not one word of complaint: 17 miles is deemed a forced march for infantry in all armies, even when passing through settled and cultivated regions, garnished with farms, villages and towns, containing all that is requisite for comfort, not to say mere subsistence. But when we compare such marches with those of thirty-six, forty, and fifty-three miles, with only a couple of hours rest, and almost entire destitution of water, and under a burning sun, with only one meal in twenty-four hours, and enveloped in dense clouds of dust, the former sink into utter insignificance—nevertheless, the California Column has done it, and done it nobly. General Canby did not hesitate to assert that it was impracticable to march a column of any considerable force from California to New Mexico, and when he learned that such a column was preparing to reinforce him, could not believe that it would consist of more than a mere scouting party, sent to watch the movements of the enemy about

Tucson. You may judge of his astonishment when he learned that the advanced guard of a squadron of cavalry, and or Lieutenant Colonel Eyre, was already on the Rio Grande, and raised the Stars and Stripes over Fort Thorne, Mesilla, and numerous other places immediately in the rear of the Texans under Colonel Steel, who had stampeded, in the belief that the column was also close at hand. In all verity, we have materially assisted in retaking New Mexico and Arizona, although without actual conflict.

HEALTH OF THE TROOPS

The percentage of sick in this column is remarkably small, far below the average of an equal number of troops elsewhere, even under the most favorable circumstances. This is probably owing to the fact that the greater number had been more or less engaged in mining, and almost all were inured to the fatigue, and life under the open sky, before joining the service. They are also nearly all men in the prime and vigor of manhood, with sufficient experience to teach them how to manage under difficulties—brave, self-reliant, and energetic. As the express is just about to leave, I am obliged to conclude for the present.

VEDETTE

ALTA, NOVEMBER 13, 1862

General Carleton's Column from California
(From the Correspondent of the ALTA CALIFORNIA,
accompanying General Carleton)
Fort Yuma, Nov. 3, 1862

EDITORS ALTA:—You last heard from me from Fort Thorn, since which time four months have elapsed, and I find myself returning to California.[217] In the meantime much of interest has transpired in relation to the movements of troops, and matters in general upon the Rio Grande, the details of which I will not attempt to give, but merely send you a running account and a review of things as they now stand. After being reinforced by two cavalry companies of regulars from Fort Craig, and it being well known that the Texans had skedaddled, our commander, Lieut. Col. Eyre, moved from Fort Thorn down the river to Las Cruces, and took up headquarters. The formality of raising our flag in Mesilla and Fort Fillmore was gone through with, and although it was

217. James P. Newcomb returned to California and went into the newspaper business in San Francisco before returning to Texas in 1867, where he was active in Reconstruction politics. Newcomb Papers.

flying in Mesilla, and had been for two weeks previous to our arrival. The people welcomed us in the warmest manner, although many of them were timid at first, having been told by the Texans that we were coming to make still more desolate their poor homes. The rear of the Texans still lingered at Franklin [Texas], but no force was sent to even reconnoitre until a week or more had elapsed, when it being well known that all the Texans able to leave had left for San Antonio, Company C, [First Cavalry] Cal. Vols., were sent down to Franklin, and found some twenty-five sick Texans in the hospital.

AN ACTIVE ADMINISTRATION

Thus matters remained until Gen. Carleton's arrival, in August, with the main body of the column, when Col. Eyre was relieved of command, and General C. took charge with a vim which soon straightened things out. The General's fine administrative power and his quick perception of the wants, necessities, and state of the country, was a happy relief from the lukewarmness of his predecessor. The lurking disloyalists were caged—troops distributed up and down the river—the people were insured of protection, encouraged to forget their past troubles and return to their business vocations, whilst the whole country was brought under strict military order and discipline. The General did not stop to rest a day upon reaching the Rio Grande, but proceeded in person from the river as far as Fort Quitman,[218] examining the posts, towne and country, disposing of troops, and establishing a good understanding of our Mexican neighbors; also dispatching a reconnoitering party of twenty men under Capt. Shirland, Co. C, 1st Cavalry, Cal. Vols., into Texas as far as Fort Davis.[219] This reconnoitering party did little else than follow the tracks of the retreating Texans. At Fort Davis they buried a poor Rebel who had no doubt been left sick by his companions and was killed by the Indians, and brought away the only living creatures that welcomed them to that inhospitable land—two dogs. On their return they were attacked by one hundred and fifty Indians, and by their gallant bravery beat them off, killing and wounding some twenty-five, and having only one man of the command slightly wounded.

218. Fort Quitman, Texas, was established on the east bank of the Rio Grande seventy miles below El Paso on September 28, 1858. U.S. troops pulled out on April 5, 1861. It was occupied occasionally by a squad of Confederates until Federal troops again raised the flag there on August 22, 1862. Hart, *Old Forts*, 130; Prucha, *Military Posts*, 100.

219. Fort Davis, Texas, was established on October 7, 1854, near the source of the Limpia River. It was intended to guard the overland trail from hostile Indians but was abandoned by U.S. troops on April 13, 1861. Confederates occupied the post in 1861 but withdrew with the advance of the Federals, who did not regarrison it. Confederates again briefly reoccupied the fort in 1864. Hart, *Old Forts*, 55, 188; Prucha, *Military Posts*, 70.

TEXAS

While on his return from Fort Quitman, the General received orders to relieve Gen. Canby, in New Mexico. Without a day's rest, he hurried on to Santa Fe, leaving Colonel West in command at Mesilla, and a better man or abler officer could not have been selected to fill the place. The troops reached the Rio Grande in fine health, and fighting trim, and they are certainly the best, most cheerful, temperate, brave, patriotic body of men in the world, and grieve over the prospect ahead, of their being cooped up in garrisons along the Rio Grande, without the hope of meeting the rebels, or participating in our struggle for the Union. I should judge our force on the river to number over 2,000 men, under the best military discipline, and sufficient to repulse any inroad the Texans might have the hardihood to undertake. The troops have comfortable quarters, plenty to eat and wear, and unsurpassed wealth. Two detachments of Company D, 1st Cav., have been sent down into Texas as escorts to two parties of Texan prisoners. They will, perhaps, go as far as Fort Clark,[220] before meeting a Confederate force. These prisoners have experienced good treatment from Uncle Sam, and will return disciples for the Union. On the last of September, Col. Rigg left Mesilla for Fort Craig, to relieve the Regulars ordered to the States. Everything is quiet and settled on the river; the people feel and act as if they were relieved from a pestilence, and business has revived to its old standard.

THE RETURN TRIP

On my return, I found troops stationed in Apache Pass. They are camped on a hill commanding the water, which they call Camp Bowie; Captain Hines is in command. This is all-important to the protection of parties travelling this road. The Indians are continually lurking in the vicinity, and scarcely a day passes without some adventure with them. I may remark, that the Indians are very troublesome on the Rio Grande, having stolen a large number of stock.

Tucson was in a flourishing condition, but rather deserted in consequence of the departure of Captain Davis, taking with him the cash and the remaining quartermaster property, etc., intended for the Rio Grande. The people are waiting with some anxiety the report of Major Ferguson in regard to bringing supplies and stores by way of

---

220. Fort Clark was established near Brackettville in southern Texas on June 29, 1852. Originally called Fort Riley, it served to protect the border region against Indian raids. Abandoned on March 19, 1861, it was occupied by Confederates in 1862 but not regarrisoned by U.S. troops until December 12, 1866. Hart, *Old Forts*, 171, 188; Prucha, *Military Posts*, 66.

Port Libertad, Sonora.[221] Fort Yuma I also found a little lonely, in consequence of the departure of Colonel Bowie. Mowry is here, swearing furiously about General Carleton; boasts of his ability to have cut up the Californians had he been so disposed, and says he will be released in a few days, and intends making Uncle Sam pay dear for imprisoning him.[222] There is nothing particularly new here; the gold excitement seems to have abated, although several persons are doing well, and others are going up to the mines. Some sales of condemned Government supplies have taken place at shamefully low rates.

PIMOS VS. APACHES

Before closing my letter, I must tell you that the Pimos are waging a bloody and successful war upon the Apaches. As I passed their villages, they were rejoicing over two successful campaigns, in which they had killed seventy Apaches, men, women, and children, and captured some fifteen children prisoners, besides horses and mules, and they are preparing for another campaign.

N.

---

221. Maj. David Fergusson was relieved of his duties as chief commissary of the Column from California in order for him to travel to the Mexican port of Libertad. His report on the roads and resources of Sonora, as well as the practicability of supplying the territories from Libertad, was promising. *OR*, 50(1):115.

222. The U.S. government never paid for losses incurred during the confiscation of Mowry's property nor for his imprisonment at Fort Yuma. For details see Altshuler, "Case of Sylvester Mowry, the Mowry Mine"; and "Case of Sylvester Mowry, the Charge of Treason."

CHAPTER 8

Arizona Dispatches, 1863

ALTA, MAY 25, 1863

Later from Arizona and Sonora.

Private letters by the military express, from Tucson, Arizona, give us the following items:

Governor Pesqueira, of Sonora, was at Fronteras, near the Arizona line, with 400 soldiers, on a campaign against the Apaches. A large number had submitted, made peace, and were settled near Fronteras, where rations were issued to them. A number of Apaches had been killed by parties who claimed the reward of $100 per scalp, offered by the Governor of Sonora. The bounty was promptly paid, and at Ures [capital of Sonora] and Magdalena a general jubilee was held, the recipients of the bounty spending their money for a general jollification.

From Arizona we learn that a new military post is to be established at Tubac, fifty miles from Tucson, on the road from the new port of Libertad,[1] to facilitate the transportation of supplies from Arizona by the new route. Capt. [Charles E.] Mowry has taken possession of the Mowry mines in the name of his brother, Lieutenant Mowry, under the recent decision of the Attorney-General and the Secretary of War in Lieutenant Mowry's favor. The mines were in full operation, and fourteen tons of bars had been shipped in April, to arrive at this port, by the Oregon. The Mowry mines are represented to be richer than ever, yielding large quantities

---

1. Libertad was located at Lobos Bay in the Gulf of California. A detachment of California Volunteers under the command of Maj. David Fergusson explored and mapped a practical land route from Libertad to Tucson in hope of relieving the critical supply shortage in Arizona Territory by finding a faster and more economical route. But strained U.S.-Mexican political relations during the war prevented use of this port on a large scale. Gen. J. H. Carleton, GO 20, Sept. 5, 1862, Dist. of Ariz., *OR*, 50(1):115.

of ore of better quality than heretofore.[2] A new lead has been opened on the estate called the "Ewell,"[3] which promises well. Mr. J. B. Mills,[4] the superintendent of the La Esperanza mine,[5] had arrived, commenced operations, and expects to ship, by the June steamer, ores and bars. He reports the mine as in superb condition, of rich metal, the machinery and stores for this mine are on the ground, and good results expected at an early day. The Olive mine,[6] between the Mowry mines and La Esperanza, gives good prospects, but the owners are somewhat troubled with water in the shaft. A great desire is manifested in Arizona to be restored to the Department of the Pacific, under command of General Wright.[7]

2. Sylvester Mowry operated the Patagonia (Mowry) Mine, which produced lead and silver, near the Arizona-Sonora border about twenty miles from Fort Buchanan. His brother, Charles E. Mowry, was four years older and made his living as a sea captain. Browne, *Mineral Resources,* 447–48; Altshuler, "Case of Sylvester Mowry, the Mowry Mine," 161–63; Senate, *Federal Census—Territory of New Mexico and Territory of Arizona,* 27 (1860).

3. In 1858 Richard S. "Baldy" Ewell, who commanded nearby Fort Buchanan's garrison of the First Dragoons, sold his interest in the Patagonia Mine to Elias Brevoort, who in turn sold out to Sylvester Mowry in 1860. Ewell and other officers invested in mining to supplement their army pay; Ewell also served as superintendent of the Patagonia mine. By the spring of 1862, Ewell was a Confederate general in the Army of Northern Virginia. Altshuler, *Cavalry Yellow and Infantry Blue,* 135; "Case of Sylvester Mowry; the Mowry Mine," 161–53; and "Case of Sylvester Mowry; the Charge Treason," 63–82.

4. John B. Mills Jr. came to Arizona with the United States and California Boundary Commission and later worked for Sylvester Mowry as his private secretary. Major Fergusson had commissioned him to draft an accurate map of Tucson in 1862. In 1863, at the age of twenty-five, Mills became superintendent of Mowry's Patagonia Mine. On December 29 the young man was waylaid by Apaches just three miles north of mine headquarters. The stripped bodies of Mills and his successor, Edwin Stevens, were found riddled with arrows and rifle balls. Browne, *Adventures,* 138, 196–202.

5. The La Esperanza Silver Mine held hope of paying a return on investment in the 1860s. It was located southwest of the Mowry Mine. Browne, *Mineral Resources,* 448.

6. The Olive Mine, just a half mile west of the Mowry Mine, produced lead and silver. Its "argentiferous galena" ore yielded from fifty to one hundred dollars per ton. Ibid., 448.

7. Confusion over the jurisdiction of Arizona resulted from changes in the military Departments of New Mexico and the Pacific. General Carleton commanded the former, while Gen. George Wright commanded the latter. Citizens and soldiers lamented shortages of supplies and raids by hostile bands of Apaches. By the spring of 1863, many in Arizona believed the Pacific Department could better supply subsistence and protection. For a full treatment of this issue, see Hunt, *Army of the Pacific;* and Altshuler, *Chains of Command.*

ALTA, MAY 27, 1863

Letter from the Column from California
From the Correspondent of the ALTA CALIFORNIA
with the Volunteers in Arizona
Tucson, May 13th, 1863

EDITORS ALTA: We have met the Apaches, and they have cause to remember our prowess, as we have given them the greatest threshing they ever received, considering the number that composed the expedition. Enclosed I send a copy of the order issued by the commanding officer of this post after the return of the expedition. Col. Bowie is expected here on the 16th, with Company D.[8] I am informed that he is ordered to proceed to Franklin, Texas, without unnecessary delay.

HEADQUARTERS, TUCSON, ARIZONA,
MAY 12TH, 1863

Order No. 8. I take great pleasure in acknowledging the very gallant and soldier-like manner in which the expedition against the Apache Indians in the Cajon de Arivaypa [Arivaipa Canyon] was conducted, and the highly creditable result of the attack on those savages, who have been devastating, robbing and murdering in this Territory and Sonora for centuries. Captain T. T. Tidball,[9] Fifth Infantry, C.V., who commanded the expedition with so much good judgement, may well be proud of it, and of the brave men under his command, who marched for five days without ever lighting a

8. Commanded by Capt. William Ffrench, Company D, Fifth California Infantry occupied Tucson on April 30, 1863. Originally organized in Sacramento, this company spent the remainder of its term of service as the Tucson garrison. In November 1864 the men marched to Las Cruces, New Mexico, to be mustered out. Orton, *California Men,* 673, 690.

9. Thomas Theodore Tidball was a California forty-niner and newspaperman in Santa Cruz. Appointed captain of Company K, Fifth California Infantry in November 1861, his company campaigned against Arizona Apaches following its posting at Fort Bowie in May 1863. Tidball's expedition against the Arivaipas did in fact become a model for future attacks against rancherias believed to shelter Apache raiders. In 1864 Arizona's first territorial legislature approved a concurrent resolution thanking "the brave and energetic Captain T. T. Tidball, and the officers and soldiers under his command, for their efficient and eminently successful campaigns against the hostile Apaches of Arizona." In 1870 the Camp Grant Massacre was almost a carbon copy of Tidball's feat, including the use of Indian auxiliaries and Tucson citizens in the strike force. Although Tidball returned to California after the war, the Society of Arizona Pioneers elected him as an honorary member in 1886 for his efforts in killing Apaches, whom the Tucsonans held in mortal terror. Orton, *California Men,* 675, 716; "T. T. Tidball," Hayden Arizona Pioneer Biography Files.

fire, maintaining silence, hiding by day and traveling by night to accomplish their object. That a handfull of twenty-five soldiers, and a few brave volunteer citizens, should so completely surprise a rancheria of the craftiest savages on the continent, traveling for sixteen hours the evening and night before the battle; over frightful precipices, through gloomy canons and chasms heretofore untrod by men, rout a numerous horde of savages, killing over fifty, wounding as many, taking ten prisoners and capturing sixty head of stock, without the loss of more than one man, is something for emulation to others in future campaigns against Apaches. We all have to mourn over the brave and generous youth who fell doing his duty, Mr. Thomas C. McClelland, the only one who fell in this brilliant little affair; he will long be mourned by those who knew him only to esteem him as good a citizen, a dutiful son, and a firm friend.

D. FERGUSON [DAVID FERGUSSON]
COL. COMD'G 1ST CAV. C.V.
S.[10]

ALTA, SEPTEMBER 11, 1863

The Californian Volunteers after the Apaches

On the 2d May last, an expedition composed of twenty-five Californian Volunteers, eight citizens, thirty-four Mexicans, and thirty-four Indians, mostly Papagos, started from Tucson to attack the Coyotero Apaches,[11] who had lately committed numerous murders and robberies about the principal settlements in Western Arizona. The expedition was commanded by Capt. Tidball, formerly of Santa Cruz [California]. The Indians were in the Cajon of Arivaypo [Arivaipa Canyon], a rugged cañon, eighty-five miles northeast of Tucson. This place is in a very mountainous region,

10. While a number of men stationed in Tucson with the Fifth California Infantry had names beginning with "S," the most likely candidate for the writer of this letter is 2nd Lt. Henry H. Stevens, Company I. Stevens had been first sergeant of Company F until promoted on February 3, 1863. Company I's hard-drinking captain, Joseph Tuttle, was replaced by 1st Lt. George Burkett from Company F, who trusted his old first sergeant, Stevens, to help him run Company I as his lieutenant. Stevens served as Col. David Fergusson's assistant adjutant at the time of the Tidball expedition and was responsible for copying or signing official communications leaving the Tucson headquarters. Stevens relinquished his position as "Post Adjutant" on February 24, 1864. GO 6, Feb. 24, 1864, Hdqrs. Tucson, Commands of J. R. West, RG 393, NARA. See also Tucson Post Returns, May 1863; Orton, *California Men,* 674, 699, 712; George Hand Diary, Oct. 3, 1862, Arizona Historical Society, Tucson.

11. Coyoteros are Western Apaches, which include the Tonto, Chiricahua, and Arivaipa bands.

which has not been visited by any white man within fifty years. A young Coyotero Apache, who had fled from his tribe, served as a guide for the party.[12] They marched the greater part of the distance at night, and finally, after a night march, they found a camp of Apaches in the Cajon.

A correspondent[13] of the Watsonville *Times* thus describes the Cañon and the attack:

12. Captain Tidball recruited forty men from Santa Cruz to form the nucleus of Company K, Fifth California Infantry. His success was due in large measure to the use of scouts and auxiliaries (Indian, Mexican American, mixed bloods, and whites) recruited from the Tucson area. Colonel Fergusson, commanding at Tucson, issued very specific orders to Tidball prior to his departure:

TUCSON, ARIZ. TER., *May 2, 1863.*
Capt. T. T. Tidball,
Fifth Infantry California Volunteers:
CAPTAIN: You will start this evening with your command. You have twelve days' rations. Should it be necessary you can remain out fifteen or sixteen days with this subsistence. The object of your expedition is to chastise Apaches. This duty I leave in your hand with confidence, therefore will not embarrass you with conditions or detailed instructions as to the modes of attack. There is a rancheria of these savages at the Cajon de Arivapa, about twenty miles from Fort Breckinridge. This I wish you to attack and destroy if possible. I am informed the preferable road to reach the rancheria is that via Canada del Oro. Jesus Maria Elias is well acquainted with this road and the trail. He and the Coyotero guide prefer the former. I agree with them. You shall have the twenty-five men selected by yourself from Companies I and K, Fifth Infantry California Volunteers, say ten American citizens and thirty-two Mexicans, with about twenty Papagos from San Xavier. Jose Antonio Saborze, who is Governor of the Papagos, you will find brave and intelligent. Jesus Maria Elias will have charge of the Mexicans. Nine tame Apaches will be sent with you as spies and guides. All will be strictly under your orders. On the morning of the third day you will arrive at the rancheria. Travel at night; make no fires; allow no firing of arms. By keeping well hid during the day and using your guides judiciously you will no doubt surprise the rancheria. All grown males are fair game; the women and children capture and bring here; also such captives as you may find among the Apaches. You are at perfect liberty to go wherever your judgement dictates after you have attacked the Arivapa Rancheria, or before if unfortunately you find that your designs are discovered. Your guides and the citizens here can give you information of the locale of the savages. Do the best you can while your subsistence will last. Provisions for twelve days have been issued to all the citizens and Indians. You will have to exercise considerable vigor to prevent the Papagos and Apaches (mansos) from killing women and children, and others from plundering when they should be fighting, but all these things will suggest themselves to you. Get as much of the savages' stock as possible. It will be equitably distributed after your return.

With best wishes for your success, I am, captain, very respectfully, your obedient servant,
D. FERGUSSON,
Colonel First Cavalry California Volunteers, Commanding.
D. Fergusson to T. T. Tidball, May 2, 1863, *OR,* 50(2):422–23.

13. Pvt. Thomas Turk enlisted in Company K, Fifth California Infantry on October 21, 1861, and was discharged at Las Cruces, New Mexico, on November 27, 1864, upon the expiration of his term of service. He was the only member of Tidball's company from Watsonville, California, and may well have been the author of this letter. In 1864 the New York-born Turk

The Cajon was a scene of unparalleled grandeur, it was an immense, narrow gorge in the mountains, with perpendicular walls of bare granite rising hundreds of feet above us, and wove into a variety of picturesque and fantastic shapes by time and action of the elements. A stately growth of ash, birch and sycamore covered the narrow bottoms, and reared their branches high up between the granite walls, as if seeking the glorious sunlight. Occasionally, as some little opening allowed the faint rays of the moon to penetrate, the weird and grotesque outlines of the rocky sides were disclosed, presenting scenes of magnificence far beyond my feeble powers of description. Thoughts of the mission of death we were upon, and the solemn stillness of the place, broken only by the rippling of the stream which coursed through it, tended to inspire all with a feeling of awe.

The Rancheria was supposed to be two or three miles above the entrance, and as it was now nearly daylight, we pressed forward as rapidly as we could with prudence. The Cajon for several miles was very narrow—not exceeding two hundred yards in any place. Every few rods we were obliged to ford the cold mountain stream, and frequently it ran for hundreds of yards through chasms where no passage was afforded except along its bed. After we had traversed about four miles of the Cajon, it was daylight—and no Indians yet. The Cajon was growing wider and the sides less precipitous. Presently we found a recently deserted Rancheria. This created a momentary excitement, and then we moved moodily along for perhaps another mile, when the guide reported Apaches ahead. The effect was electrical. Fatigue, sore feet, and hunger were forgotten; and, scarcely aware of it the whole command was pushing forward almost at double-quick.

We had proceeded but a few hundred yards, when, in turning a slight angle in the path, we came into an open grove of mesquit trees, and in full view of the Apache huts scattered through the grove, and not more than thirty or forty yards distant. A volley from the soldiers and Papagos, accompanied by demonic yells from the whole force, was the first intimation the terror-stricken savages had of our presence. They were engaged in cooking breakfast; and, completely surprised, fled in panic to the narrow fringe of willows bordering the stream in rear of their huts. But our fire was too hot for them here, and they fled up the open side of the mountain, followed by the soldiers and citizens. A few of the Mexicans and Papagos accompanied us, but the large portion devoted themselves to plundering after our first fire. About midway up this mountain, three or four hundred yards from the stream, and stretching

---

was thirty years old and living in a miserable dugout on a hillside in Apache Pass, which the volunteers knew as Fort Bowie. Orton, *California Men*, 719; Senate, *Federal Census—Territory of New Mexico and Territory of Arizona*, 50 (1864).

across its face, was a wall of rock fifteen or twenty feet in height and almost perpendicular. There were but two or three places where they could pass, and as they
clambered up these places our terrible Minie muskets[14] would tumble them head-
long to the bottom. But three succeeded in running the gauntlet of that deadly fire
and making their escape over the mountain—two of them wounded. Another
Rancheria, situated a little farther up the stream, and which we did not see for trees
and brush, escaped up the mountains. They tried to attract our attention from the
lower party by displaying a white flag: but the Captain thought the white flag trick
of the Apaches "played out," and ordered a party to send his compliments to the
flagbearer in the shape of a few Minie bullets. This caused him to seek the shelter
of the rocks. In half an hour from the commencement of the action the work was
done. No Indian was seen within range of our pieces. We had one man killed—
young McClellan [McClelland], a citizen of Tucson.

So soon as the fight came to an end, Capt. Tidball, who saw the Apaches col-
lecting on the hill about him, thought it prudent to get into the plain, where he
would be in little danger of an attack at a disadvantage. He started without delay, and
arrived safely at Tucson, having marched a hundred and eighty miles in nine days,
killed forty-seven Apaches, captured ten children, including two of Mexican
parentage, taken twenty-six horses, mules, and cattle, and managed the most successful expedition ever sent out against the Apaches by the United States authorities in Arizona.

ALTA, JANUARY 14, 1864

Letter from Arizona
(From an Occasional Correspondent)
Casa Blanca, Arizona, Dec. 20, 1863

EDITORS ALTA: Thinking that a word from the outskirts of civilization might interest you, I take the liberty of jotting a few items. The Governor [of Arizona, John N.
Goodwin] is, no doubt, inside the Territory of Arizona at last. Men lately from the

---

14. In 1855 the U.S. Army adopted the .58-caliber "Minié ball" as the standard bullet for use
in rifle muskets. Invented by Capt. Claude Minié in 1849, this expanding lead bullet greatly
improved the accuracy of muzzle-loading firearms. The Fifth California Infantry carried
Model 1855 and 1861 Springfield rifle muskets. Ordnance Returns, Fifth California Infantry,
1863, Office of the Chief of Ordnance, Returns, 1861–65, RG 156, NARA.

mines reported him at the Zuñi village,[15] in company with Major [Edward B.] Willis.[16] The Navajoes had given them some trouble, by stealing their cattle. It is reported that Major Willis has seventy-five ox-teams, loaded with supplies, for the new post that is to be established in the mines, perhaps at Walker's Diggings.[17] The post is to be called Fort Whipple,[18] in honor of the late General [Amiel Weeks] Whipple, and to be garrisoned by two companies of infantry and a detachment of cavalry. Capt. [Herbert] Enos,[19] from the Rio Grande has instructions to make a wagon road from Fort Whipple to the Colorado, to strike the river at some point below Fort Mojave,[20] if possible.

15. Abraham Lincoln signed the act creating Arizona Territory on February 24, 1863. The first governor, John A. Gurley, died en route to Arizona, but his replacement, John N. Goodwin, finally entered the territory from New Mexico in late December. Upon his arrival at Navajo Springs in northeastern Arizona, he raised the U.S. flag and took the oath of office. His California Volunteer escort, commanded by Maj. Edward B. Willis, witnessed the proceedings and selected a site near Fort Whipple for the town of Prescott, the territorial capital. Hunt, *Army of the Pacific*, 136–37.

16. Edward Banker Willis joined Company A, First California Infantry in Oroville in August 1861. He gained promotion steadily, from first lieutenant to captain and finally to major on May 6, 1863. On September 5, 1864, he mustered out in Las Cruces, New Mexico, with his regiment, but the following day he was appointed major of the First New Mexico Infantry. He was honorably discharged at Santa Fe on October 1, 1866. Willis was an excellent officer and enjoyed Carleton's favor. He was chosen to escort Governor Goodwin to the territory and located the site for the new capital. Orton, *California Men*, 325, 335–36; "Edward Banker Willis," Hayden Arizona Pioneer Biography Files.

17. Walkers Diggings were discovered in 1863 by a party led by Joseph R. Walker. Located near the head of the Hassayampa River at the confluence of Lynx Creek, miners extracted more than $2,000,000 worth of gold here during the Civil War years, making it the richest strike in Arizona Territory. Dunning and Peplow, *Rock to Riches*, 57.

18. Maj. Edward B. Willis established Fort Whipple at Del Rio Spring with Companies C, F, and G, First California Infantry and Company D, First California Cavalry. He named the post in honor of Gen. Amiel Weeks Whipple, who first surveyed a route across central Arizona in 1853. On May 18, 1864, the garrison moved the fort to Granite Creek, one mile north of Prescott, the territorial capital. Fort Whipple protected the fledgling Arizona government and became the base of offensive operations against the Yavapais and Hualapais. Altshuler, *Starting with Defiance*, 63.

19. Herbert Merton Enos graduated near the bottom of his 1852 West Point class and served in New Mexico with the Regiment of Mounted Rifles, campaigning against Navajos until the Civil War. Appointed captain and quartermaster, he came to Arizona in 1863 and participated in the establishment of Fort Whipple, but by 1864 he returned to New Mexico and was named chief quartermaster of that district. Heitman, *Historical Register*, 1:407; Altshuler, *Cavalry Yellow and Infantry Blue*, 121–22.

20. Fort Mojave was established in 1859 to protect overland emigrants at the Colorado Crossing from the Mojave, Paiute, Chemehuevi, and Hualapai Indians. Regular troops were withdrawn in May 1861, and the post was not regarrisoned until the arrival of Companies B and I, Fourth California Infantry, under the command of Capt. J. Ives Fitch, on May 19, 1863. Altshuler, *Starting with Defiance*, 44; Prucha, *Military Posts*, 92; Orton, *California Men*, 595–98, 609.

The Apaches are stealing stock from the new mines, but have committed no murders. There have been about one hundred head of horses and mules stolen in the last few days, and men are out after them. They stole seven head of horses and mules last week from Mr. White's ranch, at the Pimo villages. It is useless to make treaties with the Apaches, for they will violate them as soon as they have an opportunity to steal. Their creed is to take all the booty they can—it matters not how they get it, and until they are collected and placed under the guns of a fort, or totally annihilated—which they deserve to be—they will be nothing but a murdering band of robbers, a terror to the traveler and settler. Their many atrocious murders of emigrants and settlers was sufficient cause for the Government to subjugate them long ago. Had it not been for them Arizona would now be furnishing her millions of gold and silver, besides great quantities of other minerals much needed.

There is nothing doing in the mines. The creeks are all frozen up, and the miners are waiting "for the moving of the waters," when Old Sol shall come from the south and melt the snow on the mountains.

YOURS, &C. CORPORAL CURRY[21]

---

21. A native of Pennsylvania, Pvt. William Curry joined Company D, Fifth California Infantry at Sacramento on September 27, 1861. His company followed the California Column into Arizona and spent much of its service as the Tucson garrison, mustering out at Las Cruces, New Mexico, on November 27, 1864. Curry reenlisted in Company F, then transferred to Company D, First Battalion of Veteran Infantry on December 13, 1864, and served at Fort McRae until discharged with his company at Los Pinos on September 16, 1866. There is no evidence that the thirty-five-year-old Curry ever attained the rank of corporal, but one month after writing this letter a court-martial found him guilty of harassing a Tucson citizen while on sentinel duty. He forfeited one month's pay and was held in confinement. Orton, *California Men*, 400, 410, 692; Tucson, Company D, Fifth California Infantry, in Senate, *Federal Census—Territory of New Mexico and Territory of Arizona*, 1864; GO 4, Jan. 21, 1864, Hdqrs. Tucson, Commands of J. R. West, Special, General, and Post Orders, RG 393, NARA.

CHAPTER 9

Arizona Dispatches, 1864

ALTA, January 26, 1864

From the California Volunteers in Arizona
Fort Mojave, Arizona Territory, January 9, 1864

EDITORS ALTA:—Presuming that a short letter from this section of the universe might, perhaps, be of interest to some of your numerous readers, I propose for a brief space to lay aside the sword (or rather the musket,) and grasp the pen; try not to turn over, or shake the world, but simply inform them as to a few facts they "wot"[1] not of, concerning this, at present, comparatively unheard of country. I say "comparatively," I mean comparatively to the renown it is destined to possess ere long. But it is as much my purpose to tell of the Volunteers, in whom, I doubt not, California feels a lively interest, as of the country, to which, instead of active service in rebeldom, as we were promised when we enlisted, we have been sent to do garrison duty.

When we arrived here last May there were but few miners here, and but few discoveries had at that time been made among the vast stores of wealth, with which the mountains of the Colorado are pregnant, but enough to establish the fact that this is a miner's country.

PROSPECTING

The climate, much to our satisfaction, was voted by the military Chiefs, too warm for drill, but it was not hot enough to restrain the enterprise or arder of the "Vol.," and with half a dozen canteens slung to his person, that gave him the appearance of an iron-clad on

---

1. wot (British dialect): know.

legs, he might be seen, the hottest days, going forth across the barren plains to the grim, swarthy old mountains, whose rock-ribbed sides seemed ablaze with fire, as they threw back the fierce burning rays of old "Sol," with fiercer intensity into the deep gorges throughout which the treasure seekers must pass; and in one or two instances said treasure seekers came near paying dearly for their temerity.

In one instance a party of four started out for an unexplored district, and failing to find water where they expected, became so far gone as to stagger and fall; and one was unable to get to the river, and laid all night within four miles of the river gasping for water. He was found the next morning and saved from a most horrible death. Well, as a consequence or result of our enterprise, we are all rich men, or at least all that were ambitious that way. In truth we have "feet millionaires" among us.[2] I don't suppose there are two other companies in the service that can boast so many rich men as Companies I and B of the 4th Infantry, C.V.[3] (I should, perhaps, have mentioned that Company B was called in to Camp Drum six weeks since.) And then the beauty, if not the convenience of the thing, our wealth is so invested that we cannot spend it, unless it be in paying board bills at hotels, which we have no occasion of doing, so long as Uncle Sam's beans hold out.

THE MINES

But we are alone in the wilderness or rather desert no longer. As the weather has become cool, and I may add delightfully pleasant, fortune seekers are pouring in here from the settlements in swarms, and the mountains are being closely inspected by the inquisitive prospector, and the occasional echo of the blast tells that some are content to seek no farther, but are following up, or rather going down on their "indications." In the San Francisco District work has been commenced on five different lodes, viz: The celebrated Moss lode, the Skinner, Rosecrans, Rowell, and General Butler—all of which exhibit in the croppings most flattering prospects.[4] Of the Moss there is no

2. "Feet millionaires" refers to the fact that while many soldiers had filed mining claims, duly recording the number of feet, they had no profits to report. The author of this article, Alonzo E. Davis, cashed in on at least one of his claims, selling his interest in the Mitchell Mine to a Pittsburgh company for $10,000. Davis, "Pioneer Days in Arizona," Arizona Historical Society, Tucson, 83.

3. Companies B and I, Fourth California Infantry occupied Fort Mojave on May 23, 1863, after a fatiguing three-hundred-mile march from Drum Barracks (near Los Angeles). After the war Alonzo E. Davis remembered, "each man had to carry his musket, haversack and ammunition, making a pack of about fourteen pounds, it was a hard, hard trip." Company B returned to Drum Barracks in December 1863, but Company I stayed on until March 1865. Davis, "Pioneer Days in Arizona," Arizona Historical Society, 48; Orton, *California Men*, 596, 598.

4. Alonzo E. Davis and others in the Fourth California Infantry prospected in their spare time, filing claims and promoting the mines they held interest in. The San Francisco District, northeast of Fort Mojave and twelve miles from Hardyville, included the Moss Lode and the

need of my speaking, as the ton of rock recently sent to San Francisco speaks for it. The Rosecrans, probably a continuation of the Poindexter, and but a short distance from the Moss, shows gold in the croppings, and a most flattering indication of silver. It is the intention of the owners to push the shaft now eighteen feet down to the depth of fifty feet, where they are sanguine of striking it "big." Capt. Rowell[5] has his shaft down twenty feet, and is taking out good silver rock, and it improves rapidly as they go down. Picked samples assay at $441 to the ton.

The shaft on the Skinner is down twenty-five feet; they have not yet struck the ledge. Work on the Gen. Butler has been suspended for the want of [blasting] powder to continue. The rock at the depth of fourteen feet improves greatly in appearance; it becomes darker colored and evidently contains more silver. The top rock assays $18 per ton, which knowing ones pronounce "good indications."

IN THE IRATABA DISRICT,

Nothing has yet been done further than the commencing two or three shafts. Mr. Silverthone [George E. Silverthorn] breaks ground on the Marathon to-morrow. There is no question about the richness of these mines, as rock can be found in the croppings of most of them that assay 25 to 75 per cent., copper and some silver. And as they are within eight to twelve miles of the river, to which a good road with a down grade all the way can easily be had, their availability is all that could be wished. The only question to be solved is, are they genuine ledges? Do they hold out under ground? And of this there can be but little doubt, especially those that can be traced a distance of two or three miles, of which there are quite a number. I have next to speak

---

Skinner Mine. Capt. John Moss, Capt. John Hardy, and partner Frank Skinner had served at Fort Mojave before the war and by 1863 were reaping the rewards of their earlier prospecting. It was said Moss extracted $200,000 of gold before selling out to San Francisco capitalists for $78,000. The Rosecrans, Rowell, General Butler, and Poindexter never paid as well as the Moss Lode. Davis, "Pioneer Days in Arizona," Arizona Historical Society, 53; Browne, *Mineral Resources,* 457–60; Dunning and Peplow, *Rocks to Riches,* 63–64; Webb, "Mines in Northeastern Arizona," 247–70.

5. Converse W. C. Rowell was mustered in as captain of Company A, Fourth California Infantry at Placerville, California, on September 21, 1861. After serving in the Pacific Northwest and northern California, he was dismissed for "mutinous conduct" on April 27, 1863, per Special Order No. 17, Department of the Pacific. An energetic and capable man, he afterward poured himself into gold mining and politics in Arizona. He was elected to the Arizona Territorial Legislature and served as a justice of the peace and a district attorney. Orton, *California Men,* 601; Davis, "Pioneer Days in Arizona," Arizona Historical Society, 93; Morrow, *Mohave County Lawmakers,* 3.

of Sacramento District,[6] which I verily believe will eclipse anything on the coast for ore or pure metal.

The first lodes were discovered about three months ago by a party of three soldiers; and as they looked well, and no District had yet been organized there, we, with the assistance of a few citizens there, here organized a District, honoring it with the name of the "City of the Plains." The "indications" there found have since been vigorously followed up by both civilian and soldier, and a large number of beautiful lodes have since been determined to be certainly rich in something. What that something is, is not yet positively known . . . ore, (for such it is—not rock,) contains considerable lead. Indeed, pure galena is found in some of the lodes. It also bears evidence of containing copper and silver. A gentleman on his way to Walker's diggings, tested a small piece with a blow pipe, and obtained a very nice button of pure silver. The sample was taken from the "Union" lode. The Union is probably as fine a lode as there is in the District; it is from ten to eighteen feet wide. The ore shows a large amount of the bromide of silver and contains considerable yellow sulphate. I have been shown samples from the "Comstock"[7] that are *fac simile* of some of the samples from this lode. The lode is owned mostly by soldiers [of] the Union Company, then in number, have paid in $50 to the man to have it prospected, and it will not be long until something is known of its character under ground. I should have stated that the Sacramento District is north of the San Francisco District, on the east side of the river, and distant from the Fort thirty-five miles. It is well watered by springs, and in places heavily timbered with scrubby pine and cedar; though valueless for building purposes, it will be invaluable for smelting the ores.

6. Alonzo E. Davis and other contemporary writers rated the Sacramento District, located thirty-five miles northwest of Fort Mojave, as second only to the San Francisco District. The Union Lode and other mines were composed of "argentiferous galena" yielding silver and gold. The Union Lode was said to have a vein eight feet wide. The California Volunteers stationed at Fort Mohave mined the Cerbat and Hualapai Mountains with permission and encouragement from their officers. In 1863 they organized a mining district with mining laws modeled after those of the San Francisco District. Fully one quarter of all the claims recorded in Mojave County during the Civil War years were filed by California soldiers. Davis, "Pioneer Days in Arizona," Arizona Historical Society, 69; Browne, *Mineral Resources*, 460–61; Mohave County Mining Claims and Deed Books, 1862–65, Mohave County Courthouse, Kingman, Ariz.; Paher, *Ghost Towns*, 5.

7. Discovered in 1859 by Henry T. P. Comstock near Virginia City, Nevada, the Comstock Lode became the richest and best known of all of the western mineral strikes. Assays reporting three thousand dollars in silver per ton started a rush to the area. Lord, *Comstock Mining*, 1–12.

WHAT THE COUNTRY NEEDS

There are several things that this country is at present greatly in need of, for instance a good, reliable assayer, a stock of provisions, mining implements, etc.; a few quartz mills, in short capital; capital is what the country needs to help give it a start and it will cause the world to marvel.

There are a thousand avenues, and the best assurances for its safe and profitable investment, and last, but not least by any means, we want a good reporter to the inside world of the march of events here.

PROVISIONS, ETC

There have been half a dozen wheelbarrow loads of provisions brought in here from Los Angeles, which went off like hot cakes, at '49 prices. Bacon at sixty-three cents to one dollar per pound; flour at twenty to twenty-five dollars per cwt., and other things in proportion. But these high prices must cease, never no more to be, as soon as public enterprise gets directed this way, and a good line of boats gets started, both of which are expected with the raising of the river in the spring. The river has been at an unprecedented low stage this season, according to aborigine authority, which should be taken as good, I suppose. Yet the *Cocopah*,[8] a boat that draws eighteen inches of water, succeeded in getting up about two months since, although she was thirty days making the trip from Fort Yuma, which she usually makes in nine. But men that profess to know say, that as soon as boats get to running regularly, a channel will be formed that will always be navigable. Steamboating should be a nice business on this river, as there will be back freight of copper ore.

I was near forgetting to mention that a most formidable rival to Madame "Feet" appeared on the board a few days ago. A town has been laid out, and for awhile the new claimant seemed to be the favorite. "Town lots" was all that could be heard here, and there and everywhere it was "Lot, lot." But, as though the new comer did not bear acquaintance, the excitement has suddenly ceased, and Madame Feet is again reigning belle. Yet I must not follow the example of the fickle public, and wholly ignore the [...]

---

8. Capt. George A. Johnson launched *Cocopah* in 1859 to carry supplies from Port Isabel at the mouth of the Colorado River to Fort Yuma and Fort Mojave, 150 and 450 miles upstream respectively. This 140-foot shallow-draft sternwheeler played a role in the westernmost skirmish of the Civil War on May 20, 1863. Men of the Fourth California Infantry assigned to guard the boat came under attack by William "Frog" Edwards, a "secession desperado" who had been interned for a time at Fort Yuma with Dan Showalter's band of Rebels. Lingenfelter, *Steamboats on the Colorado*, 29, 33, 161; Tuttle, "Colorado River," 40–50; *OR* 50(2):459–60.

NEW CITY.

It is situated two miles below the Fort, on the river's bank. The site is a good one, on a high gravel bluff, safe from overflow, and where boats can have a good landing at all stages of the water. I am neither a prophet nor a son, etc., but if Irataba City[9] does not boast its thousands of inhabitant in a few years hence, in the words of Grimwig, "I'll eat my head."[10]

THE WEATHER

Of the climate, I believe we have been here long enough to knowingly speak. When we came here, last May, the weather had commenced to get decidedly warm, and it continued to grow emphatically warmer until July, when it might be said to have become positively hot, and so continued, the mercury ranging from 85 to 110 degrees. The maximum heat of the summer was 116 degrees. Since October it has been getting gradually cooler, and now it is common to see ice in the morning half an inch thick. But as soon as old Sol shows himself in the east, it is as pleasant as the May mornings of New England. The hot months here are truly unpleasant, but to no greater degree than the rest of the seasons are more than delightful—barring the fierce sand-storms with which we are occasionally treated, just to remind us, I presume, that we should be thankful for the calm and sunshine. Save two or three light showers during the months of July and August, no rain has fallen since we have been here.

RIO FRIO COUNTRY

Notwithstanding the discouraging reports that are continually coming in from the Rio Frio country [Agua Fria River, Central Arizona], there are a great many passing through here daily, en route for there—though a great many that started for there have stopped here, and many more would, if implements could be had here for quartz mining. A great portion of those that return are destitute of provisions; as a consequence, our commissary has a pretty good run of custom. The price they have to pay for "grub" enough to last them to the settlements, is the subscribing to a pretty strong oath of allegiance.

9. Iretaba City, situated on the east bank of the Colorado River just two miles below Fort Mojave, was laid out by soldier-miners in January 1864. The town never amounted to much since ferryman William H. Hardy established a rival settlement, closer to the mines, nine miles north. Hardyville soon became the "practical head of navigation" on the Colorado, and Iretaba City became a ghost town. Lingenfelter, *Steamboats on the Colorado*, 39.

10. Charles Dickens featured a Mr. Grimwig in his 1859 bestseller, *The Adventures of Oliver Twist*. Grimwig backed nearly every assertion with "or I'll be content to eat my own head, sir!" Pierce, *Dickens Dictionary*, 96–97.

Now, Messrs. Editors, I did not set out to write a long letter, nor a flashy one, but merely to state a few facts concerning the country, trusting that they might prove interesting enough of themselves to not need the embellishing flourish of the artistic correspondent. If I am right, you may again hear from

ONE OF THE CALIFORNIA VOLUNTEERS[11]

ALTA, March 26, 1864

Letter from the California Volunteers in Arizona
(From the Correspondent of the ALTA CALIFORNIA
accompanying the Column)
Fort Mojave, Arizona, March 9, 1864

PAPER CITY

EDITORS ALTA: I must acknowledge a "misscue" in my last as to the prophecy on the rise of "Irataba" City. A rival town has started, and as it has several citizens and two or three adobes, and has the start of Irataba, I feel as though I would like to withdraw my proposition to eat my head in the event Irataba did not attain her thousands. The new city is pronounced dead; for a season, at any rate. But the numerous long rows of

11. After the war Alonzo E. Davis admitted that he wrote for the *Alta* as an "occasional correspondent" during his days at Fort Mojave with the Fourth California Infantry. Born in 1839 in New York's Genessee Valley, Davis left for California in 1857 to seek his fortune in mining, ferrying, farming, and freighting. He enlisted at Oroville on October 9, 1862, in Capt. Charles Atchisson's Company I. He spent much of his time at Fort Mojave prospecting and filing claims. In February 1864 Atchisson detailed Davis to guide journalist J. Ross Browne on a tour of the mines and mineral resources of the lower Colorado River region. Browne was so impressed with Davis's knowledge that he incorporated his descriptions verbatim in his book, *The Mineral Resources of the Pacific Slope,* published in 1869. With Atchisson's encouragement, Davis read law books in the evenings, after taps, in a quartermaster supply room with darkened windows; Davis passed the bar examination shortly after his enlistment. He went on to practice law in Arizona, was appointed to public office, and was elected to the territorial legislature. He wrote for the *Alta* under the pen names "SIVAD" and "California Volunteer." He was a tireless booster of Arizona mines and defender of the Colorado River Indians, for whom he developed great sympathy. Davis met Emily W. Mathews, daughter of Hardyville businessman Frank M. Mathews, at the Fort Mojave New Year's Eve Ball of 1864–65, and they married soon after the war. On January 27, 1866, Davis wrote the editors of the *Alta:* "It is nearly a twelve month since my correspondence with the *Alta* from this territory was terminated by the powers that were. But now 'the cruel war is over,' 'Cal. Volunteer' has doffed the blue and brass of our good Uncle, and returned to the Frontier, and in the garb of a humble citizen would again contribute his mite towards bringing to notice and advancing the mighty mineral resources of our young Territory." Davis, "Pioneer Days in Arizona," Arizona Historical Society; Orton, *California Men,* 657; *Alta,* Feb. 19, 1866; "Alonzo E. Davis," Hayden Arizona Pioneer Biography Files.

stakes marked and numbered, denoting streets, plazas, etc., is evidence of the friendliness of its founders. I would advise lot-holders in Irataba to sell, if they can. I have learned that there is quite an analogy between air castles and paper cities. Both look grand and imposing, viewed through the eye glass of hope, especially to the lot-holder, inspiring bright visions of grand Gothics, fast horses, gold chronometers, champagne, oysters, etc., and the usual homage and attention.

THE PIONEER

Mr. [William H.] Hardy,[12] of Forrest Hill, Cal., is entitled to the credit of being the first capitalist that has started the steam engine of enterprise, and he is driving it most furiously, too. But instead of locating in Irataba, as we expected he would, he has gone above the Fort some six miles, and has already established a ferry, erected the walls of two or three adobes of generous size, and has the foundation laid for a large store, forty by one hundred. He has in his employ about fifteen whites and forty Indians. The site he has chosen is the best on the river. A good crossing can be had, the year round, the channel being confined by high gravel banks on either side. It is within seven miles of the San Francisco District, the nearest point to the river, and mills for working the ores of that district will probably be erected here. Mr. Hardy has a large and well-chosen stock of goods coming out that will be here as soon as the river raises, which will be in about three weeks, when mining and business generally, will surely commence a "foreward movement," as a good many men are now lying idle because of the want of proper implements, provisions, etc.

THE SAN FRANCISCO DISTRICT

Notwithstanding all drawbacks, there are a good many at work in the San Francisco District. Work has lately been commenced on several different lodes, among which are the Parsons, Hurst, Poindexter and Olive Oatman.[13] The shaft of the Skinner has

12. Born in New York, forty-one-year-old William H. Hardy was a shrewd businessman. Thanks to his partnership with George Johnson's steamboat operation, by 1865 Hardy had nearly locked up the freighting business on the lower Colorado, serving both soldiers and citizens alike. Overland travelers funneled across the Colorado at his ferry six miles above Fort Mojave, and Mormon settlements in Nevada and Utah as well as military posts and miners in central Arizona depended on his services. Hardy hired Indians to make adobes and erected a hotel/store, billiard hall, machine shop, blacksmith shop, housing, and "a fine public hall." Hardyville later became the Mohave County seat, and Hardy himself was elected to the territorial legislature. Lingenfelter, *Steamboats on the Colorado*, 39, 47–48; Senate, *Federal Census— Territory of New Mexico and Territory of Arizona*, 94 (Hardy's Landing, 1864); Davis, "Pioneer Days in Arizona," Arizona Historical Society, Tucson, 54.

13. The Parsons Lode was considered the "mother lode" for this group of mines in the San Francisco District. William H. Hardy invested $40,000 in opening it and erected a ten-stamp mill nearby. Browne, *Mineral Resources*, 459–60.

struck the ledge at fifty-feet; very rich rock is revealed. The Rosecrans, also, has struck at the depth of twenty-eight feet; the rock at that depth shows gold and considerable black sulphurets. It is to be regretted that the Moss, the most noted lode of the district, should have gone into litigation. It has been a serious drawback to the District, as the lode would have been well prospected, and it is probable we should have heard the thumping of stamps much sooner than we now will.

SACRAMENTO DISTRICT

Prospecting is going on lively in the Sacramento District. New locations are continually being made. New ledges have been discovered, every one of which is the "richest." Mr. [Edward] Carlson,[14] assayer, has arrived here, and has made several assays of the ore, and I have yet to hear of one that does not return silver. They range from nine to one hundred and fifty-four dollars per ton, about one quarter of which is generally gold. This, for croppings, I should say is good. The ores contain more or less lead, some as high as forty per cent, and some copper.

As yet there is not much being done in Irataba District (copper) although preparations are being made to open two or three of the lodes. A contract has been let to parties in San Francisco to open and work the Rip Van Winkle. One thousand pounds of ore will be shipped to San Francisco soon, for a working test.

MATTERS AT THE FORT

In consequence of the non-arrival of the steamer or trains from Camp Drum, with supplies, our commissary is in no condition to stand a siege. Were it not that Mr. [L.] Dukes,[15] (the sutler) has some beans on hand, I don't know what we would do. The beef, after a year's residence on the desert, is just about as lean as Libby [Confederate prison] prisoners. I do not know how many thousand miles they have been run the past year; they are very wild and have to be lassoed. Pork is *non est;* spuds, ditto. The sutler, providentially had a little bacon, but that is now all gone, and it is hard to tell

14. Edward Carlson immigrated from Hamburg, Germany. This thirty-one-year-old assayer had all the business he could handle as California Volunteers and civilian prospectors eagerly sought his services. Many of his clients were comrades—Carlson had served in Company C, Fourth California Infantry and later as the regimental commissary sergeant. He was discharged for disability at Fort Mojave on September 19, 1863. Orton, *California Men*, 600, 617, 799; Senate, *Federal Census—Territory of New Mexico and Territory of Arizona*, 91 (Fort Mohave, 1864).

15. Fort Mojave sutler L. Dukes had served the garrison since the summer of 1863. This entrepreneurial twenty-eight-year-old kept $2,000 worth of food and small stores for the soldiers. Low water and mechanical failures often prevented river steamers from reaching Fort Mojave on a regular schedule. Senate, *Federal Census—Territory of New Mexico and Territory of Arizona*, 91 (Fort Mohave, 1864).

where the next grease spot will come from. Relief will surely come, and in the meantime we will patiently munch our beans and bread "straight." To avoid discouraging enlistments, I will say to the uninitiated, that Uncle Sam usually sets a good table; he provides bountifully, and of good kind; unavoidable delays sometimes occur; his servants are sometimes hungry. How long we will remain here is a question that causes considerable anxiety among us all.

THE SOLDIERS LIKE THE COUNTRY

Notwithstanding many privations, inevitable in a desert country, hot weather, and the poor and scanty supplies, which some way it has been our lot to bear since we have been here, nearly all, if not every man, are deeply anxious to stay here, and it may be, be discharged here; we are all identified with the country, and probably more than half of the Company [I, Fourth California Infantry] would return here, no matter where they might be discharged. The soldiers, by exploring the country within a radius of fifty miles of the fort, have, I think, rendered a material service to the country. They discovered the Sacramento District, which would otherwise have remained unknown some time, as it is in the Walapi Mountains, and off the range of prospectors. Captain Atchison [Atchisson][16] gives us passes, and we have thus been enabled to do considerable toward developing the country. We have invested our greenbacks—some to the last dollar—in purchasing tools, etc., to sink our shafts. We have commenced five different shafts, which are being pushed forward as fast as circumstances will admit.

THE SOLDIERS' VOTE

I presume none were more surprised, or deeply chagrined, than we were at the announcement that the new Supreme Bench had disfranchised us. I am not a lawyer,[17]

16. Capt. Charles Atchisson (1824–91) commanded Company I, Fourth California Infantry from September 1861 until his resignation on June 13, 1865. The forty-year-old captain enjoyed the respect of his men and the people of Mohave County, where he returned after the war as postmaster and later served as probate judge. Atchisson made the best of difficult duty after assuming command at Fort Mojave in December 1863 after the senior captain, J. Ives Fitch, Company B, departed with his men. Atchisson encouraged his men to prospect and publicize their findings, and he promoted Alonzo E. Davis to sergeant and encouraged him to "read law" in the evenings in preparation for the bar exam. After the war he and Davis became business partners, selling drygoods. Atchisson dabbled in politics and mining as well. Throughout his life, people spoke well of him. In 1864 Gen. George Wright granted him extraordinary discretionary authority in the management of affairs at Fort Mojave "because of the high appreciation the General has of him both as a soldier and a citizen." Senate, *Federal Census—Territory of New Mexico and Territory of Arizona*, 92 (Fort Mohave, 1864); Orton, *California Men*, 598, 656; Altshuler, *Cavalry Yellow and Infantry Blue*, 12; R. C. Drum to J. F. Curtis, Apr. 21, 1864, *OR*, 50(2):823–24.

17. On October 23, 1866—just one year following his discharge as a California Volunteer—Alonzo E. Davis was admitted to the bar and began practicing law at Mohave City, Arizona Territory. "Alonzo E. Davis," Hayden Arizona Pioneer Biography Files.

and if I were, would not undertake in a letter to argue the point of law involved. For the merits of the case there is no need for a plea, as every loyal, intelligent citizen is free to acknowledge the wisdom of a law that prevents traitors from enjoying the pay and emoluments of the Government they would destroy. The right of suffrage, always esteemed a sacred privilege by the American, at this time is doubly dear. We left our homes to aid in the defence of our country. It is essential that treason should be defeated at home and abroad. Take away from us the right of suffrage, and you disarm us of our most potent weapon, and surrender us into the hands of the Philistines. The heart of the volunteer gladened when told that he could exclude from Legislative halls and seats of Justice, the traitors at home, the brothers of whom we are now in the field to meet. We were elated when told by the public journals, that our votes had kept the filching fingers of Copperheads from the public purse. We rejoiced when we were told that a Supreme Bench had been secured, composed of staunch, Union men; for we presumed that they would be called upon to pronounce upon the law. Judge then, our surprise, when the announcement came that that Court, composed of Union men, had betrayed and disfranchised us. Napoleon's soldiers, perhaps, were "machines," but I hope the learned Court does not so view the citizen soldiery that are now fighting for the preservation of republican liberty, to save their country from the toils of treason. Our hope is now, that a re-hearing may be obtained, and the decision reversed. If it is not, cannot the present Legislature do something in the matter? We must be permitted to vote for "Uncle Abe."

A CHANCE AT ACTIVE SERVICE FOILED

There was a prospect a few days ago for a bit of that much deserved "active service." Word came in that forty head of horses had been stolen by a band of Pi-Utes that infest the country around Rock Springs, with a petition from the miners there for protection. Accordingly, Capt. Atchinson immediately dispatched a detachment of fifteen men to aid in the recovery of the stolen horses. The party had been gone but one day when intelligence came that all the horses, which had strayed, had been found.[18] A courier was sent after the detachment, which overtook them at Pi-Ute Hill, with a countermand. With curses "deep, but not loud," that their first campaign should end so ingloriously, they right-about-faced for the Fort, but not until they "cleared out" a

18. Captain Atchisson believed that rumors of stock theft and Indian "depredations" had been blown up to "gigantic proportions" by excitable citizens. In his report to headquarters following this episode, the captain confirmed that the lost horses had indeed been found, adding: "In my opinion all is quiet on the road, as far as Indians are concerned, and there has been no occasion requiring a report from me other than why I sent out the detachment. I hope this explanation will be satisfactory." C. Atchisson to W. Forry, Fort Mojave, Feb. 20, 1864, *OR*, 50(2):761–62.

house of "Burbon." These, with the exception of a black eye and a skinned nose, their casualties were insignificant.

AN INDIAN TRAGEDY

Quite a tragedy occurred here a short time ago, the particulars of which are as follows. It is the custom of the Mojaves to kill their doctor when he shall have lost ten patients, and as there has been a frightful mortality among them the past winter, the slaughter among the medical faculty has been heavy. Dr. Si-noo-poo had been unsuccessful; ten times he failed by his hocus-pocus, hideous grimaces, mysterious incantations (this is the system,) to terrify the great destroyer away. His turn had come, and being the 10th to start on his trip to the spirit land, sought refuge from his executioners at the Fort, hiding away at night, trusting in the "soltous" for protection in the day time, this way he prolonged his departure some days; but he finally got careless, and one evening we were startled by hideous yells and crashing blows. We tried to catch the wretches and convince them of the white man's disapproval of such proceedings, but they eluded us, taking the body of the victim with them, which was found next morning, half consumed by fire; (they burn their dead.) Captain Atchinson summoned Chief Assokut,[19] and received his bond that this should not occur again. The Mojaves are a fine race of Indians, large, well formed, and intelligent; they are very peaceable, although a quarrel among themselves is a very frequent occurrence. Government should, and I presume will, do something for their improvement. They have rich lands, and if they were furnished with tools and learned the use of them and the science of farming, they would raise enough and more for themselves and the Mountain Indians. Had it not been for a large quantity of condemned flour in the Commissary, many would have starved this winter; about one thousand pounds of that had been issued to them per week, which has been a great help to them.

THE FIRST WEDDING

Of the country and season tool place last night, and it seems to me, as being the first, it is entitled to some notice. The bride was Miss Ah Cottio, youngest daughter of Bio-oo-hoot, Chief of the Mojaves; the groom, W. Furlong,[20] express rider. The

19. Sick-a-hote (Sic-a-hote or Sichout) was a Mojave chief often at the center of controversy in dealings with the army and white citizens near Fort Mojave. When the regular garrison at the post pulled out on May 28, 1861, Maj. Granville Haller handed over the keys to Sic-a-hote, whom he considered the head chief of the Mojaves. In 1863, when the California Volunteers arrived to reoccupy the fort, Sic-a-hote dutifully returned the keys. Tuttle, "River Colorado," 58; C. Atchisson to Lt. W. Forry, Feb. 20, 1864, Fort Mojave, OR, 50(2):761–62; Brennan, Fort Mojave, 23.

20. The express rider William "Billy" Furlong had worked around the upper Colorado crossing and Fort Mojave for five years. He may have come to Arizona with the Sixth U.S.

marriage service was performed by Parson O— [John M. Ormsbee], Private Company B, in the presence of the "Commander" [Atchisson] of Post, "Q" [Private David Quain], "M," and a few chosen guests. The marriage contract is of new form, but very full and binding. It contains a quit-claim from the Mojave tribe to the bride, "for and in consideration of two horses, one sack of flour, twenty pounds of sugar," he "W.F., to have and to hold," etc., etc.; "said Ah Cottio, free from all the incumbrances," etc. After the two were made one flesh, the gay party repaired to the house of the house of the groom, where a splendid supper was in readiness; "Old Tom" was a conspicuous guest, receiving marked attention from all. The bride seemed happy, the groom happy, and "all went merry as a marriage ball." The weather is commencing to get warm, reminding us of the hot months of last summer, which starts a perspiration.

CAL. VOLUNTEER

ALTA, May 14, 1864

Letter From Fort Mojave, Arizona
(From the Resident Correspondent of the ALTA CALIFORNIA)
Fort Mojave, Arizona Territory, April 27th, 1864

EDITORS ALTA: This is a locality more prolific of startling rumors than great events. We have not had war, but we have had a rumor of war. In these days, when every evening journal tells of civil war, bloody and terrible, it cannot be expected that bloodless rumor of Indian war here in the desert world will attract much attention, or be very interesting. Nevertheless, as a faithful chronicler of passing events, I must permit it to occupy a small space in this correspondence. With this preface for an apology for its insignificance, I will proceed to give an account of the origin and ending of the [. . .]

THREATENED INDIAN WAR.

Owing to the almost entire failure of the mesquit crop, which is the chief dependence of these Indians, they have been, through the past winter, in a condition of more than semi-starvation. Now, horse-flesh is considered by them a choice delicacy, mule more choice, and "burro" takes the superlative degree. The clamor of hunger is hard

---

Infantry in 1859 as Capt. Lewis A. Armistead's orderly. Furlong was born in Belfast, Ireland, in 1835, but Alonzo E. Davis remembered that he had gone native, living "exactly as an Indian. . . . [H]e spoke the Indian language like a native and wore no clothes other than the breechcloth." Senate, *Federal Census—Territory of New Mexico and Territory of Arizona,* 91 (Fort Mojave, 1864); Davis, "Pioneer Days in Arizona," Arizona Historical Society, 138; Tuttle, "River Colorado," 58.

to withstand, and civilized man has been known to do that which nothing else could prevail on him to do. The Indian is not perfect; he, too, has his weaknesses; and as the stock of the white strangers that have come among them offered a most seductive bait to their hunger-sharpened appetites, it is not to be wondered that they have slaughtered some of them.

But, notwithstanding that their condition is a palliation of their crime—if crime it can be called—men are averse to being left in the desert on foot, and have made complaint to Captain Atchisson, and he, in answer to the same, took the matter in hand, and caused the arrest of one, who, according to their own admission, was concerned in stock killing. Now, there is nothing that has so much terror for the Mojave as the "Calaboose," and they took the incarceration of one of their warriors as much to heart as did John Bull the detention of his traitor guests.[21] It was the intention of Captain Atchisson to get possession of a few of the leading ones and give them a flogging, and thus terrify them from committing further mischief; but through the mischievous intermeddling of some vagabond Copperheads [secessionists], by which class this country, like most of the Pacific Coast, is cursed, there came, I believe, very near being a collision between the Indians and ourselves. They told the Indians that we were about to kill the prisoner, and also commence war upon them. Their actions were proof that something was up, as they all left the Fort and vicinity, around which about a hundred are always lounging. Certain citizens had threatened to shoot the Indians if they lost any more stock, and one evening, just at dark, a person came rushing into the Fort, out of breath, with the intelligence that an Indian had been killed by a white man, and that the Indians were concentrating for an attack on the Fort. An unusually large camp fire below confirmed the report. Instantly our camp was in commotion, the guard was trebled, arms were issued to those citizens who came to the Fort, and every preparation made for repelling the anticipated attack; but night passed away, morning came, and all was yet "quiet on the Colorado." The Captain immediately despatched messengers to the mountains and wherever white men were encamped, warning them of the threatened danger, and tendering them all the protection of the garrison. Subsequent developments have proved that the report of the Indian being killed was false, and that the Indians, so far from contemplating an attack, that night were themselves concentrating, fearing an attack from us.[22]

21. "John Bull," the stereotypical Englishman, was a fictional character first made popular in pamphlets written by John Arbuthnot in 1712 to satirize Whig war policy.

22. For Captain Atchisson's account of this scare, see his report to headquarters in San Francisco, April 2, 1864, in Brennan, Fort Mojave. It seems that when the express rider, Billy Furlong, returned to the fort with the mail, things calmed down because, as Atchisson noted, he "speaks the Indian language well." Ibid., 24.

Capt. Atchisson assembled the chiefs and effected an understanding with them, they pledging themselves for the future good behavior of their tribe; and so the issuing of flour was resumed, they were again permitted to come about the garrison, and Indian and "Boston"[23] are once more friends. The Mojaves naturally class the soldier above the citizen, thinking, probably, that as with themselves, the "warrior 'Mericano" is the lion. As I said before, the trouble was all brought about through lies told by the mischievous scoundrels, who would do anything to give Union soldiers trouble. The Mojaves are very solicitous concerning Irataba, as these rascals have told them that he would not be permitted to come back again.

BACKWARD SPRING

The almanac tells us that spring has come, and well night passed, but nothing in nature corroborates it other than the heavy mantle of foliage the beautiful cottonwood, mournful willow, and thorny mesquit have donned. No bright-plumed warblers are flitting through their branches, filling the air with lively song. No sweet fragrance from violet or daisy is borne on the hot southern breeze, which frolics over these desert plains. Yet, hot weather has well set in, for several days the mercury has crawled up to a hundred in the shade, and an occasional hot breeze gives us a premonition of what we may look for the coming five or six months.

Notwithstanding the past few days of hot weather, to the surprise of every one here, the river has raised but a few inches. Everybody expected to see high water before this time. Last season was considered backward, yet at this time the river was well up, and a few days later, the *Cocopah* landed sixty tons of freight here. The natives say that the river will not "get big" this winter, by which they probably mean that it will not overflow the bottoms, which it often does. As it is reported that a good deal of snow fell last winter on the mountains that feed it, there can be but little doubt that we shall soon hear from this warm weather through the rushing, muddy waters of the Colorado; and we shall soon have the steamers tumbling their freights on our banks; and then, the complaint now so general here about scarcity of provisions, will be banished, I hope forever.

INDIAN AGRICULTURISTS

I made a trip down the river a few days since, and was greatly surprised at the large quantities of wheat the Indians were growing, and also at its fine appearance. They

23. American Indians in California and along the West Coast typically called white Americans "Bostons" because the first seamen told the natives they were from Boston. Richard Henry Dana, *Two Years before the Mast: A Personal Narrative* (reprint, New York: New American Library, 2000), 133.

select low flats, where the ground is rich, and plant in holes about a foot apart and eight inches deep, so as to get the moisture sufficient to sprout the seed. They planted last winter—in December, I believe—and it is now headed out finely, and in a short time will, I judge, be fully matured. As soon as the water recedes, which is generally in June, they plant the same ground with corn, vines, beans, etc., thus raising two crops from the same ground in one year. As I said in another letter, all they want are implements and instruction in their use, and they will raise enough to supply a large market.

FROM THE MINING DISTRICTS

Reports are continually coming in of new and rich discoveries. From the Sacramento District we hear of new leads being found that, upon assay, cause owners' eyes to sparkle, and old Washoe [Nevada] and Reese River [Nevada] prospectors to marvel. Assays made of ore selected by Dr. [G. W.] Chase, an old prospector and experienced mineralogist, are almost incredible. I will give the figures of a few assays made by him, and although I am aware that big assays do not take well, being generally considered by the incredulous public as "a puff," yet I will venture to give these, willing to wait until time, investigation, or some of your San Francisco assayers shall prove the harshness of their decision and the correctness of these figures: Upas, $315; Silver Shower, $531 80; Hancock, $2,290. These calculations are based on all being silver, and as there is a little gold in all of them, it would make the figures yet larger to give the gold its value. The Neptune is the only lode yet found in this District where the gold predominates.[24] Specimens from this exhibit free gold in considerable quantity. It is evidently very rich, but I have not the figures of an assay from it. Dr. Chase has visited every District on the river, and he give it as his opinion that the Sacramento is the richest silver district of all. He informs me, too, that the lodes are remarkably well defined, from three to thirty feet wide, and that the geological formation and general appearance of the country resembles Reese River. This District has then advantage over most Districts on the river in two great indispensables, viz: wood and water. Of the former, I am informed, there is an abundance close at hand; of the latter, numerous springs bubble out of ravines and mountain-sides, but not in sufficient quantities for a mill in but two or three places, yet there is little doubt but that tunnels will—as they

24. The glowing reports of the mysterious "Dr. Chase" notwithstanding, the Upas, Silver Shower, and Hancock lodes never amounted to much. The Neptune showed signs of promise, with a vein of gold and silver seven feet wide in walls of slate and granite. Browne, *Mineral Resources*, 460. In 1864 G. W. Chase filed mining claims in the San Francisco Mining District in Mohave County. Record of Mining Claims and Deeds, Mohave County, 1864; Roman Malach, Mohave County historian, personal communication with author, Oct. 5, 1983.

have done in Washoe—produce plenty of it. There is also an abundance of "gramma" or "Galleta," grass. From the [. . .]

SAN FRANCISCO DISTRICT

Also comes awakening reports of amazing rich discoveries. Heretofore, the noted Moss has stood among the rich lodes discovered on the Colorado unrivaled by any, but now it is given in that there are two at least equally as good. The Leland was located last Summer by Captain [Converse W. C.] Rowell. Nothing was known of it other than it was a fine large ledge of spar and quartz, until about a month ago. It is being situated in the extreme southern part of the district, where but little prospecting has been done, treasure seekers confining their searches to the vicinity of the Moss lode, but upon examining the Leland, it was found to be very rich in gold, glittering gold; the rock is thoroughly impregnated with it, not in coarse pieces, but as fine as fine powder; the rock also contains silver, or the gold is what is termed by some "silver gold." The Mitchell, a lode from four to eight feet wide, and located close to the Leland, is quite as rich, and the same kind of a lode. Upon examination, many other ledges in the vicinity of these have been found to contain gold. The Rough and Ready is another lode that is at present attracting a good deal of attention;[25] some of the rock, to use a rather inelegant phrase, is literally "lousy with gold." But there is no use to particularize. I might mention several other lodes that are full of bright promise to their owners when the day of mills dawns on the Colorado. That is what we want— mills, mills. Capital, come hither, the grandest field yield yet unimproved now lay open here on the Colorado. Cast but a few handfuls of yellow seed into the furrow of enterprise, and a golden harvest, abundant and sure, will reward you.

Of course, these mines like others situated far in the frontier where speedy and cheap communication with our great emporium is not enjoyed, will have to bide their time, and wait until by their intrinsic merit they have dispelled the fears of those that have been bit by "wild cat"—until proof a hundred times confirmed, has established the fact that the Colorado country is no humbug, but does really possess extensive mines of at least three valuable metals, viz: copper, silver and gold—then will capital build mills for us, and then will the world know that this desert country possesses

25. The Leland, Mitchell, and Rough and Ready lodes were located in the San Francisco District. Miners described them as rich in fine gold with some silver in bluish quartz. Alonzo E. Davis told journalist J. Ross Browne that, using a hand mortar, he personally had pulverized ten pounds of quartz from the Mitchell Lode and panned out gold equal to $150 per ton. Davis lamented that want of capital for proper mining and milling equipment and the danger of Indian attack were the only things that retarded the development of these mines. Browne, *Mineral Resources,* 460.

mines second to none in richness and extent. I cannot think it extravagant from present developments and evidence continually accruing to anticipate at an early day, after the ball shall have once been put in motion, a country outstriping the most flourishing, not excepting Washoe, in business and thrift. Indeed, why should I, if the mines are half as rich as every one that examines them pronounce them? How can it be otherwise, situated as they are, on a river navigable the year round for boats of light draught, at least, by which the country can be well supplied at low figures with everything needful? But pardon me if am indulging too much in speculation.

MATTERS IN GENERAL

Messrs. Butterfield and Perry [Ferry],[26] from La Paz,[27] passed by here a few days ago, on their way up the river, on an exploring tour. They are making their way in a small boat, propelled by paddles and a favorable breeze when they are so lucky as to catch one. It is their intention, if the Indians give them no trouble, to go up about two hundred and fifty or three hundred miles. Their main objects are timber and placer mines. Mr. Perry has been up on the Virgin river, and says he knows of rich placers there. He speaks the Pi Ute language, and thinks they will have no trouble with them. The will also look for coal. From the fact that coal is found on the sand-bars along the river it is certain that there is coal somewhere above.

In common with every one who is anxious to see this rebellion speedily crushed, we rejoiced to hear that General Grant was placed at the head of our armies. No change since I have been a soldier has seemed to give so much gratification—and I may say, joy to my comrades, as has this. Gladness was plainly written on every countenance as though the great battles he is preparing to fight, and perhaps while I write in fighting, had been won.

26. This may be the same Perry who, with his partner Woodworth, built a small boat to be used for prospecting at the upper crossing of the Colorado in 1862. In 1867 the people of Hardyville were all talking about a miner who survived a perilous raft journey down the Colorado—only to be rescued by "Mr. Ferry," a resident of Callville, near the mouth of the Virgin River. Beyond these reports, little evidence can be found of Mr. Perry/Ferry's existence. *Los Angeles Weekly Star*, May 31, 1862; *Los Angeles News*, Sept. 20, 1867. See also note 50: W. K. Ferris.

27. Pauline (or Powell or Paulino) Weaver, mountain man, prospector, and army scout, named the Colorado River town of Laguna de la Paz in 1862. In January of that year he discovered placer gold east of the river about 130 miles above Fort Yuma, and within a year five thousand men were working the rich deposits. In 1863 La Paz was the largest city in the newly created Arizona Territory and was named the Yuma County seat. By 1864 the gold had played out, and the fickle Colorado had changed its course, leaving La Paz high and dry. The city slowly withered as rival towns flourished on the riverbanks and near newly discovered mines. Hinton, *Handbook to Arizona*, 156; Lingenfelter, *Steamboats on the Colorado*, 33, 37, 40–41.

And pleased, too, were we beyond measure to learn that the Legislature has again pronounced that we shall retain the right of suffrage—I hope, this time, in language that the magnanimous, hair-splitting Supreme Court cannot nullify. Magnanimity to our enemies is a virtue, but not when it is treason to ourselves.

The Paymaster is expected here soon, when we will receive six months' pay, in greenbacks, that, at sixty cents on the dollar, will amount to $7.80 per month, rather small pin-money in a country like this. Perhaps it was wise in the Secretary to refuse to discriminate between the hard currency Pacific and the paper currency Atlantic; but it is rather hard on the California volunteers, and it always seemed to us rather unfair policy; but if it is wise, and the exigency of the country demands it, far be it from us to complain. The whole of our thirteen dollars per month would be the smallest sacrifice we have yet made. If a draft is made in California it will not hurt our feelings to see those at home who are groaning about high priced cotton and heavy taxes, serve their country for thirteen dollars (in greenbacks) per month to exchange home luxuries for the soldier's plain rations, perfect personal freedom for military discipline. All this could be viewed with the utmost complacency by the

CAL. VOLUNTEER

ALTA, June 26, 1864

Some Account of the Fifth Regiment Infantry, California Volunteers, in Arizona—Desperate Encounter with the Apaches

(The following is an extract of a letter received by a gentleman in this city, and kindly placed at our disposal—EDITORS ALTA)

TUCSON, A.T., JUNE 3D, 1864

* * * Your kind letter was received by me yesterday, and I hasten to return you many thanks for your kindness in sending me so much good news from the seat of war. It was the best treat that I received from any friend since I came into the army. Would to God that I could send you as good, and as late news by the mail that leaves here on the 15th inst.; but what news I could send you from the East would necessarily be stale before reaching you; consequently, I shall have to prospect the dull and monotonous town of Tucson for such local news as may call your attention for a few moments from the busy scenes of city life, and cause you to take a retrospective view of your days of soldiering, when compared with the easy and delightful days of your citizenship, which, I hope, circumstances may permit you to protract and enjoy with a good relish; and I think you can appreciate them better when you are reminded of the long cold

nights at Camps Union, Drum, Yuma, Tuttle, and Tucson:—yes, and last, but not the least of all, Camp Latham[28] and the one opposite to the creek; to say nothing about reveille, sick call, breakfast call, drill call, and divers other calls[29]—commencing roll call with a little string of thirteen non-commissioned and three commissioned officers, without including the field and staff; and all kind of detachments, and police, and guard.

BATTLE WITH THE APACHES

Our old company, J [I],[30] has achieved some great military honors since you left Tucson. On the morning of the 5th of May last, while *en route* from Fort Cummings to Apache Pass, at a place twenty-five miles beyond the latter, called Steins' Peak, just as they were entering Doubtful Cañon, they were attacked by about 200 Apache Indians, who lay concealed in the bushes and rocks until the advance guard was within fifteen feet of them, when they poured a volley of arrows and bullets into the boys, at the same time making a rush for the mules and wagons, when the fight became one of extreme interest, and the most desperate and sanguinary ever witnessed in the Territory, but terminating in a complete victory for the brave boys of Company J. The casualties sum up as follows: Indians killed, 50 (found dead) and the general supposition is that as many more were badly wounded. Company J lost two killed—private Webb, who died seven or eight days afterwards from a wound received in the action, and private Docher [Dosher]. Wounded [Private] Abbott, shot clean through the body, supposed to have been mortal, but at last accounts from Fort Bowie he was doing tolerably well. [Private] Charles Nelson, wounded with a bullet, passing through the arm at the elbow and shattering the bone; amputation was considered inevitable.

28. Capt. Joseph Tuttle organized and mustered Company I, Fifth California Infantry at Camp Union in Sacramento, California, in November 1861. The men moved on to Drum Barracks in southern California, then on to Camp Kellogg and Camp Wright en route to Fort Yuma on the Colorado River. Camp Latham was located at Ciénega, halfway between Los Angeles and Santa Monica. No record of Camp Tuttle exists—perhaps it was either a temporary camping place or an attempt to flatter Captain Tuttle, the writer's former company commander and possibly the original recipient of the letter. Orton, *California Men*, 675, 885–87.

29. The routine of military life was punctuated with many calls, sounded by bugle or drum, throughout the day: reveille (sunrise), stable call (for cavalry), breakfast call, sick call, fatigue call, drill call, guard mount, water call (cavalry), dinner call (midday), fatigue call, drill call, stable call (cavalry), supper call, retreat (sunset), tattoo, and taps (lights out).

30. Company letter "J" does not exist in any regiment in the U.S. Army. It is not known why this letter was omitted from those ten or twelve chosen to represent the companies of infantry or cavalry regiments. Some students of American military history speculate that "J" was not used in order to avoid confusion with the letter "I" in reports and other official documents. The author of this article, William B. Holmes, enlisted as a private in Company I, Fifth California Infantry. Orton, *California Men*, 714.

Sergeant C. Tobias, arrow ledged in the collar bone; not serious. [Private] P. D. Stone,[31] bullet shot in wrist; flesh wound.

ANOTHER ENGAGEMENT

But this fight was only a beginning. On the tenth day of the same month, a command of one hundred and forty-seven men strong, consisting of companies J and K, Fifth Infantry, C.V., and a detachment of cavalry, left Fort Bowie under the command of Inspector General Davis,[32] to fight Indians, and proceded to Gila River, in a northeasterly direction from this post, where they came across two or three [Apache] rancherias never seen by white man before, killing about one hundred Indians and taking sixteen squaws and children prisoners, and destroying all their crops of wheat and other property, amounting to several thousand dollars. They also captured $640 in twenty dollar pieces. The command arrived at Tucson to-day, and the town was wild with excitement, all trying to get a sight at the wornout soldiers and "captives." The boys look hard. Quarter rations, they tell me, is all they have had for ten days, and no change of clothes for twenty-five days. A great many of them were almost entirely

31. Capt. Richard H. Orton summarized the May 1864 returns for Company I, Fifth California Infantry: "On the thirtieth of April, 1864, the company left Fort Cummings, N.M., en route for Fort Bowie, A.T. On the fourth of May, when entering Doubtful Cañon, near Steins Peak, N.M., were attacked by one hundred Apache Indians. The company routed them, killing ten, and passed through the canyon. Found on calling the roll, that Pvt. Henry Dosher was missing, and that Sgt. Charles E. Tobias and Pvts. Chandler C. Abbott, Nelson, Stone, and James R. Webb were wounded. Arrived at Fort Bowie, A.T. on May fifth." It was later determined that Private Dosher had been killed in action at Doubtful Cañon, and Pvt. James R. Webb died of his wounds at Fort Bowie on May 13, 1864. The other wounded men were returned to duty and mustered out with their company when their enlistments expired on November 30, 1864. Orton, *California Men,* 671, 712–16.

32. Maj. Nelson H. Davis, General Carleton's assistant inspector general, was not a typical staff officer—inspecting posts and writing efficiency reports. A West Pointer, Davis served with distinction during the Mexican War and had seen enough combat during the Civil War to have won a brevet for gallantry at Gettysburg. When Captain Burkett's shot-up Company I, Fifth California Infantry staggered into Fort Bowie on May 5, 1864, Davis sprang into action. He organized Company I and Captain Tidball's Company K into a mobile strike force and took the war to the Apaches. Moving northwest, the command made no fires and traveled fast. In the canyon country above the confluence of the Gila and San Carlos rivers, Davis divided his command and attacked several large Apache villages, killing nine warriors and wounding many more while capturing sixteen women and children. He reported destroying fields of corn and wheat as well as vast quantities of mescal and personal property. Besides the $660 ($20 was evidently lost en route to Tucson) in $20 gold coins, Davis's command recovered horses, firearms, and a diary identified as the property of two parties of mining entrepreneurs (including John B. Mills and E. G. Stevens) that had been attacked earlier in the year in the Santa Cruz Valley south of Tucson. Davis commended the men and made special mention of Captain Tidball, Captain Burkett, and Lt. Henry Stevens for their conduct. Orton, *California Men,* 671; Browne, *Adventures,* 195–202, 212–24; Nelson H. Davis to Capt. Ben C. Cutler, June 5, 1864, Tucson, Ariz. Terr., *OR,* 50(2):869–72, 58(1):902–3.

barefooted when they came back in town to-day. There is a General Order issued by Carleton for 500 soldiers to be sent against the Apaches this summer, and the troops are now in the field, and the war will be vigorously carried on till the Apaches see the folly of longer holding out against such a formidable force. My opinion is that the days of these murderous brutes are numbered in this Territory. So mote it be.

LOCAL MATTERS

Law and order is all the rage in Tucson. Judge Howell[33] convened his (the First Judicial District) Court in the town of Tucson on the first ult. A Grand Jury of the Union-loving men in this town was empannelled, and several bills of indictment found for various crimes; so you can see that the law-loving and law-abiding citizens of this town in future can enjoy the blessing of civil liberty that they have prated so much about, and wished for so long.

The mail arrived here from the East on the 9th, just nothing later than we received from California from the East.

Company J leaves this post to-morrow for Fort Cummings.

W.B.H.[34]

33. Judge William T. Howell came to Tucson in May 1864 along with the new Arizona territorial governor, John N. Goodwin. Although Tucson was undoubtedly the most important city in the territory, General Carleton advised against making it the capital. He believed it a lawless place with too many Southern sympathizers and preferred giving the gold fields of central Arizona a boost by siting the capital at Prescott. Howell set out to clean up the territory. Working with Coles Bashford, president of the Territorial Council, he cobbled together a four-hundred-page legal code, cutting and pasting from the best ideas the other states and territories had to offer. Howell had a court system up and running by the end of May, but he did not stay long in Arizona. He reportedly told the governor that he would not "act as a judge in a district where two out of three people were barefooted, where a court was held in an adobe shack with an earthen floor, and a dry goods box was used as a rostrum." Sonnichsen, Tucson, 69–71.

34. William B. Holmes enrolled as a private in Company I, Fifth California Infantry at Sacramento, California, on December 7, 1861. Born in New York in 1833, his prewar occupation as "clerk" qualified him for the job and extra pay of an assistant clerk for the Commissary Department when his company reached Tucson in April 1863. The second lieutenant of Company I, Henry H. Stevens, was also an Alta correspondent, and the men may have worked closely together. Holmes stayed on in Tucson when his company departed for New Mexico. On February 12, 1864, he was discharged for disability in Tucson. Senate, Federal Census—Territory of New Mexico and Territory of Arizona, 69 (Tucson, 1864); Orton, California Men, 714; SO 73, Apr. 22, 1863, Tucson, Commands of J. R. West, RG 393.

ALTA, July 4, 1864

Letter from the Californian Volunteers on Duty in Arizona
(From the Resident Correspondent of the ALTA CALIFORNIA)
Fort Mojave, A.T., June 12th, 1864

EDITORS ALTA: In my last communication, I predicted an early rise of the river, as a consequence of the warm weather we were experiencing. The prophecy has been verified. The river commenced to rise about the fifth of May, and has since continued slowly to come up, until it is now a few inches higher than any time last season, and still it continues to rise an inch every day, and it would not be surprising to see the Bottoms inundated yet, as it has but three feet to go.

THE ARRIVAL OF THE STEAMER

An event long and anxiously looked for by bachelor and housekeeper, as the inaugural of a new era in domestic finance, has finally transpired. On the 20th of May, the *Cocopah* arrived, bringing a few tons of freight for Government, twenty-five tons for Mr. Hardy, and a small freight for the sutler. And now the order of things is reversed. Instead of a hungry crowd of would-be customers, wistfully gazing at empty shelves, merchants are seen standing in the doors of their well filled stores, as wistfully looking for some one to give them a call. This state of things is to be attributed to the two weeks of warm weather we had in April, and the several weeks of empty larders here. I presume that either of these plagues could have been borne singly, but, in conjunction, they were too much for men who count their thousand by tens (in fact, you understand,) and they have left the Desert country, many of them, I presume, for the shady side of Montgomery street. About the time when the pressure was the heaviest, Mr. Dukes, with commendable enterprise, started for La Paz, by trail, loaded a burro train with substantials for the starving country; and had the packers chosen to emulate Mr. Dukes' zeal, fasting would not have become so popular a custom.

For some reason, of which I am not advised, they were nearly a month on the road, and consequently, did not arrive much in advance of the steamer; and I fear our worthy merchant will have to pay for his enterprise—for steamboats can under-freight pack trains. The *Cocopah* was to have been back here several days ago, but she has not made her appearance as yet, and I doubt her being able to stem the current. I am informed by a passenger on her last trip, that she had hard work to make the "riffle" through the Cañon, and the water is four feet higher now than then. Her old triple-patched boilers can't stand the pressure of a sufficient head of steam to driver her through, I fear. The *Esmeralda*[35] would have no trouble in making regular trips, and she can bring double the amount of freight the *Cocopah* can. But the old line have the Government freight secured, as also Hardy's; and it is doubtful if they would allow their rival any of it, even if it took them another season of high water to deliver it. Government will supply the troops at Salt Lake by this river in future, and if Brigham and his people patronize the same avenue, steamboating will be lively. A Government train is expected here soon for supplies for the Salt Lake troops. Prices here now are at living rates, though of course, much higher than they will be when there is a good trade and a lively competition for it. Flour is selling at 14 cents a pound, bacon at 34, sugar at 25, and other things in proportion.

EXPLORATION

In my last I made mention of a party having gone up the river on an exploring tour. They went up some 250 miles, when they lost nearly all their provisions by capsizing of their boat, and, of course, were obliged to return. They report having found good timber of cedar and pine. They also found a very extensive mine of salt, and that of the first quality. They brought some down with them which I should pronounce a superior article. They also found a great deal of float-coal, which became more plenty as they advanced. They think they were not far from a good bed of it. Samples that they brought back look well, burn well, and are pronounced by connoisseurs excellent croppings of coal. It would be hard to estimate the value of a good coal mine to its discoverers, or the country, anywhere within striking distance. Mr. Ferry is fully persuaded that he has a good thing, and parties here at the Fort are of the same opinion, and have aided him in fitting out a small pack-train, and he and his party have started out again on rather surer footing, intending to prosecute their explorations some distance further. Mr. Ferry says the river is easily navigable, at least in high water, to Black Cañon, about 180 miles above here. As falls there forbid further advance, that will, of course, be the head of navigation. The party intend to locate there with a view that they will be the first settlers upon a site where in future a proud city will stand. If the Colorado is to be an avenue for the Salt Lake trade, there is some ground for their great expectation, to say nothing about the powerful auxiliary the mines will afford.

---

35. Sergeant Davis may have been correct in his assessment of the steamboats on the Colorado River. The *Esmeralda*, captained by Thomas E. Trueworthy, arrived on the Colorado in March 1864. Although significantly smaller than George Johnson's old *Cocopah*, *Esmeralda*'s newer engine and shallower draft may have given it an advantage on the muddy and unpredictable river. Lingenfelter, *Steamboats on the Colorado*, 161–62.

PROSPECTING

Is not being very vigorously prosecuted now, which is to be attributed mainly to the—until recently—lack of supplies. The Philadelphia [Silver and Copper Mining] Company are at work on two ledges in the San Francisco District. They are drifting for the ledge from their shaft on the Skinner. They have drifted eighteen feet and have not yet found their ledge. According to the pitch on the surface they should have struck the ledge long ago. It must, a few feet from the surface, run straight down. They have considerable water to contend with, which occasions slow progress.

In the Moss, they have struck some good silver rock, which is encouraging to those who have no faith in the permanence of gold lodes. It is not probably much will be done in this district until next fall, when there is sure to be an active campaign, for feet owners are sure they have good grounds to go on.

SACRAMENTO DISTRICT

Is the best section, for in addition to good ledges, it is blessed with a beautiful climate. It hardly seems possible that at so short a distance there can be so great a difference in the atmosphere. Yet it is a truth continually confirmed by parties returning from thence, that while here at the Fort we are sweating and fretting, with the mercury at 100ℱt, the lizards and coyotes are taking it quite cool in the dripping ravines and cool shades of the deep groves of the Sacramento District. A party from there, last night, say they were troubled to keep warm at night under two blankets, and that they days were delightfully pleasant; showers there are quite frequent. The country is verdant with vegetation, and the condition of the mountain sheep and antelope, with which the country is well stocked, is proof of the nutritious qualities of the rank "galetta" grass. I hear of parties who intend repairing there for the climate's sake, to spend the hot months. Notwithstanding its seclusion, contracts have been let upon three different lodes, with Mr. Hardy. He is to prospect them to the depth of fifty feet or more. Other parties are also making preparations to go to work there. It is reported that the Philadelphia Company will commence work there soon. I hope soon to be able to inform you how Sacramento District bears inspection underground.

FORT MOJAVE

If Fort Mojave is not the pleasantest place in the world, I do believe it is one of the healthiest, barring the fevers, which it cannot be denied are fearfully prevalent here. Had it not been for the few violent deaths that have occurred here since the country was visited by white men, I do not know how the sexton would have got a starter. But about these fevers; they may be categorically classed thus: gold fever, silver fever, copper fever, feet fever, and lately a new type called adobe fever, which is just now raging furiously. None of these maladies have as yet proved fatal, and it is said that they do so only when the victim gets one of the "ides" on the brain. Either oxyde, bromide, green-ide or red-ide is to be guarded against with vigilant care. The occasion of the adobe fever is the laying out of another new town, half a mile above the fort. Until recently, the Government reserve has covered the universally acknowledged most eligible site for a town, it being situated at a point where the river makes a curve around a high gravelly bluff, with a deep, unchanging channel. It is also closer to the fort, which will ever be the initial point of this section of the Colorado, the old Beal route crossing here, as it does.[36] It is the most central point from the San Francisco District, and a place at which it is probable the principal mills will be built. Hardy's landing is closer to the Moss lode by perhaps two miles. But the advantage of the solid road down this hard mass to the fort, over that which goes to Hardy's through a loose gravel wash, will more than offset the difference in distance. A new survey of the Government Reserve has been made, and this point, useless to the Government, but invaluable to the public, has been left out, Government taking 3,000 acres, mostly bottom lands, below, and a portion of it across the river from the fort. The founders of the town of Mojave, Messrs. Fagen and Todd,[37] have already built a new and large ferry-boat. They are now building an adobe building. The new town already boasts three stores and a saloon, that are stocked in a manner that would do credit to a place of higher pretensions. Some half-dozen adobe buildings have been commenced, and the new-born bids fair to grow and wax strong.

THE ARRIVAL OF IRATABA[38]

The ex-lion of New York and San Francisco, here last Thursday, was the crowning event of the season. Whether it is genuine Indian dignity, or whether he has learned it

36. In 1857–58 Lt. Edward Fitzgerald Beale pioneered a wagon road along the thirty-fifth parallel from Fort Tejon, California, across Arizona and into New Mexico. Fort Mojave was established in 1859 at the point the Beale road crossed the Colorado River, about three hundred miles north of Fort Yuma. Ibid., 23–24, 169.

37. P. B. Fagan and Samuel Todd were enterprising men. They mined, freighted, operated ferries, built towns, and established businesses of all kinds. Shortly after the Civil War, Todd secured the sutler contract at Fort Mojave, and Alonzo E. Davis became his business partner. Davis owed Todd a debt of gratitude: when Ira Woodworth, an angry *Alta* reader, took exception to Davis's ideas on Indian policy and went after him with a brace of loaded revolvers, Todd calmed Woodworth and likely saved Davis's life. Davis, "Pioneer Days in Arizona," Arizona Historical Society, 65, 110; Senate, *Federal Census—Territory of New Mexico and Territory of Arizona*, 92, 104 (San Francisco District, 1864); *Tucson Weekly Citizen*, Mar. 15, 1873.

38. Iretaba, chief of the Mojaves, was one of the most influential Indian leaders in the Colorado River country. He guided early U.S. military parties, including those of Sitgreaves and Whipple, and may have played a role in purchasing the captive Oatman sisters from the

while among the "hiyee" Mericano shoulder straps, I know not, but the old hero, as the boat touched the bank—the observed of all observers—stepped dignifiedly from the boat, passed through the huge assemblage of his people that had gathered to greet him, casting eye neither right or left, but steady to the front, took a bee-line for head-quarters. Arriving there, he became quite talkative. His greatest hobby seems to be the cars, which he calls bigwagons; tells his people they don't know anything; that the "Mericanos savve munchy." But he strongly objects to the ladies' costume; thinks they take up too much room. He says—"meet um Mericanno squaw; all same four soldiers." He seems to hold a high opinion of the President; says—"Abee Lincoln very good man; savve munchy; got um munchy feet; all same Irataba." I doubt if he is ever contented again with his home among the cactus and mesquit; he says he is going back to New York in one year. He sticks to his military rig heroically, but it was so warm yesterday that he had to take off his big coat and sword, and substituted his cocked hat with mud. It is a custom they have of doing their hair up in mud occasionally. They fix it up something like a Turkish turban, which makes them look quite fierce. He had his orderly at his heels, bearing his coat and sword. I think *Harpers'* would bid high for a picture of him and his suite, as thus upon from his old stamping ground.

ITEMS

I may here mention that the weather, at date of my last communication, was decidedly warm; for about two weeks the mercury ranged from ninety to one hundred and four degrees, and we thought that before the season had advanced thus far, we should have been pretty well *seasoned*. But the climate changed for the better, and we have had a month of very agreeable weather. And now, again, it is getting hot; day before yesterday the thermometer showed 108 degrees in the shade.

Talk about the veterans of the Potomac—brave though they have proved themselves many times, under fire—I doubt their meeting one of the hot breezes in the Colorado Desert, so unflinching as can the Salamanders of Company I.

Yavapais and Olive Oatman's eventual return to authorities at Fort Yuma. Generally friendly toward whites, Iretaba worked to restore peace after the Mojave uprising of 1858–59. Mining entrepreneur John Moss escorted the chief on a tour of the East that included a visit to Washington, D.C., and a meeting with Abraham Lincoln in 1863. In February 1864 the chief met and reminisced with Olive Oatman, who had become the subject of a best-selling book and a national celebrity, in New York City. Iretaba returned to Fort Mojave in the uniform of a U.S. Army general and with new respect for the power of the whites who now occupied his country. In 1865 the Colorado River Reservation became one of Arizona's first Indian reservations and is still home to the Mojave people. Thrapp, *Encyclopedia of Frontier Biography*, 704–5; Tuttle, "River Colorado," 60–61; McGinty, *Oatman Massacre*, 176–77.

The Express has been changed from semi-monthly to tri-monthly; a matter of congratulations to us, for now, while the exiting struggle between Grant and Lee is pending, express day—always anxiously looked for—is most impatiently awaited by those denizens of the desert who believe in loyalty. The only satisfaction the rebs here are able to obtain from the late despatches is, as they say, that as the Confederate lines are becoming more compressed, they will be able to oppose the advance of the Union armies with more concentration; about the same consolation the old woman derived in her sigh, "blessed be nothing."

Oh! Dixie, we see your last gutter, even now, crawling with the vermin of treason, the chivalry of a conceit-bloated Aristocracy. The type of your chivalry has printed a record of barbarity, cold-blooded malignity, in the blood of every battlefield you have not been chased from, from bloody Manassas to Fort Pillow—a record that India Sepoys would blush to own.[39]

CAL. VOLUNTEER

ALTA, August 6, 1864

Our Letter from Arizona
(From the Resident Correspondent of the ALTA CALIFORNIA)
Fort Mojave, July 19th, 1864

THE POLITICAL CAULDRON

EDS. ALTA:—Do the good folks inside ever remember that there is an outside world? I can't see why it is, but it is as natural, seemingly, as breathing, for Arizonians to speak of Los Angeles and beyond as the "inside," giving common assent that we are on the "outside" of the world. I know not why it is, I say, unless politics and politicians have been foreigners to the land of cactus and lizards. But if that is it, then open, ye doors! and admit ye Arizona Salamanders to the inside ring, for lo the Goths are among us! Yes, good people of the inside, yes. While I sat the other evening ruminating upon the chances and prospects of this portion of Paradise how long it would be until we should read in the ALTA about "silver bars" and "bullion" received from Mojave—until lightning [telegraph] connected us with the "inside world," and

39. Union and Confederate armies fought two battles at Manassas (Bull Run), Virginia, in 1861 and 1862—both Southern victories. Confederate general Nathan Bedford Forrest's attack on Fort Pillow, Tennessee, in April 1864 resulted in the massacre of the black soldiers who constituted half of the fort's garrison, prompting public outrage and a congressional investigation in the North. By the time of the Civil War, the Indian Sepoy Mutiny of 1857 was synonymous with disloyalty in the English-speaking world. Boatner, *Civil War Dictionary*, 295–96.

steamboats were as common as sunrise—and how long until the blessing of Politics should light upon us, when three scores of would-be patriotic *hombres,* anxious to serve their country in Arizona in almost any capacity—so the pay is good—would come out of their way, fawningly smile upon you, and extend their honest palm for a soul-greeting squeeze, and then so gently induce you to wend your way to some shady grotto to take a smile—(Ah! though, how long until such blessings flow)—when I was disturbed from my meditations by the announcement that a convention was to be held that very night at Mojave, for the purpose of nominating two Representatives to the Territorial Legislature. Rather short notice to serve upon a community that had hardly dreamed, as yet, a political dream. But in a country unblessed by telegraph or postal facilities, things become commonplace, that in more favored lands would seem extraordinary.

The steamer brought a communication addressed by the Union Committee at La Paz to the citizens of Fort Mojave and El Dorado Cañon, urging upon them the importance of taking immediate steps to nominate to Representatives and send by return boat the names of the candidates, so that they could place them upon their ticket. They had already nominated the two Councilmen and three of the Representatives the District was entitled to, and as the election was almost at hand it was given that Mojave and El Dorado Cañon would have to acquiesce in the arrangement and take just such a share of the loaf as their neighbors saw fit to mete out to them. As it was impossible to send to El Dorado Cañon and get their nomination in time, it was determined to make both nominations here. Accordingly, Wm. Watters [Watter][40] and E. D. Tuttle[41] were declared the unanimous choice of the people of Mojave and vicinity to represent them in the first Territorial Legislature. Both of the nominees were staunch Union men. But a few days had elapsed after the nominations had been

40. William Walter was a twenty-nine-year-old miner from Pennsylvania. He had labored in the San Francisco District above Fort Mojave for nearly a year, making him one of the old hands in the region. Senate, *Federal Census—Territory of New Mexico and Territory of Arizona,* 104 (San Francisco District, 1864).

41. Edward Deen Tuttle lived in upstate New York until the gold rush drew him west in 1852. He joined the Fourth California Infantry as second lieutenant of Company A at Placerville, California, in September 1861. Promoted to first lieutenant of Company H, he won the praise of superiors while stationed at Fort Yuma and in service along the Colorado River. After resigning his commission Tuttle turned to mining and farming near Mohave City, and in 1864 he was elected to Arizona's first territorial legislature. He served only one term before returning to military service as first lieutenant of Company F, Fourth California Infantry in June 1865. After the war he worked for the Quartermaster Department at the Yuma depot and then as agent for the Colorado Steam Navigation Company. Tall and handsome, Tuttle was well liked wherever he lived and worked. When he died at the age of ninety-four, Tuttle was assisting the Arizona state historian with writing a history of the territory. Tuttle, "River Colorado," 50; Orton, *California Men,* 601, 637, 651; Morrow, *Mohave County Lawmakers,* 1.

sent down to La Paz, when one evening we were again startled by a call for another Convention. A political courier, regardless of the price of mule meat, had hastened through from La Paz with the information that one of their nominees for Councilman had shown signs of being shaky on the "goose;" that he was in the keeping of secesh trainers, and his backers were afraid to risk him, and had therefore concluded to drop him, and start another candidate. But this time less haste was made, and instead of engine on water, it was "Injun" on land that was depended upon for the express. Notice was given to the whole country around, and the Convention was well attended. A set of Union resolutions were adopted that were the very essence of loyalty stewed down to a pill, which, though sweet to most of the Convention, were wormwood and gall to some. Mr. Bourke, of Red Dog, Cal., and Mr. G. Noble, present foreman of the Philadelphia Company, were placed in nomination.

The Convention called for an endorsement of the resolutions by the candidates. Mr. Noble was absent at El Dorado Cañon, but friends came forward and vouched for his loyalty and his endorsement of the resolutions. Mr. Bourke was called for, but he was not "thar," though he had been but a few hours before. He had got wind of the resolutions that would be offered, and it was not taken as a very appropriate way of dodging them by making himself scarce. The friends who offered his name were called for, but they would not answer for Mr. B., and of course that let him out. Mr. Noble was then unanimously elected Union candidate for Councilman. Upon his return, however, he publicly declined the honor of being the candidate, as private business made it impossible for him to serve.

At the earnest solicitation of the Union men here, Colonel Allen announced himself as the independent candidate for the office;[42] of his loyalty the Colonel has given proof on battle fields in rebeldom, and bears scars as medals for his services. But Secession was astir, too, at La Paz. A sweet batch of traitors were nominated, composed of Mexicans and mongrel Americans. "Captain John Moss" announced himself a candidate, and ran here on the Copperhead ticket.[43] Yesterday the polls were

42. John P. Bourke, an Irish miner working in the San Francisco District, missed out on his chance for elected office. George Noble, a thirty-two-year-old Pennsylvanian, arrived in the San Francisco District five months before the election. He declined the honor of serving the territory because of his responsibilities as foreman of the Philadelphia Silver and Copper Mining Company. A miner named H. T. Allen, thirty-eight years old and from Mississippi, was listed in the 1864 special census for Arizona. Little is known of him other than the fact that he was the wealthiest man in the San Francisco District. Senate, *Federal Census—Territory of New Mexico and Territory of Arizona*, 103–4 (San Francisco District, 1864).

43. Frontiersman John Thomas Moss made a name for himself in 1861 by recording the first gold strike in El Dorado Canyon, some sixty miles above Fort Mojave, and opening the San Francisco Mining District. He dressed in fringed buckskin like a trapper and was known as the "mining Kit Carson." He enjoyed being the center of attention but never stayed long in one place. Moss had lived with Paiutes, Hopis, Yavapais, Pimas, and Mojaves. Hoping to win the

opened at Lindsay's Ranch, thirty-eight good Union votes were polled and thirty-two Secesh. We are hopeful, but it will be some time before we shall know whether Copperheads or Union men have the majority. Dr. Leibe [Leib],[44] for Delegate to Congress, ran on the Union ticket here. Colonel Poston,[45] also a Union candidate, came through from the capital a few days since, which he says has been moved from Goodwin City, fourteen miles southwest of Fort Whipple, to a place called Prescott,[46] which he describes as a most beautiful place, with deep shade trees and a stream of lovely water. The Colonel came through alone. He and Irataba and staff left for La Paz, per canoe, the day following his arrival here.

THE GLORIOUS "FOURTH," OF 1864

Among the things that were, it yet seems to me that its memory deserves a passing notice. It was announced here by the thundering anvil at early dawn.[47] The slumbering garrison rolled out rubbing their eyes, but instead of the growl and the scowl with which the hour later reveille is usually received, it was greeted with smiling countenances and a

---

appointment as Indian agent for the Colorado River tribes, he toured San Francisco and Washington, D.C., with Mojave chief Iretaba and Antonio Azul of the Pimas. Moss continued prospecting in Arizona, California, and Colorado and even dabbled in California politics. He died of a gunshot wound in 1880. Thrapp, *Encyclopedia of Frontier Biography*, 1026; Lingenfelter, *Steamboats on the Colorado*, 32–33, 37–39.

44. Dr. Charles Leib's bid for Arizona delegate to Congress was unsuccessful. A physician from Pennsylvania, Leib came to Prescott with the original Fort Whipple founding party in December 1863. He and his wife, Mary, lived in Yavapai County and provided valuable medical service in Arizona Territory. Senate, *Federal Census—Territory of New Mexico and Territory of Arizona*, 111 (Yavapai County, 1864).

45. Charles Debrille Poston was a flamboyant character associated with Arizona since the 1850s. In 1854 he partnered with Maj. Samuel Heintzelman to develop the Cerro Colorado Mine near Tubac. A tireless booster, Poston was elected Arizona's first delegate to Congress in July 1864, and President Lincoln appointed him Arizona's superintendent of Indian affairs. Poston established the Colorado River Indian Reservation and has been called the "Father of Arizona" for his role in influencing key congressional leaders to pass the bill creating the territory in 1863. Browne, *Adventures*, 235–54; Sonnichsen, *Tucson*, 51, 66–71.

46. The miners at Granite Creek in Yavapai County named their little camp Goodwin City in hopes of it becoming the territorial capital. With the help of California officers, the governor located a more favorable site eighteen miles southwest of Fort Whipple along Granite Creek in the heart of the Walker District, first discovered by the ubiquitous Pauline Weaver. The capital city was named for historian William Hickling Prescott, who had popularized interest in the Southwest with his *Conquest of Mexico* and other writings. Will C. Barnes, *Arizona Place Names*, rev. and ed. Byrd H. Granger (Tucson: University of Arizona Press, 1985), 354–55.

47. By the time of the Civil War, the Fourth of July was often rung in with an "anvil chorus." This practice involved placing one anvil on top of another with a charge of gunpowder in between. When ignited, at great risk to the igniter, the thunderous blast lifted the top anvil sufficiently for it to clang down on the bottom anvil. Arthur Woodward, personal communication with author, Mar. 1, 1982, Sonoita, Ariz. Woodward interviewed old-time blacksmiths and even experimented with anvil firing.

good-natured word of jest about their noisy disturber. There are but few citizens left here now, and some of them can find no glory in the birthday of freedom. But a few, full of patriotic zeal, joined in with a will with the soldiers to pay tribute of respect to the day. Mr. Dukes [Fort Mojave sutler], especially, took active part, and contributed largely in personal service and "store-fixings," to the little manifestation at Fort Mojave. And the soldier, too, gave proof, that despite very poor commissary supplies, and greenbacks at fifty cents, he still retains his share of that patriotism which first sent him to the ranks.

At 4 P. M. citizens, soldiers and aborigines all assembled under an awning at the Fort, where they listened to the reading of the Declaration of Independence, followed by a very elegant and impressive address from Captain Price.[48] Corporal Davis[49] being persistently called for, responded in a half-hour's patriotic talk. While cheers were going up for the "old flag," the Union, etc., the noisy anvil joined the chorus, and with its smoke the patriotic crowd dispersed. The day passed off very pleasantly, and the total absence of black eyes and skinned noses next morning was good proof of the pacific qualities of the last importation of grog by the Mojave storekeepers.

RIVER MATTERS—EXPLORATIONS

In my last communication I made a statement relative to the river, which I now hasten to correct. It was, that the head of navigation must necessarily be at Black Cañon, as the falls there prevent a further advance. At the time I wrote, my information respecting the country and river beyond El Dorado Cañon, was imperfect. I also made

---

48. New York–born George F. Price became captain of Company M, Second California Cavalry on November 4, 1861, and served in Nevada and Utah until the summer of 1864, when he led a detachment that surveyed a wagon road from Fort Mojave to Salt Lake City. Captain Price's 114-day expedition covered more than thirteen hundred miles. Orton, *California Men,* 175–76, 181–84.

49. The Fort Mojave section of the 1864 Special Arizona Census, completed early in the year, still listed Alonzo E. Davis as a corporal in Company I, Fourth California Infantry, but on November 1, 1864, Captain Atchisson promoted him sergeant. Davis took soldiering seriously and made a good impression on the officers. "I will now describe," he wrote after the war, "the soldier's make up for guard duty. He must be clean from cap to shoes; the cap, with its shining patent leather visor, blue cloth and small brass buttons at each temple; the blouse, with its rows of brass buttons, must also be clean and buttons polished; the belt, with its heavy brass buckle, the cartridge box that the belt held, the haversack and canteen, the musket and bayonet—all had to be faultlessly clean and bright. The soldier's clothes had to fit—and there is a soldier ready for guard duty!" Davis, "Pioneer Days in Arizona," Arizona Historical Society, 41, 53; Senate, *Federal Census—Territory of New Mexico and Territory of Arizona,* 92 (Fort Mohave, 1864); Orton, *California Men,* 657. See also "Alonzo E. Davis," Hayden Arizona Pioneer Biography Files.

mention of Mr. Ferry[50] having gone out on a second exploring trip up the river. The party have since returned, and, as I believe it would be interesting to many of your readers, I give Mr. Ferry's account of the exploration:

Leaving El Dorado, you next come to Black Cañon, which is fifteen miles in length, and the channel through it is as good and easy to navigate as any part of the river, though on either side precipitous walls of rock loom up all along, sometimes almost overhanging the river, as if threatening to drop off and dam the stream. After running along the channel fifteen miles further you come to Veagus Wash, the point to which Lieut. Ives explored,[51] and which he declared the head of navigation. An island here divides the channel, and as the water in the lesser one tastes brackish, in consequence of seeping through the sand, Lieut. Ives supposed it to be the Virgin river; but the Virgin comes in at thirty miles above this point. At a point about twelve miles above the Veagus Wash, called Circle Valley, Mr. Ferry thinks the Salt Lake trade will land, as following the river up takes you farther from Salt Lake, for the river bears away to the east, while Salt Lake is north of this point. From here it is fifty miles to the old Spanish trail—the old Salt Lake and Los Angeles which it avoids, as it also does the terrible deserts that have to be encountered in getting to Los Angeles. This Circle Valley is the head of navigation for the Salt Lake trade, from which there is a land carriage of 420 miles, with a road supplied with good fuel and water. There can be but little doubt that all or nearly all the Salt Lake importations will soon go over this route.

TIMBER, COAL, AND SALT

Green River and the Little Colorado form a junction about 140 miles above here. As you proceed, the country loses its desert appearance, and at the junction, timber begins to show, and up Green River, say at a distance of 20 miles, you come into a well timbered country, resembling the forest of the Sierra Nevada. The Indians told Mr. Ferry that it was two sleeps from one end of the timber to the other, by which he infers it is about 80 miles in length; but how far it was back from the river he did not learn. He went 15 miles back, and at that distance the timber became of larger growth; sugar

50. Mr. Ferry may have been Washington Knapp Ferris, who came to Arizona prospecting for gold in 1864. His search for the precious metal took him all the way to New Zealand, but he finally settled in Arizona's Bradshaw Mountains south of Prescott. *Prescott Arizona Miner,* June 11, 1870; *Prescott Courier,* June 22, 1886.

51. Lt. Joseph Christmas Ives served under Capt. Amiel W. Whipple on the 1853–54 railroad survey of the thirty-fifth parallel. In 1857 he traveled up the Colorado River on the U.S. Army steamer *Explorer.* His surveys and writings are among the earliest and most accurate of the lower Colorado region, though he did confuse the Las Vegas Wash (also known as Veagus Wash) for the Virgin River, located some forty miles farther up the Colorado. Lingenfelter, *Steamboats on the Colorado,* 10, 21, 169; Thrapp, *Encyclopedia of Frontier Biography,* 710–11.

pines, four to five feet through, were common. So the question of timber for the Colorado is settled, and Arizonians are happy. Furthermore, a vein of No. 1 coal, two feet in thickness, crosses the river in this timber country. It comes out at the eastern end of a long mountain, at the other extremity of which . . . [illegible] make use of. There is a small town located here, called "Toco," or Black Town. About twenty miles from the Colorado, and on the Virgin River, they found three mountains of the very best salt. Mr. Ferry brought back huge chunks as specimens, some of which you should have in your cabinet, as they look like blocks of the purest ice.

CEVINCE INDIANS[52]

There is a tribe of renegade Indians inhabiting this country, called the Cevince Indians, from whom the timber mountains take their name. They number about two hundred and fifty warriors and receive their civilized visitors very coolly. Fortunately, Mr. Ferry could converse with them in the Piute tongue, and probably thereby avoided trouble, as they at first forbade him making any farther advance into their country; but they could not afford, after coming so far, to turn back without half a sight, and by presents of what food, tobacco, and blankets they could spare, the explorists prevailed upon the chief to accompany them two days. The redskins dogged their steps, and the Chief said his people were greatly displeased with him and he dare not stay with them longer; so he urged them to turn back, which, as their party consisted of but four, they deemed prudent to do.

LOCAL MATTERS

Captain Price, of Company M, Second Cavalry, C.V., arrived here three weeks ago, from Salt Lake, he came through for the purpose of surveying a road for transportation. He reports favorably of the route. They started back to-day, and a hard trip some of the boys will find it, as they lost some of their horses coming through, and will have to take it "Dough-Boy" style back again.[53]

---

52. Although there is no record of a Cevince tribe, the Shivwits Paiutes and Chemehuevis spoke a Uto-Aztecan/Paiute language. The Hualapais living along the Colorado River may also have been able to converse in Paiute, even though their language is of Hokam/Yuman origin. Both the Hualapai and Chemehuevi mountains border the Colorado and are visible from Fort Mojave. The Hualapai Mountains, to the north, would have been the best source of timber in late 1864. Swanton, *Indian Tribes*, 482–83. See also Holt, *Beneath the Red Cliff.*

53. Although the word "doughboy" today is commonly used to denote a World War I American soldier, here "'Dough-Boy' style" refers to walking or traveling on foot. The origin of this term is not certain, but during the Mexican War "doughboy" referred to an infantryman or foot soldier, presumably because the dust-covered men looked like bakers' doughboys. The term was still in common use during the Civil War. Dickson, *War Slang*, 54–56.

The new town of Mojave is flourishing, in anticipation of a heavy emigration here next fall. Several adobe buildings are going up, which, when completed, will add greatly to its appearance.

A company has commenced work on the Alacran Lode, Sacramento District, and at last accounts they were down fifty feet; at that depth they have met prospects even more flattering than their sanguine hopes anticipated, as the vein widens and increases in richness. It is cheering to hear so favorably from the first lode opened, and that, too, from one classed, at best, second rate.

Hanne [W. P. Hanna] & Co will break ground on the Neptune in a few days. They have brought with them a complete stock of tools and ammunition for a six months' campaign, which if vigorously prosecuted is expected to reveal a rich deposit. I can tell your folks we have rich ore here, and we can prove it, which we intend to do.

Work is still going on in the San Francisco District. A shaft is going down on the Mojave—a portion of the Moss lode. Work has been suspended on the Sparkamali, in consequence of the difficulty of procuring workmen. Every one seems to be holding off for fall. The steamer *Copala* [*Cocopah*] has made two trips here in the past month. She is expected here again soon. Mr. Hardy is receiving a lot of goods of every description by her. Word came in from Walker's the other day that a pack train would be doing well there now. Beyond doubt the country possesses rich quartz mines. Mr. Dukes has started a semi-monthly express between this place and the capital.

The river came near overflowing the bottoms, but the past two weeks it has been rapidly falling and is now at a nice stage for navigation. The mesquit season is at hand and the Mojaves are getting fat; their corn and pumpkins are also fit for use.

Irataba has gradually got skinned down to a very dirty shirt, and ditto unmentionables, though on extra occasions he appears in glittering uniform, cocked hat and all. Though he depends but little on meskeet beans himself, he has his squaws gathering them largely for winter use.

THE SOLDIERS AND THE MINES

The term of enlistment of the members of Company I, expires in about three months. Nearly all hope to be discharged here, as it will save them a tedious trip, and most all intend to stick to the country, for they feel confident they have got their "golden-egged goose" cooped, sure. There has been considerable grumbling here and elsewhere, even in the ears of military chiefs at "Frisco," I understand, because the soldiers have availed themselves of the opportunities offered for taking up "feet." They complain that the "soldier" has taken up all the good claims and will not or cannot work them, and will not let others work them; thus keeping back the country. Now this is no new song; it is one that, here on the Colorado, has been piped since the first three months of our stay, and is nearly worn threadbare. When the copper mines were first discovered in the Irataba district, a score of lazy louts were loitering in the shades of the cottonwoods with the natives, and after the first week of their discovery, when every day lodes were being located, the drones commenced the growl about the enterprise of the soldier; that he had got all the best claims, and it was no use to prospect now; yet months later, and even recently, lodes have been found that outward appearances rank with the best. In the Sacramento District the soldiers went out in an unexplored country, took the chance of being scalped by the Walapies, or perishing with thirst, and found probably one of the best mineral districts on the river. Them came in and publicly announced their discovery—told its locality—publicly called a meeting, cordially inviting citizens to assist in organizing the district. The laws governing the district were drafted by a soldier, and contained a provision that a soldier could not hold but three claims, but those should not be subject to re-location until ninety days after the expiration of his term of enlistment. The citizen was unlimited, but was required to work on his claims after the 1st of January, 1865. And as many of the soldiers' time expired in October and September, it will be seen that we yielded to the citizen an advantage, because we wished to refute the cry of "soldier monopoly." But some of the citizens, as if cut to shame by it, called for the striking out of the limitation clause, and the soldiers were granted the rights of men, though they have given themselves to their country for a time. Now, who has done the most to develop the country—these grumblers or the soldiers? We worked last winter all it was possible for us to do; invested our greenbacks, at a disheartening discount, to the last dollar; sunk shafts 45, 27, 20, 15 and 14 feet deep. Now, we have, besides, attended to our duty as soldiers; have given protection to the "grumbler," without which his life or property would not be worth a day's purchase. Yet the ingrates growl. No doubt it would rejoice them exceedingly to see the record of our claims torn up, and we cooped up in garrison, denied the right to claim anything outside of our rations and a chance of dividing them with them.

We never have interfered with the citizen; there never has been a time when he could not have a better chance by far than us for prospecting, for he is his own master. But he never has improved it, and thus it is he grumbles. I do not mean to speak of citizens at large, or the mass of them, but of that minority who claim that soldiers have no rights outside of army regulations, the jealousy, coppery, indolent set that nothing but fear of a draft into the army—or some other place—could ever have inspired with energy enough to emigrate to Arizona.

The heat during the past month has not increased, and has lately slightly abated; the worst is thought to be over, and the maximum heat attained is 110°.

CAL. VOLUNTEER

ALTA, October 3, 1864

Our Letter from the California Volunteers at Fort Mojave
(From the Resident Correspondent of the ALTA CALIFORNIA)
Fort Mojave, A.T., Sept. 10, 1864

COOLER WEATHER

EDS. ALTA:—With the return of fall we have a most agreeable change of weather; the nights have become cool; the sun pours not its rays upon us with such burning fierceness; no longer are we trembling lest the next breeze that sweeps from the south may be a blast from a little hotter portion of that hot place, supposed to be Jeff. D.'s last ditch, and commonly known as purgatory. No, the weather has become quite endurable—in fact, pleasant.

The change has quite a visible effect upon the Arizonians; the shades are deserted; every one seems to have something to do; pack animals are seen striking towards the mountains with heavy loads; prospectors are seen climbing over the rugged mountains, and the mountain sheep bound over the craggy step, chased by the echo of the miners' artillery.

All is life and animation. Thus opens the business season on the Colorado. It will be curious if the seeming energy with which the ball opens has not the effect of developing some of the numerous gold, silver, or copper lodes of the different districts.

SACRAMENTO DISTRICT

Dr. Jones has just come in from the Sacramento District.[54] He has been doing work on his ledges sufficient to hold them for a season. He stuck the "Alacran" at the depth of 51 feet, found a vein of good looking ore four feet in thickness, cased in talcose late, with every evidence of a permanent mine. The doctor is well satisfied with his prospects, but business calling him into Colorado, compels him to suspend operations for the present.

He lately found a large, well defined lode of gold-bearing quartz, in the district; the rock is of a red, rusty color, and though showing no gold in the rock, it is surprisingly rich.

---

54. In April 1864 the territorial census taker at Fort Mojave recorded that Dr. Wilson W. Jones was a thirty-eight-year-old Virginian who had come to Arizona in 1863. His occupation was listed as "Minerologist" and his property valued at $200. Six years later Jones owned a freighting business in Prescott worth $11,000. Senate, *Federal Census—Territory of New Mexico and Territory of Arizona*, 91 (Fort Mohave, 1864), 212 (Prescott, Ariz. Terr., 1870).

I saw two ounces pulverized in a mortar, and washed out, and a finer prospect is seldom obtained. The black sand, or sediment, after washing, was perfectly gilded with gold, as fine as flour. Messrs. Hanna & Co. are obtaining good ore from their prospecting shaft on the "Neptune." Mr. Hardy has just commenced work on two different lodes and other parties are preparing to go to work.

SAN FRANCISCO DISTRICT

It seems certain parties are particularly interested in running down the San Francisco District. They very likely have an object in view. I notice in the [San Francisco] *Bulletin* of August 27th, an article taken from the San Jose *Mercury,* that is certainly one of the most glaring libels I remember ever seeing in print. The whole statement is so wholly devoid of truth that surely the author can have but little regard for his reputation; and probably if the public knew him—whether they know anything about the "Moss" or not—there would be little need of going to the trouble of correcting his misstatements. But presuming he is not so far-famed as "Jim Beckwith,"[55] I propose, with your permission, to give a denial to his misstatements, which every truthful man that ever visited the "Moss" lode will bear me witness, are wholly untrue. Under the heading, "Is the Wonderful 'Moss' lode a Humbug, after all?" the *Mercury* says: "An intelligent and disinterested gentleman of this city has recently returned from a prospecting tour in that region, and informs us that he visited the 'Moss,' and is satisfied that the whole concern is not worth three cents an acre. The Philadelphia Company has stopped work, and the whole lode turns out to be nothing but granite. He worked diligently for two hours, with proper tools and implements, on various parts of the lode, and could not even find 'the color.' The rich specimens brought from the mine, he says, were found in a small pocket in the outer casing of the granite—no more such pockets can be found; and in fact there is no quartz ledge there."

To the first proposition of "Intelligent and disinterested Gentlemen" I have nothing to say, as it is quite immaterial whether he values the concern at three cents or three millions an acre. But next he says that the Philadelphia Company have stopped work, and that the whole lode turns out to be nothing but granite. The Philadelphia Company ran a tunnel in one of the extensions of the Moss, that struck the lode at about 40 feet below the surface of its croppings. They found the lode to be very much broken up, and the quartz greatly decomposed. Now, does any one believe that the ample piercing of the lode in one place, where at the surface it was badly shattered and bro-

55. Jim Beckwourth, a mountain man of great ability, told tall tales and was known by some to be a "gaudy liar." His autobiography, *The Life and Adventures of James P. Beckwourth,* first published in 1856, was still popular reading in the 1860s. Thrapp, *Encyclopedia of Frontier Biography,* 86–87.

ken up, proves, because it had not at the depth of 40 feet become solidified, that the whole lode is worthless and nothing but granite. I have been told by parties who have been at the tunnel, that a more unfavorable place for prospecting the lode could not have been selected.

Again, says the "disinterested gentleman," "the rich specimens came from a small pocket in the outer casing of the granite," etc. Now, there is not a particle of truth in this part of his statement. The ton of rich rock shipped to San Francisco for working, was blown from the side of the ledge where it rises up like a wall to a height of 15 or 20 feet, from a surface of perhaps eight feet square—merely a chip from the lode. I have examined the place from which it was taken, and know that gold is visible all over the surface of this fracture. Nor is this the only place where gold is found. I know, myself, of three places where rich rock can be found; and nearly every company located on the lode—about a dozen in all—claim to have found rich rock in their claims.

Finally, the "disinterested gentleman" winds up by declaring that there is, in fact, no quartz there. How palpably false! The truth is, the ledge is traceable at least two and a half miles by its immense croppings of the best looking quartz, 3 to 10 feet thick, walling up in places from 20 to 40 feet. The ledge can be seen for a distance of from three to five miles. In fact, it forms one of the prominent landmarks of the country. So much for the "disinterested gentleman's" story.

NEW POCKET FOUND

If I had not already occupied too much space with this subject of the Moss lode, I would remark that no doubt greatly exaggerated reports have been published concerning the Moss. Very rich specimens have been exhibited as samples of a huge ledge twenty feet thick, many miles in length, etc. Of course this is all gas. Gold, though found in many different parts of the ledge, does not abound in the whole lode. Very recently another "pocket" has been found that for richness surpasses all others. The gold lies in leaf in fine seams of the quartz, twice the thickness of gold foil. I was shown some of this character the other day, an inch long and half an inch wide. Under the superintendence of Mr. France[56] a shaft is being sunk on the lode that will strike it at a depth of one hundred feet. The work is being pushed forward night and day, and I hope soon to be able to tell you something relative to its appearance at that depth. Very rich silver rock is said to have been found on the Dayton lode [near the Moss lode]; a few feet below the surface it is in the form of bromides.

56. The Special Arizona Census for 1864 lists William France as a thirty-two-year-old Welsh teamster living in the San Francisco District. France had lived in the area for three years— longer than any other resident recorded in the census. Senate, *Federal Census—Territory of New Mexico and Territory of Arizona*, 104 (San Francisco District, 1864).

MORE PLACERS IN ARIZONA

Considerable excitement has been occasioned here by a report brought through by some men from Prescott, that very rich gold placers had lately been found by "King Woolsey"[57] and his party, away out in the Apache country, southeast of Prescott. They say that he sent in dust to corroborate the report. Rumor tells of Indians in that country who shoot gold bullets; the credulous think Woolsey has found the place where they grow. The reports may be true, but people will do well to keep cool and wait until they are well confirmed. We shall soon know all about it.

Dukes & Co. have established a semi-monthly express from here to Prescott, by which we get regularly the *Arizona Miner,* a real live little journal, that keeps us well posted regarding the news from that quarter.

They experience great trouble by the hostility of the Indians. Men dare not venture out except in sufficient force to take care of themselves. A gang of about twenty attacked W. Bottsford [Botsford], express carrier for Dukes & Co., a few [12] miles this side of Prescott. Thanks to a good mule, he was able to make his way back to Prescott, but not with out getting an arrow stuck in his back, which, however, fortunately had no serious result. The express now goes with an escort.[58]

THE FORT MOJAVE ROAD

As the travel to and from California and the capital of Arizona—now considerable—must necessarily go increasing, it is of the first consequence to the public

57. King S. Woolsey, an Alabama-born frontiersman and prospector, accompanied Albert Sidney Johnston's band of secessionists from California eastward in 1861. Woolsey found enough fighting in Arizona, however, and left the party near Maricopa Wells. He devoted a good deal of time to hunting and killing Apaches, whom he hated with a passion, and reportedly explained his Indian policy to Carleton thus: "I fight on the broad platform of extermination." Woolsey preferred to live, prospect, ranch, and farm on the fringe of white settlements and always ready to do battle with Apaches—killing adult males by ambush, poison, or hand-to-hand fights. He accompanied Walker's gold seekers in 1863 and established a ranch along the Agua Fria River, becoming one of Arizona Territory's best-known and wealthiest citizens. As late as October 1864, California officers and agents were suspicious of Woolsey's Southern sympathies, fearful that his band of Indian fighters were really Rebels. Nicholson, *Joseph Pratt Allyn,* 76; Gustav Brown, government detective, to Capt. A. Jones Jackson, provost marshal, Southern Dist. of Calif., Oct. 16, 1864, *OR,,* 50(2):1018–19.

58. Captain Atchisson reported that William M. Botsford's arrow wound was in the shoulder. The thirty-two-year-old Virginian survived his ordeal, and Atchisson requested permission to allow California soldiers to escort Dukes Express between Fort Mojave and Prescott—a four-day, 155-mile ride. Small detachments of four to five men were authorized, and the mail went through. Charles Atchisson to O. H. Lee, acting AAG, Drum Barracks, Aug. 25, 1864, in Brennan, *Fort Mojave,* 28; Senate, *Federal Census—Territory of New Mexico and Territory of Arizona,* 91 (Fort Mojave, 1864).

which route is the best: especially as the best must ever be hard, passing as it does through two hundred miles of desert country. It is a fact universally conceded by all, I believe, who have passed over the two roads, that the one from Los Angeles to Fort Mojave is better supplied with water and grass, and has less sand than the road from the former place to La Paz. In reference to the road from Prescott here, the Arizona *Miner*, of August 10th, has the following:

"The arrival of Messrs. Bowers,[59] sutlers at Fort Whipple, with their train, the return of Mr. Keunk, one of our trusty citizens, and his report, and the establishment of an express by Dukes & Co., have awakened a lively interest in the Walker and Weaver mines regarding the Mojave road. As these columns have heretofore shown, we have accounted it one of the best, if not the very best, route from California to Central and Northern Arizona.

"A very little work would remove every serious obstacle, while of water and grass there is an abundance at all seasons."

The report of Captain [Herbert M.] Enos, who came through last winter, surveying the route, gives the distance from Fort Whipple to Fort Mojave, 156 miles, which he says can be shortened fifteen miles.

These are items for consideration by those contemplating visiting the Walker and Weaver country.

Dr. Willing,[60] the explorist and discoverer of the continuation of the Comstock lode, two hundred miles southeast of Washoe, arrived here some days ago, and after a few days rest, took the trail for San Juan river, where he says gold can be had for the picking up. Notwithstanding his promise of vast riches, he was unable to get a recruit to his party.

---

59. The Bowers brothers, Herbert (forty-two), George (thirty-five), Nathan (thirty-four), and Edward (twenty-six), came to central Arizona to prospect and mine. Herbert and Nathan found their fortunes at Fort Whipple, where they became post sutlers doing business as "Messrs. Bowers" and later "Bowers Bros." The entrepreneurial brothers engaged in a wide range of businesses in Yavapai County. *Prescott Arizona Miner*, Oct. 26, 1864, Sept. 20, 1867, July 24, 1869.

60. Dr. George M. Willing came to Arizona in 1864 in search of gold. Superintendent of the Pennsylvania-based Willing Mining and Exploring Company, Willing had a proven record of mineral discoveries in California and Nevada. Later that year he finally assembled an exploring team to investigate the Colorado River mines and central Arizona. An Arizona newspaper reported shortly before his death that "Dr. Willing is known to many of our residents as the same gentleman who was exploring Arizona in 1865, but had narrowly escaped death at the hands of the Apaches. In his wanderings during the time he was dodging Mr. Lo [Lo, the poor Indian], the Doctor made some of his most valuable discoveries. He is grateful for having escaped on that occasion and thanks the late Gen. Carleton for his rescue." *Prescott Arizona Miner*, Mar. 20, 1874; *Tucson Citizen*, Jan. 10, 1874.

Professor Silliman[61] made a geological examination of the various districts here a short time ago. It is thought his report will not agree with some of the wiseacres that have honored us with a visit.

THE ELECTION IN ARIZONA

The election here resulted in the election of W. Walters [William Walter] and E. D. Tuttle, Union candidates, for Representatives; though, unfortunately, Colonel Aiken, for Council, was beaten by a few votes. The Union vote was badly divided, the field being full to repletion of candidates. Colonel Poston's majority is 400. The total vote of the Territory was 1,076—a very light vote, which may be attributed to the Indian war, and the fact that most of the Colorado people were inside, dodging the hot weather. Irataba, with some of his subordinates, has gone to Fort Yuma to have a "big talk" with the chief of the Maricopahs, with which tribe the Mojaves are not on good terms. Mojave hucksters are very numerous; melons, green corn, and pumpkins— luxuries in the absence of fruit—are plentiful and cheap.

We have had to patrol the road to Rock Springs twice a month with twenty men lately, but it is discounted now. No trouble need be apprehended from the Indians between here and Los Angeles.

It is but a few days since that Company "I" was called to mourn the loss of Mrs. Pierson [Pearson], wife of Corporal Pierson, of our company.[62] By her good qualities of heart, Mrs. Pierson has endeared her memory to all with whom for the past three years she has been in the constant society. Not one of the whole company that followed her to the grave, but was a deep and sincere mourner. This is the first death

---

61. Prof. Benjamin Silliman Jr. taught chemistry at Yale and by 1864 had become the leading expert on petroleum. He was also respected as a mining consultant. Johnson and Malone, *Dictionary of American Biography*, 17:163–64.

62. Cpl. Winfield S. Pearson originally enlisted as a private in Company F, Third California Infantry but transferred to Company I, Fourth California Infantry when Col. P. E. Connor's Third Infantry marched for Utah in 1862. Pearson's wife, Elizabeth, may have been the company laundress. She died at age thirty-one, leaving behind four children, Nancy Jane (ten), Charles A. (six), George H. (two), and baby William W., who was born in California just two months before the regiment arrived at Fort Mojave. Pearson's company commander, Captain Atchisson, believed him to be "of good morals, fair intelligence and a reliable man." The captain pleaded the corporal's case to headquarters, explaining that "this family of children cannot be properly cared for here." Atchisson respectfully requested that Pearson be honorably discharged or given a leave of absence until his term of service expired on February 24, 1865, so that he might take the children to relatives in Sacramento. Headquarters, in its wisdom, chose to send Pearson to Fort Vancouver, Washington Territory, where he was mustered out. Orton, *California Men*, 574, 657; Senate, *Federal Census—Territory of New Mexico and Territory of Arizona*, 91–93 (Fort Mohave, 1864); Capt. Charles Atchisson to Lt. Col. R. G. Drum, AAG, San Francisco, Sept. 7, 1864, in Brennan, *Fort Mojave*, 29.

that has occurred in our garrison since we have been here—some sixteen months; it speaks well for the health of the country.

CALIFORNIA VOLUNTEER

ALTA, OCTOBER 17, 1864

A Soldier's Letter from Arizona Territory
(From an Occasional Correspondent of the ALTA CALIFORNIA)
Fort Goodwin,[63] *Arizona, Aug. 29, 1864*

EDITORS ALTA: In the belief that anything which concerns the welfare of the California Volunteers must be of interest to the readers of your valuable paper, I have sent this note to you for publication.

MILITARY MATTERS

It is now a fixed fact that the troops on active service in Arizona and New Mexico, viz., the First Cavalry and the First and Fifth Regiments of Infantry, are to be discharged in these Territories after completing their full terms of enlistment—most of them, in fact, some weeks after their full terms of enlistment shall have expired. Although indications of such an event has been foreshadowed from time to time, yet it is only recently that the full conviction of the consummation of this great outrage upon the rights of the soldier has been forced upon us. We placed implicit confidence in the good faith of the Government, which, by act of Congress, promised to return us to the place of enrollment at the expiration of our term of service; we had confided in the Governor of our State and her Representatives in Congress to see that no injustice was done to her Volunteers. Keenly alive to the sinking condition of our ship, we scanned the northern and eastern horizon long and anxiously for the help which we had a right to expect; but it came not, and our worst fears are realized. We are well aware that the leading officers in this Department are responsible for this outrage. If any blame can be attached to the authorities of our State, or to our Representatives in Congress, it is for a faith too implicit in the representation of Carleton & Co., who have strained every nerve and scrupled at no means, however base, to accomplish their end. Taking advantage of the well known fact of the existence of mineral wealth in

63. Col. Edwin A. Rigg established Fort Goodwin in May 1864 with companies of the First California Cavalry and the First and Fifth California Infantry. The post was intended to be a jumping-off and resupply base for operations against Apache bands in the upper Gila River valley 120 miles northeast of Tucson and 50 miles from the New Mexico border. As volunteer enlistments began to expire late in 1864, offensive operations ceased. New Mexico Volunteers and then regulars eventually relieved the Californians. Altshuler, *Starting with Defiance*, 27–28.

these Territories, they have represented to the country that the Volunteers wished to be discharged here in order to secure rich claims in the mines, most of them being practical miners.

This statement, although glaringly false, has appeared so plausible to the outside world that it has been taken for granted, and we are not surprised that the delusion should extend even to California, where a better knowledge of these mines is supposed to exist than among the people of the Atlantic States.

THE MINES, ETC.

It is hardly necessary to inform your readers that the famous mines of this country are a humbug, so far as supporting a large mining population is concerned. Companies of men with large capital and extensive machinery may be able to secure a good dividend, in localities where water can be obtained, but a poor man cannot do worse than come to Arizona for the purpose of mining. These facts are as patent to Carleton & Co. as they are to us, but they have "an axe to grind," and their "grindstone" is located right upon these deserts; anxious to brighten a dark record at the War Department, they would not only enlist more veteran troops, but even secure those whom they have illegally enlisted. Well they know that our discharge in California, in accordance with law and justice, would defeat these ends.

THE SOLDIERS' TROUBLES

Two thousand men, suddenly thrown upon their own resources, in the midst of a desert country, infested with hostile savages, and unsafe to traverse, except in large and well armed bands, fifteen hundred or two thousand miles from their homes, with the necessaries of life at starvation prices, and allowed only the pitiful sum of eighty dollars for rations and transportation back to the place of their enlistment; unable to purchase provisions from Quartermasters, on account of their refusal to sell to citizens; delayed in their transportation from post to post, or denied it altogether; surrounded by coils of "red tape"[64] at every step of their progress; bullied and insulted by men "clothed in a little brief authority;" can it be a matter of surprise if many should succumb to the adverse circumstances surrounding them, and again resume the musket as the least of two evils? more especially such as are addicted to habits dissipation or prodigality? We could not justly complain of our discharge in this country at the expi-

64. Clearly the writer is frustrated with military bureaucracy and authority. Twill cotton tape, dyed red, was commonly used to tie bundles of government documents in the days before staples and paper clips. During the Civil War this "red tape" became symbolic of the bureaucracy that stood in the way of common-sense decision making. To speed up the process of untying the bundles of paper, one would "cut through the red tape."

ration of our term of enlistment, provided we had the same facilities of transportation which troops in the Atlantic states enjoy. There, a few days by railroad or steamboat takes them to their homes, without fatigue, and with comparatively little expense; but here the case is far different; our homes are reached only by long and fatiguing marches on foot, accompanied with great expense and loss of time. Unjustly as we have been treated at the close of our military career, it is but a capping stone to this monument of oppression, which, when the historian shall have done his perfect work, will be found to eclipse everything in the annals of American warfare, not even expecting the [1857–58] Mormon expedition of Mr. [President James] Buchanan. From the first inauguration of this expedition, the laws of justice and right have been steadily and persistently ignored. Under the leadership of such men as [General Joseph R.] West, no right has been respected which stood in the way of the accomplishment of ends however nefarious. The same men who pampered well known secessionists with fat contracts in Los Angeles county, swindled the Government by wholesale at Fort Yuma, and returned women to slavery in New Mexico, have consistently denied to us our rights. We are telling plain truths, for we are plain men, living in plain times, and unable to discover any line of demarkation between the welfare of the country and the welfare of its defenders.

VIDE[65]

65. *Vide* (Latin): see. The identity of Vide is a mystery. Considering the critical and controversial content of his letter, the writer probably hoped to maintain his anonymity. Regulations stipulated that "deliberations or discussions among any class of military men, having the object of conveying praise, or censure, or any mark of approbation toward their superiors or others in the military service; and all publications relative to transactions between officers of a private or personal nature, whether newspaper, pamphlet, or hand-bill, are strictly prohibited." It is probable that Vide was an enlisted man stationed at Fort Goodwin in either Company D, First California Infantry, or Company A, C, or E, Fifth California Infantry. A petition demanding additional compensation for soldiers discharged in the territories circulated among the disgruntled troops. The *Alta* printed one such petition that repeated the complaints made here by Vide. Among the soldier signatories were four men who belonged to the companies stationed at Fort Goodwin in August 1864: Sgt. W. W. Davis and Cpl. E. J. Morton, Company D, First California Infantry; and William Elliot and Joseph Thompson, Company E, Fifth California Infantry. Private Elliot was the only signer to have been discharged at Fort Whipple (on September 5, 1865). The morale of the men in Company D was especially low. Their captain, Francis S. Mitchell, was court-martialed and cashiered for desertion shortly before his hard-campaigning command reached Fort Goodwin. Orton, *California Men*, 324–51, 630–35; *Alta*, Dec. 21, 1865; *Revised U.S. Army Regulations of 1861*, 38.

ALTA, December 24, 1864

Interesting Letter from Arizona
(From the Resident Correspondent of the ALTA CALIFORNIA)
Fort Mojave, A.T., December 10, 1864

THE ELECTION

EDITORS ALTA:—Of course the great triumph of Loyalty over Modern Demo-cracy has ceased to occupy the public mind of those communities where the echo of the Nation's voice is borne to them by the electric wire [telegraph], and other events and other issues are exercising the huge brain and active tongue of your busy city. But you will remember that ours is not the privilege of reading from the ALTA to-day what occurred on the Atlantic side yesterday; and though it is well nigh the eleventh hour, I hear our three times three for the Union and its great victory. Though of course the result was a foregone conclusion, yet when the express did arrive with the glad news, everybody—that is, everybody worth counting—joined in wild huzzas, much to the evident disgust of a few Copperheads I noticed in the back ground, whose counte-nances seemed at once to drop even lower than Confederate money. I remember, too, that the "coyotes," that usually "make night hideous" with their howling, were forced to howl that night, probably out of sympathy for their Copperhead allies. The polls were opened here election day, and Company "I" gave a unanimous vote for "Uncle Abe." One exception, (who recently got inside of "Uncle Sam's" warm clothes, and has become fat on his pork and beans,) refused to vote at all, not having the courage to brave the scorn and contempt of his comrades at the polls and vote for his kind. Another *fellow* scratched from the Union ticket Lincoln's name, and wrote on, [Gen-eral George B.] McClellan. Holding up the ballot, he said: "You sees I pose no plack Ablish," and then passed it in, voting Lincoln electors without a scratch—a fair sam-ple of the intelligence left in the once glorious Democratic party.

TERRITORIAL MATTERS

The first Territorial Legislature of Arizona has adjourned. That honorable body will pass in history as one remarkable for the amount of work done in a short time. It is claimed by the uncharitable that three dollars in greenbacks, per diem, had some-thing to do towards the despatch of business. A code of statute laws, (taken from those of New York and Michigan, principally,) which are said to be excellent, were adopted. Judge Howard [William T. Howell] has gone East to attend the printing of them. They also passed a code of mining laws, which are discussed a good deal, and criticised not a little. The law does not find favor among the people. The universal sentiment seems to be against a special Territorial mining code, and in favor of district laws being *the* law. The law requires the recording of all claims with the Probate Clerk, with good fat fees, and provides that all claims shall have a shaft or tunnel run in them thirty feet; a house built on the claim, occupied by the owner, within a year from the date of location, and a certificate of compliance from the Probate Judge gives the owner a title in fee. The operation of this portion of the law, it is after provided, is suspended for two years, in consequence of the hostility of the Indians.

Thus every district in the Territory is laid over for three years. In some districts the reasons given will hold good; but not in any of those along the Colorado. Many of these districts have already been laid over from year to year, and now comes the sweeping proclamation that locators have three years wherein to sink thirty feet. The Territory is divided into three counties, viz.: Yapapi [Yavapai], Yuma, and Mojave; the latter is to commence at Bill Williams' Fork and extend north to the northern boundary of the Territory, and east about eighty miles—county seat at Mojave. A charter has been granted to parties for building a toll-road from Prescott to Mojave, which we trust will result soon in our having a No. 1 wagon road to our capital. In this connection, I would make mention of a work that has lately been completed chiefly by the volunteers, that would reflect credit upon any community. A meeting was called, and 142 days work subscribed to for improving the road from here to Silver Creek, which has been well applied. Both the hills—as the travellers who have passed over the road will remember, were very steep—have been graded down so that a horse attached to a buggy can trot up them with ease. A better piece of road than from here to Silver Creek could not be asked, it being nearly all the way over a hard mesa.

THE MINES

We have been strong in the hope that cold weather would be the signal for active operations in the way of prospecting, but as yet very little has been done. Our hope has been that capital would seek investment, and that some of our claims in the different districts would be prospected; but we have come to learn not to put our faith in princes. Three years ago on the croppings we can exhibit we could have got a bushel of money, now we can elicit no notice. If our claims were in Washoe or Reese River [Nevada] it would not be hard to get help to prospect them. "Every dog has his day," is a true saying, and we still have confidence—not in capitalists; but in our ledges, and our own capital, in the form of muscle, to finally prospect them. Our little experience with capitalists has not really tended to give us any great desire to have them among us. About a year ago it was heralded here that an Eastern company with a capital of

$3,000,000 was going to invest in our mines, and we should soon have mills running, and lively times generally. Well, the company came, and the result is that to-day the reputation of the mines of the Colorado are most seriously injured, and not a ledge prospected, not a mill in sight. The company extended a good deal of time doing very little work on the Skinner and Moss ledges, and because they did not strike it rich at a depth of forty or fifty feet, reported to the many in California and elsewhere that were waiting the company's developments, that the San Francisco District was a humbug. With every respect for the gentlemanly members of that company, it seems to me that they would do better in the plough-fields or coal-beds of Pennsylvania, than hunting silver mines on top the ground. Time, we feel confident, will bring things all right, and it is again reported that we are soon to have a mill here for the San Francisco District; but there have been so many false alarms about mills that we are determined to keep cool until we see it.

They are now taking very rich gold rock from the shaft on the "Moss" at a depth of sixty feet. Mr. France, the Superintendent of the Moss, has a large quantity of rock at his cabin, which for richness eclipses anything I ever saw or heard of. Chunks weighing one to three pounds, one-third gold, I do not think would be an exaggeration. If a mill comes here the San Francisco District will tell its own story.

The Moss is not the only ledge that contains gold, as there are many others that will pay largely for working. A cut is being run on the Leland lode, and very rich rock is being taken out. The gold in this lode, unlike the Moss, is very fine, and it is said to be hard to find a piece that, upon crushing and washing, will not yield a fine prospect.

SACRAMENTO DISTRICT

I recently made a trip to the Sacramento District, and it is hard to believe that so fine a country can exist so close to the barren plains and mountains that lie along the Colorado. Crossing the first range of mountains twenty miles from the river, you come upon a broad plain covered with a rank growth of *galeta* and *gamma* grass, and although there is no surface water on these plains it is evident that plenty could be had at a depth of twenty to forty feet.

As we were riding leisurely along a herd of about fifty antelopes made their appearance a short distance ahead of us. These beautiful creatures would stop and look at us for a moment, and then toss their pretty heads most coquettishly over their shoulders and gallop off a few hundred yards and stop again, look a moment, then wheel and bound back again across our trail at not more than a quarter of a mile distant. This they continued to do until, at length, having evidently satisfied their curiosity, they took off to the north and were soon lost in the distance. My poetical friend, the "Doc.," said it was brutish in me, but I can't help it—I was in agony that I did not have a Springfield musket with me.[66]

The mountains of the Sacramento District are very lofty and rugged, but with deep ravines, furnishing excellent facilities for driving tunnels deep into the mountains. In many of the ravines small springs of good water bubble up. The north and east side of the mountains are covered with scrub cedar and pinion pine; they will be invaluable for the working of the mines. The principal formation is granite, lime, pophyry, and what I believe is termed serpentine rock. The ledges have a uniform course of southeast and northwest, with a gentle dip to the east; some of them cross very boldly and can be traced with the eye for a long distance. The ledges might be divided into three different classes. First—A fine looking quartz, heavily stained with copper, both blue and green, giving it a beautiful appearance; free gold is occasionally met with, and, upon pulverizing and washing, a good prospect is invariably found; of this class the Neptune, Burnside, Peacock and Minnesota are No. 1. The second class are those that are heavily impregnated with iron, lead and antimony, with some copper stain. The Union, of this class, is from ten to fifteen feet wide; the quartz is full of iron pyrites. In the centre of the lode is a vein, two feet in thickness, of pure mineral, encased with a white and yellow ash. In this vein is found coarse galena that breaks in cubes and has a pigeon-blue color, then turning to a black-looking lead and antimony streak, with iron and copper sulphurets. There are small veins of a half to an inch in thickness, which appear on breaking like the finest steel. Assays of this are vouched for that group in the thousands. The third class are those that bear the quartz a hard black mineral that assays from $50 to $300 per ton. There is some galena and copper stain in these lodes. The No. 1 lodes of this class are the "Upas," "Mt. Buch," "Hancock," and "Alacran." The different classes of lodes are in separate sections of the District, the lodes in the same mountain generally having similar character. Yet another character might be added—first-class copper ore. In the Antietam, native copper is found—the only ledge known in the district in which it exists. These ledges are also quite rich in gold. The lodes of the district are, as far as I have seen, encased in a kind of mineral ask from six inches to two feet in thickness, and the mineral is in chimneys of from 20 to 400 feet in length on the lead. But little prospecting has as yet been done. Fifty-one and fifty-eight feet is the lowest depth yet reached. At this depth the lodes are encased well, and the mineral changes a little in appearance, and assays a little better than at the

66. The men of the Fourth California Infantry were issued the standard .58-caliber Model 1855, 1861, or 1863 Springfield rifle musket, so called because it was manufactured in large numbers at the U.S. Arsenal in Springfield, Massachusetts. Ordnance Returns, Fourth California Infantry, 1861–65, Office of the Chief of Ordnance, Returns, 1861–65, RG 156, NARA.

surface. It is not probably that they will change materially until water is reached. But more of the Sacramento District anon.

Of the thirty-six of Company I, that recently went to Camp Drum to be discharged, twenty-seven will return as soon as they get their "Eagle Bird."[67] This shows the confidence felt in our mines by those best qualified to judge. These men are nearly all practical miners, and will invest their greenbacks and labor in the development of their claims. Quite a number of Company B, who left this post, have recently returned here, and are commencing work upon their copper claims in the Irataba District.

THE COLORADO RIVER

The steamer *Esmeralda* has proven that the Colorado river is navigable at the low stage of water. Last season the people went hungry along this river for the want of the provisions that remained at the mouth of the river awaiting transportation, because, it was alleged, the river was too low to be navigated. But there was no *Esmeralda* on the river then. Since she came up, the *Co-co-pah* has made two trips with freight, going the last trip as far as El Dorado Cañon. The people of Central and Northern Arizona cannot appreciate too highly the important service rendered them by the constant navigation of the river.

INDIAN MATTERS

The measles have made sad havoc among the Indians along the Colorado river, this winter, and *Doctor* killing, as a consequence, is a very common affair. You will remember it is their rule to kill a doctor when he shall have lost ten patients. A great many will rejoice, while others will mourn, to learn that "Eagle Sky," a kind of renegade Pah-Ute (who made a trip to Los Angeles a year and a half ago), has fallen a victim to Indian superstition. He set himself up for a doctor, failed, and paid the penalty. They also killed three of his family with him, to make the sacrifice more complete— one a beautiful young squaw, said to be his daughter.

The Mojaves took warning by last winter's famine, and laid in a good supply of "mesquit" and pumpkins, and are wintering finely, or would be if it were not for the measles.

MAIL MATTERS

The reduction of our mail communication from tri-monthly to monthly, affords cause of serious complaint, especially to citizens who cannot get their mail regular

---

67. "Eagle Bird" was soldier slang for an honorable-discharge certificate, so called because the elaborate parchment bore the U.S. coat of arms, showing a large eagle with wings spread across the top of the document. *Revised U.S. Army Regulations of 1861*, 30–31.

even then. As it is sometimes large, it cannot be bought by the transportation furnished by Government. Mr. Dukes has applied for the contract of carrying it, and it is hoped we shall soon have at least a regular semi-monthly mail running clear through to Prescott.

COLD WEATHER

Log fires and great coats are becoming very popular, and the yellow crispen foliage tells that Jack Frost has been around; and if the above is not evidence enough of cold weather, an event transpired here a few days ago that makes the evident replete, to wit:

"By Alcalde [Samuel] Todd, Miss ——— Fears to Mr. Wm. Armstrong."[68]

Fearing that I have already intruded too far upon your precious columns, I will *halt.*

CALIFORNIA VOLUNTEER

68. On November 12, 1864, Judge (and ferryman) Samuel Todd performed the marriage ceremony for blacksmith William C. Armstrong and Mary Catherine Mounce. The fifty-year-old Armstrong endured more than the usual ribbing from his frontiersmen friends. A letter to the *Arizona Miner* reported that following the wedding in Hardyville, "The happy couple were spending the honeymoon under the umbrageous arms of a cottonwood, where the boys visited them for musical purposes, but 'Bill' came out like a man, and the band adjourned to the Saloon of Silverthorn & Mathews—for luck." Senate, *Federal Census—Territory of New Mexico and Territory of Arizona,* Mohave, 1864; *Prescott Arizona Miner,* Dec. 14, 1864.

Arizona Dispatches, 1865

ALTA, January 29, 1865

Interesting Letter from Arizona
(From the Resident Correspondent of the ALTA CALIFORNIA)
Fort Mojave, A.T., January 5, 1865

"EN AVANT" [FOREWORD]

EDITORS ALTA: The holidays are past, the violin is hushed, dancing has ceased, and the turkey sleeps with its head under its wing with impunity. All is again "quiet on the Colorado." To those who remember this portion of Arizona, as it was a year ago, it may look as though your correspondent was drawing on his imagination, and wickedly trying to deceive the world into the belief that in the short space of three hundred and sixty five days we have imported such gems of civilization as fair ladies, and, of course, Christmas dinners and balls; but nothing of the kind. It is a veritable fact, that Arizona is taking rapid strides towards the front of civilization. That within the past year her Territorial government has been organized; laws made; a judiciary put in operation; a printing press running; politicians pulling wires, and last, but not least, this community has received the important accession of women, "lovely women,"[1] and as

---

1. Alonzo E. Davis fell head-over-heels in love on the night of the 1864–65 New Year's ball at Fort Mojave. The object of his affection, Emily W. Mathews, was the daughter of Hardyville businessman Frank M. Mathews. Mr. Mathews gave Sergeant Davis permission to correspond with his daughter in September 1865 as Company I boarded the steamboat for Yuma and mustering out at Drum Barracks. The couple married in Los Angeles on February 10, 1867. Orton, *California Men*, 657; Davis, "Pioneer Days in Arizona," Arizona Historical Society, Tucson, 83, 114; "Alonzo E. Davis," Pension Files, Records of the Record and Pension Office, 1784–1917, RG 94, NARA

a consequence, society has leaped into existence, and the land of "cactus" and "choyas" [cholla] is becoming the vale of roses and lilies. But to be more definite and less poetic, as the first in our community's history, I think they are entitled to this notice. Christmas Eve was celebrated by a grand ball at Hardy's Landing, and New Year's Eve but ditto, at Mojave. The miners poured in from the mountains, everybody seemed to think it a religious duty to attend the first "grand ball" of the country, and everybody seemed determined to make the most of the occasion, and the meeting a festive one. I could not help thinking that if the votaries of fashion could, fresh from their stiff assemblies, take a peep in upon our social and mirthful gatherings, and witness the true cordiality among the gray shirts and calico gowns of the frontier, that they could not help renouncing the rigid circles of aristocratic fashion, and seek a rural home. The two balls, each and severally, mustered but eighteen ladies, but the disparity of numbers between the two sexes was well made up by the superior quality of the one, and I believe the glorious eighteen danced the whole male assemblage weary.

GREAT EXPECTATIONS

Now, taking the past year's improvement as a basis for calculation, who shall essay the sage that can mark the point of our advancement five years hence? I can tell you Arizona has great expectations, and why should she not? With chains of mountains coursing her whole length and breadth that are pregnant with every kind of mineral in the known world, and especially rich in the precious metals of gold, silver and copper; with a climate as health-giving as those of Italy, embracing every degree of temperature, from torrid to frigid; with plains of the best pasturage, and valleys rich and productive, with all this why should we not predict a future for Arizona glorious beyond precedent. The numerous ruins of forts and lodges scattered through the mountains and valleys of central and southern Arizona, are evidence that the country once supported a large population. And there can be no doubt that under the superior culture of the white man it can be made to do it again. But we are aware that with all these natural advantages we are at the mercy of capital. We must have capital to get the wheels of industry and enterprise in motion. Mills must be built; merchandise must be furnished; labor must be bought and sold. The hope that capitalists would come forward and assist in developing and working the mines, has been the nourishment of the spirit of the hardy pioneer, whose only capital is that of his enterprise and muscle. We hear, at length, that hope is soon to be turned to fruition—most. When it comes you will hear the story of our mines in gold and silver bullion. Within the past few days quite a number of men have arrived here from Salt Lake and the Boise mines. I know not what they will do. They want work, but there is no one here at present to give them employment, and they are nearly destitute. A poor man can make no greater mistake than coming here at present, unless he can be his own employer. There are too many poor men here now, and not enough capital.

PRICES CURRENT

I will agree the prices of the principal staples of life, and it will be seen therefrom that the cost of living will not justify a man in being long idle, unless he has a well filled larder. Flour, 14 cents per pound; sugar, 30 do.; coffee, 40 do.; bacon, 35 do.; fresh beef, 20 do.

THE MINES

Are returning flattering assurances for the little work that has been plied towards their development. The Neptune, in the Sacramento District, is the only ledge upon which anything has been done worthy in the name of prospecting. An incline has been run under the lode making its lower casing the roof of the incline. At a depth of 55 feet Mr. Hanney [W. P. Hanna] tapped the lode, and, rather to his disappointment, found his vein but two and a half feet thick, and greatly broken up and decomposed. But Mr. Hanney is a miner, and was not discouraged. His lode was beautifully cased, and the clay partings on each side were cut clean from the granite and presented a surface as smooth as a mirror. This told him he had a lode; he has continued down, taking out the vein as he went. At a depth of 70 feet, it commenced to get solid and wide and become more perpendicular, and now, at the depth of 80 feet, he has a vein of ore 6 ½ thick, of a bluish-grey color, that is thought to be rich in silver—no assay has yet been had of it. From any of the rock taken from the lode a splendid prospect of flour gold may be obtained.

A very rich gold ledge has recently been struck in the Sacramento District. The rock assembles somewhat that of the "Moss," and judging from the single specimen I have seen, should say it is (as is claimed) quite rich as that noted lode. The discoverers have gone out with powder and drills, to examine their newly-found "millions." The name of the lode is at present contraband. The "Moss," "Dayton," and "Leland" are the only lodes upon which work is being done in the San Francisco District, and all are turning out rock that bears ocular proof of its richness. The Dayton is a most beautiful character of ore. Choice samples show free gold very thick to the naked eye, and little masses or drops of horn silver are scattered very plentifully through the rock.

IN THE IRATABA DISTRICT,

Five companies are at work. Some of them are stripping the surface to the depth of five to ten feet, with a view to making the veins pay as they go. One or two lodes will be prospected to the depth of fifty to seventy-five feet. The "Long Island," "Brother Jonathan,"[2] and "Evening Star" lodes are yielding good ore from the surface. The ores of the "Irataba" District are usually very rich, and are of the classes known as "horse-flesh," [copper iron sulfide] "peacock," [bornite] and "viterous" [vitreous] copper ores; and in a few lodes, yellow sulphurets, or copper pyrites, are found. The mines are from seven to nine miles from the river, with a good natural wagon road. There is no water nearer than six miles, (Sacramento Springs,) which necessitates packing or hauling—a great inconvenience. The "Irataba" District is on the west side of the river, and in San Bernardino County, California. If there is anything in indications, these mines will yet be a source of pride to California, and great profit to their owners. But I shall be better able to speak of them after a few months work has helped to reveal their true character.

THE CARRYING TRADE

The *Esmeralda* is between here and La Paz with freight for the Mormon settlements at Santa Clara.[3] *Thus it will be seen that the great trade destined to be carried by the Colorado has commenced.* The river is four inches lower than the lowest mark last season, and if the *Esmeralda* succeeds in getting up, she will have to do some light running. L. Dukes & Co. have the contract for carrying the mail from Los Angeles to Prescott; it will be carried semi-monthly from Los Angeles to Mohave, and monthly from the latter place to Prescott. These arrangements are really cause for glorification to the people of Arizona as for months we have had but monthly communication with Los Angeles, which left us too far behind the times; and in these dark days of war was really agonizing.

2. The California miners of the Iretaba District came up with a playful variety of names for their lodes, veins, and outcroppings. "Brother Jonathan," a legendary Yankee icon since the American Revolution, became synonymous with "American" by the time of the Civil War. By the end of the war, though, Brother Jonathan was overshadowed by the popular image of Uncle Sam. Brother Jonathan's exit from cartoons and jokes may have been hastened by the disastrous sinking of the side-wheel steamer *Brother Jonathan* on July 19, 1865, off the California coast. Two hundred and fifty passengers and crew drowned, including the former commander of the Department of the Pacific, Gen. George Wright. Hunt, *Army of the Pacific*, 360–61. See also Paulding, *John Bull and Brother Jonathan*.

3. During the Civil War, Mormon leaders sent colonists to the Santa Clara and Virgin river basins in the hope of establishing agricultural communities that would produce cotton, hemp, and other semitropical crops to eliminate their dependence on the outside world. Steamboats on the unpredictable Colorado River could not be relied upon to supply the needs of these colonies in southern Utah. See Arrington, *Great Basin Kingdom*.

PRESCOTT

Mr. Caulkins, of Prescott, has just arrived here from that place. He reports considerable snow at the capital, and that he encountered snow three feet deep 90 miles east of here. "Health is excellent, but times are very dull about Prescott." Mr. Caulkins came through for the purpose of looking out a route for the toll road, upon the eastern end of which work has already been commenced. We hope soon to have a good wagon road connecting us with Prescott.

The county of Mohave will soon have its governmental machinery in motion. The Governor has appointed Col. S. Aiken County Judge; M. G. Moore, Sheriff; J. [I.] D. Woodworth, County Clerk, and Wooster Hardy, County Treasurer.[4] The Judge, Sheriff and County Clerk constitute a Board of Commissioners. Lawyers now have a chance in.

A Union League was organized here a few nights since. The weather is delightful. The community is healthy. Doctors are cursing the country; community laughs and grows fat.

CALIFORNIA VOLUNTEER

4. Twenty-five-year-old Ohioan Milton G. Moore enlisted at Nevada City, California, on December 10, 1861. He served as a corporal in Company I, Fourth California Infantry at Fort Mojave and mustered out at Drum Barracks on December 10, 1864, upon the expiration of his three-year enlistment. Jerome B. Calkins was a thirty-four-year-old miner from New York working in the San Francisco District. Ira D. Woodworth was a twenty-five-year-old Indiana miner working at Hardy's Landing. Wooster Molton Hardy was the first postmaster at Hardy's Landing when the post office was established on June 7, 1865. Orton, *California Men*, 657; Senate, *Federal Census—Territory of New Mexico and Territory of Arizona*, 93 (Fort Mohave, 1864), 106 (Yavapai County, 1864), 94, 127 (Hardy's Landing, 1864).

ALTA, February 23, 1865

ARIZONA ITEMS

We are permitted to make the following extract from a private letter from an Army officer[5] stationed at Tubac, Arizona Territory, dated Jan. 1st, recently received at Benicia:[6]

"Company L, First California Cavalry, is the only command at this post. Lieutenant Norton[7] is Post Quartermaster. Lieutenant Vose[8] is Acting Assistant Quartermaster at Las Cruces. I think he is likely to be promoted Captain of Company H, First Cavalry, California Volunteers. Colonel Brown[9] is in command of Fort Craig [New Mexico]. Captain Stombs[10] is at San Elizario [Texas]. Lieutenant

5. The identity of this officer is unknown but the only two Company L officers not mentioned in this "private letter" were Capt. John L. Merriam and 1st Lt. Leonard M. Gardner. Lieutenant Gardner joined the company in Stockton on March 11, 1863, was promoted from second to first lieutenant on February 25, 1864, and resigned his commission on January 31, 1865, just thirty days after this letter was posted. Merriam was an extraordinary soldier. He enlisted as a twenty-five-year-old private in Company E, Second California Cavalry on September 20, 1861, but within a year he had been promoted to corporal and transferred to Company F. On May 6, 1863, he gained a commission as first lieutenant of Company L, First California Cavalry. On February 7, 1864, he received his captain's bars and became the commander of Company L. Captain Merriam commanded at Tubac from the time of his arrival in June 1864. He organized scouting parties and guarded the border against incursions by French and Mexican Imperial forces. He continued active campaigning against Apaches when he moved Company L to Fort Bowie in the summer of 1865. Merriam mustered out at the Presidio in San Francisco, for disability, on October 31, 1865. Orton, *California Men*, 156, 239, 244; Senate, *Federal Census—Territory of New Mexico and Territory of Arizona*, 56 (Revanton and Calabasas, 1864); SO 54, Apr. 11, 1864, Hdqrs. Tucson, Commands of J. R. West, Special, General, and Post Orders, RG 393, NARA

6. Benicia, California, near San Francisco, was the site of the only U.S. arsenal in the Far West. Originally established in 1849 as a quartermaster depot, during the Civil War Benicia Barracks housed thousands of resident and transient volunteer soldiers, and a thriving community developed nearby. Hunt, *Army of the Pacific*, 20, 37; Prucha, *Military Posts*, 60.

7. Alfred W. Norton joined Company L, First California Cavalry as first sergeant on March 6, 1863, at San Andreas, California. He was promoted to second lieutenant on February 7, 1864, and advanced to first lieutenant on April 29, 1865, but was never officially mustered at this rank. Norton and Company L mustered out at the Presidio in San Francisco on June 28, 1866. Orton, *California Men*, 157.

8. On December 31, 1864, 1st Lt. Rufus C. Vose of Company M, First California Cavalry was promoted to captain of Company H, First Cavalry. Orton, *Records of California Men*, 97, 142, 162.

9. Oscar M. Brown became colonel of the First California Cavalry on November 6, 1864. Orton, *California Men*, 87.

10. Thomas A. Stombs joined Company F, First California Cavalry on April 24, 1863. He commanded the cavalry portion of the homeward-bound California Column when it left the Rio Grande near Las Lunas, New Mexico, on October 15, 1866. Stombs and his company were finally mustered out at the Presidio in San Francisco on December 31, 1866—one of the last California companies to leave U.S. service. Orton, *California Men*, 86, 130.

Toole[11] is retained in the service and on duty as Quartermaster at Franklin, Texas. Major Gorman[12] is in command of Fort Goodwin, Arizona Territory, with Company I, First California Cavalry, and a company of New Mexican Infantry. Lieutenant Abbott[13] is now Acting Regimental Adjutant of the First California Cavalry. Lieutenant Colonel Bennet [Bennett] is now, or shortly will be, in command of Fort Bowie, at Apache Pass.

"All sorts of reports are in circulation here about 'guerillas' along the line, only about twenty-eight miles south from this place. Rumors were prevalent about two weeks since that we were on the brink of an attack by them. I have heard that one company left Sonora some weeks since for Texas by the way of Sinaloa and Chihuahua. That there are a large number of reckless characters in this Territory, there is little doubt; but of the absolute truth of the above reports, I can't say. But of one thing I feel pretty confident, and that is, that they require a *much larger* number of troops here (in this Department [of New Mexico]) than they now have, to do anything at all. There is quite an element of disloyalty, and a FEW Apaches left in this country, and the troops are wofully scattered. * * *

11. James H. Toole joined Company G, Fifth California Infantry at Placerville, California, on November 26, 1861. He demonstrated an aptitude for quartermaster duties and was promoted to first lieutenant and regimental quartermaster on September 7, 1862. Toole joined Company C, First California Veteran Infantry in 1863; by 1864 he ran the Tucson depot during a difficult time of supply shortages. Lieutenant Toole mustered out at Franklin, Texas, on April 5, 1865. He returned to Tucson, where he became a successful banker until ruined in the Panic of 1884. He committed suicide that year. Orton, *California Men*, 394, 676, 690, 703; Altshuler, *Cavalry Yellow and Infantry Blue*, 334.

12. James Gorman had a checkered career. Born in Massachusetts, he made his way to the California gold fields and by the time of the Civil War lived in Calaveras County. He entered the service in December 1863 as captain of Company L, First California Cavalry. The morale of this company deteriorated under Gorman's leadership. He was so unpopular that, while riding to Tucson in April 1864, his men—disgruntled over excessive guard duty—cut off the flowing mane and tail of the captain's horse. Promoted to major on February 7, 1864, Gorman took command of the Tubac garrison in June. In August he took his company to Fort Goodwin, which he also commanded for a time. Gen. John Mason thought him a heavy drinker and an unfit officer, ordering him to Fort Bowie, "where he can do less harm in his intercourse with Indians." Gorman resigned on February 27, 1866. Orton, *California Men*, 78, 87, 156; Altshuler, *Cavalry Yellow and Infantry Blue*, 142–43; J. S. Mason to R. C. Drum, July 16, 1865, *OR*, 50(2):1281–83.

13. Massachusetts-born John Abbot rose steadily through the ranks. In 1864 thirty-two-year-old Corporal Abbott got his sergeant's stripes in Company G, First California Cavalry. Promoted to second lieutenant of Company I, he was soon advanced again—on November 7, 1864, First Lieutenant Abbott was named regimental adjutant. His military career ended ingloriously on August 2, 1865, when he was dismissed from the service. Orton, *California Men*, 87, 136, 147; Senate, *Federal Census—Territory of New Mexico and Territory of Arizona*, 81 (Tucson, 1864).

"Maj. Gorman came very near leaving this planetary sphere a few weeks since from an attack of typhoid fever, but is now well again. This valley is a terrible place for malarial fevers in the summer and autumn."

ALTA, April 3, 1865

Our Letter From Arizona Territory
(From the Resident Correspondent of the ALTA CALIFORNIA)
Fort Mojave, A.T., March 20th, 1865

EDITORS ALTA.—The long looked for and much dreaded order has at length come, and Company "I," Fourth Infantry, C.V., will start to-morrow for Drum Barracks. Company "C" [Fourth Infantry, C.V.] relieves us, and upon them will devolve the important duty of guarding this part of Uncle Sam's domains. I trust their stay here may be as agreeable and profitable as ours has been, and the former will depend much on the latter, for I will be candid and own that, aside from the mines and the glittering allurements of "feet," there is nothing particularly attractive about the country. The dry, arid plains and barren mountains that form the scenery along and on either side of the river, is not particularly calculated to impress one with an idea of Paradise. When we came here—not a man but the first few months was thoroughly disgusted with and sick of the country. But now, prospecting commenced. Parties would go out, and in a few days return loaded to the guards with rock—samples of ledges located by them that could be traced for miles. Connoisseurs would examine the numerous samples, and never one but that contained certain *indications* of silver, sometimes the color of gold and scarce ever a sample exhibited but that some one had seen its *facsimile* in Washoe [Nevada].

MINING INTEREST

Of course all this tended to breed "feet" fever, and I am not sure but that some of us had it on the brain for a time. Then we commenced to like the country, and began to dread the coming of the order that would remove us. We have prospected a good deal, explored not a little new country, have got lots of feet, and I will be frank and confess that some of them, by a bare possibility, may not be worth much; and for that confession I must be entitled to credit when I say that we have got *some* good claims that we *know* of. The first summer we were here, I thought this was the last place, and that the climate was one of the most disagreeable. Now I am fully persuaded that if this is not a glowing Eden, it is the United States Mint, and that if the weather is a little too warm for comfort a few months in the year, it is one that challenges Italy the rest of the year; and as for health, I don't believe there is so health-giving a climate in all the world. Sickness is unheard of, and if all the world was like Arizona, in point of health, I am inclined to think that the Medical Faculty would wear tolerably poor clothes.

THE HEATED TERM

And here I would speak of an article I saw in the [San Francisco *Evening*] *Bulletin*, last fall, that told of the extreme heat of Arizona; that several had died of sunstroke within a few days. The thermometer—if I remember right—was said to attain 142° in the shade. Now such stories are only laughed at by those who know the country, but those who do not know would probably form an idea of Arizona strongly coupled with Purgatory. The maximum heat here, (and it is much better along the river than it is a few miles back,) of 1863 was 116°, in the shade; of 1864, 115°. The average heat during the four hot months, commencing at the first of June, would not exceed 94°, and as for sun-stroke, there has never a case occurred that I have heard of in this part of the Territory. I have passed seven years in the Sacramento Valley, and I am certain that the heat there is quite as oppressive as here, but it does not last so long. So much for the climate.

THE MINES, ETC.

One year ago I had hoped to have my continued averments about the mineral wealth of Arizona backed by shipments of bullion. "But alas for hopes," those princes in whom we put our trust have not as yet appeared with the long-talked of and promised mills. That our mines are rich, none that have taken pains to examine them for themselves can deny. The Moss lode, in the San Francisco District, contains some of the richest quartz that ledges ever bear. Say some, "It is too rich to be permanent: it is a pocket lode." That may be true, but no one *knows* it to be so. It is certain that the pocket out of which the rich rock has been taken is sixty-five feet deep, rich rock having been struck in the shaft at that depth. But there are many lodes in the District that contain gold and silver too; the Dayton rock is full of fat globules of horn silver that melts into the genuine article in the flame of a candle.[14] The Leland is well stored with gold, and it cannot be urged that this is a pocket lode, unless the whole ledge is a pocket, as gold is found on all portions of it. The same made be said of several other lodes. So all that is wanting to make this a lively mining camp is mills for working the ores. Silver is found in limited quantities in the croppings of most of the lodes, and it seems reasonable to argue that rich ore might be obtained upon reasonable prospect-

14. Horn silver is a miners' term for cerargyrite (silver chloride), a soft silver ore.

ing. But as yet no ledge has been prospected at a greater depth than 65 feet; that (the Moss) contains some silver at that depth, though not rich. When shafts or tunnels have been run so as to prospect to the depth of 150 to 300 feet, then if rich rock is not obtained it will be perhaps time to declare that these mines are not as good as those of Washoe.

Another valuable discovery was made a few days since in the San Francisco District that I must not omit to mention. The lode was located more than a year ago, but until late it was not known how rich it is in gold and silver. It is of the same character as the Dayton, and is very rich in horn silver. The owners are putting up arastras,[15] and this will be the first lode out of which money will be taken. The gold of the rock is very fine, and evenly infused through the ledge.

THE COPPER MINES

Of the Irataba District are giving a good account of themselves. The Evening Star and Long Island Companies have each out twenty to thirty tons of valuable ore. There are several other companies at work taking ore from the croppings, other sinking shafts to prospect their mines. The Brother Jonathan Company have their shafts down 40 feet. They have a mineral vein of black oxide, varying from three to 16 inches in width. The ledge, however, from wall to wall, is 10 feet with every indication of permanency, and there is good reason to believe that at a proper depth a valuable mine will be found. The result of prospecting in the copper mines below the needles in the various districts has thrown a damper on the copper mines of the Colorado. The trouble in these districts seems not to have been so much in finding rich ores as in finding ledges. It is a noted fact that as soon as you get below the needles the mountains assume an entirely different appearance. There is no regular formation. The stratas of rock running and standing in every shape and direction. In short they suggest to one the idea that they have been lifted up, turned over and permitted to drop, and thus stove in to a confused and broken mass. This will, of course, account for the fact that the lodes are not continuous, but are like Paddy's flea—now you have them, and now you don't have them.

I speak not of this to disparage the copper mines below here, but to set people right, who, knowing the nature of these mines, would naturally infer that those of Irataba district were naturally of the same character. But it is not the case. The ledges of this district have a uniform course from northeast to southwest, and can be traced

---

15. *Arrastra* is a Spanish word for an ancient animal-powered, ore-reducing mill. Typically, a circular pit, lined with flat stones, holds the ore to be crushed. Mules or donkeys circle the pit, dragging large stones over the ore. It is a primitive process almost entirely supplanted by stamp mills in the United Sates by the time of the Civil War. Browne, *Adventures,* 255.

miles by their continuous croppings. They are well cased, and their chimneys contain rich ores of copper glance oxides, carbonates, and horse flesh ore. The flattering prospects met with upon the little work done has turned the head of the community from gold and silver to copper. I do not wish to convey the impression that any one is turning Copperhead, politically speaking, for since the fall of Charleston there has been a sensible shuffling for the opposite side.

The more ready availability of the copper mines offer to the poor man strong inducements. They need not be so dependent upon capitalists, as they can take out ore from the top and make it pay. Several tons will be got out in this way this spring. The heavy snow storms and cold weather of Sacramento district last winter had the effect of freezing out the miners of that district and at present nothing is being done there. However, there is a probability of livelier times there the coming summer.

MILLS, TRADE, ETC.

A five-stamp mill will be here in a few days. It is being brought out by Mr. Hardy, and will be put up at his landing. It is intended to crush the Moss rock at present. I trust that this will give milling a start, and that as soon as a result of a few months' crushing is known we shall have machinery of heavier calibre here. Wood can be had now for four dollars per cord, and it will be a long time before it will cost more than ten dollars. Ores, then, should be crushed for twenty dollars at most.

Mr. Ravenna [Manuel Ravena],[16] at La Paz, has established a general merchandise store at Mohave. He has a large and well assorted stock, but it takes a great deal to buy a little here now. Flour is selling at eighteen dollars per hundred, bacon forty cents per pound, and other things in proportion. It will be seen from this that the cost of living is heavy, and what wonder that in the absence of capital to employ the poor men here, that times are extremely uncomfortable for the pioneers, and that may have left until times mend, because they could not stand the pressure.

INDIANS, TRAVEL, ETC.

It is extremely unfortunate for Arizona, that the road over which her emmigration from California must pass has been disturbed by the Indians, and it is more vexatious that the depredations that have from time to time been committed has been done by a

16. Manual Ravena was one of the most successful merchants in La Paz. Born in Italy, he had hawked his wares in Colorado River mining communities for three years. Now, at age fifty, he had come to Mohave to take advantage of the boomtown prices that a shrewd salesman might demand. Ravena represented Yuma County in the Second Legislative Council in 1865 and later served as a member of the Yuma County Board of Supervisors. Senate, *Federal Census—Territory of New Mexico and Territory of Arizona*, 100 (La Paz, 1864). See also *Prescott Weekly Arizona Miner*, Mar. 2, 1872.

squad of renegades, of probably not more than fifty in all. Persons at a distance do not know of this, and distance always magnifies such matters, and no doubt that their troubles will be as damaging to the interests of Arizona as though there was really a formidable force of them. There is now and henceforth will be ample protection on the road. There is a good deal of talk, and, it seems to me, unjust fault found with Uncle Sam for not having the road stocked with troops before the late difficulty occurred, but the road has been deemed safe. Reports have come in from time to time that a small band of Indians were saucy on the road. Scouts were always sent out when the information appeared reliable, but were never able to find the Indians. Had there been open and positive acts of hostility committed, no doubt but that the road would have been guarded by Uncle Sam long ago.

INDIAN TROUBLES

Colonel Curtis[17] paid this post a flying visit a short time after the Indian troubles, and left instructions to have a party of twenty make a raid down the Chimawava [Chemehuevi] Valley, and, if possible, capture twenty of that tribe and hold them as hostages, until the renegades should be brought in, it being supposed that the gang that had been doing the mischief were composed of Chimawavas and Pi-Utes. Accordingly, the scout was made, and we had the glory of "marching up a hill and marching down again." Not an Indian could we see after leaving the Mojaves, the Chimawavas having all removed to their large valley about sixty miles this side of Fort Yuma.

The Mohaves express great indignation towards the Chimawavas, and only need encouragement and backing by the military authorities to take the war path against them. I don't think it would do any harm to let them fight one another, as it would tend to advance the inevitable finale of the race. So go in, red-skins, kill, cut and gouge all you like. But that won't do; they want the "sold-ers" to back them; they are afraid of the Chimawavas alone, but would no doubt make valuable allies.

The Chimawavas are said to number about six hundred warriors; the Pi-Utes eight hundred to one thousand; the Mojaves about five hundred. The Mojaves will never be an open enemy to the Americans, so long as Irataba lives, at any rate; for he has a wonderful control over them. They not only respect him but fear him. He is an extraordinary man, and possesses such a high superiority over his tribe that it is at once marked

17. James F. Curtis was an active member of the California State Militia prior to the Civil War and chief of police in San Francisco. In May 1861 he joined the Second California Infantry as its major. He transferred to the Fourth California Infantry as lieutenant colonel on June 25, 1863, and on May 9, 1864, became colonel of the regiment. Orton, *California Men*, 305, 431, 595, 599.

by all who observe them. He knows too much to ever think of being bad friends with the white man. But the other tribes—the Pi-Utes and Chimawavas—will probably have to be cleaned out and broken up, as much so as the Apaches.

MISCELLANEOUS

The river raised quite suddenly about a month ago, and is now at good stage for navigating. The *Esmeralda* did not go (though she might have easily) to the new Mormon settlement [Callville],[18] at the proposed head of navigation, some forty miles above El Dorado Cañon. She got near there, and upon learning that most of the Mormons had left, and were not there to take the merchandise he had on board, Captain Trueworthy[19] turned back, and his boat is now tied up at El Dorado Cañon, he having gone to Salt Lake to perfect future arrangements regarding freight. The *Esmeralda* towed up a barge with eighty tons of freight.

In a former communication I made an error in stating the county divisions, which you will please permit me to correct. I stated that it was divided into three—Yavapai, Yuma, and Mohave, to which should be added Pimo county.

The Prescott and Mohave toll road is fast approaching completion. It goes through Union pass twelve miles north of Beale's pass, and strikes the river five miles above Hardy's landing. It thus affords a good road to Sacramento district, a very important consideration.

A PHENOMENON

A loud noise, supposed to be the report of a meteor, was heard a few weeks ago about ten o'clock at night. It was distinctly heard for twenty miles up and down the river, and also in the San Francisco district. It sounded like a heavy blast. In the Irataba district the report was very heavy, and it is claimed that the place where it struck has

18. Mormon leader Brigham Young and the Deseret Mercantile Association dispatched Anson Call to establish warehouses to receive freight from Colorado River steamers one hundred miles above Fort Mojave in Pah-ute County, Arizona Territory (ceded to Nevada Territory in 1866). Although Callville became the head of navigation on the Colorado, the difficulty of beating against the river's current and seasonal low water doomed the experiment, and the Mormon settlement was soon abandoned. Lingenfelter, *Steamboats on the Colorado*, 47–48.

19. Capt. Thomas E. Trueworthy started a steamboat line on the Colorado River in 1864, determined to break George A. Johnson's monopoly of the river trade. His Union Line operated the *Esmeralda* and later the *Nina Tilden*, which towed barges to increase their freight capacity. Trueworthy worked to establish a viable trade route to Salt Lake City, and his boats landed supplies as far as the Mormon settlement at Callville, Nevada, more than four hundred miles above Yuma. Trueworthy gave up on the cutthroat river trade, eventually selling out to Johnson in 1867. Lingenfelter, *Steamboats on the Colorado*, 43–49.

been found there. The rocks and earth are said to be rent and torn up fearfully. If it was a meteor, it might be profitable to mine there for aerolites.[20]

CALIFORNIA VOLUNTEER

ALTA, July 24, 1865

Our Arizona Advices
The California Troops Leave Arizona—Condition of Affairs
in that Territory
(From the Correspondent of the ALTA with the California Column)
Headquarters, District of Arizona, Tubac,[21] *A.T., June 19, 1865*

EDITORS ALTA:—As General Mason[22] starts the express in the morning to the Maricopa Wells, I thought I would send you a letter to let you know the shape of affairs here. The train left Fort Yuma at 4 o'clock A.M., May 21. Nothing unusual tran-

20. Aerolites, or meteorites, were prized as collectibles by museums and rock hounds in the mid-nineteenth century. General Carleton himself was fascinated by them. When he arrived in Tucson, he confiscated blacksmiths' anvils that had been fashioned from spectacular meteor fragments. These specimens he shipped to San Francisco and later the Smithsonian Institution. Lockwood, *Arizona Characters*, 36. See also Buchwald, *Handbook of Meteorites*, 98, 1280.

21. Gen. John Sanford Mason wrote back to Department of the Pacific headquarters that "Tubac is a worthless town, containing about thirty worthless adobe houses. It was deserted entirely until within a very few months. The houses are nearly in ruins, and could not be made available for any military purpose." J. S. Mason to R. C. Drum, June 18,1865, *OR*, 50(2): 1261–63.

22. General Mason took command of the newly organized District of Arizona on March 1, 1865. An able regular-army officer with war service in the East (and the brevets to prove it), Mason took to his new assignment with energy and efficiency. He urged the recruitment and equipping of the Arizona Volunteers—four regiments made up of Pimas, Maricopas, and Mexican Americans—for service against the Apaches. Mason doubled the number of military posts in Arizona and replaced the original California Volunteer regiments, which had mustered out or consolidated and reorganized as veteran volunteers, with the Seventh California Infantry, a battalion of Native Cavalry (Californios who enlisted with a will once the U.S. government made it clear that it would not recognize the French puppet government in Mexico under Maximilian), and a company of the First California Cavalry. The general attempted to alleviate the critical food and clothing shortages in Arizona by authorizing the shipment of supplies by way of Guaymas. He understood that his mission included both patrolling the Mexican border to check the French invaders and taking the fight to the Apaches, advocating a harsh policy of death to all adult Apache males and attempting to have all of his units simultaneously strike hostile bands within their reach. General Mason gave up his Arizona command on June 3, 1866, and returned to the regular army as a major. Altshuler, *Cavalry Yellow and Infantry Blue*, 22–23; and *Chains of Command*, 39–50; J. S. Mason to R. C. Drum, May 3, 1865, *OR*, 50(2):1247–48; GO 10, Hdqrs. Dept. of the Pacific, Feb. 20, 1865, ibid., 1137. Gen. Irvin McDowell ordered Mason to take command of the District of Arizona as soon as he was relieved of his duties as provost marshal of San Francisco. See also J. S. Mason to R. C. Drum, July 16, 1865, ibid., 1281–83.

spired on the road till we reached the Maricopa Wells. On the road to the last named point we passed parties on their way to California, who gave rough accounts of the state of the country in regard to the Indian troubles and the scarcity of provisions. We reached the Maricopa Wells on the 29th of May, and laid over till the first of June. While there the General made arrangements to have a receiving post established, as it is the most available point in the Territory, and the Government can there obtain considerable quantities of grain of the Maricopa and Pimo Indians. General Mason, in connection with Governor Goodwin, has made arrangement to arm for the field two hundred Indians of the above named tribes, to fight the Apaches.[23] I think it is a good idea. They were out on the war-path and had a brush with some of the Apaches just before we came. They took two of their women prisoners. The General had them before him, in order to find out where their tribe would most likely be found, but he could learn nothing, except that their tribe had taken the war path against the whites, and all Indians who would not join them. It appears that they had sent to the Yumas to join, but they had refused to take stock. It strikes me very forcibly that the troops are not sent in as quick as they might be to this District. Their detention has hindered the operations of the General somewhat, but there was no apparent need of half of the delay which has occurred. Gen. Mason gave orders to fit out the expedition more than a month before he arrived at Wilmington. Who is to blame for not having a mule in his corral when wanted? Gen. Mason has from the first manifested a great deal of energy in getting the troops in their proper posts, but the lack of transportation has been the main cause of all the delay.[24]

23. On May 30, 1865, General Mason wrote that he intended to recruit two hundred Pima and Maricopa warriors to help campaign against Apaches, Hualapais, Yavapais, and those Navajos that had not already been interned by Carleton at the Bosque Redondo Reservation along the Pecos River. Mason hoped to launch coordinated attacks against these tribes, leaving them no place to hide or retreat. The Pimas and Maricopas were enlisted, armed, and accoutered. The general insisted on outfitting his Indian allies with red shirts trimmed to identify their tribe—probably an attempt to prevent misidentification by his soldiers. Officered by former California Volunteers, the Arizona Volunteers, as they were recognized by the territorial legislature, performed well during their one-year enlistments. The Third Arizona Legislature commended these men for killing between 150 and 175 enemy warriors and inflicting "greater punishment upon the Apaches than all other troops in the territory." J. S. Mason to R. C. Drum, May 30, 1865, *OR*, 50(2):1247–48; Underhill, "Arizona Volunteers," 1, 15, 76, 92.

24. Mason discovered, much as Carleton had in 1862, that the dry desert air and scorching sand had desiccated his rolling stock—wagon wheels shrank and the iron tires got loose. Mason reported that while his horses and mules were in good shape, troop movements and active campaigning would be delayed until the wagons could be repaired and civilian teamsters and wagonmasters hired. J. S. Mason to R. C. Drum, May 30, July 16, 1865, *OR*, 50(2):1247–48, 1281–83.

When we arrived there were very few troops in the Territory. The people have gained confidence, and think the Government means to protect them. Gen. Mason has divided his District into Sub-Districts, under the commands of Col. Lewis,[25] Lieut.-Col. Bennett,[26] and Lieut.-Col. Boulware.[27] The post of Tubac is evacuated, and one is to be established at Calabasas,[28] which is to be the headquarters of the Seventh Infantry. It commands the only available route to Sonora, and is splendidly situated to mount a battery on, as there is a nice hill back of the post commanding the valley all around, so that it cannot be attacked with any hope of success. There is also to be a post in the Tonto Basin (so called), which will be named Fort McDowell,[29] in honor of the Commander of the Department of the Pacific.

25. Charles W. Lewis took command of the Seventh California Infantry in January 1865. By spring he had arrived in Arizona, and on June 15 General Mason ordered him to take charge of the newly created Southern Subdistrict of Arizona. Lewis was a capable and popular officer. After his discharge in May 1866, he returned to Arizona and established a ranch near Tubac and later served one term in the territorial legislature. Altshuler, *Cavalry Yellow and Infantry Blue*, 202–3; Orton, *California Men*, 763, 766; GO 4, June 15, 1865, Hdqrs. District of Arizona, Tubac, *OR*, 50(2):1261.

26. Clarence E. Bennett was a professional soldier. He graduated from West Point and served with the Tenth U.S. Infantry in Utah from 1857 to 1860. After marrying Toodie Whitlock, a Mormon girl, he was forced to resign his commission due to the strong anti-Mormon sentiment within the army. In 1863 Bennett served as major, then lieutenant colonel, of the First California Cavalry, commanding for a time at Fort Yuma and in 1864 at Fort Bowie. General Mason named Bennett to command the Eastern Subdistrict of Arizona. Altshuler, *Chains of Command*, 48; Orton, *California Men*, 87.

27. Madison Boulware joined the Seventh California Infantry as its lieutenant colonel in December 1864. General Mason posted him at Fort Yuma with Companies A and K. Boulware mustered out at San Francisco in March 1866. Orton, *California Men*, 766; *OR*, 50(1):1274.

28. Calabasas was a well-known stopping place in the Santa Cruz Valley on the road from Tucson to Sonora. It was fifteen miles from Tubac and only eight miles from the Mexican border. Spanish missionary priests had used the place as a temporary *visita*, and U.S. dragoons had established Camp Moore here two years after the Gadsden Purchase of 1854. In August 1865 Col. Charles Lewis established Fort Mason, named for his superior, Gen. John S. Mason, with Companies D, E, and G of the Seventh California Infantry. In September Maj. John C. Cremony's Native Battalion arrived to reinforce the garrison, which suffered a high mortality from disease. Altshuler, *Starting with Defiance*, 41, 47; Browne, *Adventures*, 144, 152–55.

29. Fort McDowell was established by Lt. Col. Clarence E. Bennett, First California Cavalry, on September 7, 1865. He located the post at the Verde River near its confluence with the Salt. Three companies of the Seventh California Infantry launched offensive operations from this point until these volunteers were replaced by regulars in the spring of 1866. Bennett named the fort to honor Irvin McDowell, who had been appointed to replace General Wright, commander of the District of California, formerly the Department of the Pacific. McDowell's failures as a field commander in the eastern theater of the Civil War, especially the 1861 Bull Run debacle, were not representative of his efficient and energetic leadership in the Far West. Hunt, *Army of the Pacific*, 28; Hageman, *Fighting Rebels and Redskins*, 9; War Dept. GO 118, June 18, 1865, Washington, *OR*, 50(2):1268.

There is a deal of trouble between the officers of Company A, First C.V., also among the men. The Company is a splendid one, but it is in a bad state. The General will bring this up all right in due time.

W.C.W.[30]

ALTA, December 21, 1865

General Carleton's Men Ask for Relief

The following Petition, which is about to be presented to the Legislature, sets forth in clear and explicit terms the claims which a portion of our California Volunteers have, for relief, upon the State. These claims would seem to be founded in equity, and we think that our citizens generally would consent to bear the burden of the slight taxation necessary to enable the State to refund the money expended by these soldiers of the Union under such peculiar circumstances. Other States have paid out millions to meet such demands, and we can surely afford to do justice to the few men we have called out to send into distant fields to fight for the Union and the honor of our State.

To the Honorable Legislature of the State of California:

We, the undersigned, late Members of the California Volunteers, under command of Brigadier-General Carleton, do most respectfully petition your Honorable body to grant us relief in the amount and for the reasons hereinafter specified:

Enlisting in good faith and solely from patriotic motives, to do our country's service in the field, and fill our State's quota [approximately 16,000 men], we were taken to the Territory of New Mexico and to the State of Texas, where, for over two years, we were busied either in building fortifications; making tiresome marches of from twenty to forty-five and fifty miles per day; frequently obliged to subsist upon half-rations; short of clothing, and suffering for the want of water; scouting for and skirmishing with the Indians; entirely subduing the Navajoes, and repeatedly whipping the Camanches and Apaches. Finally, upon the expiration of our term of enlistment, after repeated calls upon the State's Executive, through the medium of the Press, to pro-

30. W.C.W. appears to be very well informed. His information and opinions seem to mirror General Mason's own dispatches to Department of the Pacific headquarters. This writer is most likely William C. Walker, a civilian traveling with Company E, Seventh California Infantry, though Pvts. William Wenzel and William Wilt are possible candidates. Wenzel enlisted at Mokelumne Hill, California, on November 29, 1864. Wilt joined Company E on November 24, 1864, at San Andreas, California. Both men mustered out at the Presidio in San Francisco on June 28, 1866. Orton, *California Men*, 764, 781; *Alta*, June 17, 1865.

cure our return, we were discharged—nearly two thousand miles from the place of our enlistment, with neither provisions or transportation, but obliged to receive from seventy-five to one hundred and twenty-five dollars in lieu thereof. The expense incurred by us in returning amounting to from three hundred and fifty to four hundred dollars, the difference in figures is due to our having been discharged at different places, necessitating different routes of travel.

Felling [*sic*] as we do, that under these circumstances the actual expenses attending our return, in excess of the amount furnished by the Government, is needed by and due us from the State.

WE ARE, WITH GREAT RESPECT, ETC.,
ELWIN DAVIS, CO. E, 1ST INF.,
JOSEPH THOMPSON, CO. E, 5TH INF.,
C. H. WARREN, CO. E., 1ST INF.,
WM. ELLIOTT, CO. E, 5TH INF.,
PETER P. HOIN, CO. E, 1ST INF.,
WM. H. TROY, CO. B, 2D CAV.,
JOHN S. HANCO, CO. H, 5TH INF.,
FRANK STOW, CO. B, 1ST CAV.,
FERDINAND LANG, CO. E, 1ST CAV.,
JOHN UPTON, CO. B, 1ST INF.,
ELLIOTT WESCOTT, CO. E, 1ST CAV.,
ROBERT CRANE, CO. B, 1ST CAV.,
HOWARD MORRISON, CO. E, 1ST CAV.,
H. A. BURNS, CO. H, 1ST CAV.,
W. W. DAVIS, CO. D, 1ST INF.,
JOHN SENNETT, CO. H, 1ST CAV.,
LOUIS H. LOHSE, CO. K, 1ST INF.,
P. O. SAPER, CO. E, 1ST INF.,
H. S. O. ROBINSON, CO. B, 1ST CAV.,
JOHN HIGGINS, CO. I, 5TH INF.,
GEO. L. EGAN, CO. E, 1ST INF.,
E. J. MORTON, CO. D, 1ST INF.

Epilogue

In 1890 General Richard H. Orton, adjutant general of California, had occasion to ride a Southern Pacific Railroad passenger train across Arizona. As the steam locomotive chugged through Picacho Pass, he saw the familiar jagged volcanic plug standing alone in the broad, flat valley. At the narrowest point in the pass, Picacho Peak loomed large, and the engineer began a slow, almost imperceptible, turn to the northwest and into the setting sun. The general's eyes followed the dusty trace that marked the old Butterfield stage road as it meandered through the saguaros and

Capt. Richard H. Orton made his mark on the sandstone rock called El Morro in New Mexico before leading the last contingent of volunteers across Arizona and home to California in October 1866. Orton was the last California Volunteer to be mustered out of U.S. service, January 4, 1867. Photo by Don Bufkin.

mesquite thickets parallel to the railroad tracks. Then he saw what he was looking for—Lieutenant Barrett's grave. The marker, only twenty feet from the tracks, flashed past his window in an instant and was gone. Orton had last seen this place twenty-five years before, as a youthful captain of the First California Cavalry. He wondered that Barrett's sister Ellen, last reported to be living in Albany, New York, had never claimed her brother's remains or had them properly buried in California. Even the two enlisted men, Johnson and Leonard, who had died beside him had been reinterred at the military cemetery in Tucson, and when Fort Lowell was deactivated, they would be moved again to the national cemetery at the Presidio in San Francisco. But Barrett, the first to fall, had been forgotten.

Orton often thought of the war and the role played by the California Volunteers in the Arizona desert. Many of his comrades were active in the Grand Army of the Republic—GAR posts had sprung up everywhere, from coast to coast—but the Californians often sat silently as the old soldiers from the Army of the Potomac prattled on about great battles in the East: Chancellorsville, Gettysburg, and Appomattox ad nauseam. The march of the California Column had been all but forgotten—buried, it seemed, with Barrett.

In the mixed company of veterans from East and West, it was hard to even broach the subject of desert marches, Apache fights, and saving the gold-rich territories for the Union. But when old California Volunteers got together, they remembered. Some, with grandchildren on their knees, would eagerly scan new history texts and encyclopedias for even a mention of the Civil War in Arizona, only to be disappointed.

As time passed and the veteran ranks began to thin, interest in the Civil War grew, as if the nation recognized that something precious would soon be lost. Congress authorized the publication of the Official Records of the War of the Rebellion *(128 volumes in all), and in 1890 (the same year the U.S. Census Bureau declared the western frontier to be closed) the state of California commissioned a war record of its own. General Orton would compile and publish in a single volume the extant records of the California Volunteers.*

This flurry of historical activity soon passed, however, and as the twentieth century began, only rare mentions of the Civil War in the West could be found in print. In Arizona, stories of the Column from California were found occasionally in newspaper obituaries. Hundreds of California soldiers had stayed in or returned to Arizona after the war. They had built homes and businesses, raised families, and become community leaders. Newspapermen in the prosperous cities of Phoenix, Prescott, Tuc-

*son, and Yuma now wrote sentimentally, even reverentially, of the passing pioneers—
"the boys of '63." By the time of the Second World War, the last GAR post in Arizona
had closed and bolted its door forever—the records of its California Volunteer members
lost or dispersed.[1]*

1. Orton, *California Men,* 5, 47; E. E. Eyre to R. C. Drum, May 14, 1862, *OR,* 50(1):120. The
gravesites had been marked and were visible, on the right side of the tracks, from the windows
of westbound trains. Julius Hall, "Wild West." "In Memory of Alexander G. Bowman [Co. B,
Fifth California Infantry] (1842–1915)," written by Bowman's niece Ida Louise Estes Franklin,
is a 1957 manuscript detailing his bitter disappointment over the lack of recognition the California Volunteers received in published histories. Franklin remembers that her uncle "sat
silent in groups of Civil War veterans discussing the battles of Gettysburg or Appomattox." Special Collections, University of Arizona Library, Tucson.

Bibliography

UNPUBLISHED SOURCES

Arizona State University Library, Tempe
  Alonzo E. Davis, "Pioneer Days in Arizona by One Who Was There," ed. Louise Van Cleve, Jessie White, and Rae Van Cleve [1916], Arizona Historical Foundation
  Bert Fireman, "Jack Swilling, the New Father of Arizona," Arizona Collection
  Hayden Arizona Pioneer Biography Files
Arizona Historical Society, Tucson
  Edward E. Ayer, "Reminiscences of Edward E. Ayer, 1860–1918"
  Clarence E. Bennett Diary and Papers
  Sidney B. Brinckerhoff, "Last of the Lancers: The Native California Cavalry Volunteeers, 1863–1866"
  Alonzo E. Davis, "Pioneer Days in Arizona by One Who Was There" (typescript)
  David Fergusson Biographical File
  George Hand Diary, 1861–63
  Hayden Arizona Pioneer Biography Files
  Marriage Register for Yavapai County (typescript)
  George Oakes Reminiscence
  A. B. Peticolas Diary
  Edith C. Tomkins Manuscript, Small Collection, John Spring Papers, 1850–1921
Bancroft Library, University of California, Berkeley
  Edward E. Ayer, "Reminiscences of the Far West and Other Trips, 1861–1918"
  D'Heureuse Photograph Collection
  William McCleave Papers
Beinecke Library, Yale University, New Haven, Conn.
  George H. Pettis Papers, Western Americana Collection
William Addison Bushnell Diary, 1865 (typescript in author's possession)
California State Library, Sacramento
  Clothing Account Books of California Volunteer Regiments, 1861–66
  Moses Patterson Diary, December 1863–April 1866

Irene Newton, "Column from California"

Center for American History, University of Texas at Austin
James P. Newcomb Papers, Journals, and Diaries, 1857–71

El Dorado County Museum, Placerville, Calif.
Photograph Collections: Hitchcock Collection
Aaron Cory Hitchcock Letters, 1864–66, Joanne Grace Private Collection
(copies in author's possession)

Huntington Library, San Marino, Calif.
Thomas T. Tidball Diary
Edward D. Tuttle Letters

Mohave County Courthouse, Kingman, Ariz.
Mohave County Book of Claims, 1864–66

National Archives Records Administration, Washington, D.C.
Record Group 92: Records of the Office of the Quartermaster General
Record Group 94: Records of the Office of the Adjutant General, Letters
Received; California Volunteers, Regimental Letter Books, 1861–66
Record Group 95: California Volunteers Clothing Accounts; California Vol-
unteers Descriptive Lists
Record Group 98: U.S. Army Commands, Fort Bowie Letters Received,
1862–71
Record Group 109: Records of Organizations from the Territory of Arizona;
War Department Collection of Confederate Records
Record Group 156: Benicia Arsenal Letters Sent, 1846–1923; Office of the
Chief of Ordnance, Returns, 1861–65; Office of the Inspector General,
Extracts of Inspection Reports, 1864–65; Records of the Chief of Ord-
nance, "Records of Arsenals and Armories, 1794–1944"
Record Group 393: Department of the Pacific, General, Special, and Post
Orders, 1861–66; Department of California, Letters Sent, 1861–62;
Department of the Pacific, Letters Sent, 1861–66; Records of the U.S.
Army Continental Commands, Commands of J. R. West, Special, General,
and Post Orders, 1861–65

San Augustin Cathedral, Tucson
Marriage Registry, 1864–67

Sharlot Hall Museum, Prescott, Ariz.
Charles A. Wyckoff, "Journal of Company C, Seventh Infantry, California
Volunteers, May 20, 1865, to March 26, 1866" (typescript by Aurora Hunt
of original at Sutter's Fort Museum, Sacramento, Calif.)

Stanford University Libraries, Palo Alto, Calif.
James H. Carleton, "Papers Relating to Service in Arizona and New Mexico,
1851–1865"

University of Arizona Library Special Collections, Tucson
Thomas Akers Diary, October 8, 1861—December 6, 1865
Alexander Grayson Bowman Diary, December 20, 1861–February 22, 1865
(typescript)

"Diary of Corporal A. Bowman, Pace-counter, Co. B., 5th Infantry, California Volunteers"

Charles D. Poston, "History of the Apaches," 1886

Ida Louis Estes Poston, untitled reminiscences of Alexander G. Bowman (uncle), 1957

Oury Family Papers

Edward D. Tuttle Diary

University of Southern California Library, Los Angles

De la Guerra Papers, Owen Coy Room

Yavapai County Courthouse, Prescott, Ariz.

Book of Deeds and Claims No. 1

PUBLISHED SOURCES

Agnew, S. C. *Garrisons of the Regular U.S. Army, 1851–1899.* Arlington: Council on Abandoned Military Posts, 1974.

Ahnert, Gerald T. *Retracing the Butterfield Overland Trail through Arizona: A Guide to the Route of 1857–1861.* Los Angeles: Westernlore, 1973.

Alberts, Don E. *The Battle of Glorieta: Union Victory in the West.* College Station: Texas A&M University Press, 1998.

————. *Rebels on the Rio Grande: The Civil War Journal of A. B. Peticolas.* Albuquerque: University of New Mexico Press, 1984.

Allyn, Joseph P. *The Arizona of Joseph Pratt Allyn.* Edited by John Nicholson. Tucson: University of Arizona Press, 1974.

Almada, Francisco R. *Diccionario de Historia, Geografía, y Biografía Sonorenses.* Chihuahua, Mexico, 1952.

Anderson, Fred, and Andrew Cayton. *The Dominion of War: Empire and Liberty in North America, 1500–2000.* New York: Viking, 2005.

Altshuler, Constance Wynn. "Camp Moore and Fort Mason." *Council on Abandoned Military Posts Periodical* 26 (Winter 1976): 34–37.

————. "The Case of Sylvester Mowry, the Charge Treason." *Arizona and the West* 15 (Spring 1973): 63–82.

————. "The Case of Sylvester Mowry, the Mowry Mine." *Arizona and the West* 15 (Summer 1973): 149–74.

————. *Cavalry Yellow and Infantry Blue: Army Officers in Arizona between 1851 and 1886.* Tucson: Arizona Historical Society, 1991.

————. *Chains of Command: Arizona and the Army, 1856–1875.* Tucson: Arizona Historical Society, 1981.

————. *Latest from Arizona!: The Hesperian Letters, 1859–61.* Tucson: Arizona Historical Society, 1969.

————. "Military Administration in Arizona, 1854–1865." *Journal of Arizona History* 10 (Winter 1969): 215–38.

————. "Poston and the Pimas: The 'Father of Arizona' as Indian Superintendent." *Journal of Arizona History* 18 (Spring 1977): 23–42.

————. *Starting with Defiance: Nineteenth Century Arizona Military Posts.* Tucson: Arizona Historical Society, 1983.

Archambeau, Ernest R. "The New Mexico Campaign of 1861–1862." *Panhandle Plains Historical Review* 37 (1964): 3–32.

Armstrong, A. F. "The Case of Major Isaac Lynde." New *Mexico Historical Review* 36 (January 1961): 1–35.

Arrington, Leonard J. *Great Basin Kingdom: An Economic History of the Latter Day Saints, 1830–1900.* Salt Lake City: University of Utah Press, 2000.

Athearn, Robert G. "West of Appomattox: An Interpretive Look at the Civil War and Its Impact beyond the Great River." *Montana The Magazine of Western History* 12 (April 1962): 2–12.

Avillo, Phillip V. "Fort Mojave: Outpost on the Upper Colorado." *Journal of Arizona History* 2 (Summer 1970): 77–100.

Bailey, Lynn R. "Thomas Varker Keam: Tusayan Trader." *Arizoniana* 2 (Winter 1960): 15–19.

Bancroft, Hubert H. *History of Arizona and New Mexico, 1530–1888.* San Francisco: History Co., 1889. Reprint, Albuquerque: Horn and Wallace, 1962.

————. *History of Mexico.* 6 vols. San Francisco: History Co., 1888.

Bandel, Eugene. *Frontier Life in the Army, 1854–1861.* Glendale, Calif.: Arthur H. Clark, 1932.

Barnes, William C. "Arizona Place Names." *University of Arizona General Bulletin* 2 (1935).

Barney, James M. "Battle of Apache Pass." *Arizona Highways* (January–February 1936).

————. "Colonel Edward E. Eyre." *Sheriff Magazine* (March 1952).

Barr, Alwyn. "Texas Civil War Historiography." *Texas Libraries* 26 (Winter 1964): 160–69.

Baylor, George Wythe. *John Robert Baylor: Confederate Governor of Arizona.* Edited by Odie B. Faulk. Tucson: Arizona Pioneers' Historical Society, 1966.

Beck, Warren A., and Ynez D. Haase. *Historical Atlas of New Mexico.* Norman: University of Oklahoma Press, 1976.

Bellah, James Warner. "The Desert Campaign." *Civil War Times* (April 1961).

Benet, William Rose. *Reader's Encyclopedia.* New York: Crowell, 1969.

Bensell, Royal A. *All Quiet on the Yamhill: The Civil War in Oregon.* Edited by Gunther Barth. Eugene: University of Oregon Books, 1969.

Boatner, Mark M. *The Civil War Dictionary.* New York: David McKay, 1966.

Brady, Francis P. "Portrait of a Pioneer, Peter R. Brady, 1825–1902." *Journal of Arizona History* 16 (Summer 1975): 171–94.

Brandes, Ray. *Frontier Military Posts of Arizona.* Globe, Ariz.: Dale Stuart King, 1960.

Brennan, Irene J., ed. *Fort Mojave, 1859–1890: Letters of the Commanding Officers.* Manhattan: MA/AH Publishing, Kansas State University, 1980.

Brinckerhoff, Sidney B. *Boots and Shoes of the Frontier Soldier, 1865–1893.* Museum Monograph 7. Tucson: Arizona Historical Society, 1976.

————. "Soldiers Came, Fought, and Stayed." *Arizona* 15 (1975): 76–81.

Browne, J. Ross. *Adventures in the Apache Country*. New York: Harper and Brothers, 1869. Reprint, edited by Donald M. Powell, Tucson: University of Arizona Press, 1974.

———. *The Mineral Resources of the Pacific Slope*. New York: D. Appleton, 1869.

Buckwald, V. F. *Handbook of Meteorites*. Berkeley: University of California Press, 1975.

Byars, Charles. "Documents of Arizona History: The First Map of Tucson." *Journal of Arizona History* 7 (Winter 1966): 188–200.

Byrne, Henry L. "Early Journalism in California." *Society of California Pioneers Quarterly* 3 (1926): 108–44.

Carleton, James H. *Correspondence between Carleton and Governor F. F. Low Concerning Complaints of California Volunteers Discharged in Arizona*. Sacramento: O. M. Clayes, state printer, [1865].

Carlson, Edward. "Martial Experiences of the California Volunteers." *Overland Monthly* 7 (May 1886): 480–90.

Carmony, Neil B., ed. *The Civil War in Apacheland: Sergeant George Hand's Diary, California, Arizona, West Texas, New Mexico, 1861–1864*. Silver City, N.M.: High-Lonesome Books, 1996.

Carroll, Thomas F. "Freedom of Speech and of the Press during the Civil War." *Virginia Law Review* 9 (1923): 516–51.

Casebier, Dennis G. *Camp El Dorado, Arizona Territory*. Tempe: Arizona Historical Foundation, 1970.

———. *Carleton's Pa-Ute Campaign*. Norco, Calif.: Tales of the Mojave Road Publishing, 1972.

———. *Fort Pa-Ute*. Norco, Calif.: Tales of the Mojave Road Publishing, 1974.

———. *Mojave Road*. Norco, Calif.: Tales of the Mojave Road Publishing, 1975.

———. *The Mojave Road in Newspapers*. Norco, Calif.: Tales of the Mojave Road Publishing, 1976.

Clendenen, Clarence C. "A Confederate Spy in California: A Curious Incident of the Civil War." *Southern California Quarterly* 45 (September 1963): 219–34.

———. "An Unknown Chapter in Western History." *Westerners Brand Book, New York Posse 1* (Summer 1954).

———. "Dan Showalter—California Secessionist." *California Historical Quarterly* 40 (December 1961): 309–25.

———. "General James Henry Carleton." *New Mexico Historical Review* 30 (January 1955): 23–43.

———. "Southwestern Chronicle: Was Sylvester Mowry a Secessionist?" *Arizona Quarterly* 10 (Winter 1954): 260–66.

———. "Southwestern Chronicle: A Little More on Sylvester Mowry." *Arizona Quarterly* 10 (Winter 1954): 358–60.

———. "The Column from California." *Civil War Times Illustrated* 9, no. 9 (January 1971): 20–28.

Colton, Ray C. *The Civil War in the Western Territories: Arizona, New Mexico, and Utah*. Norman: University of Oklahoma Press, 1959.

Conkling, Roscoe P., and Margaret B. Conkling. *The Butterfield Overland Mail, 1857–1869.* 3 vols. Glendale, Calif.: Arthur H. Clarke, 1947.

Connell, F. S. "The Confederate Territory of Arizona as Compiled from the Official Records." *New Mexico Historical Review* 17 (April 1942): 148–63.

Conner, Daniel E. *Joseph Reddeford Walker and the Arizona Adventure.* Edited by Donald J. Berthrong and Odessa Davenport. Norman: University of Oklahoma Press, 1956.

Cook, F. A. "War and Peace: Two Arizona Diaries." *New Mexico Historical Review* 24 (April 1949): 95–129.

Cooke, Philip St. George. *Cavalry Tactics, or Regulations for the Instruction, Formulations, and Movements of the Cavalry of the Army and Volunteers of the United States.* Philadelphia: J. B. Lippincott, 1862.

Cremony, John C. "The Apache Race." *Overland Monthly* 1 (1868): 201–12.

———. "How and Why We Took Santa Cruz." *Overland Monthly* 6 (1871): 335–40.

———. *Life among the Apaches.* New York: A. Roman, 1868.

Cullum, George W. *Biographical Register of the Officers and Graduates of the U.S. Military Academy.* New York: Houghton, Mifflin, 1891.

Dary, David. *Red Blood and Black Ink: Journalism in the Old West.* (Lawrence: University Press of Kansas, 1998.

DeLong, Sidney R. *History of Arizona.* San Francisco: Whitaker and Ray, 1905.

Dickson, Paul. *War Slang: Fighting Words and Phrases of Americans from the Civil War to the Gulf War.* New York: Pocket Books, 1994.

Duffen, William A. "Overland Via 'Jackass Mail' in 1858: The Diary of Phocion R. Way." *Arizona and the West* 2 (Spring, Summer, Autumn 1960): 35–53, 147–64, 279–92.

Dunlay, Tom. *Kit Carson and the Indians.* Lincoln: University of Nebraska Press, 2000.

Dunning, Charles, and Edward H. Peplow. *Rock to Riches.* Phoenix: Southwest, 1959.

Dutton, Bertha P. *Indians of the American Southwest.* Englewood Cliffs, N.J.: Prentice-Hall, 1975.

Edrington, Thomas S., and John Taylor. *The Battle of Glorieta Pass: A Gettysburg in the West, March 26–28, 1862.* Albuquerque: University of New Mexico Press, 1998.

Elson, Mark D., and William H. Doelle. *Archaeological Survey in Catalina State Park with a Focus on the Romero Ruin, Technical Report No. 87–4.* Tucson: Institute for American Research, 1987.

Evans, George S. *List of Electors Resident of California in the Military Service of the United States.* Sacramento: State Printing Office, 1865.

Farish, Thomas E. *History of Arizona.* 8 vols. San Francisco: Filmer Brothers Electrotype, 1915–18.

Finch, L. Boyd. "Arizona in Exile: Confederate Schemes to Recapture the Far Southwest." *Journal of Arizona History* 33 (Spring 1992): 57–84.

————. "Arizona's Governors without Portfolio: A Wonderfully Diverse Lot." *Journal of Arizona History* 26 (Spring 1985): 77–99.

————. "The Civil War in Arizona: The Confederates Occupy Tucson." *Arizona Highways* 65 (January 1989): 14–17.

————. *Confederate Pathway to the Pacific: Major Sherod Hunter and Arizona Territory, C.S.A.* Tucson: Arizona Historical Society, 1996.

————. "Sanctified by Myth: The Battle of Picacho Pass." *Journal of Arizona History* 36 (Autumn 1995): 251–66.

————. "Sherod Hunter and the Confederates in Arizona." *Journal of Arizona History* 10 (August 1969): 139–206.

————. "William Claude Jones: The Rogue Who Named Arizona." *Journal of Arizona History* 31 (Winter 1990): 405–24.

Fireman, Bert M. "What Comprises Treason? Testimony of Proceedings against Sylvester Mowry." *Arizoniana* 1 (Winter 1960): 5–10.

Forbes, Jack D. *Warriors of the Colorado: The Yumas of the Quechan Nation and Their Neighbors.* Norman: University of Oklahoma Press, 1965.

Forbes, Robert H. *Crabb's Filibustering Expedition into Sonora, 1857.* Tucson: Arizona Silhouettes, 1952.

Fountain, Albert J. *The Life and Death of Colonel Albert Jennings Fountain.* Edited by A. M. Gibson. Norman: University of Oklahoma Press, 1965.

Frazier, Donald S. *Blood and Treasure: Confederate Empire in the Southwest.* College Station: Texas A&M University Press, 1995.

Garate, Donald T. *Juan Bautista de Anza: Basque Explorer in the New World, 1698–1740.* Reno: University of Nevada Press, 2003.

Gilbert, Benjamin F. "California and the Civil War: A Bibliographic Essay." *California Historical Society Quarterly* 40 (December 1961): 289–307.

————. "The Confederate Minority in California." *California Historical Society Quarterly* 20 (1941): 154–70.

Gorley, Hugh A. *The Loyal Californians of 1861.* Commandery of California, Military Order of the Loyal Legion, War Paper 12. San Francisco, 1893.

Granger, Byrd H. *Arizona Place Names.* Tucson: University of Arizona Press, 1960.

Greene, Laurence. *The Filibuster: The Career of William Walker.* New York: Bobbs-Merrill, 1937.

Grinstead, Marion C. *Life and Death of a Frontier Fort: Fort Craig, New Mexico, 1854–1884.* Socorro, N.M.: Socorro County Historical Society, 1973.

Gulton, Maurice G. *Lincoln County War.* Edited by Robert N. Nullin. Tucson: University of Arizona Press, 1980.

Gustafson, A. M., ed. *John Spring's Arizona.* Tucson: University of Arizona Press, 1966.

Guth, Jerry. "The Battle of Picacho Pass: The Turning Point for the Southwest in the War of the Rebellion." *American West* (1969).

Hageman, E. R., ed. *Fighting Rebels and Redskins.* Norman: University of Oklahoma Press, 1969.

Halaas, David Fridtjof. *Boom Town Newspapers: Journalism on the Rocky Mountain Mining Frontier, 1859–1881.* Albuquerque: University of New Mexico Press, 1981.

Halaas, David Fridtjof, and Andrew E. Masich. *Halfbreed: The Remarkable True Story of George Bent—Caught between the Worlds of the Indian and the White Man.* Cambridge, Mass.: Da Capo, 2004.

Hall, Julius C. "In the Wild West: Arizona at the Outbreak of the Rebellion. . . . Campaigning across the Arid Plains in 1862." *National Tribune,* October 20, 1887.

Hall, Martin H. "Colonel James Reily's Diplomatic Missions to Chihuahua and Sonora." *New Mexico Historical Review* 31 (July 1956): 232–44.

———. "The Mesilla Times, a Journal of Confederate Arizona." *Arizona and the West* 5 (Winter 1963): 337–51.

———. "Native Mexican Relations in Confederate Arizona, 1861–1862." *Journal of Arizona History* 8 (Autumn 1967): 171–80.

———. *Sibley's New Mexico Campaign.* Austin: University of Texas Press, 1960.

———. "The Skirmish at Mesilla." *Arizona and the West* 1 (Winter 1959):343–51.

———. "The Skirmish of Picacho." *Civil War History* 4 (March 1958): 27–35.

Hall, Martin H., and Sam Long. *The Confederate Army of New Mexico.* Austin: Presidial, 1978.

Hamilton, Patrick. *The Resources of Arizona.* Prescott: Arizona Territorial Legislature, 1881. Reprint, Tucson: Pinon, 1966.

Hart, Herbert M. *Old Forts of the Far West.* Seattle: Superior, 1965.

Heitman, Francis B. *Historical Register and Dictionary of the U.S. Army, 1789–1903.* 2 vols. Washington, D.C.: Government Printing Office, 1903.

Heyman, Max L. *Prudent Soldier: A Biography of Major General E. R. S. Canby, 1817–1873.* Glendale, Calif.: Arthur H. Clark, 1959.

Hicks, James E. *Notes on United States Ordnance.* 2 vols. Mount Vernon, N.Y.: privately printed, 1940.

Hinton, Richard J. *Handbook to Arizona: Its Resources, History, Towns, Mines, Ruins, and Scenery* San Francisco: Payot, Upham, 1878.

Holt, Ronald L. *Beneath the Red Cliff: An Ethnohistory of the Utah Paiutes.* Albuquerque: University of New Mexico Press, 1992.

Hughes, T. "Anonymous Journalism." *McMillans Magazine* 5 (December 1861): 157–68.

Hulse, F. S. "Migration and Cultural Selection in Human Genetics." Special volume, *The Anthropologist* (Delhi, India: University of Delhi, 1969), 1–21.

Hunsaker, William J. "Lansford W. Hastings' Project for the Invasion and Conquest of Arizona and New Mexico for the Southern Confederacy." *Arizona Historical Review* 4 (July 1931): 5–12.

Hunt, Aurora. *The Army of the Pacific: Its Operations in California, Texas, Arizona, New Mexico, Utah, Nevada, Oregon, Washington, Plains Region, Mexico, etc., 1860–1866.* Glendale, Calif.: Arthur H. Clark, 1951.

———. "California Volunteers." *Historical Society of Southern California Quarterly* 36 (June 1954): 146–54.

———. "California Volunteers on Border Patrol, Texas and Mexico, 1862–1866." *Historical Society of California Quarterly* 30 (December 1948): 265–76.

———. "The Far West Volunteers." *Montana: The Magazine of Western History* 12 (April 1962): 49–61.

———. *Major General James Henry Carleton, 1814–1873: Western Frontier Dragoon.* Glendale, Calif.: Arthur H. Clark, 1958.

Hutchins, James S. "The United States Mounted Rifleman's Knife." *Man at Arms* 13 (March/April 1991): 10–21.

Hutton, Paul A., ed. *Soldiers West: Biographies from the Military Frontier.* Lincoln: University of Nebraska Press, 1987.

Illsley, G. W., A. Finlayson, and B. Thompson. "The Motivation and Characteristics of Internal Migrants." *Milbank Memorial Fund Quarterly* 41 (1963): 217–48.

Irwin, Bernard. "The Apache Pass Fight." *Infantry Journal* 22 (1928): 1–8.

Johnson, Allen, and Dumas Malone, eds. *Dictionary of American Biography.* Vol. 17. New York: Scribner's, 1937.

Johnston, William P. *The Life of General Albert Sidney Johnston.* New York: D. Appleton, 1878.

Josephy, Alvin M. *The Civil War in the American West.* New York: Alfred A. Knopf, 1991.

Julyan, Robert. *The Place Names of New Mexico.* Albuquerque: University of New Mexico Press, 2001.

Karolevitz, Robert F. *Newspapering in the Old West.* Seattle: Superior, 1965.

Keleher, William A. *Turmoil in New Mexico, 1846–1868.* Santa Fe: Rydal, 1952.

Kemble, Edward C., and Helen H. Bretnor, eds. *A History of California Newspapers, 1846–1858.* Los Gatos, Calif.: Talisman, 1962.

Kemble, John H. *The Panama Route, 1848–1869.* Berkeley: University of California Press, 1943.

Kennedy, Elijah R. *The Contest for California in 1861: How Colonel E. D. Baker Saved the Pacific States to the Union.* Boston: Houghton, Mifflin, 1912.

Kerby, Robert L. *The Confederate Invasion of New Mexico and Arizona, 1861–1862.* Los Angeles: Westernlore, 1958.

Kibby, Leo P. "California, the Civil War, and the Indian Problem: An Account of California's Participation in the Great Conflict." *Journal of the West* 4 (April, June 1965): 183–209, 377–410.

———. "California Soldiers in the Civil War." *California Historical Society Quarterly* 40 (December 1961): 343–50.

———. "A Civil War Episode in California–Arizona History." *Arizoniana* 2 (Spring 1961): 20–22.

———. "Some Aspects of California's Military Problems during the Civil War." *Civil War History* 5 (September 1959): 251–62.

———. "With Colonel Carleton and the California Column." *Historical Society of Southern California Quarterly* 41 (December 1959): 337–44.

Knight, Oliver. *Following the Indian Wars: The Story of the Newspaper Correspondents among the Indian Campaigners.* Norman: University of Oklahoma Press, 1960.

Knightley, Phillip. *The First Casualty: From the Crimea to Vietnam, the War Correspondent as Hero, Propagandist, and Myth Maker.* New York: Harcourt Brace Jovanovich, 1975.

Kroeber, A. L. *Handbook of the Indians of California.* Berkeley: California Book, 1953.

Lasker, G. W. "The Question of Physical Selection of Mexican Migrants to the U.S.A." *Human Biology* 26 (1954): 52–58.

Lewis, Oscar. *The War in the Far West: 1861–1865.* Garden City, N.J.: Doubleday, 1961.

Lingenfelter, Richard E. St*eamboats on the Colorado River, 1852–1916.* Tucson: University of Arizona Press, 1978.

Lockwood, Frank C. *Arizona Characters.* Los Angeles: Times-Mirror Press, 1928.

———. "John C. Cremony, Soldier of Fortune." *Westways* 41 (March 1946): 18–19.

———. *Life in Old Tucson, 1854–1864.* Tucson: Tucson Civic Committee, 1943.

Lonn, Ella. *Desertion during the Civil War.* Gloucester, Mass.: Peter Smith, 1966.

Lord, Eliot. *Comstock Mining and Miners.* Berkeley, Calif.: Howell-North Books, 1959.

Lord, Francis A. *They Fought for the Union.* New York: Bonanza Books, 1960.

Martin, Douglas. "The California Column and the Washington Press." *Arizoniana* 1 (Winter 1960): 10–11.

Mathews, Mitford M., ed. *A Dictionary of Americanisms on Historical Principles.* Chicago: University of Chicago Press, 1966.

McChristian, Douglas C. *Fort Bowie, Arizona: Combat Post of the Southwest, 1858–1894.* Norman: University of Oklahoma Press, 2005.

McChristian, Douglas C., and Larry L. Ludwig. "Eyewitness to the Bascom Affair: An Account by Sergeant Daniel Robinson, Seventh Infantry." *Journal of Arizona History* 42 (Autumn 2001): 277–300.

McGinty, Brian. *The Oatman Massacre: A Tale of Desert Captivity and Survival.* Norman: University of Oklahoma Press, 2005.

McClintock, J. H. *Arizona: Prehistoric, Aboriginal, Pioneer, Modern.* 3 vols. Chicago: S. J. Clark, 1916.

McNitt, Frank. *Navajo Wars.* Albuquerque: University of New Mexico Press, 1972.

Meketa, Charles, and Jacqueline Meketa. *One Blanket and Ten Days Rations.* Globe, Ariz.: Southwest Parks and Monuments Association, 1980.

Memorial and Affidavits Showing Outrages Perpetrated by the Apache Indians in the Territory of Arizona for the Years 1869 and 1870. San Francisco: Arizona Territorial Legislature, 1871.

Miller, Darlis A. *The California Column in New Mexico.* Albuquerque: University of New Mexico Press, 1982.

———. "Carleton's California Column: A Chapter in New Mexico's Mining History." *New Mexico Historical Review* 53 (1978): 5–38.

———. "Historian for the California Column: George H. Pettis of New Mexico and Rhode Island." *Red River Valley Historical Review* 5 (Winter 1980): 74–92.

———. *Soldiers and Settlers: Military Supply in the Southwest, 1861–1885.* Albuquerque: University of New Mexico Press, 1989.

Miller, Robert R. "Californians against the Emperor." *California Historical Society Quarterly* 37 (September 1958): 193–214.

Morris, William G. *Address Delivered before the Society of California Volunteers.* "Combats with the Indians of Arizona and New Mexico." San Francisco: Society of California Volunteers, 1866.

Morrow, Robert E. *Mohave County Lawmakers.* Kingman: Mohave County Miner, 1968.

Mowry, Sylvester. *Arizona and Sonora: The Geography, History, and Resources of the Silver Region of North America.* 3d ed., 1864. Reprint, New York: Arno, 1973.

———. *The Geography and Resources of Arizona and Sonora.* San Francisco, 1863.

Mulligan, R.A. "Apache Pass and Old Fort Bowie." *The Smoke Signal* 11 (Spring 1965).

———. "Sixteen Days in Apache Pass." *The Kiva* 24 (1958): 1–13.

Mullin, Robert N., ed. *Maurice Garland Fulton's History of the Lincoln County War.* Tucson: University of Arizona Press, 1968.

Myers, Lee. "The Enigma of Mangas Coloradas' Death." *New Mexico Historical Review* 41 (October 1966): 287–304.

Myers, R. D. "The Confederate Intrusion into Arizona Territory, 1862." *Cochise Quarterly* 2 (Spring 1972): 1–27.

Neeley, James L. "The Desert Dream of the South." *The Smoke Signal* 4 (1961).

Newmark, Harris. *Sixty Years in Southern California 1853–1913.* 4th ed. Edited by M. H. and W. R. Newmark. Los Angeles: Zeitlin and VerBrugge, 1970.

Nicholson. John, ed. *The Arizona of Joseph Pratt Allyn. Letters from a Pioneer Judge: Observations and Travels, 1863–1866.* Tucson: University of Arizona Press, 1974.

North, Diane M. T. *Samuel Peter Heintzelman and the Sonora Exploring and Mining Company.* Tucson: University of Arizona Press, 1980.

Office of the Mohave County Historian. *Book of Claims, 1864–1866.*

O'Meara, James. "Early Editors of California." *Overland Monthly,* n.s., 14 (1889).

Ordnance Manual for the Use of the Officers of the United States Army. 3rd edition. Philadelphia: J. B. Lippincott, 1861.

Orton, Richard H. *Records of California Men in the War of the Rebellion, 1861–1867.* Sacramento: State Printing Office, 1890.

Paher, Stanley W. *Northwestern Arizona Ghost Towns.* Las Vegas: Gateway, 1970.

Paulding, James K. *The Diverting History of John Bull and Brother Jonathan.* New York: Innskeep and Bradford, 1812.

Pearce, T. M., ed. *New Mexico Place Names: A Geographical Dictionary.* Albuquerque: University of New Mexico Press, 1965.

Perry, James M. *A Bohemian Brigade: The Civil War Correspondents Mostly Rough, Sometimes Ready.* New York: John Wiley and Sons, 2000.

Pierce, Gilbert A., with additions by William A. Wheeler. *The Dickens Dictionary.* New York: Kraus Reprint, 1965.

Pitt, Leonard. *The Decline of the Californios: A Social History of the Spanish-Speaking Californians, 1846–1890.* Berkeley: University of California Press, 1966.

Pettis, George H. *The California Column.* Monograph 11. Santa Fe: Historical Society, 1908.

———. *Frontier Service during the Rebellion, or a History of Co. K, First Infantry, California Volunteers.* Providence: Rhode Island Soldiers and Sailors Historical Society, 1885.

Pierce, Gilbert A. *The Dickens Dictionary.* New York: Kraus Reprint, 1965.

Pomeroy, Earl S. "Military Roads in Arizona." *American Railroad Journal* 38 (January 1965).

———. *The Territories and the United States, 1861–1890.* Philadelphia: University of Pennsylvania Press, 1947.

Prezelski, Tom. "Lives of the Californio Lancers: The First Battalion of Native California Cavalry, 1863–1866." *Journal of Arizona History* 40 (Spring 1999): 29–52.

Prucha, Francis P. *Guide to the Military Posts of the United States, 1789–1895.* Madison: State Historical Society of Wisconsin, 1964.

Quebbeman, Francis E. *Medicine in Territorial Arizona.* Phoenix: Arizona Historical Foundation, 1966.

Randall, James G. "The Newspaper Problem in Its Bearing upon Military Secrecy during the Civil War." *American History Review* 23 (1918): 303–23.

Rathbun, Daniel, and David V. Alexander. *New Mexico Frontier Military Place Names.* Las Cruces: Yucca Tree, 2003.

Revised Regulations for the Army of the United States, 1861. Philadelphia: J. G. L. Brown, 1861.

Revised U.S. Army Regulations of 1861. Washington, D.C.: Government Printing Office, 1863.

Rice, William B., and John Walton Caughey, eds. *The Los Angeles Star, 1851–1864: The Beginnings of Journalism in Southern California.* Berkeley: University of California Press, 1947.

Rickey, Don. *Forty Miles a Day on Beans and Hay.* Norman: University of Oklahoma Press, 1963.

Riggs, John L. "William H. Hardy, Merchant of the Upper Colorado." Edited by Kenneth Hufford. *Journal of Arizona History* 6 (Winter 1966): 177–87.

Roberts, Gary L. *Death Comes for the Chief Justice: The Slough-Rynerson Quarrel and Political Violence in New Mexico.* Niwot: University Press of Colorado, 1990.

Robinson, John W. *Los Angeles in Civil War Days.* Los Angeles: Dawson's Book Shop, 1977.

Robrock, David P. "Edward D. Tuttle: Soldier, Pioneer, Historian." *Journal of Arizona History* 30 (Spring 1989): 27–50.

Rodenbaugh, T. F. *Army of the United States.* New York: Maynard, Merril, 1896.

Rogers, Fred B. *Soldiers of the Overland.* San Francisco: Grabhorn, 1938.

Ruhlen, George. "San Diego in the Civil War." *San Diego Historical Society Quarterly* 7 (April 1961): 17–22.

Ryan, Andrew. *News from Fort Craig, New Mexico, 1863: Civil War Letters of Andrew Ryan with the First California Volunteers.* Edited by Ernest Marchand. Santa Fe: Stagecoach, 1966.

Sacks, Benjamin. *Be It Enacted: The Creation of the Territory of Arizona.* Phoenix: Arizona Historical Foundation, 1964.

Salmon, Lucy Maynard. *The Newspaper and the Historian.* New York: Oxford University Press, 1923.

Scheiber, Harry N. "The Pay of Troops and Confederate Morale in the Trans-Mississippi West." *Arizona Historical Quarterly* 18 (Winter 1959): 350–65.

Schellie, Don. *Vast Domain of Blood.* Los Angeles: Westernlore, 1968.

Schreier, Konrad F., ed. "The California Column in the Civil War, Hazen's Civil War Diary." *San Diego Journal of History* 22 (Spring 1976): 31–47.

Scott, Henry L. *Military Dictionary.* New York: Van Nostrand, 1864.

Sloan, Richard E., and Ward R. Adams. *History of Arizona.* 4 vols. Phoenix: Record, 1930.

Sonnichsen, C. L. *Tucson: The Life and Times of an American City.* Norman: University of Oklahoma Press, 1982.

Spaulding, Imogene. "The Attitude of California toward the Civil War." *Historical Society of Southern California Publication* 9 (1912–13): 104–31.

Spicer, Edward H. *Cycles of Conquest: The Impact of Spain, Mexico, and the United States on the Indians of the Southwest, 1533–1960.* Tucson: University of Arizona Press, 1962.

Splitter, Henry Winfred. "The Adventures of an Editor, in Search of an Author." *Journal of the West* 1 (October 1962): 1–10.

———. "Newspapers of Los Angles: The First Fifty Years, 1851–1900." *Journal of the West* 2 (October 1963): 435–58.

———, ed. "Tour in Arizona: Footprints of an Army Officer by 'Sabre.'" *Journal of the West* 1 (October 1962): 74–97.

Spring, John A. "A March to Arizona from California in 1866, or; Lost in the Yuma Desert." *Journal of Arizona History* 3 (1962): 1–6.

Stanley, F. *The Civil War in New Mexico.* Denver: World, 1960.

Stone, Charles P. *Notes on the State of Sonora.* Washington, D.C.: Henry Polkinhorn, printer, 1861.

Stratton, Royal B. *Life among the Indians: Being an Interesting Narrative of the Captivity of the Oatman Girls, among the Apache and Mohave Indians.* San Francisco: Whitton, Townet, 1857.

Swanton, John R. *The Indian Tribes of North America.* Washington, D.C.: Government Printing Office, 1952.

Swartz, Deborah L., and William H. Doelle. *Archaeology in the Mountain Shadows: Exploring the Romero Ruin.* Tucson: Center for Desert Archaeology, 1996.

Sweeney, Edwin R. *Cochise: Chiricahua Apache Chief.* Norman: University of Oklahoma Press, 1991.

———. *Mangas Coloradas: Chief of the Chiricahua Apaches.* Norman: University of Oklahoma Press, 1998.

Swift, R. "The Civil War's Forgotten Battle, Picacho Pass." *Point West* 4 (April 1962): 42–50.

Tevis, James H. *Arizona in the 50s.* Albuquerque: University of New Mexico Press, 1954.

Thian, Raphael P. *Notes Illustrating the Military Geography of the United States, 1813–1880.* Austin: University of Texas Press, 1979.

Thompson, Major Dewitt C. *California in the Rebellion.* San Francisco, 1891.

Thompson, Gerald. *The Army and the Navajo: The Bosque Redondo Reservation Experiment, 1863–1868.* Tucson: University of Arizona Press, 1976.

————. "'Is There a Gold Field East of the Colorado?': The La Paz Rush of 1862." *Quarterly of the Southern California Historical Society* 67 (Winter 1985): 345–63.

Thompson, Jerry D. *Westward the Texans: The Civil War Journal of Private William Randolph Howell.* El Paso: Texas Western, 1990.

Thrapp, Dan L. *Encyclopedia of Frontier Biography.* 3 vols. Lincoln: University of Nebraska Press, 1988.

Todd, Frederick P. *American Military Equipage, 1851–1872.* 3 vols. Westbrook, Conn.: Company of Military Historians, 1978.

Tuttle, Edward D. "The River Colorado." *Arizona Historical Review* 1 (July 1928): 50–68.

Twitchell, Ralph E. "The Confederate Invasion of New Mexico, 1861–62." *Old Santa Fe* 3 (January 1916): 5–43.

Underhill, Lonnie. *Index to the Federal Census of Arizona for 1860, 1864, and 1870.* Tucson: Roan Horse, 1981.

U.S. Congress. Joint Special Committee to Inquire into the Condition of the Indian Tribes. *Report of the Commission Appointed March 3, 1865.* Washington, D.C.: Government Printing Office, 1867.

U.S. Infantry Tactics. Philadelphia: J. B. Lippincott, 1863.

U.S. Senate. *Federal Census—Territory of New Mexico and Territory of Arizona, [1860, 1864, 1870].* 89th Cong., 1st sess., 1965. S. Doc. 13.

U.S. Senate. Executive Document 1, pt. 1. 35th Cong., 2d sess. Serial 974.

Utley, Robert M. *Frontier Regulars: The U.S. Army and the Indian, 1866–1891.* New York: Macmillan, 1973.

————. *Frontiersmen in Blue: The U.S. Army and the Indian, 1848–1865.* New York: Macmillan, 1967.

————. *Historical Report on Fort Bowie.* Santa Fe: National Park Service, 1958.

Virden, Bill. "The Affair at Minter's Ranch." *San Diego Historical Society Quarterly* 7 (April 1961): 23–25.

Wagoner, Jay J. *Arizona Territory, 1863–1912.* Tucson: University of Arizona Press, 1970.

Walker, Franklin. "Bohemian No. 1." *Westways* 29 (September 1937).

————. *San Francisco's Literary Frontier.* New York: Alfred A. Knopf, 1943.

Walker, Henry P. "Freighting from Guaymas to Tucson, 1850–1880." *Western Historical Quarterly* 1 (July 1970): 291–304.

————, ed. "Soldier in the California Column: The Diary of John W. Teal." *Arizona and the West* 13 (Spring 1971): 33–82.

Walker, Henry P., and Don Bufkin. *Historical Atlas of Arizona.* Norman: University of Oklahoma Press, 1986.

Wallace, Andrew. "Fort Whipple in the Days of the Empire." *The Smoke Signal* 26 (Fall 1972).

War of the Rebellion: The Official Records of the Union and Confederate Armies. 139 vols.. Washington, D.C.: Government Printing Office, 1880–1901.

Washburn, H. S. "Echoes of the Apache Wars." *The Arizona Graphic* 1 (March 24, 1900): 6–7.

Watford, W. H. "The Far-Western Wing of the Rebellion, 1861–1865." *California Historical Society Quarterly* 39 (June 1955): 125–48.

Webb, George E., ed. "The Mines in Northwestern Arizona in 1864: A Report by Benjamin Silliman Jr." *Arizona and the West* 16 (Autumn 1974): 247–70.

Webster's American Military Biographies. Springfield, Mass.: Merriam, 1978.

Wellman, Paul I. *Death in the Desert.* New York: Macmillan, 1935.

Wheat, Carl I. *Mapping the Trans-Mississippi West, 1540–1861.* 5 vols. San Francisco: Institute of Historical Cartography, 1963.

Whitford, William Clark, D.D. *Colorado Volunteers in the Civil War: The New Mexico Campaign in 1862.* Denver: State Historical and Natural History Society of Colorado, 1906.

Willis, Edward B. "Volunteer Soldiers in New Mexico and Their Conflicts with Indians in 1862–63." *Old Santa Fe* (April 1914).

Wilson, John P. *When the Texans Came: Missing Records from the Civil War in the Southwest, 1861–1862.* Albuquerque: University of New Mexico Press, 2001.

Woodruff, Charles A. *The Work of the California Volunteers as Seen by an Eastern Volunteer.* Commandery of California, Military Order of the Loyal Legion, War Paper 13. San Francisco, 1893.

Woodward, Arthur. "Irataba, Big Injun of the Mohaves." *Desert* 1 (January 1938): 10–11.

———, ed. *Man of the West: Reminiscences of George W. Oaks.* Tucson: Arizona Pioneers Historical Society, 1956.

Wright, Arthur A. *The Civil War in the Southwest.* Denver: Big Mountain, 1964.

Wyllys, Rufus K. *Arizona: The History of a Frontier State.* Phoenix: Hobson and Herr, 1950.

Young, John Phillip. *Journalism in California.* San Francisco: Chronicle Publishing, 1915.

Zabriskie, James A. *Address to Arizona Pioneers.* Report of the Board of Regents, University of Arizona. Tucson, 1902.

DISSERTATIONS, THESES, AND PAPERS

Dayton, Dello G. "California Militia, 1850–66." Ph.D. diss., University of California, Berkeley, 1959.

Fireman, Bert M. "Extending the Civil War Westward to the Bloodied Banks of the Colorado River." Paper presented at the Arizona Historical Convention, Tucson, March 16–17, 1962.

Hastings, Virginia. "A History of Arizona during the Civil War." Master's thesis, University of Arizona, 1943.

Killin, Hugh E. "The Texans and the California Column." Master's thesis, Texas Technological College, 1931.

Lewis, Albert L. "Los Angeles in the Civil War Decades, 1851–1868." Ph.D. diss., University of Southern California, 1970.

Masich, Andrew E. "Civil War in Arizona: The Impact of the California Volunteers, 1861–1866. Master's thesis, University of Arizona, 1984.

———. "Columnists with the California Column: The California Volunteers in Arizona, 1862–1866. Honors thesis, University of Arizona, 1977.

Murray, Richard Y. "The History of Fort Bowie." Master's thesis, University of Arizona, 1951.

Underhill, Lonnie. "A History of the Regiment of Arizona Volunteers." Master's thesis, University of Arizona, 1979.

Yoder, Phillip D. "The History of Fort Whipple." Master's thesis, University of Arizona, 1951.

NEWSPAPERS

Arizona Daily Star (Tucson)

Arizona Enterprise

Arizona Miner (Prescott)

Calaveras (Calif.) Chronicle

Downieville (Calif.) Sierra Democrat

Dutch Flat (Calif.) Enquirer

Los Angeles News

Los Angeles Weekly Star

Oakland (Calif.) Tribune

Prescott (Ariz.) Courier

Sacramento Record Union

Sacramento Union

San Francisco Call

San Francisco Evening Bulletin

San Francisco Daily Alta California

San Francisco Herald and Mirror

San Francisco Weekly Alta California

Santa Fe Gazette

Santa Fe New Mexican

Tucson Arizona Citizen

Wilmington (Calif.) Journal

Index

All references to illustrations are in italic type.

Regular Army units are designated as U.S. units. State Volunteer military units are grouped by State (e.g. California First Cavalry vs. conventional text designation of First California Cavalry).

Abbot, John, 320n13
Abbott, Chandler C., 283n31
Adventures in the Apache Country (Browne), *91, 100*
African Americans, 147n7, 290n39
Agricultural production, 131, 196–97, 277–78, 317n3. See also Maricopa Indians; Pima Indians
Agua Fria River, 268
Aiken, S., 318
Alamo Express, 209n124
Alcohol/alcoholism, 16, 49, 96–98, 101n40, 128, 320n12
Aldrich, Levi, 99
Allen, Gabriel, 158n11
Allen, H. T., 292n42
Allen, J. B., 98
Allen, William, 247n211
Alta. See San Francisco Daily Alta California
American Indians: CV campaigns, 5–6, 59–60, 130; CV marriage to, 92, 107, 274–75; CV relations with, 195; extermination policies toward, 11, 61–62, 67, 86, 118, 146–47, 152, 172n51, 228, 262, 302n57, 327n22; as government contractors, 95–96; intertribal warfare, 325–26; military service of, 65–66, 126–27, 213–14, 256n9, 328n23; newspaper accounts of, 151–52; preserving culture of, 90, 92; rituals and religion, 199–201;

superstitions, 274, 312. See also Reservations, Indian; specific Indian tribe/band
American Museum of Natural History, 90
Ammunition. See Weapons and equipment
Anderson, Allen L., 110
Antelope Peak station, 165n31, 168, 192
Apache Indians: Arizona Volunteers and, 327n22, 328n23; bands defined, 12n5, 257n11; as captives in Tucson, 48; Cremony and, 158n10; CV encounters with, 50–52, 129, 215, 225–27, 282–84; CV tactics with, 256n9; hostile actions in Arizona, 12, 30–31, 60–65, 147–48; hostile actions in New Mexico, 52; as scouts and guides, 258n12. See also American Indians; specific Apache bands
Apache Pass, battle of: artillery use in, 72, 216n135; Chiricahua Apaches and, 51–52; dispatch reports of, 225–27, 236–43; newspaper accounts of, 147–50, 153–54
Arivaipa Apaches, 63, 256n9, 257n11
Arivaipa Canyon, 63, 147, 256–60 & 258n12
Arizona (motion picture, 1941), *135*
Arizona Brigade, 117–18
Arizona City, *31*, 94, 97, 191n99

Sibley, Henry Hopkins, 11, 13, 153, 160n22, 232n176
Sic-a-hote (Mojave chief), 274n19
Sierra Bonita Mountains, 62
Silliman, Benjamin, Jr., 304n61
Silver. *See* Gold and silver mining
Silverthorn, George E., 265
Singer, William, 167n36
Skinner, Frank, 265n4
Slavery: Carleton and, 156n3; Confederate plans for Indian, 11; as CV issue, 16; Indian captives in, 48; racism and, 147n7
Smith, E. Kirby, 118
Smith, John Y. T., 130–31 & n36
Smith, Joseph, 185n87
Smith, William, 248n213
Smithsonian Institution, 92–93, 327n20
Society of Arizona Pioneers, 256n9
Society of California Volunteers, 163n25
Solarse, José Victoriana (Papago chief), 182n81
Sonora, Mexico, 157n5, 170nn42–45, 202n109, 210–14, 254
Southern Pacific Railroad, 42n9, *138*
"Spanish Ranch," 64, 65n18
Spanish trail, 295
Spring, John, 128
Stanford, Leland, 46, *139*, 185n86
Stanton, Edwin M., 132
Stanwix Station, 33, 38, *39*
Stark, Conrad, 248n212
State militia. *See* California militia
Steele, William, 232n176
Steins Peak, N.Mex., 283n31
Stevens, Edwin, 255n4
Stevens, Henry H., 257n10, 283n32, 284n34
Stombs, Thomas A., 319n10
Stone, Charles Pomeroy, 242n193
Stone, P. D., 283n31
Sumner, E. B., 160n20
Sumner, Edwin V., 12, 70n27
Supplies and equipment: advance unit, 31–33, 38, 42; civilian teamsters and, 22, 58, 158n11; Colorado River steamers for, 83, 267n8; drinking water, 26, 38, 103–04; food and provisions, 104–06, 224; government contractors for, 24, 59, 75–76, 94, 105, 111, 131, 211n127, 221n149; illegal trade in, 99–100; logistics importance, 19, 45, 67–68, 80–81; maintenance of, 80–81; from Mexico, 58, 185, 207, 211; river steamboats for, 57, 83, 94–95, 270n12, 271n15, 286n35, 312, 317, 326nn18–19; supply routes for, 57–58, 108–11, 202n109, 254n1; uniforms and shoes, 15n10, 24–25, *27*, 73–77, 242n191, 294n49. *See also* Horses and equipment; Weapons and equipment
Sutton, Jesse, 194n103
Swilling, Jack, 38–39, 45, 131, *133*, 237n179
Swilling Irrigation and Canal Company, 131

Tanks stage station, 32–33
Tánori, Refugio, 123
Taylor, Edward G., 217n140
Teal, John W., 68, 222n150, 239n182, 240
Teel, Trevanion T., 233n177
Telegraph, 290–91
Territorial government: Carleton as military governor, 48–50, 131–32, 209–10; code of statute laws, 308–09; county and, 318, 326; CV role in, 129–30; elections in, 85, 132, 291–92, 304; establishing, 56, 82–86, 112, 129, 284n33; extermination policy, 61, 86. *See also* Arizona Territory; Politics
Tevis, James H., 11, 46n17, 170n41
Texas, 10, 12–13, 113, 115–17, 132, 152, 209n124. *See also* Rio Grande
Texas Hill. *See* Grinnell station (Grinnell Ranch)
Texas Rangers, *162*, 186
Texas Second Mounted Rifles (CSA), 11, 172n51, 186n92
Texas Seventh Mounted Regiment (CSA), 232n176
Thompson, William A., 14, 72, 166n33, 216n135

Tidball, Thomas Theodore, 63—*64*,
  147–48, 256n9, 258n12, 283n32
Tilden, Alphonso F., 95
Titus, Henry P., 208n121
Tobias, Charles E., 283n31
Tobin, William C., 40n7
Todd, Samuel, 288n37, 313n68
Tohono O'odham, 182n81. *See also*
  Papago Indians
Tonto Apaches, 36–37, 111, 169n38,
  181n76, 257n11
Toole, James H., 96, 320n11
Training: CV, 163, 165; garrison routine
  and, 102–03; infantry, 28–29; tactics
  and, 61
Transportation and roads: District of
  Arizona, 110; Fort Mojave road,
  302–04; Fort Mojave-Salt Lake City,
  294n48; Gila Trail, 38, 110; Mojave-
  Fort Whipple road, 60; Prescott-
  Mojave toll road, 309, 318, 326;
  railroad survey, 295n51; Rio Grande-
  Tucson road, 231; supply routes, 28;
  surveying and mapping, 108–11, 296;
  Tucson-Lobos Bay, 109; Tucson-
  Sonora road, 329n28; wagon trains,
  58; Yuma-Tucson route, 57. *See also*
  Butterfield Overland Mail route;
  Overland Stage route; San Antonio-
  San Diego Mail line; Supplies and
  equipment
Trueworthy, Thomas E., 95, 286n35,
  326n19
Tubac, Ariz., 60, 103, 123, 152, *219*,
  254, 293n45, 327n21, 329
Tucson: Apache attacks around, 12,
  30–31, 60; Confederate garrison at, 4;
  Confederate withdrawal, 190; CV
  garrison at, 35–38, 46–47, 256n8,
  282–83; CV withdrawal from, 113–14;
  economic development, 84–85;
  ethnic composition, 48; law and
  order in, 96–99, 205–06, 284;
  strategic importance of, 45–46;
  supply routes for, 108–09, 202n109;
  survey and mapping of, 110
Turk, Thomas, 258n13

Turner, William, 160n20
Tuttle, Edward Deen, 85, *87*, 92, 98,
  115–16, 291n40
Tuttle, Joseph, 115, 257n10, 282n28
Twiggs, David E., 176n64

Uniforms. *See* Weapons and equipment
Urrquides, Fernando, 98
U.S. Army: African Americans in,
  290n39; Articles of War, 101;
  California enlistments in, 9–10; Civil
  War history of, 6, 334; CV
  replacement by, 113–14, 128;
  "Dough-boys," 296n53; enlistment
  bonuses, 126, *136*; "red tape"
  bureaucracy, 306n64; regulations,
  119, 145, 171n48, 220n148, 307n65;
  weapons and equipment, 17–27;
  withdrawal from Arizona, 10–11
U.S. Army of the Potomac, 334
U.S. First Cavalry, 128
U.S. First Dragoons, 4, 12, 14, 16–17,
  18, 165n29, 175n62
U.S. Fourteenth Infantry, 128
U.S. Fourth Cavalry, 132
U.S. Government: army demobilization
  by, 67; interests in Mexico, 121–22;
  recognition of Arizona Territory,
  10–11 & n4, 48, 56; soldier's right to
  vote, 272–73, 281
U.S. Grand Army of the Republic,
  334
U.S. Military Academy. *See* West Point
U.S. Ninth Infantry, 159n15
U.S. Regiment of Mounted Rifles,
  261n19
U.S. Second Dragoons, 232n176
U.S. Tenth Infantry, 172n50, 329n26
U.S. Third Artillery, 13, 22, 157n8
U.S. Third Cavalry, 232n175
Utah, 270n12, 329n26. *See also*
  Mormons

Vallecito station, 158n12
Van Alstine, Nelson, 202n110
Veck, William S., 158n11
Venable, Thomas, 202n110